Dear H[...]

Brendan — a serious student of history. I hope you enjoy my little book.

Please be careful in your dangerous and important work!

Peter

The Big Picture

The Past, The Present, & Your Children's Future

Peter W. Hauer

authorHOUSE®

AuthorHouse™
1663 Liberty Drive
Bloomington, IN 47403
www.authorhouse.com
Phone: 1-800-839-8640

© 2011 Peter W. Hauer. All rights reserved.

No part of this book may be reproduced, stored in a retrieval system, or transmitted by any means without the written permission of the author.

First published by AuthorHouse 9/30/2011

ISBN: 978-1-4208-1535-1 (e)
ISBN: 978-1-4208-1536-8 (sc)

Printed in the United States of America

Any people depicted in stock imagery provided by Thinkstock are models, and such images are being used for illustrative purposes only. Certain stock imagery © Thinkstock.

This book is printed on acid-free paper.

Because of the dynamic nature of the Internet, any web addresses or links contained in this book may have changed since publication and may no longer be valid. The views expressed in this work are solely those of the author and do not necessarily reflect the views of the publisher, and the publisher hereby disclaims any responsibility for them.

DEDICATION

To my Mother and Father, who showed me there is no greater blessing on earth, than the love of devoted parents.

AUTHOR'S PROMISE:

    This book explains why society is the way it is today, and what life will be like for your children. In order to give you a full understanding of such a broad topic, this book had to include many subjects, such as psychology, economics, religion, politics, and history. However, you will find my discussion about these subjects refreshingly different from anything you may have learned before. This book explores important ideas that your college professors were probably too afraid to bring up.

    After reading this book you will have a sounder understanding of economics than most economists. You will have a firmer grasp of history than most historians. You will understand our world and where it is going. You will see, "The Big Picture."

WHY I WROTE THIS BOOK

Several years ago I was using the treadmill at my local gym. The television directly in front of me was showing a news story about the plight of homeless people. The older fellow on my right blurted out, *"Most of those guys are drug addicts or alcoholics. It's their fault they're homeless."*

I was surprised, because people rarely talk openly about controversial topics at the gym. Before I could think of a reply, the younger man on my left chimed in with something like, *"How can you say that? They still need help. How they got homeless doesn't matter now."*

The older fellow snorted back something about tax money being wasted, and then the younger man turned away in disgust. Both men quickly decided they wanted nothing more to do with each other. Suddenly it dawned on me. I had just witnessed the great divide in Western culture. It all took place in less than fifteen feet, and in less than ten seconds. I was in the middle. I felt sorry for the homeless people, yet I also had nagging doubts about what they had done to become homeless.

If I could see both points of view, then why were these other two men so polarized? Why do liberals and conservatives think so differently about poverty? Why do liberals and conservatives also think differently about society, government, and every controversial issue we face today? For nearly four years I searched for explanations, through books on history, politics, religion, and economics. I found the answers.

As my understanding grew, I began to see the proverbial "big picture." I discovered where conservative and liberal ideas came from. More importantly, I could see where these ideas were taking us. This gave me a surprising view into the future. The future will not be what you expect. The 20th century saw a fatal change in Western culture. This change will destroy Western culture in the 21st century, unless we act quickly. As things stand now, the 2,400 year old struggle between conservatism and liberalism will soon be settled by a third force, which is poised to destroy them both.

TABLE OF CONTENTS

CHAPTER ONE	THE ORIGINS OF CONSERVATISM	1
CHAPTER TWO	THE EVOLUTION OF LIBERALISM	31
CHAPTER THREE	MODERN LIBERALISM RISING	58
CHAPTER FOUR	ECONOMICS 101 (IMPROVED)	115
CHAPTER FIVE	PSYCHOLOGY REVISITED	183
CHAPTER SIX	POLITICS FOR THE SOUL	239
CHAPTER SEVEN	HOW TO AVOID TYRANNY	266
CHAPTER EIGHT	OUR PRESENT	325
CHAPTER NINE	THE FUTURE	362
REFERENCES		381

CHAPTER ONE

THE ORIGINS OF CONSERVATISM

June 15, 1215, Runnymede England. The signing of the Magna Carta.

The Royal page briskly entered King John's tent. He halted to attention and announced, *"His Eminence, Stephen, Archbishop of Canterbury, Primate of all England."*
"*Yes yes, enough of your pomp. Show him in!*" growled the King.
A middle-aged cleric, dressed in a rich white robe and a purple cape, entered the large tent. Three important nobles were already seated with King John. First and foremost was William Marshall, the Earl of Pembroke. The Archbishop noticed that Pembroke was sitting immediately next to the King, leaning towards him, with their shoulders almost touching. Obviously he was the King's confidant. The other two men were seated more appropriately, facing the King and several feet away from him. They were the Earls of Chester and of Warwick.
King John looked up at the Archbishop and blurted, *"I won't stand for etiquette when my crown is being wrested away from me!"*
The archbishop understood that gruff remark as the King's explanation for why these three nobles did not stand up when he entered the room. After all, the Archbishop of Canterbury was God's representative here in England. By normal protocol they should have stood up for him. Still, the Archbishop decided that he himself ought to follow some custom, and so he bowed briefly to the King.

"Sit my friend," said the King, in a calmer tone of voice, trying to make up for his earlier temper. *"There are almost a hundred treasonous barons camped on the other side of this field. They want me to sign this blasphemous compact or else they'll unleash their dogs on me."*

The archbishop had already heard about the document the King was referring to. It would later become known as the "Magna Carta." It was an effort to force King John to limit his powers.

The King spoke on, *"The worst part is this damned clause, what was it? Number sixty–one?"* The Earl of Pembroke nodded in agreement. *"It says that a convention of twenty-five barons can vote to take away my Royal castles and all my Royal estates...merely by their damned vote! Why don't they just vote to crucify me?!"*

"Your majesty, there is no need for blasphemy," the Archbishop gently chided.

"Well what in the name of God is this document if not a blasphemy?"

The Earl of Pembroke quietly spoke up, *"Your Majesty, our enemies have over twice the number of knights and freemen that we can muster. Remember, we'll receive no help from Ireland either."*

"Damn the Irish pigs," growled the Earl of Warwick. The Earl of Chester grunted in agreement.

Pembroke continued, *"The other problem is that if we fight, then the King of France will surely take the opportunity to conquer your Royal possessions in Aquitaine. So it appears that you have no choice but to sign the infernal document, at least for now."*

The King grimaced and clenched his fist reflexively. The Archbishop and the two lesser nobles glanced at each other nervously, but Pembroke went on smoothly. *"But your majesty, remember you can always recant this thing at a later time, when your fortunes improve. That will be acceptable under the law, because you were forced to sign the devilish paper in the first place. That's right, you were forced. You cannot be bound to a promise that you made under fear of death."*

King John closed his eyes in heated thought. He knew Pembroke was correct, but it was still hard for the King to admit the truth. He had no choice but to sign the document. Pembroke had merely stated what the King already knew.

"And the Pope will absolve you, uh....of any oath you are forced to sign," added the Archbishop.

The King drew a slow breath. *"Very well,"* he hissed in an angry half-whisper. *"Send for two of the barons to witness this."*

The signing of the Magna Carta was a milestone in the struggle between individual liberty and government power. The Magna Carta was also an early battle in the war between conservatism and liberalism. In many ways, the modern struggles between conservatives and liberals are just re-enactments of the conflict at Runnymede.

TRUE CONSERVATIVES VS FALSE CONSERVATIVES

The contemporary news media often misidentify politicians within the Republican Party as "neo-conservatives." However, the name neo-conservative does not really describe any type of conservative. Nearly all of the so-called neo-conservatives (e.g. Richard Nixon, Gerald Ford, the two Bush presidents, Bob Dole, Orin Hatch, Trent Lott, Arlan Specter, John McCain, etc.) are actually liberal politicians who merely pay lip service to conservative ideals. In fact they nearly always support liberal policies, such as expanding the size and power of the government.

For example, neo-conservatives support nearly every part of the great social welfare complex that liberals have created. Occasionally a neo-conservative might make a pretense of cutting back slightly on a particular government program, but they never question the general validity of the social welfare state. Neo-conservatives also support global government almost as fervently as liberals do. Neo-conservatives can be more accurately called "pseudo-conservatives" (false conservatives).

"STATUS-QUO CONSERVATIVES"

There are basically two different types of true conservatives in America today. They hold similar positions on most issues, but they have very different reasons for doing so. These two types of conservatives have fundamentally different views of government and society. The first type of conservative we will discuss is the *Status-Quo Conservative*.

Status-Quo Conservatism is very much an English and American phenomenon. The Status-Quo Conservative wants to preserve as much as possible the traditions, moral values, political institutions, and religious beliefs of his Anglo-Saxon forefathers. Status-Quo Conservatism is an attempt to preserve the legal, cultural, and political traditions that developed in England from 580 AD to 1774 AD.[1] A Status-Quo Conservative will resist any change in society unless he sees some convincing evidence in favor of the proposed change. The idea of a social experiment is unacceptable to a Status-Quo Conservative.

Some liberals do not view Status-Quo Conservatism as a true belief system. Instead they see Status-Quo Conservatism as more of a personality trait, or a mind-set; i.e. an attitude that seeks to preserve the traditions, institutions, and even the prejudices of the past. Yet as we will soon see, Status-Quo Conservatism is much more that just fear of change or love of nostalgia. There are important civil rights and freedoms that are woven into the complex tapestry of Anglo-Saxon culture. Besides, even preserving tradition for its own sake can be beneficial for society. The great historian Will Durant recognized that tradition helps to maintain social order:

"Tradition is to the group what memory is to the individual; and just as the snapping of memory may bring insanity, so a sudden break with tradition may plunge a whole nation into madness, like France in the Revolution."[2]

The greatest intellectual proponent of Status-Quo Conservatism was Edmund Burke (1729-1797). Burke was an Irish born Member of Parliament and an intellectual giant. Burke's commentaries on government power and individual liberty still make useful reading today. Burke was perceptive enough to foresee the fates of different societies based upon the types of governments they possessed. For example, three years before the Reign of Terror in France, Burke predicted that the French Revolution would degenerate into a bloody dictatorship. He was completely correct.

Burke gave his greatest intellectual support for the theory that the government should not try to change society. Burke believed that the collective wisdom of millions of people working together to maintain society and tradition was superior to the cleverest plans of any government committee. Burke also believed in free-market capitalism, with minimal government interference. Burke's support of property rights naturally caused him to oppose socialism. Regarding individual liberty, Burke argued that history and tradition guaranteed certain rights for all Englishmen. These traditional rights included: free speech, jury trial, property rights, and habeas corpus. (Habeas corpus prevents the government from keeping you in prison indefinitely, without a trial.) Burke believed that these rights were sacred, and so the government could never legitimately take these rights away.

THE ORIGINS OF STATUS-QUO CONSERVATISM: "THREE FOUNDATIONS OF LIBERTY"

Edmund Burke may have perfected Status-Quo Conservatism, but he certainly did not invent it. It had been developing for centuries before he was born. To find out where modern Status-Quo Conservatives obtained their ideas about individual liberty, we must dig deeper into history. In fact we must go all the way back to pre-Christian northern Europe, namely the Dark Ages. Long before the Norman Conquest, English culture of the post-Roman era possessed three conservative ideas that together formed the foundation of Anglo-Saxon liberty:

1. "Government by consent." The first idea was that the government could only rule with the consent of the governed. This concept naturally led to democracy, and it is the basis for our modern republican form of government.

2. "The law of the land." The second idea was that certain rights are permanent, and can never be taken away. This concept tended to prevent tyranny.

3. "Property rights." The third idea was that the government could not arbitrarily take an individual's private property. Historically speaking, the right to own property is the oldest civil right of all. Now we shall examine each of these three foundations of Anglo-Saxon liberty.

FOUNDATION #1: GOVERNMENT BY CONSENT

Most people have a fairy tale idea about how democracy originated in Anglo-Saxon culture. The fairy tale goes something like this: After the fall of Rome, primitive Europeans in the Dark Ages were ruled by tyrannical kings who wielded absolute power over their pitiful subjects. Then the scholars of the Renaissance re-discovered democratic ideas from ancient Athens and Rome. Next, the rational intellectual movement known as the Enlightenment inspired Europeans to put these ancient democratic ideas back into practice. In reality, nothing could be farther from the truth.

Peter W. Hauer

The truth is, after the fall of Rome, England in the Dark Ages was heavily influenced by the Scandinavian and Germanic cultures of the Angles, Saxons, and Danes. All of these cultural groups believed that the king could only rule with the consent of the inferior lords who supported him. Therefore, if those same lords lost confidence in their king, then they could legitimately depose that king and put a new ruler on the throne. These rough and uneducated barons had never heard of silly fictions such as "the divine right of kings." That dangerous idea would have to wait until the Renaissance. In the meantime, any man who would be king (even the son of the former king) would have to obtain the support of his lesser nobles before he could rule any of the separate kingdoms that made up England during the Dark Ages.

The English coronation ceremony still retains a vestige of primitive democracy from those early Anglo-Saxon days. Before the new monarch can be crowned, the Archbishop of Canterbury asks the assembled people if they consent to be ruled by the proposed monarch who stands before them. A majority of the people in the hall must voice their agreement. In this way the new king is, in theory at least, "elected" to rule over the people. In fact, this part of the coronation ceremony is even called "The Election." Several archbishops in English history actually made serious use of this election during the coronation ceremony, in order to avoid being personally blamed for having crowned a bad monarch.

In the middle of the 6th century, the Angles and the Saxons began conquering England from the native Britons. From the 6th through the 9th centuries, England did not have a central government. England consisted of several separate kingdoms, each with its own monarch. Moreover, each of these monarchs was highly dependent upon local lords for support. There was no Parliament yet, but there were numerous local councils which met to advise the local lords on matters of importance. This was an Anglo-Saxon tradition, and it is the root from which England's national council gradually evolved. This we know today as Parliament.

After 855 AD, the Danes began conquering large parts of England. Soon they held everything except the southwest corner of England, known as Wessex. The only English king to earn the accolade "The Great" was Alfred of Wessex. This was because Alfred the Great succeeded in defeating a large Danish army in 878 AD. The Danes were forced to permit the Anglo-Saxon race to live in peace at Wessex. This also saved the English language from extinction.

Yet the northern and eastern portions of England still remained under Danish control. Here the Danes established their own rule of law, and hence their region was called "the Danelaw." For the next eighty years, the Anglo-Saxons pushed back against the Danes, shrinking the territory of the Danelaw every year. Finally, the Danes were evicted entirely from England in 954 AD. That was the year that the Anglo-Saxons reestablished their own "law of the land." In most important respects, Anglo-Saxon law and Danish law were very similar.[3] Anglo-Saxon culture was in many ways similar to Scandinavian culture.

It is not surprising that the very word "freedom" originates from Scandinavia. In Norwegian it is "frihet," and in Swedish it is "vridom." Both of these Scandinavian words stem from a common ancient runic root word meaning "family member." In effect, to have "freedom" meant you had the rights of a family member; not a servant or a slave. This also implied a certain amount of equality, since all members of those Scandinavian societies were considered as roughly equal brothers and sisters within those societies. Anglo-Saxon villages had a long history of holding democratic town meetings, long before the arrival of Christianity. Exactly when this democratic tradition began among the northern European tribes is unknown.

Both egalitarianism (equal rights for all) and pure democracy tend to disappear when people organize into larger socio-political groups. Historically speaking, small autonomous tribes generally permitted significant individual freedom and were generally not socially stratified. These smaller groups of people always had a chief or "big man" in charge, but other members of the group had considerable freedom. Furthermore, the chief was nearly always subject to demotion by the consensus of the group. On the other hand, large complex societies have historically been characterized by less individual freedom and more strictly enforced class distinctions.[4]

In fact, the farther back you go in Scandinavian history, the more democratic and egalitarian it becomes. When the Scandinavians lived without any centralized authority, the free men in most villages would meet regularly to vote on major issues. These people had never heard of the Roman Assembly or Athenian democracy. Yet pre-Christian

Scandinavia had local governments that were just as democratic as ancient Athens or any town meeting in 19th century Vermont.

Of course as a matter of practice, different individuals held vastly different amounts of influence throughout both Scandinavia and England. A goat herder was not considered the social equal of a great land owner. Nor did the goat herder enjoy the same sway over his fellows as did the wealthy land owner. These social and political class distinctions grew stronger as time went on. Eventually, as local autonomy gave way to kingdoms and centralized authority, the governments of Scandinavia (including their settlements in England) grew less democratic and less egalitarian.

In Norway, this process of reducing democracy began in the 9th century when King Harold the Fair Haired united that country under his central authority. Yet the overall change was still gradual. The Scandinavian settlements on Iceland and Greenland were founded in the 10th century, and yet they remained models of democracy for many generations. In fact, some historians believe that the Vikings who settled these lands did so partly to escape the centralized authority that was begun by King Harold.

The Norman Conquest of England (1066 AD) hastened the trend toward social stratification. The Normans brought with them the very strict form of feudalism they had learned from the French. The Normans also brought with them the French idea that kingship should be hereditary. However, the tradition of "no rule except by the consent of the governed" was still firmly rooted in the minds of English noblemen. This concept survived the Norman Conquest. Of course, by the time of the Magna Carta, 1215 AD, the only consent that really mattered was that of the powerful nobles.

The first Parliament similar to the one we know today did not occur until 1265, almost 200 years after the Norman Conquest. By that time, England had finally developed into a united nation with a strong central government, consisting of the King and Parliament. Of course the territory of England was far too large to practice true democracy. So the English gradually replaced the early Scandinavian tradition of true democracy with a representative system of government. This was to become the foundation for the type of government we now call a republic. In a republic, the people vote for representatives who in turn vote on laws and taxes. The important thing to remember is that the right to vote comes from very ancient Scandinavian roots. It was not learned from either Rome or Athens.

FOUNDATION #2: THE LAW OF THE LAND

The second foundation of Anglo-Saxon liberty is the idea that there are certain rights which are so fundamental, they can never be taken away by the government. This principle is known as "the law of the land." This Anglo-Saxon idea also survived the Norman Conquest. The law of the land is the opposite of the later Renaissance idea, called "lex regia," which means the person in power makes the law. Under lex regia there is no permanent law. The law changes with each new ruler, or with each new election.

The law of the land is a barbarian tradition from northern Europe, which can be traced back to at least the 5th century in France, and back to the 6th century in England. The law of the land cannot be changed by the individual who happens to sit on the throne. Therefore, Englishmen may enjoy these rights despite the tyrannical wishes of an over-reaching monarch. The English coronation oath still requires the new monarch to swear he will uphold and enforce *the law of the land*. It does not give him the power to change this law.

Therefore, by the time of King John (1199-1216) English nobles had long been accustomed to having certain rights regardless of what king was in power. So when King John tried to usurp some of these rights, and tried to rule without the consent of these powerful "constituents," they forced him to back down. In 1215 the nobles, along with some powerful abbots and a few rich commoners, forced King John to sign a written promise to honor their ancient rights. This written promise was called the "Magna Carta" or "Great Charter."

In this sense the Magna Carta was a conservative document. It was an attempt to preserve old rights which the nobles were not willing to yield to a powerful central government. The Magna Carta was a crucial victory for conservative Anglo-Saxon law over the statist innovations that the Normans had learned from the French. The 63 articles of the Magna Carta guaranteed the right to a trial by jury, the right to confront witnesses, the right to habeas corpus, and the principle that no one, (not even the king), was above the law.

Yet the most overlooked concept contained within the Magna Carta was the idea of "no taxation without representation." Of course the Magna Carta did not phrase this idea in such modern terms. The nobles bluntly told the King that he could not levy any taxes on them or their lands without first calling a parliament to vote on such taxes. This had a profound side effect. This restriction on the king's power to tax tended to limit the power and size of the central government. The king could still raise money from royal lands and rob the Jews, but he could not levy taxes on the entire kingdom without the consent of the governed, i.e. without the consent of Parliament.

Various English kings tried to tax and rule without the approval of Parliament, and some achieved limited success in this regard. However, Richard II failed miserably. In 1399 he was deposed after he foolishly proclaimed, *"The laws are in my mouth."* The great Tudor King Henry VIII was perhaps the most successful in trying to impose his personal will as law. He was able to generate substantial income for royal spending by confiscating and selling off farmland that had been owned by the Catholic monasteries in England. He also murdered his political opponents with the aid of a secret tribunal called the Star Chamber.

In the 17th century, King Charles I was heavily influenced by the new ideas about royalty coming from the Italian Renaissance. These ideas encouraged Charles to imitate the absolute rulers of the Roman and Persian Empires. Full of these pompous delusions, Charles I tried to rule Great Britain as an absolute monarch. He failed to realize that a despotic monarch such as Henry VIII was the exception in English history, not the rule. Charles' attempts to reign as an absolute monarch violated "the law of the land." The English Parliament refused to put up with Charles' usurpations and revolted against him. He was tried and executed. A bloody civil war broke out in which the forces of Parliament defeated the Royalists.

Ironically, the most despotic ruler of all English history was the commoner who next controlled Parliament, Oliver Cromwell. He even threw out the Presbyterian members of Parliament who opposed him, and ruled for awhile with the consent of a docile "Rump Parliament." Soon Cromwell became a complete dictator, giving himself the title "Lord Protector of the Realm." When Cromwell died, his son Richard assumed power. He ruled England feebly until Charles II (son of the executed Charles I) landed back in England with an army to challenge the Cromwell dynasty. Neither Parliament nor the young Cromwell could muster enough support among the English people to effectively oppose the young Charles II.

After this unhappy experiment with civil war and dictatorship, the English people were generally willing to accept Charles II as their king. Unfortunately this new Charles proved too dull to learn from his Father's mistakes. He too tried to impose his royal will by "divine right." His equally foolish son James II tried the same thing, although he was not quite as obnoxious about it as his father was. But after James II sired a male heir (who would obviously become a Catholic king), the English Parliament finally lost all patience and tossed James II from the throne with a show of military force. Parliament then invited William and Mary to jointly rule Great Britain with Parliament's approval. James II fled the country.

Yet what exactly is this "law of the land" that the Stuart kings violated? According to the English legal scholar Blackstone, the law of the land can be boiled down to three fundamental rights which can never be abolished. He described them as; *"...the absolute rights of every Englishman: the right of personal security, the right of personal liberty, the right of private property."*[5]

FOUNDATION #3: PROPERTY RIGHTS

This third aspect of the law of the land (the right to property) is so important that it must be discussed separately as the third foundation of Anglo-Saxon liberty. It must also be discussed separately because this right has recently been so threatened by over-reaching politicians. There is an unfortunate tendency among modern politicians to divide our rights into different categories such as "property rights," "civil rights," and "human rights." This is usually a trick employed by leaders who want to take away our property rights. By placing the right to own property in a separate category all by itself, we are led to believe that it can be taken away without affecting our other, "more important" rights.

But if your right to keep your own property is taken away, then you are totally dependent upon the government for support. You cannot oppose the government because you would be fighting against your source of food and shelter. This is why Ayn Rand argued that property rights are really the most important rights of all:

"Without property rights, no other rights are possible. Since man has to sustain his life by his own effort, the man who has no right to the product of his effort has no means to sustain his life."[6]

The Founding Fathers certainly would have agreed with the reasoning that Ayn Rand used to argue that property rights are the most important rights of all. Alexander Hamilton put it best: *"A power over a man's substance (wealth)...amounts to power over his will."*[7]

The right to own property is also the oldest civil right of all. It certainly predates free speech, free press, free religion, and even the right to vote. Perhaps the only right which is more fundamental is the right to self-defense. (Self-defense will be discussed in Chapters Five and Seven.) Before civilization, primitive human beings were nomadic and so individuals did not own land. Early humans were hunter-gatherers who shared whatever food any individual happened to find or kill. Eventually, as man established permanent agricultural communities, he nearly always established the private ownership of both land and livestock.[8]

Archeological evidence indicates that nearly all of the earliest settled cultures permitted individuals to own their property. Examples of this come from Mesopotamia, Egypt, the Indus River Valley, Shang China, and ancient Anatolia. For example, the earliest written records from Sumerian culture were etchings cut into flat stones, long before the invention of clay tablets. These most ancient of records contain contracts for the sale of land, livestock, barley and beer, all of which were privately owned. The earliest complete set of laws that we have discovered is the famous code of the Babylonian King, Hammurabi. It contains complex rules for protecting the property rights of merchants, farmers, land owners, and widows.

So the right to own property was clearly recognized by the earliest civilizations, long before the right to vote or any other right for that matter. Some modern authors would have us believe that property rights were invented by Adam Smith, or perhaps by the earliest capitalists of the industrial revolution. However, the truth is property rights are very old indeed. In contrast, the communal living and sharing of resources in the Polynesian long houses that so enchanted Margaret Meade and other liberal anthropologists are the exception, not the rule.[9] In the vast majority of cases, whenever a tribe settled down into permanent communities, the people quickly began to honor individual property rights.

Therefore, it is not surprising that all of the world's major religions also protected the right to own property. Judaism, Christianity, Buddhism, Islam and Hinduism all prohibit stealing. All of these religions also try to prevent envy, because envy is the primary motive behind stealing and most social conflict in general. It is reasonable to assume that the earlier religions of our oldest ancestors probably prohibited stealing as well, for the very same reasons.

The first philosopher to sit down and try to write a non-religious justification for the right to own property was Aristotle (384-322 BC). His reasons were far more practical than theoretical. First of all, Aristotle assumed that men are most happy when they are given the most freedom. Freedom to Aristotle meant the ability to control one's own life and one's own wealth. Secondly, Aristotle argued that every man would put more care and effort into his own business enterprise, rather than if he were forced to work on some large collective project. Thirdly, Aristotle realized that a man cannot do any good for his fellow man if he himself is without any resources, i.e. without wealth. So ambitious men must be allowed to keep enough of their profits in order to make charity possible.

Aristotle merely supported property rights because he thought they were useful. Aristotle never bothered to think up an intellectual or moral justification for property rights. It wasn't until a century later, during the Roman Republic, that the statesman Cato (234-149 BC) first proposed that the right to own property was *natural, eternal, and fair:*

"By 'Liberty' I mean the power which every man has over his own actions, and his right to enjoy the fruits of his labor, art, and industry, as far as he hurts not society or any members of it, by taking from any member or by hindering him from enjoying what he himself enjoys. The fruits of a man's honest industry are the just rewards of it, ascertained to him by natural and eternal equity, as is his title to use them in the manner which he thinks fit. And thus with the above limitations, every man is the sole lord and arbiter of his own actions and property."[10]

Ancient Rome also gave us the philosopher Cicero, (106-43 BC) who first theorized that *the right to own property is the very reason for government to exist:*

"The chief purpose for the establishment of states...was that individual property rights might be secured...It is the peculiar function of the state...to guarantee to every man the free and undisturbed control of his own property."[11]

Under the guidance of Roman conservatives such as Cicero and Cato, the citizens of Rome enjoyed a republican form of government. This republican government provided the following safeguards of liberty:
(1) a representative government with a significant right to vote,
(2) a written constitution, which restricted government power, and
(3) the right to own property.

Of course the Roman Republic was not perfect. The Romans owned slaves and also gave no political rights to women, although Roman women did enjoy significant property rights. However, the Romans came closer than any other ancient people to creating an ideal form of government. It was only after the powerful liberal politician Julius Caesar seized power that this form of limited government was finally ended.

As we have discussed, the barbarian tribes of northern Europe had independently developed similar ideas about government by consent, the law of the land, and the right to property. The northern European tribes already had these three traditions long before they heard about Roman law. So our barbarian forefathers did not borrow their ideas about property rights from Cato or Cicero.

The barbarian origin for our property rights is illustrated by an episode from early French history. In the late 5th century, a Gallic priest approached the Frankish King Clovis I to ask a favor. Apparently one of Clovis' warriors had looted a valuable ceramic chalice from a local church. The local priest wanted it back. At this particular time the King was eager to curry the favor of the Catholic Church, and so King Clovis went to the warrior and personally asked if he wouldn't mind giving up the chalice. The warrior flatly refused. Under the traditional laws of the Frankish tribe, the ceramic chalice was now the warrior's rightful property. Therefore, King Clovis could not take it away.

King Clovis left empty-handed and humiliated. The King did nothing to punish the warrior. In fact, he could not.[12] The King was bound by the traditional property rights his tribe had customarily honored. This episode illustrates that property rights existed long before other rights, such as freedom of speech and freedom of religion.

THE AMERICAN EXPERIMENT

The three traditional foundations of Anglo-Saxon liberty (government by consent, the law of the land, and property rights), were not fully codified into one document until 1789, when the American Founding Fathers set them all down in the Bill of Rights, which promptly became part of our Constitution. This means that almost two thousand years after the Roman Republic, the world once again saw a representative government, limited in its power by a written constitution, along with guarantees of property rights.

The rebels behind the American Revolution were devoted to both liberty and limited government. In this way, they supported most of the same ideals that the later "classic liberals" of 19th century England did. However, this is the only sense in which the American rebels were "liberal." By our modern use of the terms liberal and conservative, the American rebels were primarily *conservative* thinkers because they were inspired by very conservative principles. The freedoms they sought to protect were in fact old rights their ancestors had enjoyed for countless generations as Englishmen. The patriots' slogan, "no taxation without representation" had its origins in the Middle-Ages, and was supported by the Magna Carta, although that slogan had not yet been coined.

So the revolutionaries of 1776 were hardly revolutionary thinkers. In fact, they were conservatives, fighting to restore their ancient birthrights as free born Englishmen. So while the Declaration of Independence was in one sense a revolutionary document, it was also (like the Magna Carta) a very conservative document. This explains why the conservative English statesman Edmund Burke sympathized with the American rebels. Burke admitted, *"We are being haunted now by the ghosts of our ancient liberties."* One of the greatest lawyers in the American colonies was John Adams. He knew full well he was fighting to preserve the traditional liberties of Anglo-Saxon culture:

"The patriots of this province desire nothing new; they wish only to keep their old privileges."[13]

Of course the American rebels also consciously imitated some aspects of the old Roman Republic when they set up their constitution, such as calling their upper legislature the "Senate." However, this does not mean that they actually got their ideas about individual liberty from the Romans. Their ideas about individual liberty were rooted in the damp fields of East Anglia and the dark forests of Wessex. They did not sprout from the Greek agora or the Roman forum. In England, widespread knowledge of the ancient Romans only dated from the 16th century, during the rebirth in classical learning known as the Renaissance. So long before most Englishmen had even heard about Roman law, they had already become accustomed to centuries of individual freedom under Anglo-Saxon law.

Significantly, the American patriots who wrote the US Constitution went even farther than merely restoring the three Anglo-Saxon liberties of: 1) government by consent, 2) the law of the land, and 3) property rights. Our Founding Fathers also added additional, newer rights, such as freedom of speech, press, religion, and association. When the Founding Fathers added these newer rights to the Constitution, they added these rights to the American version of "the law of the land."

The American Founding Fathers did not invent these newer rights all by themselves. They were influenced by centuries of English common law, as well as by the great political philosophers of the Enlightenment. Yet the addition of these newer civil rights did not diminish the importance of the oldest civil right of all, the right to own property. For example, the Enlightenment thinker who most influenced the Founding Fathers was John Locke. Locke agreed with Cicero that property rights were so fundamental, they were the very reason that governments exist:

"The great and chief end of Men uniting into commonwealths and putting themselves under government is the preservation of their property."[14]

The American Founding Fathers were scholarly men who read and understood both Cicero and Locke. This may partly explain their great concern about protecting property rights. The following statement by John Adams was typical:

"The moment the idea is admitted into society that property is not as sacred as the laws of God and that there is not a force of law and public justice to protect it, anarchy and tyranny commence."[15]

THE HAPPY ACCIDENT

For all the evil that modern liberals try to lay at the feet of Western Christianity, they forget that Western Christian culture was the first culture in the world to abolish slavery. It was also the first culture in the world to grant equal rights for women. Western Christianity was the first culture in the world to abolish abortion and infanticide.[16] It was even the first culture in the world to permit freedom of speech. The Founding Fathers understood their debt to Christianity:

"The general principles upon which the [Founding] Fathers achieved independence were...the general principles of Christianity." (John Adams)"[17]

"The religion which has introduced civil liberty is the religion of Christ and his Apostles...and to this we owe our free constitutions of government."[18] (Noah Webster)

At least one very intelligent non-Christian recognized the unique value of Christianity as a powerful force to fight totalitarianism. According to Albert Einstein, during the Nazi rise to power in Germany, the only institution inside Germany that dared to oppose Hitler was the Christian Church:

"Being a lover of freedom...I looked to the universities to defend it, knowing that they had always boasted of their devotion to the truth; but no, the universities were immediately silenced. Then I looked to the great editors of the newspapers...but they, like the universities were silenced in a few short weeks...Only the Church stood squarely across the path of Hitler's campaign for suppressing the truth. I never had any special interest in the Church before, but now I feel a great affection and admiration because the Church alone has had the courage and persistence to stand for intellectual truth and moral freedom..."[19]

Of course for many centuries the Western Christian Church failed to support one important civil right, freedom of religion. During the Middle-Ages, Christian Church leaders were as intolerant as radical Muslims are today. So exactly how did Christianity become a force against tyranny and a support for individual liberty? This brings us to a happy accident of history. Christianity happens to possess three important teachings which support the three Anglo-Saxon foundations of liberty (government by consent, law of the land, and property rights).

First of all, Judeo-Christian teachings supported the Anglo-Saxon concept of government by consent. All the way up until the Renaissance, Christian Church fathers in the West had taught that the relationship between the individual and the government is based upon mutual agreement, or as John Locke later called it, "the social contract." This tradition can be traced all the way back to the covenant that Moses obtained from God on Mount Sinai. It was even present throughout the Middle Ages in the feudal system. According to the early American preacher John Cotton: *"...all civil relations are based on covenant."*[20]

This means that the government only has power over us because we the people consent to it. We voluntarily agree to follow its rule. The American nation can be traced all the way back to just such a covenant in 1620. It was called the Mayflower Compact. The new government only held power because the individual members of the new society voluntarily agreed to be ruled by it. The Mayflower Compact was not a unique agreement. Several such "compacts" were agreed upon by the early settlers of different colonies. Not surprisingly, all of these covenants explicitly invoked God and Jesus Christ.

A government by mutual consent is also the foundation for the right to vote. If the consent of the people is to be maintained or renewed, then the people must periodically be allowed to select new rulers by voting. Of course the right to vote did not originate with Christianity. As we discussed earlier, Scandinavian and Anglo-Saxon men enjoyed voting rights in their primitive villages long before they converted to Christianity. Yet Christianity (especially the Protestant variety) helped to preserve the principle that the government is only legitimate as long as the people agree to support it.

In regard to the second foundation of Anglo-Saxon liberty (the law of the land), the northern European tribes were very unusual. In most cultures throughout ancient history, the ruler was considered divine. Therefore, his will was the law, regardless of what earlier kings or earlier traditions might have said. The Chinese Emperors, Egyptian Pharaohs, Japanese Emperors, Persian Emperors, and Mongol Khans, were all regarded as God's representatives on earth. This gave them absolute power to make any laws they wanted.

In contrast, the opposite was true for the tribes of northern Europe. This included the Britons, Galls, Saxons, Angles, Jutes, Danes, Franks, and Normans. In all of these northern European tribes, the King was considered to be a mere mortal. This explains why northern European kings did not have the power to change the laws and customs that their people had lived by for time immemorial. The barbarian northern tribes were not the only Europeans who refused to worship their rulers. To their credit, the ancient Greeks and the Romans also tended to view their rulers as mere mortals. Sadly, the Romans regressed during the reign of Augustus, as they fell under the influence of Middle Eastern cultures. This was when the Romans began to worship their emperors. The northern European tribes never fell into this political trap.

The Christian religion also teaches us that earthly rulers are not divine. Christianity obtained this idea from Judaism. God may have favored some rulers, such as King David and King Solomon, but they were not divine. Under both Judaism and Christianity, earthly rulers also have no power to change God's eternal laws, which can be found in the Ten Commandments.

This is similar to the northern European tribal concept that the king cannot change the ancient laws of his people. When northern Europeans adopted Christianity, their native concept that the king was not divine was reinforced by the Judeo-Christian concept which taught exactly the same thing. Moreover, the idea that there was a permanent set of laws that could not be changed was bolstered by an identical teaching from Christianity. This combination created a powerful cultural deterrent to prevent northern European kings from behaving like oriental despots. It was only much later, (after the Renaissance) that English kings such as Henry VIII and the Stuarts tried to become absolute rulers.

The third foundation of Anglo-Saxon liberty, property rights, was also reinforced by Christianity. This point will be demonstrated fully in Chapter Five. For now, it is only important to note that both Christianity and Judaism teach their followers not to envy the wealth that other people have. This teaching tends to prevent socialism. Christianity values free will and voluntary giving, instead of forced transfers of wealth. Because charity is voluntary, it encourages moral virtue. Socialism is not voluntary. Therefore, socialism does not encourage moral virtue. People are not being virtuous if they merely pay their taxes as required by law.

WHO ARE THEY?

The vast majority of conservatives in America are Status-Quo Conservatives. Significant individuals include William F. Buckley, Russell Kirk, M. Stanton Evans, Thomas Sowell, Rush Limbaugh, Michael Savage, Bill O'Reilly, Daniel Flynn, Robert Bennett, and Robert Bork. Status-Quo Conservative politicians include only a few members of the Republican Party. Institutions include the Christian Coalition, the Heritage Foundation, the American Conservative Union, the Family Research Council, the Club for Growth, the American Legion, the Eagle Forum, and the National Rifle Association.[21] Christians who are conservative on social issues (e.g. abortion, homosexual marriage, prayer in public school, etc.) are nearly always Status-Quo Conservatives.

"LIBERTARIAN CONSERVATIVES"

The second type of conservative is the Libertarian Conservative. Often times these people are called "paleo-conservatives." This label is misleading. "Paleo" means old. In fact, historically speaking, Libertarian Conservatism is the newest of all the belief systems discussed in this book. Libertarian Conservatism is easy to understand. Basically it maintains that the government should not be allowed to do anything that an individual is not allowed to do. So if an act is a crime when committed by an individual, then it would also be a crime for the government to commit the same act.

Here is an illustration: Joe is standing in the public square. Joe sees a poor old woman who appears to need money. Joe also sees Felix, who is known to be very wealthy. Joe forcefully robs money from Felix, and then gives most of that money to the poor old woman. Joe keeps a small amount as compensation for his trouble. Joe has committed a crime. Likewise, when the government does the same thing through a social welfare program, the government commits the same crime. Because man (in nature) is entitled to keep the possessions he finds or manufactures, then taking his possessions is a crime against nature.

If this idea sounds a bit extreme, you should note that the famous French socialist, Pierre Paul Prudhon, declared the exact opposite; *"Property is a crime, and the attempt to possess it should be punished."* Other famous enemies of private property include the communist Karl Marx and the socialist George Bernard Shaw, who preached, *"Private property is robbery."* When you compare these two ideas (one saying there is a *right* to own property and the other saying it is a *crime* to own property), our natural instinct tells us that the Libertarian Conservatives are correct. Owning property must be a right, not a crime.

Let's go back to our example of Joe, Felix and the old lady. According to Libertarian Conservatives, as long as Felix did not make his fortune by cheating the old lady, the government should not do anything to redress their different levels of wealth. The government should only establish agencies to prevent fraud and deceptive business practices. This allows people to compete fairly in a free market. Beyond that, Libertarian Conservatives believe that the government should have nothing to do with the wealth of its citizens, or how they live.

Modern liberals often criticize Libertarian Conservatives for being obsessed with their property rights, and therefore, "selfish." But Libertarian Conservatives are not just concerned with property rights. In a nation run by Libertarian Conservative principles, the common people would also enjoy all their other traditional civil liberties. You see, if it is wrong for an individual to take away your right to free speech, (or free religion, or free association, etc.) then it is also wrong for the government to do that same thing. The logic of Libertarian Conservatism protects all of our rights equally well.

THE ORIGIN OF LIBERTARIAN CONSERVATISM

The creation of Libertarian Conservatism is a much simpler story than the creation of Status-Quo Conservatism. It was a joint effort spanning just two centuries and two different men. It began with the first great martyr of the civil rights movement, Algernon Sidney (1623-1683). The concept of natural law that Sidney devised was clearer and more truly "universal" than any other idea about natural law, either before or since. To Sidney, all law should be based on, *"The great natural law, that no one may do anything to someone else that they would not want done to themselves."* This is really just a restatement of the Christian golden rule, "Do unto others as you would have them do unto you."

However, Sidney went one step farther. Sidney claimed that right and wrong were absolute concepts. Therefore, if an action was wrong for a common person to do, then it was also wrong for the government to do the same thing.[22] So if your next door neighbor cannot rightfully take away your free speech or your money, then neither can the government. Sydney understood that the only difference between theft by government and theft by highwayman was a mere legal difference, not a moral difference.

Almost two hundred years later, a French libertarian elaborated upon Sidney's basic concept to finally produce Libertarian Conservatism. He was a 19th century politician and philosopher named Frederic Bastiat (1801-1850). Bastiat used Sidney's basic theory to devise a cogent polemic in favor of limited government, and against socialism. In 1848, Bastiat wrote his most insightful arguments into a slim booklet entitled "The Law." This little book was a deliberate response to the Communist Manifesto of Karl Marx; another little book, which had just been published a few months earlier.

Bastiat was a more penetrating thinker than Marx. "The Law" contains incisive logic not present in Marx's call to arms. Bastiat agreed with Sidney that if an action is evil if done by an individual, it is also evil if it is done by the government. Yet Bastiat thought of a crucial defense for Sidney's theory. It was Bastiat who effectively refuted the statist claim that the government has special privileges to do things which an individual is not allowed to do. Bastiat pointed out that the government is really nothing more than a small band of individuals, who happen to possess great power. Our rulers simply control enough deadly weapons that they can impose their will upon the rest of us by force. So the government is simply a group of individuals who are better equipped to commit robbery than any other group.

According to Bastiat, the mere fact that a ruler is elected by popular vote does not legitimize his taking money away from his subjects. Bastiat understood that every government (elected or not) ultimately collects taxes from the barrel of a gun. The government's seizure of private wealth may be dressed up with elections, tax codes, and judges, but it really boils down to the brutal realization, "Might makes right." If you don't believe this, just try telling the IRS that you refuse to pay your income tax! They will come to your home…with guns.

In a republic, the power of government is held by elected rulers. In a dictatorship power is held by one self-appointed ruler. In either case, the result is the same for the helpless tax-payer. In either case, the tax-payer is plundered by leaders who want his money in order to stay in power. In a republic, the government robs the tax-payer after he is outvoted. In a dictatorship, the government robs the tax-payer without the formality of an election. Either way the tax-payer ends up exploited like a serf.

At this point a socialist will argue something like, *"The tax-payer had his one vote just like everyone else, and his candidate lost the election. That's fair. The majority rules."* But how exactly is majority rule "fair?" Without a strictly enforced constitution, majority rule is really just tyranny by the majority, or mob rule. What if the majority voted to impose a special tax on Jews? Couldn't we then say, *"They had their vote and they lost. That's fair. The majority rules."* Without strictly enforced property rights, democracy will always degenerate into class warfare of some sort, whether based on race, religion, or income. Bastiat recognized that French elections in his own lifetime had become mere charades to justify plunder.

Bastiat was not opposed to all taxes. He recognized two exceptions to his general rule that the government had no right to take your property. These two exceptions are also *the only two legitimate functions of government:*
1) to prevent invasion by foreigners, and
2) to prevent citizens from harming each other.

Any other use of government power (or tax money) is illegitimate, according to Bastiat. So under Bastiat's logic, the government can properly tax people to pay for national defense, in order to prevent foreign invasion. The government can also tax people to pay for police, prisons, food inspections, and agencies which regulate consumer affairs. All of these powers are legitimate under the government's responsibility to prevent citizens from harming each other.

Therefore, Bastiat was not an absolutist. He conceded that the government can do certain things that an individual cannot do. For example, the government has the power to throw you in jail for committing a crime. An individual does not have this power. Only the government can do this, *under its duty to prevent citizens from harming each other.* Likewise, an individual cannot force you to fight or to risk your life in combat. However, the government can indeed force people to fight, *under its duty to prevent foreign invasion.*[23]

A small portion of Bastiat's theory has been overtaken by modern technology. In our densely populated cities, we need the government to regulate necessary utilities, such as water, natural gas, and electricity. However, in most situations Bastiat's logic still applies today. For example, under Bastiat's system, the government would not be paying farmers to destroy food. The government would not be in the business of educating children. The government would not be running a vast welfare system, a national retirement system, or health care. Under Bastiat's thinking, none of these burdens would have befallen us. Libertarian Conservatism fulfills the old political adage: *"That government is best which governs least."*

Regrettably, most contemporary conservatives have long since forgotten Bastiat's profound ideas. If more conservatives had embraced the ideas of Bastiat and Sidney (as liberals have embraced the ideas of Rousseau and Marx) then conservatism might have blossomed into a formidable intellectual movement. Unfortunately this did not happen, perhaps because Bastiat's logical arguments were too emotionally unappealing for most people. However, on rare occasions you can still hear faint echoes of Bastiat's ideas in popular conservative literature. In 1955, the National Review (back when it was truly conservative) opined:

"It is the job of centralized government to protect its citizens' lives, liberty and property. All other activities tend to diminish freedom and hamper progress. The growth of government...must be fought relentlessly."[24]

"NATURAL LAW?"

Some authors prefer to label Libertarian Conservatives as "Natural Law Conservatives." After all, their view of government, society, and the individual is based on their belief that every person has a *natural right* to speak his mind, to keep his property, to follow the religion of his choice, and to raise his children as he thinks best. However, the term "natural rights" (just like the term "natural law") means different things to different people. Thomas Aquinas was the first important Westerner to contemplate natural law, but just like all the philosophers who followed him, Aquinas failed to prove why his ideas about right and wrong were truly "natural."

This explains why the terms "natural law" and "natural rights" are so subjective as to be meaningless. Whatever policy a political philosopher happens to prefer, he will call "natural." For example, Hugo Grotius claimed that all natural law was based upon the intellect, by which he really meant *his own intellect*. Thomas Jefferson generally followed John Locke's ideas about natural law and natural rights. The truth is both Locke and Jefferson inherited these rights from English common law. They both greatly admired the legal traditions of their Anglo-Saxon forefathers. Just like Grotius before them, whatever rights Locke and Jefferson admired, they too called "natural."

Thomas Paine was far less religious than Locke or Jefferson. This may explain why Paine incorporated socialism (enforced transfer payments) into his concept of natural law. Once again however, Paine's famous collection of rights that he grandly called "The Natural Rights of Man" was really just the set of rights that he personally valued. Because there is no consensus on what natural law is, the term does not have any real meaning. Therefore, for our discussion, the intellectual followers of Sidney and Bastiat cannot be called "natural law conservatives." We must refer to them as "Libertarian Conservatives."

WHO ARE THEY?

Libertarian Conservatives make up only a small minority of American conservatives. This is because very few conservatives have even heard of Frederic Bastiat, much less read his book. Libertarian Conservatives are usually well educated. Significant individuals include Ludwig Von Mises, F.A. Hayek, Ayn Rand, Leonard E. Read, David

Kelly, Henry Hazlitt, Robert Higgs, and Robert Welch. Politicians who are Libertarian Conservatives are rare, and include men such as Congressmen Ron Paul. Institutions include the Cato Institute, the National Center for Policy Research, and the Libertarian Party.

WHAT'S THE DIFFERENCE?

Both types of conservatism favor individual freedom over government power. However, they do so for different reasons. Status-Quo Conservatives want to protect our individual rights because they are *part of our Anglo-Saxon cultural heritage*. In contrast, Libertarian Conservatives want to protect these same rights because they are *natural for our species*.

However, Libertarian Conservatives go one crucial step further. They seek to protect our *"moral freedom"* from government meddling. Libertarian Conservatives believe that we should be allowed to do whatever we want, as long as we are not harming anyone else. This is why Libertarian Conservatives support the legalization of gay marriage, prostitution, gambling, and narcotics. In contrast, Status-Quo Conservatives seek to impose moral standards by using government power. In terms of policy issues, this is the primary difference between the two types of conservatism.

Generally speaking, Libertarian Conservatism is better equipped to fight against contemporary liberalism than Status-Quo Conservatism is. For example, in response to a proposed social welfare program, a Status-Quo Conservative can only point to the unintended harms it might cause. He can only point to things like the smothering of ambition, the spread of habitual dependency, and the wasteful distribution of resources to unproductive people. So the Status-Quo Conservative can only complain about the practical drawbacks of the social welfare system.

Yet a Libertarian Conservative can do much more. He can argue that taxing productive people to pay for other people's living expenses is actually immoral. He can claim that this is a wrongful taking of property. He can argue that taxation for this purpose violates a man's right to enjoy his own property. In this way, the Libertarian Conservative can take the moral high ground away from liberals who advocate socialism. For example:

"What do liberals mean by 'Social Justice'? Is it 'justice' to take money away from workers trying to feed their wives and children and then give that money to a drug addict? Or to a woman living on welfare with four kids by four different men? Is that 'justice?' No it is not. It is giving into envy. It is placating greed. It is rewarding irresponsible behavior. It is encouraging the very worst instinct in mankind; the desire to live off other people. So-called 'social justice' is really the height of injustice."[25](Stephen Klink)

"...socialism, or any form of collectivism, is not just inefficient, it is immoral. It is a degrading expression of envy, of malice, of the lust for power in the few who rule and the fear of freedom in the many who submit."[26](David Kelly)

Status-Quo Conservatism also suffers from a poor historical reputation that it can never seem to shake off. For decades, Status-Quo Conservatives defended ugly traditions, such as slavery, racial segregation, and anti-miscegenation laws. Status-Quo Conservatism also opposed giving women the right to vote. Status-Quo Conservatism by its very nature tends to oppose change, and therefore it tends to perpetuate ancient injustices.

In contrast, Libertarian Conservatism has no such blemishes on its historical record. Under Libertarian Conservatism slavery would have been considered a harm committed by one citizen upon another. So under Libertarian Conservatism, the government has a duty to abolish slavery. Other laws that discriminate based on race would also be considered invalid under Libertarian Conservatism, because the government has no power to make Jim Crow laws. Such laws have nothing to do with the two sole purposes of government, which are: (1) to prevent invasion and (2) to prevent people from harming each other.

Status-Quo Conservatism is not entirely useless. It can engender caution, which leads to deliberation and even prudence. However, as we will soon discover, it is a feeble opponent against the many ideologies contained within modern liberalism (e.g. Marxism, socialism, authoritarianism, feminism, materialism, nihilism, humanism, secularism, multiculturalism, environmentalism, elitism, collectivism, and globalism). Finally, we must understand that the two types of conservatism are not always mutually exclusive. A Status-Quo Conservative may well appreciate the theories of Frederic Bastiat. Likewise, a Libertarian Conservative may also have a deep appreciation for the Anglo-Saxon legal system. For example, the John Birch society routinely supports ideas from both conservative camps.

IS CONSERVATISM AN IDEOLOGY?

Most conservatives passionately insist that their views do not amount to an ideology. Conservatives generally believe that all ideologies are unreliable, and that most of them are dangerous as well. After all, some ideologies have brought us terrible suffering. Nazism, fascism, and communism are the classic examples. Here are two conservative explanations for why ideologies are so dangerous:

"The ideologue believes he possesses a truth that others have missed…the key to earthly redemption. Ideology contains no such power, but if you believed that it did, dishonesty, repression, murder and other sins might be seen as a mere pittance to pay when you're providing deliverance to humanity. When you're saving the world, what's wrong with telling a few lies? If you're making heaven on earth, what's wrong with sacrificing a few people to save the rest? But heaven is in heaven and not on earth, and demands for human sacrifice necessarily make any cause suspect."[27] (Daniel J. Flynn)

"Ideology…is an instrument of power; a defense mechanism against information; a pretext…for approving evil with a clean conscience; and finally a way of banning the criterion of experience, that is, of completely eliminating…the pragmatic criteria of success or failure."[28] (Thomas Sowell)

An ideology is a belief system which does three things:
1) It dismisses (disregards) any evidence that tends to disprove the ideology.
2) It calls upon people to change their behavior to conform to the rules of the ideology.
3) It promises a utopian existence as a reward for people who implement the ideology.[29]

In regard to the first part of an ideology (dismissing evidence to the contrary), an illustration may help. Communists claim that anyone who offers evidence against Marx's theories must certainly be a closet capitalist or a bourgeois stooge. Communists believe that any such opponent is simply blinded by his own self-interest in maintaining the corrupt capitalistic system. Therefore, any evidence he offers against communism should be ignored.

In regard to the second part of an ideology (calling upon people to change their behavior), we can use the same example. Communists believe that all property should be owned by the state. This certainly changes human behavior. You cannot be a landlord under communism. You cannot start a business under communism. You cannot even work without government approval. So your behavior is very limited. In regard to the third part of an ideology (promising utopia for people who implement the ideology), communism teaches that if the nation abolishes private property, then society will become an earthly utopia known as "the workers' paradise."

The reason that conservatism is not an ideology is because *neither type of conservatism contains all three parts of an ideology*. First of all, Status-Quo Conservatives generally do not ignore evidence that tends to undermine conservatism. If a liberal offers them some evidence that the social welfare system works, then Status-Quo Conservatives will generally examine that evidence to determine if it is accurate, reliable, and complete. They generally will not dismiss the evidence outright.

On the other hand, Libertarian Conservatives are indeed likely to dismiss the evidence, not because it is false, but because it is irrelevant. This is because Libertarian Conservatives believe that taxing some people to support other people is immoral. So to a Libertarian Conservative, any evidence showing that a welfare program is beneficial for society is simply not relevant.

In regard to the second part of an ideology, only Status-Quo Conservatism seeks to change individual behavior. It seeks to preserve traditional moral values by banning vices such as prostitution, gambling, narcotics, and pornography. It also seeks to preserve the institution of marriage as exclusively heterosexual. However, Libertarian Conservatism lacks this second element of an ideology. Libertarian Conservatism does not require individuals to change their personal behavior. Instead, it seeks the opposite. Libertarian Conservatism seeks *to remove any unnecessary restrictions on human behavior.*

Finally, the most important reason that conservatism (of either type) is not an ideology is because neither type of conservatism contains the third element of an ideology. *Conservatism never promises utopia for its followers*. Conservatism never promises to eliminate injustice, poverty, or war. Instead, conservatism only promises to avoid some of the more egregious pitfalls that have been committed under radical ideologies such as communism, socialism, fascism, and Nazism. For this reason, conservatism may be understood as an "anti-ideology."

Far from offering utopia, conservatism denies that utopia can ever exist here on earth. Instead, conservatism offers only a very imperfect society. Conservatives claim that such an imperfect society is actually *the best possible society*, i.e. the society with *the most individual freedom and the most opportunity to improve one's material and spiritual condition*. Whether this claim is true can only be determined after we study the opposing view, which is offered by liberalism. This brings us to our next chapter.

CHAPTER TWO

THE EVOLUTION OF LIBERALISM

Munich, August 13, 1783. Inside the home of Dr. Adam Weishaupt, revolutionary socialist.

    Dr. Weishaupt was beside himself with worry. For two years he had secretly recruited talented men for his great project to liberate mankind from the three great tyrannies: private property, nation states, and Christianity. He had promised his eager revolutionaries that they would soon share in a new morality, one that was superior to the Christian religion. Weishaupt had just recruited the influential Marquis of Savioli, largely based on Weishaupt's boasts about the lofty moral standards of his secret brotherhood. Now, just before Savioli was about to arrive to meet with the other members of the Order, they had nearly all shown themselves to be vile and morally depraved.
    Weishaupt reached for his quill and began to write. As he wrote, he instinctively used the secret code names for group members in case the letter was intercepted.
    "My dear brother Cato (alias Zwack of Regensburg Switzerland, first name unknown), What shall I do? I am deprived of all help. Socrates, (alias uncertain, but possibly the Bishop of Spire) who would insist on being a man of consequence among us, and who really is a man of talents, is eternally drunk. Augustus (alias unknown) is in the worst estimation imaginable."
    These words made Weishaupt pause to reflect once again as to why "Augustus" decided to rape the virgin daughter of his own

tenant, when he had enough money to obtain all the whores he wanted. Weishaupt wondered idly if "Augustus" was able to finish his business before he was caught. Then he continued writing:

"*Alcibades (alias unknown) sits all day long with the vintner's pretty wife. A few days ago Tiberius (alias unknown) tried to ravish the wife of Diomedes, (the Marquis of Constanza) and her husband came in upon them. Good heavens! What Areopagitoe I've got. When the worthy man Marcus Aurelius (the Marquis of Savioli) comes to Athens (Munich) what will he think? What a meeting of dissolute, immoral wretches, whore-masters, liars, bankrupts, braggarts and vain fools! When he sees all this, what will he think? He will be ashamed to enter into an Association.*"

After a few more minutes of writing out his fears to his old friend, Weishaupt sealed the letter with wax, and walked over to a chest of drawers. He took some effort to bend down and unlock the bottom drawer. He carefully pulled the drawer open and inspected his five small bottles of poison. He selected the bottle that was least full.

Weishaupt thought to himself, *"She's a small woman; this ought to be plenty to finish her."*

He did not stop to think how ironic it was that he was about to murder the beloved sister of his friend Cato (Zwack), the man to whom he had just written complaining about the immoral conduct of other members of their group. Weishaupt never judged himself. He knew he was above judgment. After all, he was on a noble mission to improve humanity. It would be foolish to let outdated moral standards jeopardize his cause. Besides, the silly girl had gotten herself pregnant with Weishaupt's child. Weishaupt had not intended to get her pregnant, so it was obviously her fault. Worst of all, she had refused to drink an abortion remedy.

"Stupid irresponsible girl," he thought to himself as he carefully checked the cork to see that it was tight. Then he slipped the bottle into his pocket. *"This problem will be resolved tonight."*

The word "liberal" has had several contradictory meanings over the past few centuries. At first the term liberal did not have any political connotations at all. It had various meanings, all of which described personality traits, such as generous, open-minded, or even unstructured. For example, two hundred years ago one might have properly said, "His nature was most liberal in pouring forth his largess," or "Harsh punishments violated her liberal temperament."

The first time the word liberal conveyed a purely political meaning was in 1808, during the Spanish resistance to Napoleonic rule. The Spanish freedom fighters were called "liberales." So the first political use for the word liberal simply meant someone who opposed the military rule of a foreign power. However, as we will soon see, by the 20th century, the word liberal had evolved to mean an individual who wants to change society by increasing government power.

Yet even before the Napoleonic occupation of Spain, the word liberal had already taken on some political overtones. During the American Revolution, to someone like Thomas Jefferson, the term liberal connoted the tendency to favor individual freedom over government authority. That is why Jefferson variously described himself as having both "liberal" and "republican" opinions. To men like Jefferson, Thomas Paine, Ben Franklin, and John Adams, the word liberal still held the meaning of its Latin root, *libertas*, meaning freedom from restraint. In England, the 18th century conservative statesman Edmund Burke was using the term liberal to convey a similar political meaning.

CLASSIC LIBERALS VS MODERN LIBERALS

These men were what we now call "classic liberals." Classic liberalism was closely related in meaning to our modern concepts of both "liberty" and "libertarian." To men like Jefferson, Paine, Adams and Franklin, the term liberal did not refer to a reformer or an economic socialist. Those modern connotations would have to wait until the 20th century. Back in the 18th and 19th centuries, liberal simply meant a lover of liberty. So classic liberalism was directly opposed to the ideas of someone like Thomas Hobbs, who favored a powerful central government instead of individual liberty.

This helps to illustrate the most important difference between the classic liberals of the 18th and 19th centuries and modern liberals. The classic liberals of the past despised the powerful government which Hobbs advocated. Conversely, modern liberals generally embrace Hobbs' vision of an all powerful government. Furthermore, the old classic liberals favored a free market economy, with little or no interference from the government. On the other hand, contemporary liberals generally favor the government's broad regulation of most commercial activities. Because of these fundamental differences, *classic liberalism is the opposite of modern liberalism.* In fact, classic liberalism is nearly identical to modern conservatism.

THE BIRTH OF POLITICAL PARTIES

The violent political upheavals of 17th century England, which we discussed in the previous chapter, gave birth to a very modern institution: the political party.[30] Before the 17th century, political factions were primarily based upon personal loyalties or perhaps religion. However, by the close of the 17th century, England had seen the birth of true political parties. These were groups of individuals who banded together to advance their own agendas for social, economic, and political change. By the end of the 17th century, two political parties dominated English politics, and they would continue to do so until 1832.

The English Tory Party favored keeping most of the political power in the hands of the king. In fact the name Tory is a derivation of the Irish oath of allegiance, "Ta-ra-re," which means "Come oh King."[31] In revolutionary America, loyalty to England was identified with loyalty to the English monarchy. This is why the colonists who wished to remain loyal to England were derisively called "Tories" by the American revolutionaries. The Tories were originally founded to support King James II and the Stuart family's claim to the English throne. The Tories also supported the landed aristocracy over the merchant class.

Conversely, the Whig party wanted to reduce the king's power and increase the power of Parliament. The Whigs supported the interests of the merchant class instead of the old landed aristocracy. The Whigs originated from a faction within Parliament that favored the royal claim of the Protestant William of Orange, instead of the Catholic James II. The English Whig Party gave us most of the classic liberal politicians who favored expanding the right to vote. The name "Whig" comes from the Scottish word for a driver of horses. This name implied that the new party would be united and driven hard, like a team of draft animals.

Eventually, as Parliament forcefully reduced the king's power in the 17th century, the Tory Party fell into decay. This happened because nobody (not even the Tories) wanted a strong monarch any longer. Therefore, the Tories had lost their main reason to exist. The remaining Tories formed a new political party, called the Conservative Party. It retained certain Tory policies, such as supporting the British Empire and keeping taxes low. But it completely dropped its previous support for a strong monarchy.

Likewise, seeing no further threat to the power of Parliament, the Whig party also lost most of its reason to exist. Some of the Whig members went on to form the Liberal party, which would be a major force in English politics until 1922, a span of nearly a hundred years.

The important thing to note is that by the 19th century, the term liberal had become so politically charged that an entire political party was even named the "Liberal Party." Yet liberals back then were not much different from conservatives. The 19th century classic liberals strongly favored maintaining the British Empire, as did the conservatives. In fact, both the liberals and conservatives of that era favored a mercantile sort of British Empire. This meant that the British colonies would ship raw materials to England at favorable prices and then purchase English manufactured products in return. This system was palpably exploitative.

In matters of Imperial policy, the only significant difference between the Liberal Party and the Conservative Party was that the conservatives looked upon colonies exclusively as sources of raw materials and economic exploitation. On the other hand, the Liberal Party also viewed colonialism as a way to "civilize" primitive cultures. To contemporary liberals, the old Liberal Party's attitude appears paternalistic, even arrogant. But in the 19th century nearly everyone understood that Western culture was superior to any other culture in the world.

The old Liberal Party in England did favor two important policies that today's liberals would certainly admire: pacifism and the expansion of the right to vote. Liberals wanted to maintain the British Empire, but they were less willing to fight than were the more hawkish conservatives. For example, in the 19th century, a Liberal Party government was toppled from power for not pursuing a more aggressive military policy in the Sudan.[32]

The classic liberal effort to expand the voting franchise was called the Chartist Movement, which began in England with the Reform Act of 1836. This expansion of democracy was a return to the more democratic and egalitarian society that had existed in Anglo-Saxon England. So while the move toward a wider voting base is often viewed as a modern innovation, it is really just a resurrection of an ancient

Scandinavian tradition. The only thing truly new about our modern right to vote is the inclusion of women. It should also be noted that the Conservatives sponsored the biggest expansion of the English right to vote with the Reform Act of 1867. This law gave virtually all adult males in England the right to vote.

THE LABOUR PARTY

The leftward march of the Liberal Party was too slow for the most reform-minded of English men and women. After World War I, the most ambitious social agitators in England switched over to a new party that was even more "liberal" than the nominal Liberal Party. This new group was called the Labour Party. It was based upon the union movement, as its name implies. However, it also embraced a wide spectrum of social reforms, including social welfare programs, and extreme pacifism in the form of anti-Imperialism.

The Labour Party was founded in 1893 by a socialist named Keir Hardie, but it did not gain a wide following until 1923. Up until 1922, the Labour Party was considered to be a mere radical fringe group. However, after the disastrous showing of the Liberal Party in the English election of 1922, it was finally disbanded. Most of its former members joined the more radical Labour Party. A smaller group went over to the Conservative Party. These were people who were either frightened off by the socialist rhetoric of the Labour Party or else people who disliked the Labour Party's anti-Imperial policy. The Labour Party was genuinely antagonistic towards the British Empire. The Labourites considered the Empire to be both a waste of public monies and immoral as well.

Unlike the old Liberal Party, the new Labour Party was committed to socialism. However, even the Labour Party was not truly radical by the standards of continental Europe. The English Labour Party favored the *gradual* implementation of socialism. It favored public ownership of the means of production, but only when the government could afford to pay the capitalists a fair compensation for their investments. The English Labour Party has never supported the violent seizure of capital, or revolutionary socialism.

LIBERALISM IN CONTINENTAL EUROPE

In this way the English liberal movement was much more moderate than the radical liberal movement which spread across the European continent. After all, the radical liberal movement was founded on the European continent, not in England. As far back as ancient Greece, Plato called for a powerful central government, in charge of everything from distributing food to raising the nation's children. He described this all powerful state in his classic book, *Republic.*

It should not surprise us that ancient Athens was the birthplace of what we today call "liberalism." After all, for many years Athens was a democracy. Democracy inevitably leads to a certain temptation among politicians. This temptation is to tax the wealthy in order to bribe the poor for their votes. This leads to political factions, such as the faction of the aristocrats (who want to keep their money), and the faction of the poor, (who want to take the aristocrats' money). In modern times, we generally call the party of the aristocrats "conservative" or "capitalist," and we call the party of the poor "liberal" or "socialist." In ancient Rome they were called the "optimares" and the "populares." The names are the only things that change over time.

So the idea of gaining political support by taking money from one class and giving it to another class is at least as old as ancient Athens and the Roman Republic. For example, the powerful Gracci family used government subsidies to keep the price of bread low in Rome. In exchange, the Roman population who voted in the Assembly always supported the position favored by the Gracci.[33] The technique of using the public treasury to buy votes was mastered by the greatest of all ancient liberal politicians, Julius Caesar. He broke up the large land holdings of his wealthy opponents and distributed the land to poor people, who then became his most ardent supporters. Julius Caesar later decreed a moratorium on all debts when he was Proconsul. These policies so pleased the Roman mobs that they voted to make Caesar dictator for life.[34]

Purchasing votes does not necessarily mean that Julius Caesar was personally immoral, or that liberal politicians in general have immoral motives. We should bear in mind that Caesar's reform-minded goals included citizenship for all freeborn males throughout the Empire, a universal code of laws (including the radical reform of granting a few basic rights to slaves who were owned by the state), and of course free trade within the Empire. Only Caesar's untimely death prevented him from implementing these reforms.

However, as noble as Caesar's goals for humanity were, it is undeniable that liberal politicians such as Julius Caesar do indeed hand out money from the public treasury with the expectation that the people who receive this money will vote to keep those same liberals in power. Buying votes is the simplest form of political corruption. Even revolutionary communists know that they cannot gain power without first appealing to the selfish interests of their audience. For instance, during the Bolshevik revolution Lenin promised the peasants generous land redistribution so the peasants could own their own farms.[35] So even the Bolsheviks practiced the ancient art of gaining support by promising loot. Of course Lenin never intended to keep that promise. In fact the Bolsheviks soon did the exact opposite. They collectivized the farmlands within their empire.

Our modern world has not changed. American politicians routinely use the public treasury to buy votes. On rare occasions they even admit to this. For example, back in the 1930's a liberal advisor to FDR named Harold Ickes assured Democratic Party insiders that he had a sure-fire method to win reelection for FDR. Mr. Ickes famously boasted, *"We will tax and tax and spend and spend, and elect and elect!"*[36] However, the Democrats are not the only party willing to plunder the US treasury for votes. The first political party in American history to use plunder politics was the Republican Party. During the 1880's and 1890's, Republican congressmen passed generous pension benefits for Civil War veterans of the Union Army. These benefits were excessive and clearly intended to buy votes.

More recently, after the Republicans took control of Congress in 1994, they went on a decade long spending spree. At the time of this writing, (2010) the Democrats are working to increase government spending even more. The Democrats tend to spend more money on welfare and so they receive more votes from the poor. The Republicans spend more money on the military and so they receive more votes from service-members and defense contractors. Either way, the damage to the economy is the same, as we shall see in Chapter Four.

SETTING THE MODERN STAGE: THE RENAISSANCE

After the fall of the Roman Empire, liberalism went into hibernation all over Europe. Liberalism remained dormant throughout the Dark Ages and the Middle Ages. Only after the intellectual movements known as the Renaissance and the Enlightenment did liberalism find new roots in European culture.[37]

The Renaissance lasted from about 1390 to 1640.[38] It was the rediscovery of ancient Greek and Roman philosophy and culture. The Renaissance had a great impact on European thinking. First, it acquainted Europeans with the logical methods and rhetorical devices of the ancient Greeks. The Europeans quickly learned to apply these same techniques to everything from philosophy to political science. Second, the Renaissance encouraged intellectuals to question the traditions and institutions upon which society was based. It is impossible for a person to read Plato's book, *Republic* without dreaming about how he or she might change society *if only they had power over other people.*[39]

This desire to follow Plato's ideas about re-making society led to a totally new attitude toward government. Politically speaking, the Renaissance marked the beginning of the end for limited government. The Renaissance gave birth to a new idea; statism. Statism is the belief that the government should be centralized and very powerful.

THE ENLIGHTENMENT

The next great intellectual movement was the Enlightenment. It lasted from about 1640 to 1814. It began after the close of the Renaissance, and it continued until the mass destruction of the Napoleonic wars.[40] Previously, during the Renaissance, the Roman Catholic Church worked hard to make sure that the techniques of observation and reason were not applied to either natural science or religion. However, this effort ultimately failed during the Enlightenment. During the Enlightenment, reason and observation were applied to everything. The Enlightenment represents the triumph of knowledge through science over knowledge through religion. It was the intellectual victory of reason and observation over divine revelation. After the Enlightenment, most educated Europeans accepted observation and reason as the primary sources of knowledge, with the Bible playing a subservient role, if any.

In fact, most of the philosophers behind the Enlightenment were either atheists (Hume and Diderot), or agnostics (Montesquieu), or pantheists (Spinoza), or mere deists (Descartes, Benjamin Franklin, Jefferson, Thomas Paine, Voltaire, and Jakob Fries). Most of them were certainly not traditional Christians. True believers in Christianity (such as John Locke, Isaac Newton and Adam Smith) were but a small minority. The following statement by David Hume is typical of how most of the Enlightenment's learned men felt about Christianity:

"Does it contain any abstract reasoning concerning quantity and number? No. Does it contain any experimental reasoning concerning matter of fact and existence? No. Commit it then to the flames. For it can contain nothing but sophistry and illusion."[41]

It is primarily for convenience that most historians have chosen the Napoleonic bloodbath as the end of the Enlightenment and the beginning of our modern intellectual era. Yet this may be very appropriate, because modern philosophy is dominated by nihilism; a dark and self-destructive philosophy which concludes that suicide is the most rational course of action.

The dismal philosophy of nihilism is truly the offspring of the Napoleonic debacle. The Napoleonic Wars caused the greatest wave of death in Europe since the Black Plague. Arguably this was not what Napoleon intended. The liberal social policies of Napoleon (new rights for women, land reform, the abolition of serfdom) were intended to liberate the peasants and other working classes of continental Europe. He intended to initially conquer Europe by military force. However, Napoleon wanted to then maintain his conquests via the goodwill generated by his enlightened social policies.

Unfortunately nationalism and anti-French sentiment prevented his plan from working. Napoleon soon found he could only keep his Empire together by garrisoning French soldiers in the conquered territories. Worst of all, Napoleon tried to save money by having his troops "live off the land," which meant stealing food from the native populations. This further inflamed anti-French animosity. Perhaps if Napoleon had instead used the methods of the Gracci, he might have created a European super state two hundred years before our present European Union, and prevented four major European wars. Instead,

Napoleon's rule became oppressive, and his constant warfare damaged both the economy and society of Europe.

The widespread destruction of the Napoleonic wars caused a surge of cynicism throughout continental Europe. This clearly weakened the traditional religious beliefs of many Christians. Previously, in the 18th century, it was only the intellectuals who accepted observation and reason as the basis of knowledge. However, in the 19th century, (after Napoleon's blood-letting) more and more of the European common people began to adopt this new world view.

Unfortunately, logic and reason by themselves (without the spiritual comfort of religion), lead to materialism, which makes for a society that is both self-indulgent and depressing. Materialism holds that nothing exists except for the objects we find in this world. To a materialist there is no God, and so there is no afterlife. Of course if there is no spiritual reward in the afterlife, then our lives here on earth are meaningless. This is the ultimate conclusion of nihilism; that human existence is meaningless. So after the Enlightenment led to materialism, then materialism led directly to nihilism.

GOVERNMENT POWER VS INDIVIDUAL FREEDOM

In order to understand the developments which have brought us where we are today, it is vital to understand the relationship between government power and individual freedom. This relationship is easily explained by the following simple axiom:

"Government power and individual freedom are inversely related."[42]

This means that as government power goes up, individual freedom goes down. Any increase in government power means that the government will have more authority to force people to obey the government's will. This means the common people will have less freedom to make their own decisions. Therefore, it is undeniable that as government power grows, individual freedom must shrink. Likewise, as government power is reduced, individual freedom grows.

A few examples may help to illustrate this phenomenon. As the government gains the power to run health care, you will lose your right to select your own options for treatment. As the government gains the power to tear down your home to make way for a Walmart store, you lose the right to stay in your own home. As the government gains the power to ban firearms, you lose your right to effective self-defense. As the government sets aside contracts for minorities and school admissions based on race, you lose your right to equal protection under the law.

The same dynamic also happens when the growth of government power is manifested in high taxes. As the government taxes almost half of your total income, you lose the freedom to do many things for yourself and your family. For example, as the government gains the power to take away 14% of your income, (to shore up the faltering Social Security system) you lose your financial freedom to save for your own retirement. Fourteen percent of your income has already been taken away.

As the government taxes your property to pay for failing public schools, you don't have enough money left to pay for decent private education for your own children. You lose that freedom. This list of freedoms we are losing through high taxes is virtually endless. High taxes even take financial freedom away from poor people. Regressive taxes such as sales tax, Medicare tax, utility tax, telephone tax, gasoline tax, and Social Security tax, always hit poor people hardest.

THE BIRTH OF MODERN LIBERALISM: THE PHILOSOPHES

To discover the origins of modern liberalism we must travel back to France at the beginning of the 18th century. We must revisit a small group of French intellectuals called the "philosophes." At the risk of sounding flippant, modern liberalism is actually the creation of a half dozen disgruntled Frenchmen. In fact, these French free-thinkers helped to create all five of the main elements of modern liberalism, i.e. collectivism, authoritarianism, globalism, elitism, and socialism.

The first of these avant-garde Frenchmen was a disillusioned French priest named Charles Irenee Castel, also known as the Abbe de Saint-Pierre, and most commonly as, "Saint-Pierre." Saint-Pierre rose to become a high level French diplomat. Saint-Pierre was instrumental in negotiating the 1713 Treaty of Utrecht, which created an international peacekeeping alliance, in order to prevent war. It was Europe's first baby step towards *global government*.[43] A hundred years later, the Congress of

Vienna was created, for the same reason. Nearly a hundred years after that, the League of Nations was created, again for the same purpose.

Saint-Pierre published several related essays between 1712 and 1737. In these essays, he called for five basic changes in society. Surprisingly, all five of his goals are perfectly compatible with contemporary liberalism. In fact, the five goals of Saint-Pierre still comprise the central elements of modern liberalism:

1) An international government to replace sovereign nations. This global government would prevent war.

2) An educated elite, to rule over the population with wisdom and virtue. This was a repeat of Plato's call for an oligarchy of "philosopher kings." Marx merely changed the name to "the dictatorship of the proletariat."

3) All schooling to be done by secular teachers, without any influence from Christianity. Saint-Pierre was almost certainly an atheist.

4) High taxes, including a progressive income tax, and a high inheritance tax.

5) A vast social welfare system, to be run by the government. This would be paid for by high taxes.[44]

Saint-Pierre's wish list is strikingly similar to Marx's Communist Manifesto of 1848. The only important part missing was Marx's call to abolish private property. Yet even this was really not a significant departure from the socialist goals of Saint-Pierre. The massive redistribution of wealth envisioned by Saint-Pierre was intended to accomplish the same thing. Marx simply voiced this same idea more dramatically. So anyone who is familiar with Saint-Pierre's work will recognize how his ideas clearly influenced Karl Marx.

As we shall see in Chapters Five and Six, these same ideas of Saint-Pierre were supported by left-wing activists throughout the 20th century. For example, we find the same ideas repeated in 1962, in the Port Huron Statement of the radical S.D.S. (Students for a Democratic Society). Saint-Pierre was the creator of the two movements we now know as socialism and globalism. Because of this, Saint-Pierre was the father of contemporary liberalism.[45]

Even during his own lifetime, Saint-Pierre's ideas had some powerful repercussions. Almost immediately the liberal agenda of Saint-Pierre took hold over the intellectual elites of continental Europe. For example, Saint-Pierre inspired the first intellectual support for socialism in Germany. As early as 1715, the great German intellectual and mathematician Leibniz published a favorable commentary on Saint-Pierre's 1712 essay. It especially praised the government-run social welfare programs envisioned by Saint-Pierre.

Closer to his home, Saint-Pierre influenced many of the 18th century French philosophers known as the philosophes. The philosophes accounted for some of the cleverest minds of the Enlightenment, including Voltaire, Diderot, Rousseau, Helvetius, Montesquieu, d'Alemburt, and Condorcet. The philosophes adopted most of the ideas of Saint-Pierre (such as secular education and globalism) and used them to encourage both revolution and the recreation of all social institutions. However, several significant philosophes (most notably Voltaire and Diderot) rejected the socialism of Saint-Pierre. In fact the only noteworthy philosophe who showed any real sympathy for socialism was Jean-Jacques Rousseau.[46]

The philosophes had a tremendous impact upon Europe's first truly modern revolution: the French Revolution of 1789. For four decades before the French Revolution began, the radical ideas of the philosophes dominated the conversations of politically active Frenchmen. In this way, the philosophes transmitted the ideas of Saint-Pierre to the most radical of the French revolutionaries, the Jacobins. Yet of all the philosophes, Rousseau was the one who most heavily influenced the Jacobins.

THE TROUBLE WITH ROUSSEAU

Even for us in the 21st century, Rousseau is still the most influential of all the philosophes. This is ironic, because during his lifetime Rousseau was shunned by most of the other philosophes. Several of the other philosophes actually thought that Rousseau was insane. Some historians do not even consider Rousseau to have been a member of the philosophes. This is because Rousseau emphasized emotion and feeling, while all the other philosophes stressed logic and reason.

Rousseau lived for most of his life as an impoverished outcast from society. This was actually quite appropriate, because Rousseau was an immoral wretch of a man. In his brutally honest autobiography, Rousseau admits to being a sexual masochist, an exhibitionist, and a peeping tom. Normal sexual relations apparently brought him little pleasure. His long-suffering mistress was a pretty young servant girl of sub-average intelligence. She could not count money or even keep track of the days of the week. She gave birth to five children by him. Rousseau cruelly forced her to abandon each infant at the local foundling shelter. According to historian Will Durant, such abandonment was a virtual death sentence for a newborn baby in 18th century France. Rousseau also stole from at least two employers. Finally, if he was not paranoid, at the very least he suffered from a strong persecution complex.[47]

Yet despite his many personal flaws, Rousseau has influenced more people than any of the other philosophes. His overwhelming influence on contemporary liberalism has been noted by liberal and conservative scholars alike. Rousseau's influence began with the French Revolution, and has remained strong ever since. According to his conservative contemporary, Edmund Burke:

"Rousseau is their (the French Revolutionaries') canon of holy writ... to him they erect their first statue. Him they study, him they mediate..." [48]

A hundred years later, the liberal scholar Gustave Lanson also acknowledged Rousseau's profound influence on modern liberalism:

"For a century now, all the progress of democracy, equality, universal suffrage...the war against wealth and property, all the agitations of the working and suffering masses, have been in a sense the work of Rousseau."[49]

Rousseau read Saint-Pierre with keen interest and was greatly influenced by him. In 1756 Rousseau even wrote his own summary of the twenty-three volumes that Saint-Pierre had written about war, peace, education, and politics. Rousseau wanted to make the ideas of Saint-Pierre accessible to a wider audience.

Rousseau's most important contribution to liberalism was to provide a moral justification for changing society. In effect, Rousseau created a moral justification for implementing the radical ideas of Saint-Pierre. The reason Rousseau offered was simple. He claimed that society was responsible for all the evils of mankind. Therefore, if society causes evil, then we can eliminate evil by changing society.

Rousseau's underlying premise was that children are born naturally good, but that society and traditional institutions change children into evil human beings. Therefore, according to Rousseau, if we can perfectly restructure society, then we can remove the cause for human evil. As a result, man will revert back to his natural condition, which is innocent and childlike. Rousseau's rationalization for destroying the old social order was exactly the excuse used forty years later by the Jacobins during the Reign of Terror in 1793.

Unfortunately, there are serious flaws in Rousseau's thinking. First of all, Rousseau's simplistic premise (that children are born naturally good) is false. Rousseau fails to consider the fact that infants are naturally quite selfish. Babies are only concerned with getting food and being pampered. Young children are also primarily concerned with their own pleasures. The social habits of sharing and being kind to others must be taught over several years. Adult care-givers, such as parents, teachers, or day care workers, teach children how to share and how to care about other people. These adult care givers are obviously part of society. Therefore, society actually *improves* the moral character of infants and children. It is revealing that Rousseau never actually raised a child in his entire life. His theory about the natural goodness of children was based purely upon idle speculation, not experience.

Another fatal flaw in Rousseau's thinking was his illogical assumption about the nature of primitive man. Rousseau imagined that primitive man (i.e. "natural man") was a completely independent person, wandering around on his own, doing whatever he thought best for himself. Rousseau's imaginary "noble savage" was under no obligation to follow anyone else's ideas about morality or religion. According to Rousseau, our natural state is wandering through forests all by ourselves, having brief sexual couplings with random people that we might encounter. To Rousseau, a lasting love between a man and a woman is *"unnatural."*

Even more absurd, Rousseau claimed that the love of parents for their own children is also unnatural. It should be noted that Rousseau's mother died soon after childbirth, and his father later abandoned him. So poor Rousseau never experienced normal parental love or affection. His ideas about parenthood and society were obviously poisoned by his own abysmal childhood.

Of course Rousseau's ideas about humanity contradict everything we know about human beings, from the sciences of anthropology, archeology, and psychology. It is *natural* for parents to love their own children. Furthermore, early man *always lived in groups*. It was the only way for him to survive in a world full of large carnivores. This means that human beings have *always* been born into a society of some sort. Therefore, following social customs and cooperating with other humans has always been the *"natural"* condition of man. If early man had tried to live the way Rousseau imagined, then our species would have died out in one generation.

Because it is natural for human beings to live in family groups, then it follows that it is natural for children to learn the knowledge, skills, prejudices, and religious beliefs of their parents. Likewise, our parents learned these very same things from their parents. Over several generations, this collection of wisdom and folly grew into a culture, full of traditions and values. Traditions taught people to behave in certain ways in order to maintain social harmony. Therefore, it is *natural for man to be influenced by society*. The completely independent existence imagined by Rousseau would have been quite unnatural, and impossible.

REDEFINING "FREEDOM"

An equally serious flaw in Rousseau's thinking is his bizarre definition of "freedom." According to Rousseau, freedom can only be found by *"obeying the general will."* So according to Rousseau, freedom means submitting to someone else's will! Of course, this is the exact opposite of what freedom really means. To any rational person, freedom is the absence of compulsion. Therefore, Rousseau's system would produce the exact opposite of freedom. Here is an example of the topsy-turvy language of Rousseau:

"Whoever refuses to obey the general will shall be COMPELLED to do so by the whole body. This means nothing less than HE SHALL BE FORCED TO BE FREE." [50] (Emphasis added.)

The essence of Rousseau's twisted logic can be expressed as *"Compulsion will set you Free."* This is just as illogical (and dangerous) as the Nazi slogan that was posted at the gates of their slave labor camps, *"Work will set you Free."* The greatest of the philosophers tried to tell us that the grass is blue and the sky is green, i.e. that "compulsion is really freedom." Rousseau's most important ideas are both false and absurd. Yet Rousseau's ideas for how society should be run (largely adopted from Saint-Pierre) are the foundations for the ideology that we in the 21st century now call liberalism.

Rousseau's absurd definition of freedom also begs another troubling question: What if the "general will" seeks to do evil? Rousseau was a dogmatic idealist. Rousseau believed that the general will of the people must always be good, by definition. Therefore the general will must always be obeyed, even if it crushes a few minorities in the process. This means that Rousseau was both a radical democrat and also a ruthless authoritarian. Rousseau wanted the government to impose social policy with an iron fist:

"The social compact...gives the body politic ABSOLUTE POWER over all its members."[51]

Of course if any government wields absolute power, it will surely crush dissent and trample individual freedom. This evil result is perfectly consistent with the dangerous ideas of Saint-Pierre:

"...anybody who does not obey orders will be treated by the others as a quadruped."[52]

So Rousseau did not invent the idea of a democracy with absolute power. He inherited this radical concept from Saint-Pierre. But it was Rousseau more than any other person, who wove *authoritarianism* into the fabric of contemporary liberalism. As we will see in later chapters, Rousseau's brand of radical democracy offers no protection against tyranny or injustice. It merely enforces the tyranny of the majority, and breeds authoritarian government.

This explains why the type of "liberalism" that Rousseau advocated really produces the opposite of freedom. It creates a repressive government that rigidly stamps out any dissent. Thus, the social system that Rousseau claimed was so natural and free actually turns out to be very unnatural and restrictive. Ironically, Libertarian Conservatism is an attempt to get back to the original state of nature that so enchanted Rousseau. If the natural state for human beings is to be truly free, then

Libertarian Conservatism is the belief system that can bring us closest to that idealized state of nature.

The most likely reason that Rousseau is still popular among liberals today is because most of them only have a superficial knowledge of his ideas. They only know about Rousseau's call to tear down old traditions in order to rebuild society from scratch. This part of Rousseau is a message that contemporary liberals seem to enjoy hearing. However, most contemporary liberals are probably unaware of the absurd logic that Rousseau employed in order to reach his radical conclusions.

Despite all the flaws within Rousseau's ideas, liberals have been following Rousseau for almost three centuries. Because of this, Rousseau's ideas are still generating far reaching consequences. After thousands of years of civilization, Rousseau inspired men and women to sit down and question the very foundations of the societies into which they were born. Rousseau started mankind off on the heady experiment to deliberately reconstruct a better society, in order to improve the moral condition of our species. After 2,200 years, the experimental ideas of Plato were beginning to be put into practice.

However, not all of the European intelligentsia appreciated this reawakening of Platonic liberalism. English and American conservatives, such as Edmund Burke, Walter Scott, John Adams, and Thomas Jefferson, naturally opposed any effort to tear down the existing social structures. They also feared that any government without strict limits on its power would eventually degenerate into tyranny. Modern liberal scholars tend to view the struggle between liberals and conservatives as the struggle between "the optimism of Rousseau vs. the pessimism of Burke." However, it would be better described as the struggle between *the tyranny of Rousseau vs. the liberty of Burke.*

EARLY ATTEMPTS AT SOCIAL ENGINEERING

Of course long before Rousseau, other leaders had deliberately changed their societies. Lycurgus of Sparta restricted the accumulation of wealth and demanded that all male children be raised in common barracks. However, his "reforms" were only intended to keep Sparta strong militarily. He was not trying to improve the human race.

Shih Huang Ti (the First Qin Emperor of China) uprooted Chinese society by replacing Confucianism with Legalism. However, his motive was primarily political. He wanted to ensure that his dynasty would continue for many generations beyond his death. He failed miserably. His heir was overthrown after ruling for just seven years. The new Han dynasty let China return to traditional values and customs.

Only Rousseau left a lasting legacy which encouraged social upheaval. However, his premise was false, his logic was flawed, and his conclusions were dangerous. Tragically, Rousseau's influence is very much alive today. As we will see in Chapters Six and Seven, any liberal politician who wants "to change the world" is still following the siren song of Rousseau.

THE ILLUMINATI & THE JACOBINS

By the time of the French Revolution (1789), Rousseau's idea about changing society had already been accepted by a radical political group called the Jacobins. The Jacobins were simply the French branch of a group of revolutionary Masons who called themselves "Illuminati,"[53] and sometimes, "the Order." The Illuminati was founded in Bavaria in 1770 by a radical socialist and underground revolutionary named Adam Weishaupt, also known by the alias "Spartacus." We visited him in his home at the start of this chapter.

In 1776, the Illuminati headquarters was raided by the Bavarian police. Thereafter, the members lay low, hoping to avoid arrest. However, by 1783 enough evidence of revolutionary conspiracy was collected to finally get them exiled from Bavaria. The members of the Illuminati sought refuge in Switzerland at first, and then they dispersed to Prussia and to France. In France, they quickly began to recruit new members from the larger French Masonic lodges in Paris and Lyon. Within a few years these radical followers of Weishaupt dominated both the French and German Masonic networks. In France, the most influential chapter of the Illuminati was located in Paris. Some of these lodge members formed a new radical political salon, which became known as the "Jacobin Club." Most historians think the Jacobins derived their name from the fact that they briefly met in a rented hall owned by an order of Jacobin monks.[54]

The Jacobin clubs of Lyon, Orleans, and Paris were especially active, and they eventually became the notorious political faction which dominated France during the latter part of the French Revolution. None

The Big Picture

other than George Washington recognized a connection between the Bavarian Illuminati and the French Jacobins. He was even worried that their revolutionary ideas might infect America:

"It was not my intention to doubt that the doctrine of the Illuminati and the principles of Jacobinism had not spread in the United States. On the contrary, no one is more satisfied of this fact than I am..."[55]

Within the confines of their meeting halls, the French and German Masons were freed from the traditional social restraints that normally kept them from speaking their minds openly. For example, inside his lodge, a butcher could freely criticize both king and pope. He could even criticize the ideas of the magistrate or local lord who was sitting next to him. On frequent occasions the butcher might even hold a higher rank within the Masonic hierarchy. Talk which could have been punished with execution outside the Masonic lodge (such as questioning the legitimacy of monarchy) was freely permitted among its members. According to one contemporaneous historian:

"...in those hidden assemblies, (Masonic Lodges) free communication of sentiment was highly relished and indulged...the church dreaded the consequences and tried to suppress the Lodges, but in vain...The Lodges became schools of skepticism and infidelity..."[56]

THE FRENCH REVOLUTION

It is no coincidence that most of the Jacobins who influenced the French Revolution (The Duke of Orleans, Marat, Robespierre, Mirabeau, Carrier, Cloontz, and Danton) were all active and high ranking Masons. Two anecdotes will illustrate the power of the Masonic Jacobins in France. In 1788, the Duke of Orleans was elected Grand Master of the Masonic Order in France. A year later, and just a few months before the uprising at the Bastille, he had his agents go throughout the French countryside buying up consignments of wheat flour.[57] Then he strategically withheld these wheat supplies from Paris. The supply of bread shrank and the price soared. Two poor harvests had already made the food situation bad to begin with, but the manipulations by the Duke of Orleans turned a bad situation into a crisis. As a result, the mobs of Paris called out for not just liberty and equality, but for bread as well.

The Duke of Orleans also provided the money to pay off street rabble, so they would form mobs for the many riots that sent the royal family into a panic. Usually the Duke employed intermediaries to make the payoffs, but sometimes events overtook him, and he was forced into the streets of Paris to hand out gold coins personally.

"The armed mob which came from Paris to Versailles on the 5th of October, importuning the King for bread, had their pockets filled with crown pieces; and [the Duke of] Orleans was seen by two gentlemen with a bag of money so heavy that it was fastened to his clothes with a strap, to hinder it from being oppressive, and to keep it in such a position that it should be accessible in an instant."[58]

Before his execution, the Duke of Orleans even admitted to having paid the equivalent of 50,000 in pound sterling as bribe money to the Gardes Francois so they would not fire on the rioting crowds. The ambitious Duke had hoped that the revolutionaries would select him to replace the reigning King. He was gravely mistaken. The revolutionaries did not want to merely exchange one monarch for another. The Jacobins in particular wanted to change society from the ground up.

In 1793 the Jacobins seized control of the revolution from a more moderate faction called the Girondists. Now that the Jacobins had power, they quickly revealed the full radicalism of the liberal movement on the European continent. Virtually all members of the ruling class were either exterminated or exiled. The Jacobins even turned on their fellow conspirator, the Duke of Orleans, and executed him.

Under Jacobin influence, the revolutionary government also became aggressively secular, and it persecuted Christianity. The seeds of secularism that were sewed by the Enlightenment finally bore their bitter fruits. Religious marriage was abolished. Clerics (priests, nuns and monks) were not permitted to teach. In fact, clerics who refused to renounce their faith were beaten and often murdered. Priests who insisted on performing the sacraments of the Roman Catholic Church faced execution. In 1793 over 600 priests were killed in Paris alone.

The new regime even tried to invent a brand new state religion to replace Christianity. At first, the Jacobins tried to replace the Christian Trinity with a new duality, called "Holy Liberty, and Holy Equality." When these two vague deities failed to inspire people, Robespierre replaced them in 1794 with "the Goddess of Reason." Robespierre even made himself the high priest of this new state cult.

The Jacobins sought to eliminate three institutions from the old regime, namely: 1) private property, 2) Christianity, and 3) the nation state itself. This is extremely important, because these same three institutions were exactly the ones which were attacked by later collectivists, such as the socialist Robert Owen, and the communist Karl Marx. In fact, communism was actually first attempted during the French Revolution. The new regime wanted to make everyone equal.

The Jacobins tried so hard to prevent the accumulation of wealth, that many factories were not merely seized, they were literally destroyed. Lamentably, this orgy of destruction wrecked the important French industrial center of Lyon. As a result, the French economy was in shambles just as France's enemies were moving to invade France to force the return of monarchy. Eventually this political and economic chaos created the opportunity for Napoleon to step in and seize power a few years later. Anarchy is nearly always the midwife for dictatorship.

In regard to destroying the nation state, the Jacobins were determined to create a global government, under their own enlightened rule of course. The Jacobins obtained the idea of globalism from their German comrades, the Illuminati. The following is a letter of instruction from the head of the Illuminati telling his subversive brethren how to teach young recruits about the benefits of global government:

"After the mind of the pupil has been warmed by pictures of universal happiness, and convinced that it is a possible thing to unite all the inhabitants of the earth into one great society...it may frequently be no hard task to make him think that PATRIOTISM IS A NARROW MINDED MONOPOLIZING SENTIMENT, and even incompatible with the more enlarged views of the Order, namely the UNITING OF THE WHOLE HUMAN RACE INTO ONE GREAT AND HAPPY SOCIETY."[59](Emphasis added.)

CHRISTIANITY AND LIMITED GOVERNMENT

The Illuminati and the Jacobins were the final death blows to limited government in continental Europe. However, they did not start the process. Ironically, this process was started by the same institution that had previously supported limited government: the Roman Catholic

Church. Before the Protestant Reformation, the Catholic Church could send its agents into any part of Western Europe to ferret out heretics. The Church did not need strong central governments and so it did not encourage them. After all, a powerful central government might have challenged the Pope.

The Protestant Reformation changed all that. After the Protestant Reformation, the Roman Catholic Church began to support the concentration of power into the hands of strong monarchies, specifically in Portugal, Spain, and France. The Roman Catholic Church abandoned her traditional opposition to strong central government because now she wanted powerful governments to help her stamp out heresy. She wanted the support of strong kings in nations that were still Roman Catholic, in order to enforce religious orthodoxy. This is why the Roman Catholic Church accepted the new Renaissance idea that the state should be run by a powerful central government. In this sense, the Reformation induced the Catholic Church to accept the dangerous political ideas of the Renaissance. This change in policy eventually backfired. As the Catholic monarchies became more powerful they stood up to the Church. This was dramatically illustrated when the Jesuits were soon thrown out of Portugal, Spain and France.

Meanwhile, the Protestant faith of Martin Luther (which dominated northern Germany and Scandinavia), did a somewhat better job of preserving Christianity's medieval role as the defender of individual liberty. Later, this was even more true for the Protestant sects which dominated the American colonies. In both northern Europe and the American colonies, the Protestant Reformation had blunted the Renaissance ideal of an all powerful state. These Protestant faiths were also less autocratic in their own church administrations than the Roman Catholic Church was. In Scandinavia and Germany the culture of limited government managed to live on for four more centuries.

Yet as we saw in Chapter One, the culture of limited government was able to thrive best of all in the American colonies, due to the extreme form of political liberty that was taught by the Puritan, Quaker, Anglican, Congregational, and Calvinist denominations. These freedom loving Protestant churches dominated the American colonies. These Protestant churches taught men to read the Bible, and to think for themselves about God. Men who thought for themselves in matters of religion also tended to think for themselves in matters of government.

Of course, as we also saw in Chapter One, Christianity in England throughout the medieval era supported limited government, and the rights of the individual over the state. From Thomas a' Becket to Thomas Moore, English church leaders traditionally looked out for the rights of the individual against the government. So Christianity in England had been a liberating force against the cruelty of tyrants long before the Protestant Reformation, and for a considerable time afterward. This was because of the happy accident that fused Anglo-Saxon traditions with medieval (Roman Catholic) Christianity, a development that we have already discussed in Chapter One.

This long tradition of English churchmen defending individual liberty against the encroachments of government was brought over to the American colonies. For example, before the American Revolution, one of the most widely read American preachers was Reverend John Cotton. Reverend Cotton consistently preached that limited government was the only guarantor of liberty:

"It is necessary, therefore, that all power that is on earth be limited, church power or other…It is counted a matter of danger to the state to limit prerogatives; but it is a further danger not to have them limited."[60]

During the American Revolution, Tory members of Parliament complained bitterly about their real enemy in the colonies, the so-called *"black regiment"* of puritan, Calvinist, and Anglican preachers who boldly called for revolution against Mother England.[61] Edmund Burke was forced to admit that the American rebels' obsession with individual rights came in part from their Protestant religious heritage:

"Religion, always a principle of energy, in this new people is in no way worn out or impaired; and their mode of professing it is also one main cause of this free spirit…The religion most prevalent in our northern colonies is a refinement on the principle of resistance; it is the dissidence of dissent, and the Protestantism of the Protestant religion. This religion, under a variety of denominations agrees in nothing but the community of the spirit of liberty…"[62]

The Anglo-Saxon political tradition, together with Christianity, combined to preserve limited government in England and America longer than anywhere else. Anglo-Saxon Christianity was able to extend the life of limited government for a few centuries, but not forever. Sadly, limited government was finally lost completely during the first half of the 20th century. It no longer exists anywhere on earth. There is no longer any nation on earth that lives under a fixed constitution, which protects individual liberty from the ambitions of government leaders.

MEANWHILE, ON THE OTHER SIDE OF THE WORLD...

This book focuses on the development of Western political thought instead of Asian, Middle Eastern, Latin American, or African political thought, for one simple reason. Western political thought has deeply influenced all of the other cultures and societies that make up humanity around the globe. However, the reverse is not true. Non-Western political traditions have had little or no impact on Western political thought. Confucianism, Shinto Imperialism, Pre-Columbian kingdoms and African monarchies have had no discernable effect on Western political thought, from Aristotle to Arianna Huffington.

For the sake of brevity we will discuss only a single example of this one-way influence. China has the oldest existent culture on earth. China has also enjoyed a longer continuous flow of political philosophy than any other nation or culture. The ancient Chinese "Book of Changes" was first written down in 600 BC, but it is based on Chinese verbal traditions that probably go back to at least 1000 BC. Confucianism was developed into a mature philosophy by 400 BC, and still continues to influence Chinese political thought. Legalism, Taoism, and Buddhism also influenced Chinese political thinking.

Yet even this proud and ancient culture has been greatly influenced by Western political traditions. In the 19th century, the Chinese intelligentsia learned about shocking Western ideas, such as voting, republican government, and free market capitalism. The famous Chinese "May 4th Movement" was only one of several new political movements that were influenced by Western ideas. These new revolutionary movements called for abolishing the old imperialist system for an entirely new type of government, based on Western models. By the time of the great 1911 rebellion, Western ideas had penetrated deeply into the Chinese body politic. The Chinese patriot Sun Yat Sen initially favored the classic liberal ideas, such as free markets and republican government. However, in his last few years, Sun Yat Sen embraced more radical Western ideas, such as socialism and even communism.

Based on these statist Western ideas, Mao Tse Tung took China down an authoritarian (but still Western) path, to communism and centralized planning. Yet in doing so Mao ignored China's own native tradition of socialism. Mao seemed unaware that Confucius had called for the redistribution of wealth to help widows and poor children. Mao also ignored China's ancient attempts to implement socialism during the Han and Sung dynasties. (These attempts will be discussed in Chapter Four.) Instead Mao learned about socialism from purely Western sources, such as Karl Marx and Frederick Engels.

The same thing has happened in Africa, Asia and Latin America. Governments are generally based on Western models and Western political ideas. Unfortunately, these nations nearly all adopted the radical liberalism of continental Europe, instead of the classic liberalism of 18th century England and the USA. As we will see in the next few chapters, continental liberalism favors a strong central government. Most non-Western cultures already had strong traditions of authoritarianism. Therefore, they adopted the ideology that supported powerful government (the continental "liberalism" of Saint-Pierre, Rousseau, and Marx), instead of the belief system that supported individual freedom, (the classic "liberalism" of Locke, Burke and Jefferson).

Limitations of space prevent us from exploring other developments in Western liberalism, such as the Methodist reform movement, Comtian socialism, the Manchester liberal movement, the Paris Commune, the Fabian Society, and the many liberation movements of Latin America. Suffice it to say that the radical form of liberalism that developed in continental Europe only gradually came to dominate England and the USA. How this happened (and how liberalism evolved into its modern form) brings us to our next chapter.

CHAPTER THREE

MODERN LIBERALISM RISING

London, February 4, 1896.

It was well past midnight, and the dark London docks were nearly deserted. The gas lights on the nearest street were a feeble gesture against the enveloping gloom. The only real light was the distant quarter moon, and even it was masked by the dripping fog. Lord Nathan Rothschild paced back and forth nervously alongside his carriage. He had every reason to be agitated. He was engrossed in planning what he should say to the great man who was about to disembark from the South African freighter at the dock. Lord Rothschild saw the dark humor in this situation. Here he was, the second richest man in the world, about to tell the richest man in the world (Cecil Rhodes) that he has been acting like a complete fool.

Cecil Rhodes had carelessly sent two letters to Lord Milner in London. In these letters, Rhodes boldly admitted his involvement in the Jameson raid. This was the provocative military attack which started the English war to conquer Dutch territory in southern Africa. This English conquest would later be known as the Boer War.

In the wrong hands, these letters would prove that they all had a hand in starting the war. Worst of all, in the second letter, Rhodes even dared to provoke a showdown in Parliament, over the English government's failure to support *"the grand little war that we have begun."* Fortunately the explosive letters were not intercepted. But Lord Rothschild was still amazed at his friend's lack of caution.

The Big Picture

If Rhodes were to tell the Select Parliamentary Committee the truth (that Lord Chamberlain knew about the Jameson raid ahead of time) then this would surely bring down the entire Salisbury government! All of their plans for the great South African Union would be ruined. Rothschild knew it was imperative that he speak to Rhodes before anyone from the press got to him.

"It would be just like Rhodes to brag about his role in the Jameson Raid to the newspapers," Rothschild thought to himself. *"If he were a Jew, he would have learned a lot more discretion by now."* Rothschild thought in just a second or two about the hundreds of years his own people had to carefully think about what they did, and what they said, while living among an entire continent of hostile Christians.

"Milner was wise to send me," mused Rothschild. *"Rhodes would not listen to anyone else. He won't respect anyone who is not a man of power."*

As the gangway from the ship was being tied down, Rothschild could see his old friend, the great Cecil Rhodes, barreling downward, intent on being the first man on shore. Rothschild waved at him, and called out, *"Hello!"*

Rhodes looked over and saw Rothschild. Rhodes shouted, *"Natty, you old goat!"* Instantly Rothschild smiled in delight, and with a sense of relief. Rhodes always liked to call his friends by their nicknames. Tonight this habit prevented Rhodes from calling out Rothschild's real name in public, in front of so many people. *"Thank God,"* Rothschild muttered to himself.

This meeting between Cecil Rhodes and Nathan Rothschild in February of 1896 was a turning point in history.[63] At stake were both modern liberalism and the British Empire in Africa. Both survived the dangers of that evening. The British Empire only lived on for another half century, but modern liberalism thrived and is now stronger than ever. This episode is just one illustration of the tremendous power that a few influential liberals held at the dawn of the 20th century. In fact the influence of such people has only increased since then.

The previous chapter explained how the term "liberal" has had various meanings throughout history. It also demonstrated that liberalism meant one thing to Englishmen and Americans, but something far more radical to continental Europeans. Yet what is "modern liberalism" and where did it come from? In regard to England and America, *modern* liberalism is over a hundred years old. As we will soon see, it became firmly established in England during the 1890's, as a synthesis of two main goals: *socialism and globalism*.

Previously, the classic liberals of 18th and 19th century England had borrowed all three foundations of Anglo-Saxon liberty from conservatism. First, the classic liberals embraced the conservative principle that rulers can only govern with the consent of the people. Second, they accepted the Anglo-Saxon law of the land, meaning that certain rights can never be restricted by the government. Third, the classic liberals supported the ancient right to own property.

So in England and North America, liberalism did not really distinguish itself from conservatism until the dawn of the 20th century. Only then did English speaking liberals adopt both *socialism* and *globalism*. This fusion of socialism and globalism marked the establishment of "Modern Liberalism" in England and the USA. Throughout the rest of this book, the term Modern Liberalism will be typed with capital letters, as a proper name. This is because Modern Liberalism is a unique subset of ideas within the general category of liberalism, just as Libertarian Conservatism is a unique subset of ideas within the general category of conservatism. Also by using capital letters we can avoid any confusion between "classic liberalism" and "Modern Liberalism." As we saw in the last chapter, Modern Liberalism is nearly the opposite of classic liberalism.

Modern Liberalism does not simply mean "contemporary" or "present day" liberalism. In fact, Modern Liberalism began in continental Europe three hundred years ago, with the essays of Saint-Pierre in 1712. His ideas outlived classic liberalism. His ideas became so dominant in our present day that they can still properly be called *Modern* Liberalism. Today, Modern Liberalism incorporates many tertiary beliefs, such as feminism, pacifism, humanism, secularism, multiculturalism, and environmentalism. These represent the *social values* of Modern Liberalism. However, as we will see in the next four chapters, the most important values of Modern Liberalism are its *economic and political values*. These are the values originally proposed by Saint-Pierre. They are: collectivism, authoritarianism, globalism, elitism, and socialism.

The Big Picture

WHAT IS SOCIALISM?

According to the famous French socialist Henri de Saint-Simon (1760-1825, no relation to Saint-Pierre), socialism is government ownership of the means of production and the redistribution of wealth. However, in practice, "socialism" changed somewhat during first half of the 20th century. In Europe, up until the 1960's, socialism in practice meant that the government should own only certain basic industries, including transportation, utilities, and communications. Now (after James Callaghan in England and Barack Obama in America), socialism has gone back to the more radical concept of Saint-Simon. Currently under the quasi-socialist economies of England and America, the government can own any large company. According to a 2010 report by the Department of Commerce, the US government controls 35% of the national economy, or "the means of production."[64]

The other half of socialism is redistributing the wealth via transfer payments. This part of socialism has also grown dramatically. In our modern era approximately one quarter of the US population (seventy-four million people) depend on the government for some type of financial support.[65] Furthermore, as of 2009, 40% of the US population received *more money from the government* than they paid in taxes.[66] Of course this 40% figure includes government employees. However, even these people are still the net beneficiaries of other people's money.

Henri de Saint-Simon's concept of socialism required a powerful central government in order to redistribute the nation's wealth. However, not all of the early socialists agreed with this idea. The first definition of socialism presented in the English language came from the 19th century socialist and utopian, Robert Owen (1771-1858). He argued that socialism meant the means of production should be *owned by the workers themselves*, not by the government. Owen understood that government leaders and the workers are two different groups of people, with different interests.

At the present time, most socialists believe that the *government* should own and control the economy, not the workers. So the majority of today's socialists have chosen to follow Saint-Simon, instead of Robert Owen. Therefore, for a working definition of socialism, we will follow the modern trend and use the concepts of Saint-Simon. Socialism then is, *"An economic system in which the government owns the means of production and redistributes the nation's wealth."*

Socialists have long defended the redistribution of wealth with their famous slogan *"From each according to his ability and to each according to his needs."*[67] Under this principle, the government taxes productive people based on their ability to pay (i.e. taxing wealthy people at a higher percentage than poor people), and then the government hands that money over to poor people, based on how much they need. To many people this sounds quite fair. Socialism even sounds pragmatic, because it would appear to prevent the lower classes from rioting and looting due to their poverty. In fact, these are exactly the two reasons that most people living in Western industrialized nations have accepted socialism; it seems both fair and pragmatic.

Whether or not socialism is truly fair and pragmatic will be discussed in Chapters Four and Seven. Later on we will see that the theory of socialism described in the previous paragraphs is very different from the practice of socialism. In theory, socialism only takes from the rich and only gives to the poor. However, as we will see throughout the rest of this book, in reality, socialism often takes money from the poor and middle class, and then gives that money to the rich.

Most of the Modern Liberal news media have consistently supported socialism for the past fifty years. For example, in the following statement, the New York Times celebrated the creation of a:

"...new philosophy of social welfare that seeks to establish the status of welfare benefits as rights, based on the notion that everyone is entitled to a share of the common wealth."[68]

In December of 2010, Republicans tried to extend tax cuts for everyone, including the wealthy. Democrats did not want wealthy people to receive any tax cuts, for purely socialist reasons. Democrat Senator Dianne Feinstein was typical, saying, *"I don't know a single millionaire who needs a tax cut right now."*[69] This statement is perfectly consistent with the main principle of socialism that we just discussed, "From each according to his ability, and to each according to his need." According to this thinking, rich people do not deserve to keep their wealth. The government can take whatever it wants from them, *because the government can decide how much money everyone "needs."*

This support for the main principle of socialism is virtually universal among Modern Liberals. For example, in October of 2008, when Barack Obama was challenged by a citizen to justify raising taxes on wealthier Americans, Obama used a purely socialist reason; *"I think when we spread the wealth, it's good for everybody."* Yet whenever conservatives correctly call these Democrats "socialists," the conservatives are shouted down by the mainstream media. Comparing Democrats to socialists is considered "outrageous" and "hateful." But these conservatives are merely pointing out an ugly truth.

This Modern Liberal support for socialism completely contradicts the thinking of the Founding Fathers who created our great nation. According to Thomas Jefferson, "to spread the wealth" was both immoral and undesirable:

"To take from one, because it is thought that his industry and that of his father's has acquired too much, in order to spare (help) others, who have not exercised equal industry or skill, is to violate arbitrarily the first principle of association, 'the guarantee to everyone of the free exercise of his industry, and the fruits acquired by it.'"[70]

Even Jefferson's political enemy, Alexander Hamilton, agreed that socialism and liberty were incompatible. You can have one or the other, but not both. So according to Hamilton, if you want liberty, you must be willing to accept economic inequality:

"Inequality will exist so long as liberty exists. It unavoidably results from that liberty itself."[71]

America's traditional disapproval of socialism did not die out with the Founding Fathers. It dominated American politics through the 19th century, and the earliest part of the 20th century, all the way up until the administration of Herbert Hoover. According to Abraham Lincoln:

"Private property is desirable, is a positive good in the world...Let not him who is houseless pull down the house of another, but let him work diligently to build one for himself, thus by example assuring that his own shall be safe from violence."[72]

Peter W. Hauer

AMERICAN REVOLUTION VS FRENCH REVOLUTION

The Founding Fathers' respect for property rights made them very different from the French Revolutionaries of 1789. The American rebels were nearly all capitalists, while the French rebels were mostly socialists. The most famous slogan of the French Revolution ("Liberty, Equality, Fraternity!") came from socialism. When the French revolutionaries said "Equality," they meant equality in every possible way; socially, politically, and *economically*. Yet when the American rebels sought equality, they only meant equal legal rights for all citizens.

The French concept is fatally flawed, because "liberty" and "economic equality" are contradictory. They cannot exist together in the same society. The government can either protect liberty or it can enforce equality of wealth. It cannot do both, because they are opposite actions. This illustrates that conservatism is not just different from socialism, it is the exact opposite. Under conservatism, the government exists *to protect private property*. Under socialism the government exists *to take away private property* and give it to others.

These two revolutions were different in other important ways. These differences explain why the American Revolution led to a peaceful government, while the French Revolution led to a bloodbath. First, the American rebels based their new government on the ancient foundations of Anglo-Saxon liberty (government by consent, the law of the land, and property rights). Second, the Americans accepted additional rights which came from the Enlightenment, such as freedom of speech, freedom of religion, and freedom of the press. Third, the Americans accepted Edmund Burke's concept that society should only change gradually, based on centuries of accumulated wisdom. Fourth, as we shall see in Chapter Six, the American rebels founded the United States on the moral teachings of Christianity.[73] By following this four-fold path, the American rebels created a peaceful government, with only limited power, but with great personal freedom.

In contrast, the French revolutionaries based their new government on the radical ideas of the Philosophes. First, the French revolutionaries accepted Saint-Pierre's idea that the government should re-distribute the nation's wealth. Second, they accepted Rousseau's belief that the government should have *absolute power* over the people. Third, they accepted Rousseau's idea that previous traditions should be destroyed, so that the government can create a brand new society from scratch. Fourth, they followed Voltaire's idea that the government should not be influenced by Christianity in any way. By following these authoritarian ideas, the French Revolution quickly led to tyranny and slaughter.

SOCIALISM MEANS BIGGER GOVERNMENT

Socialism naturally requires a powerful central government, in order to administer the economy, and also to constantly redistribute the wealth of all citizens. This powerful government is necessarily a "top down" arrangement. It requires a vertically structured society, where a political elite controls all the other members of society. This is true whether the political elite is elected or not.

David Hume was a brilliant historian and philosopher from 18th century England. Hume (an atheist) was a friend and ally to many of the Modern Liberal philosophes in France. However, Hume disagreed with the socialism of Saint-Pierre, because Hume saw the danger posed by any government that was powerful enough to redistribute the wealth. Hume understood why socialism leads to tyranny:

"[If we] render possessions ever so equal, men's different degrees of art, care and industry will immediately break that equality. Or if you check these virtues…the most rigorous inquisition is requisite to watch every inequality on its first appearance, and the most severe jurisdiction to punish and redress it…So much authority must soon degenerate into tyranny." [74]

In both Russia and China, the movement towards socialism and tyranny burst forth in sudden and traumatic revolts, first with the Bolshevik coup in Russia, and later with the Maoist victory in China. Nowadays in the USA and Western Europe, this movement toward socialism and tyranny is happening more gradually and peacefully.

The government (by definition) has a monopoly on political power. If you also give the government economic power, then you give it nearly complete control over the people. If the government has power over the economy, then it will control how many people will work, who will work, how long they will work, and how much money they can keep for their families. This is the danger Americans have been facing ever since the administration of FDR.

Socialism's need for a powerful government makes some conservatives suspect that socialists have an ulterior motive. These cynical conservatives suspect that the real motive behind socialism is the accumulation of power, not the redistribution of wealth. They believe that redistributing the wealth is merely the excuse that politicians use to gain power over the nation's wealth:

"...communism was a tactic employed for the assumption of power, rather than a sincere belief. These same tactics, modified only slightly, are being used today...A socialist economy—even socialism under a parliamentary system of government—concentrates power in the hands of the few who run the state...To conspirators, socialism serves as a control-the-wealth program, not a share-the-wealth program." [75] (Thomas R. Eddlem.)

During the two decades between WWI and WWII, the political elites in the West gradually accepted the socialist concept that the government should control the economy and redistribute the wealth. They also accepted the Modern Liberal idea that the government should play the primary role in improving society. From that time on, the central governments of the northern hemisphere became extremely powerful and far reaching. The central governments throughout the industrialized West grew to assume a major role in fostering everything from a healthy economy, to health care, to education, to social responsibility, and even morality.

In this way, English speaking liberals finally accepted the powerful central government that Hobbs had advocated three hundred years earlier. However, they did not do this for the reasons offered by Hobbs. Hobbs thought a powerful central government was needed *merely to keep social order*, especially in a society that was starting to develop large populations within its cities. Urban populations have always been noted for their lack of strong social bonds to family and neighbors. This feeling of alienation tends to produce a more volatile population compared to rural folk.

Instead, Modern Liberals came to accept the leviathan (large central government) for reasons that came from the Jacobins of the French Revolution. Modern Liberals knew that only a strong central government could tax the nation's wealth and redistribute it among the masses. Only a strong central government would have the power to make everyone economically equal. Only a strong central government would have the authority to experiment with society on a national scale. This Modern Liberal thinking clearly went against the classic liberal (and conservative) idea that the central government should only have *limited powers*.

There was only one short interlude, during the 1960's, when Modern Liberals briefly supported individual freedom, and opposed big government. In effect they momentarily adopted the libertarian views of conservatism and classic liberalism. During that unusual decade, Modern Liberals adopted visceral slogans of true liberty, such as "Question Authority," "Fuck the Establishment," and "Hell No, We Won't Go!" Some conservative scholars believe this development was mostly due to the adolescent spirit of rebellion.

However, adolescent rebellion was only part of the story. This brief Modern Liberal opposition to government authority was primarily due to one policy of the federal government: the Vietnam War. College students especially resented the draft, because they knew they would be subject to it upon graduation. Unfortunately this Modern Liberal flirtation with libertarianism was short-lived. It ended almost immediately after the war ended. American troops had nearly all left Vietnam by the summer of 1971, and the student unrest (along with their opposition to government power) quickly evaporated. By the late 1970's, these former radicals of the baby boom generation began to grasp the reins of government power. Not surprisingly, they quickly became ardent supporters of big government. Modern Liberalism was back on its normal track.

THE LONG ARM OF SOCIALISM

Socialism does not merely affect the economy. It can affect every part of your life, including your physical health. For example, socialized medicine is providing Europeans with low quality health care and long delays for cancer treatment. As a result, if you develop colon cancer in Europe you are most likely going to die. In contrast, in America (with our capitalist, profit motivated health care system) you are most likely going to live. For example, England has only a 40% survival rate for colon cancer. In contrast, America enjoys a 60% survival rate for colon cancer.[76] Americans are also more likely to survive heart disease, breast cancer, prostate cancer, and leukemia than Europeans. Americans are also more likely than Europeans to receive preventative tests to help detect cancer earlier, such as pap smears, mammograms, prostate exams, and colonoscopies. Now which health care system truly needs fixing?

Whenever the government takes over a social function, such as health care, it opens the door for fraud. This is because government agencies have no profit motive. Therefore, they have no motive to stop fraud, or any other form of waste. The more money an agency gives out (whether to deserving people or to criminals submitting fraudulent claims) the better the agency's chances are for an increase in the next federal budget. This explains why bureaucrats generally don't care where the money goes, so long as the money gets spent.

This bureaucratic apathy is probably the main reason that Medicare loses 60 billion dollars each year *in just one type of billing fraud.*[77] Sadly, this particular fraud has been going on for years, because the government lacks any profit motive to care about where the money is going. This dynamic alone shows that we should not be putting our health care into government hands. Private insurance companies are not perfect, but at least they have a motive to keep costs down, and to prevent money from being wasted through fraud. The government has no such motives.

SOCIALISM FINALLY TAKES ROOT

The establishment of the modern social welfare state had a false start during the abortive revolutions of 1848. Most of the revolts were easily suppressed by the monarchies of that era. However, the Prussian ruling class decided that they had better start sharing at least part of the nation's wealth with their restless working class. The model they adopted had been created by the great German corporate capitalist, Krupp. Krupp guaranteed medical care for his employees. Krupp even guaranteed a retirement pension for his employees. These new ideas were quickly adopted by clever Prussian politicians such as Bismarck. In Prussia we find Western civilization's first government-run retirement system, the precursor to the modern welfare state.

Contemporary socialists tend to exaggerate the amount of socialism that existed in Prussia's early social welfare state. It was not nearly as all encompassing as our modern social welfare state. In old Prussia, all benefits were tied to employment. If you did not work, then your family received nothing. Even the benefits were mostly paid for by the workers themselves, out of deductions taken from their salaries. The government contributed only a small share of the benefits.

Yet the Prussian model was the first successful attempt by any government to create a national retirement fund for workers.[78] It was an important first step in the long march towards the modern welfare state. A few decades later, in 1907, Kaiser Wilhelm II established a national health insurance program which covered poor Germans, so long as they participated in government "work exchanges" located in the major German cities.[79] Once again, the Prussian model still tied social benefits to work requirements.

While the Prussian government embraced social welfare programs as a vehicle to maintain power, the Prussians never accepted the other half of Modern Liberalism; i.e. globalism. The 19th century Prussians were far too nationalistic to cede any sovereignty to an international government. This explains why socialism flourished long before globalism. Nationalism naturally stands in the way of globalism, but nationalism does not stand in the way of socialism. This brings us to the issue of sovereignty.

WHAT IS SOVEREIGNTY?

Whenever a conservative complains that the United Nations is "weakening American sovereignty," most listeners become bored and disinterested. After all, sovereignty is widely seen as an arcane concept; dry and not really clear to most people. So when Modern Liberals reply that sovereignty is antiquated, and that it constitutes an obstacle to world peace, many people assume they are correct.

In truth, sovereignty is terribly important for any nation. In simple terms, *sovereignty is the right of the people to govern themselves.* So sovereignty is not just a power possessed by the government. It is also a right of the people to decide how they will be governed. In this sense, sovereignty is a very basic human right. After all, if we lose our sovereignty, then we no longer have any control over our government. Therefore, if we lose our sovereignty, all of our civil rights could easily be taken away.

Peter W. Hauer

WHAT IS GLOBALISM?

Nowadays, the term globalism has several different meanings. To some people it means the creation of a global culture. To others, it means free trade throughout the earth. However, for our purposes, globalism shall refer to; *the effort to create a GLOBAL GOVERNMENT with power over the entire human population.*

Globalism seeks to eliminate sovereign nations, and replace them with an international body that will govern the entire planet. So this global government would not merely regulate how nations interact with each other, but rather it would rule directly over the whole human population. The alleged benefit to such an arrangement would be the elimination of war. The idea is that if sovereign nations no longer exist, then it will be logically impossible for any nation to declare war.

Obviously the elimination of war is a very tempting goal. This explains why Modern Liberals have eagerly supported globalism ever since Saint-Pierre first suggested it back in 1712. For example, the philosophes all supported globalism, and so in turn did the Illuminati and the Jacobins who followed them. The Illuminati even coined the expression "citizen of the world."[80]

Globalism has been gradually imposed upon the world ever since the end of World War II. It has primarily been implemented by a series of trade agreements that require the signing states to give up increasing amounts of control over their economic decisions, including tariffs, taxes, subsidies, and sometimes even wages and working conditions. Globalism has also been fostered by numerous UN treaties and protocols that are unrelated to trade.

Globalism has progressed slowly but consistently. The supporters of globalism are very patient, working over several generations on "the great cause." As early as 1917, the British diplomat and ardent globalist, Lionel Curtis wrote:

"The world is in throes which precede creation or death. Our whole race has outgrown the merely national state and [we] will surely pass either to a great Commonwealth of Nations or else an empire of slaves." [81]

In 1950, the German leader Conrad Adenauer dreamed that the national boundaries of Europe would someday be abolished, resulting

The Big Picture

in the unification of the European continent.[82] A half century later his dream came true. Americans generally cherish their national sovereignty more than most other nations. However, even American policy makers soon began to follow the lead of their European globalist friends. In 1939, US diplomat John Foster Dulles wrote:

"The fundamental fact is that the nationalist system of wholly independent, fully sovereign states is completing its cycle of usefulness. It is imperative that there be a transition to a new order."[83]

Succeeding generations of American diplomats have long maintained this support for global government. In 1966, Henry Kissinger said:

"The ultimate goal of a supra-nationalist world community will not come quickly…but it is not too early to prepare ourselves for this step beyond the nation state."[84]

As early as 1952 the globalists in charge of the *Saturday Review* were boasting that the real goal behind the United Nations was global government:

"If UNESCO (United Nations Educational, Scientific and Cultural Organization) is attacked on grounds that it is helping to prepare the world's peoples for world government, then it is an error to burst forth with apologetic statements and denials. Let us face it: the job of UNESCO is to help create and promote the elements of World Citizenship. When faced with such a 'charge' let us by all means affirm it from the rooftops."[85]

For the past fifty years, the influential National Education Association has been working hard to undermine American sovereignty, and to encourage global government in its place. As early as the 1960s and throughout the 1970s, the NEA was distributing film strips and teaching guides that were designed:

"…to help students see the world as it is now, and explore possibilities for how it might be in the future. The filmstrips question the usefulness of our system of sovereign nation-states. They challenge the students to design an appropriate world system."[86]

Beginning in the late 1960's, some of the most powerful members of Congress (most notably Representative Wayne Hayes of Ohio and Senator Allan Cranston of California) also supported the birth of a global super state. Since 1972, nearly every important member of the US Congress has also been a member of the Council on Foreign Relations, (CFR) an influential globalist organization. Its avowed purpose is to help eliminate sovereign nations in favor of a new global super state.

The promoters of globalism are patient because they know that any sudden elimination of sovereignty would alert the common people to what is happening. By taking small steps that gradually reduce American sovereignty, the globalists are less likely to arouse suspicion. This explains why members of the powerful Council on Foreign Relations have frequently called for *a gradual erosion of American sovereignty,* instead of a sudden elimination of it. According to the journal Foreign Affairs (the publishing arm of the CFR):

"...an end run around national sovereignty, eroding it piece by piece, will accomplish much more in the long run than the old fashioned frontal assault."[87]

The chairman of the CFR, Richard Hass, endorsed this gradual assault on American sovereignty in his book *The Opportunity*. He even offered a timetable for when most sovereignty will be eliminated: *"Our policies must recognize that globalization is a reality, not a choice... Sovereignty is conditional, even contractual, rather than absolute...The world 35 years from now will be semi-sovereign."*

Unfortunately, this gradual elimination of our sovereignty will also gradually eliminate our civil rights. James Madison was correct when he warned us over two hundred years ago:

"Since the general civilizations of mankind I believe there are more instances of the abridgement of the freedom of the people by gradual and silent encroachments of those in power than by violent and sudden usurpations."[88]

As we shall see in the next few pages, the international community is quite determined to take away the individual freedoms that we enjoy as Americans.

TWO LESSONS FROM HISTORY

As long as the globalists continue to control both American political parties, the mass media, and the teachers' unions, then time is on their side. For example, it took about 50 years for the European Union to be created.[89] It all began in 1952, when six European nations signed what appeared to be a simple trade agreement. It was called the "European Coal and Steel Agreement." It created a governing body to resolve any disputes regarding these two important commodities. It also "relaxed the borders" of the six member nations. Gradually, more nations were added to the agreement, and more products and commodities were included. The result was the "European Common Market."

Just a few years later, with the 1957 Treaty of Rome, the European Common Market was transformed into the European Economic Community, (ECC). Libertarian Conservatives warned that this new arrangement might become the basis for a European super state. The mainstream news media dismissed such warnings as mere paranoia. Later events proved they were not paranoid at all. The next step was to change the confederation into the "European Community," (EC). Gradually, members of the EC began to openly discuss their plans for creating a European super state. Finally, at the dawn of the new millennium, the members of the EC changed themselves into our modern "European Union." Indeed, Europe now has a continental legislature, a continental court, and a continental executive.

The other lesson from history occurred a bit earlier. In 1819, the creation of the German unified state also began with a simple free trade agreement. It was called the Zollverein. Initially it was presented to the independent German states simply as a way to "relax the borders." It was touted as a way for the sovereign German states to open up free trade amongst themselves. However, the creator of the Zollverein, Friedrich List, had bigger ideas. In fact, he was an early globalist:

"If the whole world were united by a union like the twenty-four states of North America, free trade would be as natural and beneficial as it is now in the Zollverein."[90]

By 1834 the majority of the German states had joined in this free trade agreement, including the important states of Prussia and Bavaria. Sure enough, by 1871, about fifty years after the process was begun,

Germany finally became a unified state. Of course the Franco-Prussian War and Bismarck's diplomacy both contributed to German unification. However, the economic groundwork had already been laid by the creators of the Zollverein a half century earlier.

Remember, fifty years is also how long it took to unify Europe into a single super state. It too began with a free trade agreement. Therefore, conservatives are probably not being paranoid when they fear that NAFTA (The North American Free Trade Agreement) will eventually turn the United States into part of a gigantic super state, including what is now the USA, Canada, and Mexico. This new entity will be named the North American Union (NAU). It was negotiated by the George Bush Sr. administration with delegations from Mexico and Canada. These things take time, but they are almost inevitable once the process of "relaxing the borders" has begun.

NAFTA was signed by Bill Clinton in 1994. If history is any indicator, then approximately fifty years later (2044) the United States will likely no longer exist as a sovereign nation. It will be part of a continental super state, probably ruled from Houston Texas, which by then will be almost entirely Spanish speaking. President George Bush Sr. and Mexican leaders even negotiated the creation of a new continental currency. The name of this proposed currency has still not been officially announced, for fear of encouraging opposition to the planned NAU. However, the tentative name for this new currency is the "Amero."

GLOBALISM SUBVERTS LIBERTY

The first problem with globalism is that it would certainly reduce our civil rights. Remember, most member states of the UN are not free nations. They are mostly violent, repressive dictatorships. It is hard to imagine that representatives appointed by the King of Saudi Arabia or the strongman of North Korea will really care about our civil rights. For any American who truly values his civil rights under the US Constitution, *global government is a frightening prospect.*

The United Nations has already shown itself to be an enemy of individual freedom. For example, the UN Declaration of Human Rights is tailor made for dictatorship. First of all, it offers no right to a jury trial. Why should it? Other nations trust government appointed judges to rule on all cases. This means that if the accused is really being prosecuted because of his political beliefs, then he has no remedy. So political persecution cannot be prevented under the UN Declaration of Human Rights.

There is also no right to a speedy trial, and no right to confront witnesses against you. The UN document only promises, *"a fair trial,"* whatever that might mean. The UN Declaration of Human Rights also fails to guarantee fair compensation for any property seized by the government. So you can forget about your rights under the Fifth Amendment to the US Constitution.

Most disturbing of all, article twenty-nine of the UN Declaration contains two general caveats that could easily be used to take away all of the rights previously listed. The first caveat says that all the previously listed rights are *"subject only to such limitations…as are determined by law…meeting the just requirements of morality, public order and the general welfare in a democratic society."* Most of the nations in the UN are dictatorships. So these brutal dictators will decide how your rights may be limited. The second UN caveat is even more ominous:

"These rights and freedoms may in no case be exercised contrary to the purposes and principles of the United Nations."

So according to the UN, you have no right to free speech if your speech would contradict any purpose that the UN has adopted. This means the global government will take away your freedom of speech if your speech disagrees with its policies. What can we call a government that will not permit people to speak against its policies? It is tyranny.

GLOBALISM IS UNDEMOCRATIC

Global government would also create a huge gulf between the rulers and the people. If the common people have any vote whatsoever, i.e. by electing representatives to any global legislature, then their power to vote would be weakened. Their vote would not be as potent as it is now in traditional national elections. For example, currently in the USA, each representative in Congress answers to less than one million people in his district. However, under a global government, a typical representative would have to represent anywhere from roughly fifteen to forty million people. Otherwise the legislative body would be too big to actually work. It would have to include thousands of representatives.

Therefore, under global government, the individual voter could not possibly make his voice heard as effectively as he could under a national government. This means that the influence of the individual voter would be diluted under global government, making it *less responsive to the voters*. Therefore global government will be *less democratic* than traditional national government.

This anti-democratic tendency within globalism is not limited to the United Nations. The European Union is another globalist organization because it too seeks to erase the boundaries and laws of sovereign states. Just like the UN, it is also anti-democratic. For example, in recent years the peoples of France, Ireland and the Netherlands all voted to reject the proposed constitution of the European Union. However, the bureaucrats in Brussels who run the European Union claim these national votes had no legal effect. These bureaucrats claim that because *the governments* of these three nations had already decided to join the European Union (prior to the referendums), *the will of the people is now irrelevant*. The elitists who support globalism nearly always violate the will of the common people.

The President of the European Union is not elected by the people of Europe. The various national heads of state take turns occupying the Presidency for twelve months. Even the legislature has some very undemocratic traits. The members of the EU Parliament are themselves elected, but they cannot initiate any new laws. Only the "European Commission" can introduce new laws. Sadly, none of these Commissioners are elected. The powerful European Commission is an oligarchy of appointed bureaucrats.

GLOBALISM & GENOCIDE

The third problem with globalism is that it will probably encourage the worst human activity of all: *government sponsored genocide*. Most people mistakenly believe that war is the worst of all human activities. However, government sponsored genocide actually kills far more people than war does. Therefore, genocide is even worse than war.

For instance, throughout the 20th century, governments slaughtered one hundred nineteen million people (119,000,000) in government sponsored genocides. In contrast, the number of people killed by combat operations in the 20th century was about thirty five million (35,000,000).[91] Therefore, in terms of human lives lost, government sponsored genocide is three times worse than warfare. With a truly global government, genocide could be carried out anywhere in the world, because no sovereign nations would be left to oppose the carnage.

This brings up the most damning criticism against globalism. It is the sheer danger of giving overwhelming military power to an international body so it can *forcefully* prevent war. Such overwhelming military power will almost certainly be misused, especially when the majority of members in the global super state are dictatorships. As early as 1935, the renowned Leopold Amery (historian, Member of Parliament, cabinet secretary and First Lord of the Admiralty) was prescient enough to foresee the dangers inherent to any powerful international body:

"...a league (international body) which was to maintain peace by going to war whenever peace was disturbed. That sort of thing, if it could exist, would be a danger to peace; it would be employed to extend war rather than to put an end to it."[92]

In a very practical sense, international laws are not really laws at all, because they cannot be enforced. International laws are merely suggestions for good behavior. Sovereign states can still act as they wish, limited only by their economic and military power. This is a good thing, because the global power that would be needed to enforce international law would itself become a monstrous tyranny. If a government such as the UN had a monopoly on military force, then that government would be all powerful. Using the logic of Lord Acton, if absolute power corrupts absolutely, then the new global government will certainly abuse its power, despite any legal safeguards which might be envisioned to prevent such abuse.

The United Nations already has a history of supporting tyrants. For example, as early as 1961 the UN forcefully invaded Katanga, the southern province of Congo. The UN used overwhelming force to ruthlessly crush a popular independence movement in Katanga. Instead of supporting the rebels, the UN chose to fight on behalf of Congo's Marxist central government, which was run by a violent megalomaniac named Patrice Lumumba. In order to break the back of the popular rebellion, UN "peacekeepers" regularly bombed and burned down villages that were suspected of supporting the rebels. The UN has never apologized for this brutal aggression. After all, it was done "in the name of peace."

PEACE-KEEPING THROUGH TERROR

The Katangan debacle was only the beginning of human rights abuses committed by UN mercenaries.[93] The mainstream media prefers to call them "peace-keepers." However, UN troops certainly fit the classic definition of a mercenary, which is; *a professional soldier who is paid to fight in the service of a power other than his native country.* The term peace-keeper is a deceptive euphemism for these mercenary troops. More often than not, UN troops bring the opposite of peace, by terrorizing the local civilian population.

For example, throughout much of West Africa, UN troops are notorious for their despicable method of distributing food aid among starving villagers. They simply demand to have sex with young girls in exchange for food. If a family does not have an eight or twelve year-old daughter to give up, then they starve.

In areas that have more plentiful food supplies, such as Congo and Uganda, UN troops cannot use food as a leverage to obtain young girls. In these situations they rely on sheer force of arms to abuse the civilian population. In 2006, UN troops in Uganda committed flagrant abuse of women, including public rapes. When journalist Matt Lee exposed the UN crimes in New York City's "The Inner City Press," the UN quickly cancelled its entire operation in Uganda. Apparently the UN hierarchy feared that other press outlets might start to cover this ugly story. The UN worked quickly to make it "old news." Indeed, the national and international media largely ignored the story.

So contrary to their public image, the soldiers in those baby blue helmets are often just violent thugs. Even worse, these savages enjoy immunity from local prosecution, and even immunity from lawsuits, courtesy of the United Nations. Of course not all UN mercenaries are rapists and murderers. Some of them must surely want to prevent war. However, the incidents of abuse by UN troops are so frequent, and the incidents where UN troops are punished are so rare, that one may reasonably suspect the UN leadership of complicity in condoning these human rights abuses.

Sadly, this situation will only grow worse after global government is fully realized. After all, how much more abusive will UN troops become after the UN gains a complete monopoly on military power? In the words of Milton Friedman:

"Concentrated power is not rendered harmless by the good intentions of those who create it."[94]

CONCLUSION ON THE UNITED NATIONS

The goal of the United Nations is to impose global government. This will destroy American sovereignty, i.e. our right to govern ourselves. Without sovereignty, we will lose our civil rights. The stated benefit from global government (the end of war) will never be realized. The global government itself would start wars and become oppressive with its military power, because it would have *absolute power*. This means we are giving up our sovereignty and our civil rights in exchange for a false promise. Therefore, the United Nations is fatally flawed. It should be abolished. At the very least, the United States should withdraw from it.

"THE MILNER GROUP"

The story of how socialism and globalism were both adopted by Modern Liberals in England and America is fascinating. Of course it had much to do with the changing culture, as evidenced by the works of hundreds of Modern Liberal authors, from H.G. Wells and George Bernard Shaw in England to Upton Sinclair and John Steinbeck in America. However, to fully understand what happened, we must go back to England over a hundred years ago. We must focus on a handful of influential men who shared a grandiose dream. In 1885, the wealthy adventurer Cecil Rhodes brought together an elite group of powerful Englishmen. They began meeting to plan ways they could quietly influence official policy within the English government.

In just a few years, this group was able to establish influence within both the Liberal and Conservative Parties. Because of this, the group could never be entirely removed from power. Yet the activities of this important group have only been obliquely mentioned in less than a dozen history books. The many history books that have been written by members of the group discreetly fail to mention anything about it.

The most eminent American historian to fully document the activities of this group was the late Dr. Carroll Quigley of Georgetown University. Dr. Quigley was one of the most erudite historians of the 20th century. By the time of his death in 1976, Dr. Quigley had influenced two generations of American diplomats and government leaders. President Bill Clinton cited Dr. Quigley twice in one of his inauguration speeches. There is probably no other academician whose ideas have been more frequently championed in the prestigious journal *Foreign Affairs* than Dr. Quigley.

Yet despite his stellar contributions to scholarship, Dr. Quigley is virtually unknown outside of academia and government. Dr. Quigley is often referred to by history PhD candidates, Foreign Service Officers, and Rhodes scholars (such as Mr. Clinton), but almost never by anyone else. This is not surprising. Dr. Quigley's books are tedious reading. His seminal work, *Tragedy and Hope* is nearly 1400 pages long.

In his other seldom read book, *The Anglo-American Establishment*, Dr. Quigley describes the origins and activities of this group, which he loosely calls "The Milner Group," after its most influential early member, the Viscount (Lord) Alfred Milner. This book is extremely detailed and makes difficult reading because of Dr. Quigley's turgid writing style. His detailed descriptions of the marital connections between various group members are lengthy and dull. Yet for the patient reader, Dr. Quigley's book provides a wonderful window into the nursery of Modern Liberalism.

Cecil Rhodes conceived of the secret plan in the mid 1870's, but could not put it into action until the late 1880's. Dr. Quigley says the group really didn't gain political influence until 1891. In London, Rhodes discretely befriended a few powerful politicians and wealthy Lords of the realm. All of them shared his view that the British Empire should be expanded for the benefit of all mankind. The British Empire was then seen as the most expedient way to spread the civilizing influence of Western culture. Here was ethnocentrism on a Messianic level. Yet by the standards of their own era, these men were considered quite liberal. This fact alone helps to show that multiculturalism is not necessarily part and parcel with Modern Liberalism.

HOW TO CHANGE THE WORLD

When Cecil Rhodes created the Milner Group, he was prudent enough to bring in a few key members of the British press, in order to prevent any unfavorable publicity about their activities. For example, the most renowned English journalist of that era was William T. Snead. Rhodes quickly made Snead part of the group's inner circle. Later, the Editor in Chief of the Times of London was recruited into the inner circle of the Milner Group as well. Influence over the Times of London was considered so important by the group, that its Editor in Chief was a member of the Milner Group from 1897 to 1945. The only exceptions were three years from 1919-1922. In fact, to regain control of the highly influential Times, Lord Milner persuaded Lord and Lady Astor (also members of the inner circle) to purchase a controlling interest in the Times in 1922. This guaranteed the group's influence over the most influential news source in the British Empire.

To control the writing of any history about themselves, the Milner Group wisely created the two prestigious organs that future generations of historians would end up mining for their research. One was the British Empire's periodical *The Round Table*, and the other was South Africa's leading journal, *The State*. Later the Milner Group gained editorial control over the British National Dictionary of Biography, and also over the prestigious Encyclopedia Britannica. Virtually all the profiles about group members were written by other members of the group. Of course these articles were flattering and non-controversial.

The other two members of the original tribune (besides Rhodes himself) were Reginald Brett (Lord Esher) and Lord Milner. Together these three men influenced British education, finance, and politics. In regard to politics, Dr. Carroll Quigley notes that Lord Esher was the single most influential advisor to both King Edward VII and King George V. Furthermore, Rhodes also had numerous connections within Parliament.

In regard to education, Lord Milner had almost complete control over three of the most prestigious colleges at Oxford. These were Balliol, All Souls, and New College. This control was exercised through sympathetic chair holders who were usually members of the group's outer circle. These prestigious "chairs" (or teaching positions) were usually funded by wealthy members of the Milner Group. If a promising young man wished to enter government in the fields of politics, law, or foreign affairs, it was almost mandatory that he should obtain a fellowship at one of the three colleges controlled by the Milner Group.

In regard to finance, Rhodes brought in not just his own financial power, but he also obtained financial backing from two of the richest men in Africa, Abe Baily and Alfred Beit. Rhodes even persuaded the wealthy international banker, Lord Nathan Rothschild, to join the group. The group's first meetings took place in Rothschild's home.

Some conspiracy theorists insist that Rothschild's membership somehow proves that the Milner Group was a clandestine Zionist plot. However, Lord Rothschild was never a member of the group's governing tribunal. He was simply a wealthy man who happened to agree with Rhodes' vision of spreading Western civilization through global government. In fact, according to Dr. Quigley, Lord Rothschild began to lose interest in the group after Rhodes died in 1902. Eventually Rothschild stopped attending meetings entirely. After that he only contributed some money, but no real leadership.

Rhodes made five wills before he died. Four of these left the bulk of his enormous fortune to the Milner Group, for the stated purpose of spreading the British Empire. However, according to Dr. Quigley, other members of the group advised Rhodes to exclude the group from being mentioned in his will, for fear of exposure should his will ever become a public document. Therefore, in his fifth and final will, Rhodes left nearly all of his fortune to endow the now famous Rhodes scholarship fund instead.

This was an indirect way to accomplish the same purpose. Rhodes scholarships were intended to bring promising young foreigners from various parts of the far flung British Empire over to Oxford for their educations. In England these bright young men would be imbued with "English values." When they returned to their homelands, they would presumably take these English values back with them. The Rhodes scholarship fund was a benevolent form of cultural imperialism. Cecil Rhodes also made sure that the Rhodes scholarships would be open to any competent scholar, regardless of their race or religion. In this regard Rhodes was ahead of his time.

After Rhodes died in 1902, Lord Milner became the undisputed leader of the clique up until his own death in 1922. Under Milner's stewardship, the group's influence on British foreign policy became pervasive. This explains why Dr. Quigley named the group after Lord Milner. How great was their influence? The Milner Group had an extremely impressive list of accomplishments for an informal circle of friends. They actually plotted and helped to carry out the Jameson Raid of 1895. This provocative raid into Dutch African territory sparked the Boer War in Africa. Then the Milner Group worked hard to quell any opposition to the war in Parliament. After the British won the war, the Milner Group created the Union of South Africa in 1906.

From World War I through World War II, members of the Milner Group usually held the following government posts: Ambassador to the United States, Counselor to the Embassy, First Secretary to the Embassy, Secretary of State for the Colonies, Secretary of State for Dominion Affairs, Secretary of State for Foreign Affairs, President of the Board of Education, Secretary of State for War, Secretary of the War Cabinet, Solicitor General, Attorney General, Chairman of the Board of Internal Revenue, and High Commissioner of South Africa. The Milner Group was also represented on the Board of the Bank of England, but it did not always hold the governorship.

With access to all these positions of power, the Milner Group was able to push forward Cecil Rhodes' plan for an international government to prevent war. As we will soon see, the Milner Group was actually the driving force behind the League of Nations and later behind the United Nations. Of course the idea of global government originated with Saint-Pierre, but it was the Milner Group that finally put this idea into practice over two centuries later.

The famous Balfour Declaration obligated the British government to support a Jewish homeland in the Holy Land. It should have been properly called the Milner Declaration, since Lord Milner and fellow member Leopold Amery actually wrote it. The Milner Group was also largely responsible for the departure of British troops from India, much to the chagrin of conservatives such as Winston Churchill. The Milner Group also successfully pushed for the early independence of both Egypt and India. In fact, it was the Milner Group that transformed the British Empire into the loosely associated "Commonwealth of Nations."

The Milner Group also played a critical role in forcing the abdication of King Edward VIII in 1936. In the 1930's Lord Lothian was one of the three tribunes who controlled the Milner Group. It was Lord Lothian who told the Washington Post about the King's love affair with an American strumpet named Wallis Simpson. After American newspapers started to cover the story widely, it became impossible for the British Press to keep the story secret.[95] The resulting scandal forced the King to abdicate.

We can only speculate as to why the Milner Group wanted to dethrone King Edward VIII. Remember, as a secret group they kept no minutes of their meetings. One possible reason is because Edward was firmly opposed to the League of Nations. Another possible explanation is because the Milner Group disagreed with most of Edward's imperial policies. In any event, the abdication of Edward VIII turned out to be very beneficial for Great Britain, because Edward VIII was very much pro-Nazi. This means he would have been an extremely poor leader for England in the coming war against Nazi Germany, which began just a few years later.

One may wonder how large a group would have to be in order to possess such influence. For several decades it was a surprisingly small number of people. The tribune itself was always composed of three members. The inner circle was never more than about a dozen people at any time. From the 1890's up until the 1920's, the group's outer circle never had more than fifty or sixty members. In the 1930's, as their influence grew, membership in the outer circle increased to about a hundred. Exact numbers are impossible to determine because the Milner Group purposely did not keep records or membership lists. This was natural for a group that wanted to remain secret.

Sadly, not all of the activities of the Milner Group yielded positive results. Any group composed of human beings is bound to make a few mistakes. For example, the Milner Group completely failed in its attempt to bring Ireland back into the English fold, both politically and culturally. They even dreamed of reuniting with the United States and Canada in an "Atlantic Federation." Nothing ever came of this.

In order to drum up support for the Boer War, the Milner Group planted extensive anti-German and anti-Dutch propaganda in British newspapers. Ten years later, this propaganda had the unintended effect of making the English people all too eager to enter World War I. If England had not entered the war (and if France and Germany had eventually stopped fighting and agreed to a peace treaty), then World War II might have been prevented. Even a victory for Germany in 1918 would probably have been better than their abject defeat, which set the stage for Adolf Hitler to gain power.

After World War I, the Milner Group failed to prevent the imposition of economic reparations against Germany. These burdensome reparations were partly to blame for provoking World War II. Worst of all, in the two years before World War II, most members of the Milner Group actively supported the appeasement policy of Neville Chamberlain as a way to deal with Adolf Hitler.[96] This was a disastrous policy. It was the other major cause of World War II. Modern Liberals generally seem unable to understand that concessions do not appease tyrants. Instead, concessions merely encourage their aggressive behavior.

THE RE-BIRTH OF MODERN LIBERALISM

Yet what does a secretive group of Oxford dons, wealthy lords, diplomats, and newspaper editors have to do with Modern Liberalism? Everything, due to the influence of one inspirational young man. In 1880, Arnold Toynbee was a promising undergraduate student at Balliol College. It was then that he befriended Alfred Milner. Toynbee died only three years later. Yet in those crucial three years, Toynbee changed Milner's attitude toward humanity forever.

Toynbee was a very left-leaning thinker who passionately supported socialism. For Toynbee, socialism was a moral duty. He firmly believed that all members of society had a moral responsibility to assist all other members of society. Toynbee also believed that socialism was *"the highest development of mankind."* In three crucial years Toynbee converted Milner to his ardent brand of socialism. The conversion would last for Milner's lifetime. According to Dr. Quigley, Milner admitted that Toynbee's death had a galvanizing effect upon him. Milner then dedicated his life to fulfilling the socialist dreams of his dear departed friend.

Rhodes recruited Milner into the group just two years after Toynbee's death. Soon Milner's influence within the group became even more dominant than that of Rhodes himself. Rhodes was spending a great deal of time dealing with his declining health, so he was happy to let Milner become the unofficial leader of the group. Rhodes trusted Milner, partly because Milner shared his dream of creating an international federation of English speaking nations. Furthermore, Rhodes recognized Milner's phenomenal ability to organize the group and to motivate its individual members. As an illustration of how much Rhodes trusted Milner, here is what Rhodes told fellow group member William T. Snead in 1898: *"…If he says peace, I say peace; if he says war, then I say war. Whatever happens, I say ditto to Milner."*[97]

Lord Milner did two things that changed the group forever. First he stopped recruiting new members based solely on their devotion to the British Empire. Instead, he now required new members to also have a pronounced socialist outlook. The original group begun by Cecil Rhodes had only global government as its great goal. Milner added socialism as an equally important goal. This was how socialism became combined with globalism. In effect, Milner combined the *globalism of Rhodes* with the *socialism of Toynbee*. In doing so, Milner laid the two foundations for Modern Liberalism.

These two goals are not logically dependent upon each other. You could have socialism without global government. You could also have global government without socialism. Therefore, we need to know how these two separate goals became joined. It was Lord Milner more than anyone else who brought these two goals together.

Equally important, Milner also created permanent institutions to carry out the goals of Modern Liberalism. *Lord Milner institutionalized Modern Liberalism.* We do not know if Lord Milner read the essays of Saint-Pierre. Either way, he certainly gave those same ideas a tremendous push forward. If Saint-Pierre was the inventor of Modern Liberalism, and Rousseau its greatest theorist, then Lord Alfred Milner was its greatest champion, because he turned their ideas into reality.

LORD MILNER VS KARL MARX

That is why we have discussed Lord Milner for many pages while spending only a few paragraphs on Karl Marx. The only nation that came close to implementing the vision of Karl Marx was the old Soviet Union.[98] It lasted only seventy years. Historically speaking that's the blink of an eye. In contrast, Lord Milner's vision for changing the world was effectively implemented in 1920 when he created Chatham House, which soon became the Royal Institute for International Affairs

(RIIA). A year later Milner persuaded American members of his group to found an American subsidiary, the "Council on Foreign Relations" (CFR). Milner's vision for the world has been promoted by these two institutions for nearly a century, and still shows no sign of waning.

Of course, Lord Milner's original vision has been changed over time by the collective influence of thousands of new members who all left their individual marks upon the Modern Liberal movement. For example, Milner probably never dreamed of homosexual rights, abortion, racial quotas, or the environmental movement. However, the basic course that Milner set towards globalism and socialism has not been altered. Remember, Lord Milner was responsible for creating two permanent institutions to advance Modern Liberalism, namely the Royal Institute for International Affairs, and the Council on Foreign Relations. Years later these two groups in turn created both the League of Nations and the United Nations. These were mankind's first real attempts to live under one global government. Lord Milner left a much more lasting legacy than did Karl Marx.

Marx did not create anything. He certainly did not create communism. According to the eminent historian Will Durant, the first communist was an ancient Persian revolutionary named Mazdak, who preceded Karl Marx by over a thousand years. Ironically he also carried a red flag, to symbolize the blood he needed to spill in order to change the world. Even the term "communist" was first coined in 1835 by a secret group of French revolutionaries, not by Marx.

Marx wrote a few books and pamphlets, but none of these was particularly good. He was not an original thinker. Marx was a failed poet who borrowed ideas from other men, and the ideas he selected do not reveal sound judgment. Marx is well known for the "labor theory of value." However, this dubious theory had already been published by the German economist Friedrich List several years before Marx wrote about it. The labor theory of value assumes that labor should receive all of the money which is paid for any manufactured product. This childishly simplistic idea fails to compensate for the other costs of production, such as raw materials, transportation, and capital investment.

Many history books mistakenly give Marx credit for coining the phrase, *"From each according to his ability, and to each according to his needs."* Yet even this slogan was originally penned by the socialist Louis Blanc in 1840. Blanc himself based this expression on the ideas contained within a 1775 essay written by an early French communist named Morelly. This socialist idea is also fatally flawed. If everyone receives money and benefits "according to their needs," then no one has any incentive to work hard. Therefore, nobody will work to the fullest of his ability. As one communist worker in Poland famously said, *"We pretend to work, and they pretend to pay us."*

Most foolish of all, Marx ignored the power of capitalism to generate new wealth and even to spread wealth throughout society. Rich capitalists do not generally sit on their money. They tend to invest it for profit. This means their investments will create new wealth and new jobs. This benefits the entire economy. Marx also underestimated the power of labor unions to obtain better wages and working conditions.

Marx was greatly influenced by the German philosopher, Hegel. Hegel was an intelligent man, but he fell victim to the delusion that all history could be explained by a single theory. This method for understanding history has been called the "magic bullet" theory.[99] Hegel simplistically claimed that all history could be explained by the struggle between competing ideas. Marx borrowed this simplistic framework but changed the source of the struggle from ideas to economics.

So according to Marx, all history could be explained by the struggles between *competing economic classes*. This was perhaps the closest that Marx ever came to having an original idea. Unfortunately it was not a sound idea. This method for studying history is such an over simplification that it is useless for actually trying to understand history. Marx (just like Hegel) failed to consider the many important factors that were outside his theory. These other factors include: the personalities of individual leaders, geography, the distribution of natural resources, comparative differences in technology, cultural developments, and of course the effects of individual military genius.

Marx even suffered from a basic misunderstanding of capitalism. Marx mistakenly thought of capitalism as a fairly recent development. Yet capitalism has been around since the first caveman bartered his stone tool for some of his neighbor's food. Marx claimed that modern industrial capitalism was somehow qualitatively different from primitive manufacture and trade. He failed to adequately justify this claim. He also placed too much importance on the lack of a personal relationship between the factory owner and his workers. Marx thought this lack of personal relationship between owner and workers *defined capitalism*, because it led to exploitation. However, a wide gulf between assembly line workers and management is inevitable in any modern industrial setting, whether in a communist or capitalist nation.

Finally, Marx failed to consider basic human psychology. People are naturally selfish, so some degree of capitalism is quite natural for our species. The profit motive within capitalism also tends to encourage the development of natural resources and economic expansion. Most important of all, capitalism encourages the most efficient production of both natural resources and manufactured goods through trade. If one village has salt deposits and another village has fertile soil for food production, then trading these two items (salt and food) will obviously benefit everyone involved. This bartering was an early form of free market capitalism, i.e. *voluntary economic activity motivated by the mutual benefit for the parties involved.*

THE GREAT CHANGE

Obviously Lord Milner was not the only intellectual to support both globalism and socialism.[100] The great H.G. Wells wrote in support of both globalism and socialism throughout most of his life. In 1903 he published his famous "Outline of History," which supported both of these goals. It was the second most widely read book in the first half of the 20th century, second only to the Bible. Yet it was only Lord Milner who established an institutional structure to support both globalism and socialism. Writers such as H.G. Wells and Karl Marx were mere pitch men. It was Lord Milner who organized the network which put their ideas into action.

In doing so, Lord Milner established Modern Liberalism as the dominant political ideology in both England and the United States. Lord Milner succeeded entirely where Karl Marx had failed. Therefore, Lord Alfred Milner was almost certainly the most important person of the entire 20th century. Yet he is virtually unknown outside the tiny fraternity of Rhodes scholars.

The three foundations of Anglo-Saxon liberty (government by consent, law of the land, and property rights) now became far less important. After World War I, if any of these ancient Anglo-Saxon traditions got in the way of either globalism or socialism, then globalism or socialism would surely take precedence. This was a great sea change in Western civilization. It was arguably the *most important change in Western civilization since the fall of Rome.* Amazingly, this great change in our culture has gone largely unnoticed by Western scholars.

A PERMANENT MOVEMENT IS BORN

Lord Milner turned a small group of like minded, leftist thinkers into a large scale, self-sustaining movement. He did this by creating two permanent bureaucracies (the RIIA in England and the CFR in America) that would keep the ideals of the group moving forward after his own death, which occurred in 1922. After Milner's demise, the inner circle and the tribune became less important. The general membership of the group began to function more and more as a self-guided entity. After all, every one of its members shared a common philosophy and agreed-upon goals. Milner had laid the groundwork for this development. He had "got the ball rolling." Modern Liberalism would continue on its own indefinitely, with very little guidance from the top.

The result was an energetic body of discreet and highly influential men and women who shared common goals. One of their early goals (1895-1915) was the formation of an international federation of English speaking peoples. They wanted to reestablish the old British Empire, but held together this time by moral bonds, not military coercion. The second goal was socialism, implemented gradually and peacefully, without the violence of Marxism.

After 1915 the Milner Group expanded their goal to include non-English speaking nations. This dream was first realized after WWI, with the League of Nations. Of course that early attempt failed, but the idea of a world governing body was kept very much alive within the Milner Group. Eventually, the anti-war sentiment caused by World War II gave the Milner Group the opportunity to create a more powerful form of global government; an international body that held actual power over its individual member states. This vision was to become the United Nations. The holy grail of globalism has always been the elimination of war through the elimination of the nation state. The UN was the new way to achieve that goal.

Lord Milner's other goal was to implement government sponsored social welfare programs that would improve the lot of the lower classes.

Socialism would end the other great scourges of humanity; poverty, and the revolutionary violence that results from poverty. Socialism has in fact been firmly established throughout the developed world. It has not been as thoroughly implemented in the undeveloped world, due to a lack of financial resources.

THE LEAGUE OF NATIONS

A skeptical reader might find it hard to believe that Lord Milner and his merry band had such tremendous influence. Let's look first at the claim that the Milner Group created the League of Nations. After that we will examine the claim that the Milner Group also created the United Nations.

According to Dr. Quigley, the original idea for the League of Nations came from inner circle member Lionel Curtis, on the eve of WWI. Several years earlier, Milner, Rhodes and Lord Salisbury had tried to create a global federation of English speaking nations based upon the British Empire. It was Lionel Curtis who took the first concrete steps toward fulfilling the broader dream of a truly global organization, which would include all of the civilized nations of the world. Even the Milner Group's own publishing organ, "The Round Table Quarterly," admitted that the original idea for the League of Nations grew out of the Imperial Conferences which were held before World War I.[101] Lionel Curtis was the chief organizer of those Imperial Conferences.

One of the most powerful members of the Milner Group's inner circle was Robert Arthur Talbot Gascone-Cecil, who was the third Marquis of Salisbury, (herein "Lord Salisbury"). All five of Lord Salisbury's sons were also members of the Milner Group. His third son, Lord Robert Cecil, was the primary author of the charter for the League of Nations, as well as the most active English propagandist in favor of the League.[102] In recognition of his tireless efforts promoting the League of Nations he was awarded the Nobel Peace Prize in 1937.

Conservatives in Parliament did not support Lord Robert Cecil's initial draft for the League. They thought it gave the League too much power. These conservatives demanded an alternative version to vote upon. Lord Milner cleverly made sure that the alternative draft was also written by another group member, Lord Walter Phillimore. Phillimore's version was even less acceptable to the conservatives, so they finally gave in and accepted the original draft written by Lord Robert Cecil. Finally Lord Milner made sure that members of his group were appointed to key positions within the League of Nations.[103]

THE UNITED NATIONS

By 1938, the leaders of the Milner Group realized that the English colonies would forever reject any continuation of the old British Empire, no matter how benevolent. They were insisting on complete independence. In response, the Milner Group changed their plan in one very significant way. Instead of trying to prop up a decrepit British Empire, they worked to create a brand new international organization. This new association was based partly on the old League of Nations, but this time the organization would have more power. Instead of a loose federation of sovereign nations, the new organization would be its own sovereign government, with global authority. This new plan was the beginning of the organization we know as the United Nations.

At that point, (1938) Lionel Curtis was perhaps the most influential member within the Milner Group, second perhaps only to Lord Lothian.[104] Once again it was Lionel Curtis who organized the great propaganda effort to support the creation of this newly proposed international body, which did not yet have a name. In 1938 Curtis published a book supporting the concept. It was grandly entitled "The Commonwealth of God." The book was praised in all the media organs controlled by the Milner Group and was widely distributed among the students and faculty of Oxford.

Lionel Curtis instructed two Americans in the Milner Group to launch a similar propaganda effort in support of a powerful new international organization. These men (both former Rhodes scholars and CFR members) were Clarence Striet and Frank Aydelotte. Curtis commissioned Striet to write a supportive book for American readers. The result was an impassioned volume called "Union Now." Newspapers that were controlled or influenced by the Milner Group (the Times of London, New York Times, Christian Science Monitor and the RIIA quarterly "International Affairs") all gave favorable reviews of the new book and published supportive editorials as well.

Curtis also organized meetings of former Rhodes scholars all over the world to support the effort. He called for meetings of the RIIA in

The Big Picture

England and the CFR in America in order to get members in line behind the great project. The majority of the English and American delegates who attended the secret meeting at Dumbarton Oaks (where the UN was actually created) were either members of the Milner Group or else members of the group's daughter organizations, namely the English RIIA or the American CFR. Specifically, the American delegation was dominated by Alger Hiss, Lawrence Dugan, Noel Field, and Victor Perlo, all CFR members. They, like their English counterparts, clearly shared the Milner Group's agenda for a powerful global government.

Later, at the first official UN meeting in 1945, CFR member Alger Hiss was Secretary General. Hiss had also helped to write the UN charter itself. Then Hiss personally transported the signed charter back to Washington DC for Senate approval. According to recently released Soviet documents, both Alger Hiss and Victor Perlo were secretly working as Soviet agents when they helped to create the UN. They were communist spies. Whether they were really working to advance the interests of the Soviet Union or the Milner Group cannot be determined. Either way, they certainly were not working for the best interests of the United States. They were traitors, and the UN is the poisonous fruit of their treason.

TENTACLES OF POWER

We must remember that back in 1921, the CFR was created by American members of the Milner Group's outer circle, at the behest of Lord Milner, Lionel Curtis, and Lord Lothian. It was founded in the USA by Colonel Edward M. House (President Woodrow Wilson's chief adviser), Walter Lippman (the most prestigious American journalist of that age), Thomas W. Lamont (the CEO of J.P. Morgan's bank), and Dr. Isaiah Bowman, (a noted academician at Yale who later became president of Johns Hopkins University). These men were among the most influential in the nation, perfectly suited for the task of creating an American branch of what Professor Quigley calls, "the Anglo-American Establishment."

This little group of founding fathers was a microcosm for the future membership of the CFR. Together they represented the most influential persons in the fields of government (House), journalism (Lippman), international banking (Lamont), and education (Bowman). This was similar to the founding tribunal of the Milner Group itself two decades earlier, which also included one leading figure from government, banking, and education.

The CFR was not the only instrument which the Milner Group used to create the United Nations. The great charitable foundations also helped the Milner Group with the birth of the UN. The Rockefeller Foundation donated over eight million dollars to purchase the land for the UN building. Since 1940, the Carnegie Endowment had been "priming the pump" in support of a new international organization to replace the defunct League of Nations. The Carnegie Endowment helped the CFR to finance speakers, newspaper advertisements, and conferences in support of the new global organization.

J.P. Morgan Jr. was a vital member of the Milner Group's inner circle. Morgan died in 1943, but his bank continued his policies in support of globalism. J.P. Morgan's chief corporate officers and his lawyers have influenced the CFR ever since its creation after World War I. For example, by virtue of its representation within the CFR, the Morgan Bank was able to greatly influence the closed door conference at Bretton Woods, which created both the International Monetary Fund and the World Bank. Dr. Quigley noted:

"The Morgan Bank has never made any real effort to conceal its position in regard to the Council on Foreign Relations. The list of officers and board of directors are printed in every issue of Foreign Affairs and have always been loaded with partners, associates and employees of J.P. Morgan and Company."[105]

THE CONSPIRACY SIDE OF HISTORY

The secretive nature of the Milner Group has caused it to be exploited by an entire cottage industry of right-wing conspiracy mongers. Their inflammatory claims of conspiracy have led many modern readers to dismiss as fiction any reports of secret groups that wield political influence. This is unfortunate, because the Milner Group really did play a crucial role in the development of Modern Liberalism.

On the other hand, Modern Liberal professors are equally mistaken when they claim that no secret group has *ever* held influence in England or America. Modern Liberals prefer to believe that we are merely experiencing the ripple effect of a very potent ideology. According to them, Modern Liberalism is able to inspire support over many generations

The Big Picture

simply because it has such strong emotional appeal. As opinion makers (e.g. journalists, teachers, union leaders, lawyers, politicians, and Hollywood celebrities) join together to support the ideology, they are all acting in concert. They are all working toward common goals simply because they believe in these goals. This Modern Liberal view denies the existence of any conspiracy.

As with many other disputes, the truth lies in the middle. Contrary to some conservative fantasies, the Milner Group was not a Zionist cabal. Nor was it a sinister plot to take over the world for the benefit of the super rich, the Jews, or the Masons. However, the Milner Group was in fact a secret organization which sought to implement a dual agenda of socialism and globalism. Furthermore, the Milner Group did indeed secretly manipulate British and American policy in order to advance these two goals.

Not only do conspiracy aficionados claim that the Milner Group itself was a conspiracy, but they also claim that the Milner Group was part of a much older conspiracy, which began with the Illuminati in 1770. We will now examine whether there is persuasive evidence to connect the Milner Group to the Illuminati. It will help our search for the truth to begin somewhere in the middle, about seventy years after the Illuminati and about fifty years before the Milner Group. In 1840, there was yet another important political clique. It also supported globalism and socialism. It was a clandestine group of German radicals called the Bund der Gerechten, or "League of Just Men." They sponsored the first Communist Internationals, and they even paid Karl Marx to write the *Communist Manifesto* in 1848.

Marx demanded a "dictatorship of the proletariat," to rule society. Only a dictatorship would have the power to abolish private property, religion, and all the institutions of the old regime. Of course, a dictatorship is by nature both authoritarian and elitist. The Modern Liberal idea that an elite group of supermen should rule over the masses originated with Plato. This elitist idea was re-discovered by Saint-Pierre, who then passed it on to the philosophes. Then elitism was carried forward by the Illuminati and the Jacobins. Marx was just the next man on the ideological relay team. He passed this same goal on to our current generation of Modern Liberals.

With his famous Communist Manifesto, Karl Marx helped to guide Modern Liberalism toward the five basic goals of: collectivism, authoritarianism, globalism, elitism and socialism. Therefore, if the men who sponsored Karl Marx were really just Illuminati working under a new name, *then Modern Liberalism would indeed have its roots in the Illuminati:* a dangerous, atheistic, totalitarian conspiracy. However, there is no direct evidence to prove such a connection. No one has been able to prove a direct connection between the Illuminati and the League of Just Men.

On the other hand, there is *circumstantial evidence* which indicates that the League of Just Men was probably a collection of Illuminati members who merely adopted a new name. After their expulsion from Bavaria in 1783, many Illuminati fled to Prussia, which was then the most intellectually tolerant of all the German states. The King of Prussia had followed Bavaria's lead by suppressing the Masonic orders in his own territories. However, Prussia still offered great lenience to the various literary societies and scientific societies which had sprung up as part of the European Enlightenment.

So the Prussian branch of the Illuminati simply stopped having lodge meetings in Masonic halls and instead began to hold meetings in their newly formed literary societies. All of these Illuminati cells operated covertly, under the supervision of a secret organizing group called "The German Union for Rooting Out Superstition and Prejudice and Advancing True Christianity." We know all of this occurred because one of their disillusioned members revealed their operating instructions to a printer named Goschen in Leipzig. Goschen published the document, in order to expose their activity.[106] According to this German Illuminati instruction letter of 1789:

"...the business takes on a new external form. The Brethren speak not of the Union ...nor of a Society, nor of enlightening the people. But they assemble and act together in every quarter merely as a LITERARY SOCIETY, bring into it all the lovers of reading and of useful knowledge; and in fact [these] are the Ordinary Brethren, who only know that an association exists...for the encouragement of literary men. But by no means that it has any connections with any other similar Society, and that they all constitute one whole. But these societies will naturally point out to the intelligent Brethren such persons as are proper to be selected for carrying forward

THE GREAT WORK...The active Brethren will observe in secret, and will select those whom they think valuable acquisitions to the sacred Union. They will invite such persons to unite with themselves in their endeavors to enlighten the rest of mankind."[107] (Emphasis in the original.)

The Prussian Illuminati normally referred to themselves simply as "the Union," or even "the Sacred Union." In keeping with this name they were instrumental in preparing the many small Germanic states to accept the idea of one united Germany. Their literary societies became hotbeds of pan-German unification. This was not done out of a spirit of national pride. Instead, to the Illuminati, German unification was just the first step toward the larger goal of creating a united European super-state. Their ultimate goal was global government.

This brings up the most incriminating piece of evidence connecting the Illuminati to the League of Just Men; *both groups shared identical goals*. Both of these secretive groups wanted to unite the world under one government, to abolish traditional Christianity, and to implement the complete redistribution of wealth. Even the language that the League of Just Men used to describe themselves makes them sound an awful lot like the Illuminati. For instance, the stated purpose of the League of Just Men sounds very much like it was borrowed straight from the Illuminati handbook. Just like the Illuminati, the League of Just Men used the vocabulary of Christianity to advance their secular agenda for socialism and globalism. According to the League of Just Men, they sought:

"...the establishment of the Kingdom of God on Earth, based on the ideas of love of one's neighbor, equality, and justice."[108]

The stress on "equality and justice" was a thinly veiled call for socialism. Please note that freedom and liberty were not even mentioned as desirable goals.

Most important of all (for determining whether Modern Liberalism is rooted in conspiracy), it is disturbing to note how many goals *the Milner Group* had in common with the subversive Illuminati, the bloodthirsty Jacobins, and the radical League of Just Men. So not only do we have circumstantial evidence to connect the League of Just Men with the Illuminati, we also have circumstantial evidence *to connect the Milner*

Group with the Illuminati. The Milner Group also shared nearly identical goals. All of these secret groups supported collectivism, authoritarianism, global government, elitism, and socialism. All of them believed in the humanist idea that if wise rulers were given enough power, they would usher the world into an era of peace and prosperity.

How did they plan to create heaven on earth? According to the Illuminati, they intended to transform all humanity into perfectly rational and perfectly happy creatures:

"Princes and nations shall vanish from the earth. The human race will then become one family, and the world will be the dwelling of rational men."[109]

"...to make of the human race, without any distinction of nation, condition or profession, one good and happy family."[110]

Significantly, the Milner Group shared some of these heady fantasies about making mankind morally perfect and perfectly happy. According to an anonymous article that was written by either Lord Alfred Milner or his partner, Arnold Toynbee:

"The end of the State is to make men. And its strength is measured not in terms of defensive armaments or economic prosperity but by the moral personality of its citizens."[111]

It is also revealing that both the founder of the Illuminati, Dr. Adam Weishaupt, and the founder of the Milner Group, Cecil Rhodes, organized the structure of their groups on the model created earlier by the Jesuits. The founder of each group called himself "general," as was also true for the Jesuits. In addition, both Dr. Weishaupt and Cecil Rhodes borrowed heavily from the constitution of the Jesuits in organizing their groups.[112]

The Illuminati and the Milner Group shared another important similarity. Both groups operated in secret. The Illuminati operated in secret because they were plotting illegal activities, such as revolutions and assassinations. In contrast, the Milner Group was doing nothing illegal, but they still chose to operate in secret. At first, Cecil Rhodes was quite enamored with plans for clandestine ceremonies, fancy robes, and secret handshakes. However, Dr. Carroll Quigley tells us that as soon as Lord Milner was recruited into the group, he put a stop to such humbuggery. Milner persuaded the other members that it was unnecessary and potentially dangerous if such claptrap were ever exposed. It would have made their group look like some sort of evil cabal. In fact, it would have made them look a great deal like the Illuminati. Instead the Milner Group was secretive and anonymous (like the Illuminati), but without the Illuminati's ritualistic fanfare. According to Dr. Carroll Quigley, to keep their group secret, Milner and Rhodes purposely did not select a name for their organization:

"From Milner and Rhodes they got this idea of a secret group of able and determined men, but they never found a name for it, contenting themselves with calling it "the Group" or "the Band" or even "Us.""[113]

"...the criteria for membership...became knowledge of the secret society, and readiness to cooperate with the other initiates toward a common goal."[114]

Of course this still begs the question; if the Milner Group was not doing anything illegal, then why all the secrecy? After all, isn't secrecy some indication of conspiracy? At the very least, it appears that the Milner Group believed they would be more effective if they operated behind the scenes. This assumption was probably correct. Dr. Quigley describes the subtle but powerful methods the Milner Group employed to advance their policy goals:

"Thus, a statesman (a member of the Group) announces a policy. About the same time, the Royal Institute for International Affairs publishes a study on the subject, and an Oxford don, a fellow of All Souls (and a member of the Group) also publishes a volume on the subject...through a publishing house...allied to the Group. The statesman's policy is subjected to 'critical' analysis and final approval in a leader in The Times, while the two books are reviewed in The Times Literary Supplement. Both the leader and the reviews are anonymous, but are written by members of the Group. And finally, at about the same time, an anonymous article in The Round Table strongly advocates the same policy. The cumulative effect of such tactics...is bound to be great."[115]

The Milner Group's well orchestrated campaigns did arouse some suspicions among British conservatives, such as the great 20th century statesman and historian, Sir Winston Churchill. Churchill was angry that this small group of people should have such great influence both inside and outside the government. Here is Churchill, in 1935, describing, with grudging respect, the Milner Group's ability to push forward their own agenda for the independence of India:

"I have watched this story from its very unfolding, and what has struck me more than anything else about it has been the amazingly small number of people who have managed to carry matters to their present lamentable pitch. You could almost count them on the fingers of one hand. I have also been struck by the prodigious power which this group of individuals have been able to exert…through the vast machine of party, of Parliament, and of patronage, both here and in the East. It is tragic that they should have been able to mislead the loyalties and use the assets of the Empire to its own undoing. I compliment them on their skill, and I compliment them also on their disciples. Their chorus is exceedingly well drilled."[116]

It is understandable that Winston Churchill did not recognize the Milner Group as modern day Illuminati. Churchill only saw a connection between the Illuminati and *modern revolutionary socialists*. Winston Churchill feared that Illuminati ideas had taken root inside the revolutionary socialist movement:

"[From] the days of Spartacus-Weishaupt to those of Karl Marx, to those of Trotsky, Bela Kuhn, Rosa Luxemburg and Emma Goldman, this world wide conspiracy has been steadily growing. This conspiracy played a definitely recognizable role in the tragedy of the French Revolution. It has been the mainspring of every subversive movement during the 19th century; and now, at last this brand of extraordinary personalities from the underworld of the great cities of Europe and America have gripped the Russian people by the hair of their heads, and have become practically the undisputed masters of that enormous empire."[117]

Yet Winston Churchill never saw any reason to connect *the Milner Group* to the great Illuminati conspiracy. If Churchill had possessed evidence to make such a connection, then he surely would have used it, because Churchill disagreed with so many of the Milner Group's policies. It would have been a convenient way for Churchill to discredit his political opponents. However, this omission by Churchill does not mean that such a connection did not exist. As the previous pages have detailed, the Milner Group was disturbingly similar to the Illuminati.

The fact is, Churchill died just before Dr. Carroll Quigley's research about the Milner Group was published in the 1970's. If Churchill had read Dr. Quigley's evidence about the Milner Group's support for socialism and globalism, then Churchill almost certainly would have recognized a strong connection between the Milner Group and the Illuminati. The radical ideas of "Spartacus-Weishaupt" had spread farther and deeper than Churchill could have imagined. In fact, the Milner Group, which represents the fountainhead of Modern Liberalism, is the ideological descendent of both the Illuminati and the Jacobins. Of course Modern Liberals are less violent in their methods than were the Illuminati or the Jacobins. But their end goals are virtually identical. These goals are: world government, (to prevent war) and socialism, (to prevent poverty and revolution).

Therefore, conservatives such as Dennis Miller are not just being dramatic when they call Modern Liberals "Jacobins." They are being historically accurate. Modern Liberals are indeed the intellectual descendents of the Illuminati, the Jacobins, the League of Just Men, and finally the Milner Group. This intellectual pedigree is undeniable.

All of these groups shared nearly identical goals, and even used identical justifications for these goals. All of them operated in secret. At least two of them (the Illuminati and the Milner Group) were even established along the same organizational structure. The evidence connecting the Illuminati to both the League of Just Men and to the Milner Group is substantial, and this connection cannot be ignored if we want to understand both history and our modern situation.

CONCLUSION ON CONSPIRACY THEORY

Yet is Modern Liberalism a conspiracy? The whole question boils down to our definition of the word conspiracy. If it is *an agreement to commit a crime*, then there is no such thing. Socialism and globalism may be undesirable policies, but they are not illegal. However, if a conspiracy is simply an *agreement to change society by working in secret*, then a "conspiracy" has indeed existed for over two hundred years. Modern Liberalism has been consistently supported by a powerful network of like-minded people who are all quietly working to change society as they see fit.

Whether or not we choose to call Modern Liberalism a conspiracy, the result will be exactly the same. Either way, society will move towards more socialism and more globalism, because the people in power want it that way. Whether or not we decide to call it a conspiracy is just a question of semantics.

THE GREAT CAUSE MARCHES ON...

According to Professor Quigley, the Milner Group slowly began to lose influence after 1938. Like so many great family enterprises, the Milner Group failed to flourish beyond two generations. The grandchildren of men such as Lothian, Salisbury, Astor, and Curtis lacked the interest and ambition of their grandfathers. The prestigious chairs which the Milner Group controlled at Oxford were eventually occupied by uninspiring academics, who lacked the political ambitions of their predecessors. The Round Table groups became less influential all over the English speaking world. Most of them disappeared. Meetings of the Milner Group became less frequent and ceased entirely by the late 1970's.

There is a simple reason that the Milner Group faded away. It was no longer needed. After World War II it was gradually supplanted by the RIIA and the CFR, as well as by the two great charitable trusts, the Carnegie Endowment and the Rockefeller Foundation. So while the Milner Group itself disappeared, Lord Milner was ultimately successful in his life's mission. As mentioned earlier, Lord Milner gave Modern Liberalism a permanent infrastructure when he established the RIIA in England and the CFR in America.

Lord Milner also persuaded the two great charitable trusts to adopt the Modern Liberal goals of globalism and socialism. Unfortunately we do not know exactly how the Milner Group came to influence the policies of both the Carnegie Endowment and the Rockefeller Foundation. Remember, the Milner Group was a secret entity. It documented none of its activities. Most of the "records" used by historians are either the personal letters or diaries written by some of the group's individual members. So we have no records to explain how Lord Milner persuaded the directors of the two great American charitable trusts to adopt both globalism and socialism. All we can do is note that an overwhelming number of board members of the two great charitable trusts have also been members of the Milner Group or the CFR.[118]

For whatever reason, the Carnegie Endowment and the Rockefeller Foundation, along with J.P. Morgan and later the Ford Foundation, have given consistent support for the Milner Group's Modern Liberal agenda. Even after the Milner Group ceased to exist, the big charitable trusts continued to support the Milner Group's daughter organizations, namely the RIIA, the CFR, and the United Nations. In this way the great charitable foundations continued to support the goals of the Milner Group (globalism and socialism) long after the Milner Group itself faded away.

"COLLECTIVISM"

When Lord Alfred Milner established socialism as the dominant economic and social policy in the West, he also caused Modern Liberalism to adopt a closely related concept: *collectivism*. Collectivism is more than just redistributing the wealth. If that was all it meant, then collectivism would just be another word for socialism. Instead, collectivism is the doctrine which claims that *the individual has no value.* Only the welfare of the nation as a whole is important. This is a throw back to Jeremy Bentham's idea that government should always pursue *"the greatest good for the greatest number."*

Collectivism is vital to Modern Liberalism for two reasons. First, collectivism provides the moral justification for socialism. Ayn Rand recognized this fact when she defined socialism:

"Socialism is the doctrine that man has no right to exist for his own sake, that his life and his work do not belong to him, but belong to society, that the only justification for his existence is his service to society, and that society may dispose of him in any way it pleases for the sake of whatever it deems to be its own tribal, COLLECTIVE GOOD." (Emphasis added.)

The second reason collectivism is so important to Modern Liberals is that collectivism helps them to justify reducing individual freedom. You see, if the individual has no value, then the individual does not deserve any rights either. So collectivism is their rationalization for eliminating individual freedom, and giving all power to the state. If globalism and socialism are the foundations of Modern Liberalism, then collectivism is the keystone.

Modern Liberals know very well that the term "collectivism" has negative connotations, so they prefer to use the term "the common good." It means the same thing. The Nazis used the slogan *"Gemeinnutz geht vor Eigennutz."* or "The Common Good supersedes the Individual Good." This was their cursory excuse not only for redistributing the wealth, but also for *increasing government power over the individual.* After all, if the common good is paramount, then the individual cannot be allowed to make decisions which might harm "the common good." The individual cannot be trusted to act for the benefit of the common good. The Nazis (like all collectivists) believed that only the government can be trusted to pursue the common good. Therefore, the government must have total control over the individual.

This slavish devotion to "the common good" did not die out with the Nazis or the Bolsheviks. This thinking is still very much alive inside the minds of Modern Liberal politicians. For instance, Hillary Clinton boldly justified redistributing the wealth in terms that Lenin and Hitler would have agreed with. Mrs. Clinton declared:

"We're going to take things away from you on behalf of the common good."[119]

Hitler defined "the common good" in racial terms. In contrast, most other socialists (such as Hillary Clinton, Barack Obama, and Fidel Castro) define the common good in economic terms. Yet in regard to individual freedom, the net result of their thinking is exactly the same. Under the banner of "the common good" all of these leaders would increase government power and reduce individual freedom.

COMMUNISM, FASCISM, AND NAZISM: SAME PRODUCT WITH DIFFERENT LABELS

So the common good is not merely a rationalization for transferring wealth. The *common good is the primary excuse for increasing government power.* This is true under socialism, fascism, communism, or Nazism. Modern Liberals invariably bristle whenever any scholar includes Nazism or fascism under the category of "liberal" or "left-wing" political movements. In fact, Modern Liberal scholars have tried very hard to label both Nazism and fascism as "right-wing" movements. This effort is clever, but intellectually dishonest. In reality, there is an overwhelming number of similarities that are shared by communism, fascism, and Nazism.

Communism, fascism and Nazism all shared at least ten important characteristics. All three systems permitted only one political party, with a complete monopoly on power. All three of them denied civil rights such as; freedom of the press, freedom of speech, and freedom of association. They all permitted the state to imprison and execute political dissidents. All three allowed the state to impose punishment without due process of law.[120] All three systems maintained a government sponsored youth movement, to indoctrinate impressionable young minds. All three of them relied on a secret police to spy on the native population. In all three systems the government had strict control over the economy. All three of them imposed progressive income taxes to redistribute the wealth. All three systems had government-run social welfare programs. All three systems banned independent labor unions. Most importantly, all three of these systems placed *the welfare of the group above the rights of the individual.*

In both Nazism and communism, the social welfare programs were very extensive, including: a government retirement system, government schools, government child care, and even land redistribution. This was pure socialism. Even the name "N.A.Z.I." came from the German for National *Socialist* Workers' Party. The Nazis merely altered their form of socialism in one peculiar way. The Nazis limited their welfare benefits to the so-called Aryan race. A second difference was that Nazism (as well as fascism) stressed patriotism. In contrast, the communists saw their movement as more international in scope.

The only other significant difference was that under Nazism and fascism, an individual could still own land and factories. Under communism, all property ("the means of production") was owned by the state. Therefore, the communists more closely followed the pure socialist model of property ownership. However, this one difference is not enough to shift Nazism all the way over from the extreme left of the political spectrum to the extreme right. When comparing Nazism to communism, the most important thing to consider is not how the two systems treated *property*. The most important thing to consider is how the two systems treated *people*.

Remember that all three systems sought government control over the economy, in order to redistribute the wealth. So while the communists controlled the economy through government *ownership*, the Nazis and fascists controlled the economy through government *regulation*. Either way, the result was basically the same for the common man. The government's power grew without limits, and individual freedom was brutally suppressed.

Yet this one small distinction is still useful for us in the 21st century. Barack Obama's take over of the health care industry did not create government *ownership* of the health care industry. Therefore, conservative pundits were incorrect when they called it a "socialist" policy. Instead, Obama imposed government *regulation* of the health care industry. So it was really an example of fascism, not socialism.

Technically speaking, Modern Liberalism is not quite socialism, because most Modern Liberals still accept the right to own private property. At the same time, Modern Liberalism is not quite fascism, because most Modern Liberals still prefer free elections over outright dictatorship. Modern Liberalism is a hybrid movement. It combines the main element of socialism (redistributing the wealth) with the main element of fascism (government control over the individual). That is why Modern Liberalism leads to both collectivism and authoritarianism.

This brings up yet another similarity between Nazism, fascism, and communism. Because all three of these movements were collectivist and authoritarian, it logically follows that under all three systems, the individual should have no value. To prove this, let's start with the communist Karl Marx:

"[The idea] That each man has a value as a sovereign being is illusion, a dream and a postulate of Christianity, which affirms that every human being has a soul."[121]

The fascist Mussolini also placed no value on individuals:

"...society is the end, individuals [are] only the means and the instruments of social ends."[122]

The Big Picture

As early as 1920, the first official platform of the Nazi party not only claimed that individuals were worthless, but that individuals were a threat to society:

"National Socialism...undertakes to defend the people as a whole against the individual."[123]

Not only did communism, fascism, and Nazism all share the same low opinion of individual liberty, but they also employed exactly the same excuse for their thinking. All three of these Modern Liberal ideologies claimed that they merely wanted to protect the weak and poor from the rich and strong. According to the communist Lenin:

"Can you not see that an economic system that allows every man to do what he pleases means that the strong shall be pleased and the weak shall be crushed...There must be a reordering of economic life so that all the economic resources of a nation are bent to the good of all."[124]

Mussolini agreed completely with Lenin, his collectivist comrade:

"Any political system which asserts that the individual must be kept free from state control...leaves the weak unprotected against the strong. The State must protect the weak against the strong!"[125]

The Nazis also climbed on board the "protect the weak" bandwagon. According to the Nazi ideologue Gregor Strasser:

"We are socialists. We are enemies of today's capitalist economic system, with its exploitation of the economically weak, its unfair wage system, its immoral way of judging human beings in terms of their wealth and their money..."[126]

It is also revealing that Modern Liberal writers during the 1920's usually made no distinctions between Russian Communism and Italian Fascism. Modern Liberals back then greatly admired what they called, *"the Russian & Italian experiment."* They did not distinguish between these two examples of collectivism, because there was not much difference between them. Likewise, when the Nazis gained power in the mid

1930's, Modern Liberals once again found much to admire. Modern Liberals back then openly praised the way the Nazis reorganized society and unified their people.

For example, two of the most influential Modern Liberal authors in the first half of the 20th century were George Bernard Shaw and H.G. Wells. Both men were die-hard socialists. So it's not surprising that both men loved Mussolini, Stalin, and Hitler with equal ardor. Shaw praised all three tyrants for being *"progressive"* and for *"doing things."*[127] H.G. Wells called upon students at Oxford to become *"liberal fascisti,"* and *"enlightened Nazis."*[128] Meanwhile in America, a Modern Liberal Marxist named Rexford Tugwell was arguably FDR's most influential economic advisor. Mr. Tugwell glorified Mussolini's fascist state, saying; *"It's the cleanest, neatest, most efficiently operating piece of machinery I've ever seen. It makes me envious."*[129]

So when did the Nazis and the fascists suddenly get labeled as "right-wing" and "conservative?" Why did this change happen? It all began in June of 1941, when the Germans invaded the communist Soviet Union during World War II. Suddenly Modern Liberals needed to distinguish between Nazism and communism. Modern Liberals desperately wanted to help the Russian communists, so they needed some way to paint sinister pictures of Hitler and Mussolini, while at the same time keeping their kindly image of "Uncle Joe Stalin." This was when Modern Liberal scholars in the USA and England suddenly stopped calling the fascists and the Nazis "progressive" and "leftist." Instead, Modern Liberals began calling them "right-wing" and "conservative." This trend only accelerated after World War II ended. When news of the Jewish holocaust leaked out to the West, there was even more impetus to label the Nazis as "right-wing."[130]

The terms "left-wing" and "right-wing" come from the French Revolution. During the first half of 1789, the representatives in the French national assembly (called the "estates general") sat in two different groups. The members of the third estate (commoners) sat on the left side of the room. They generally wanted radical changes in French society. So this urge to change society was soon called "left-wing." In contrast, the members of the first estate (nobles) sat on the right. These conservative nobles naturally wanted to preserve traditional social institutions. This attitude became known as "right-wing."

Yet if "right-wing" means preserving traditional social values and institutions, then the Nazis were really the opposite of right-wing. They were not conservatives at all. In fact, they were revolutionaries who drastically changed their society by uprooting traditional morals and social conventions. For example, before the Nazis came to power, German culture had traditionally placed great value on both marriage and also on a woman's virginity before marriage. Out of wedlock births were strongly condemned. Traditionally in Germany, the fathers of such girls would often beat them, or even horse-whip them as punishment.

Hitler changed this completely. Hitler set up hundreds of youth camps, where German boys and girls from 16 to 18 could have sexual access to each other during the summer months. Nearly all the girls came home pregnant. When the shocked parents of the girls tried to object, they were quickly repressed by the Gestapo. To set an example, a few fathers who dared to punish their daughters were themselves horse-whipped in public. Some stubborn parents were imprisoned. Furthermore, the government also gave these girls monthly support money, and honored them by calling them, "Fuhrer's brides." Hitler also set up similar sex camps for adults, where SS soldiers impregnated adult German women, again without the benefit of marriage. To the Nazis, traditional institutions such as marriage meant nothing.

The Nazis and the fascists also denied individual freedom and gave all power to the state. Remember, both types of conservatives want limited government with guarantees of individual freedom. The Nazis and fascists wanted the exact opposite. They wanted all power to the state (social, economic, and political), with no individual liberty. This is another reason it is absurd to call the Nazis and fascists "right-wing" or "conservative."

Despite the fact that the Nazis and the fascists were really the opposite of conservative, the Modern Liberal propaganda effort to paint conservatives as "fascists" continues to this very day. This explains why most contemporary dictionaries now define fascism (incorrectly) as a "right-wing" political movement. However, if we look at what Mussolini really did between 1922 and 1943, we see that fascism is much better defined as: *"A system of government that places all political and economic power in the hands of one party, which uses both internal terrorism and transfer payments to maintain its power."*[131] So according to this definition, at the time of this writing (2010), "Communist" China is actually a fascist state.

This propaganda campaign to paint Nazis and fascists as conservative and right-wing is so widespread, it still infests our popular culture. On the popular television show "West Wing," the conservative supporters of school vouchers were labeled "fascists."[132] This was done despite the fact that supporting school vouchers is really *the opposite of fascism*. School vouchers take power away from the government, and give that power (school choice) back to the people. To call this "fascist" is to turn the world upside-down. This is the same trick as calling the Nazis "right-wing." Ironically, the real fascists are the people who oppose school vouchers. They are determined to keep poor kids trapped in bad government schools.

In fact, there are many disturbing similarities between Mussolini's fascism and Modern Liberalism. The economic power that Roosevelt seized for the federal government in the 1930's gave the American government the same control over the economy as in Mussolini's fascist state. In the 1930's, John T. Flynn was a journalist for the New Republic. He saw that FDR's New Deal was just fascism with a new name:

"[Mussolini] organized each trade or industrial group or professional group into a state-supervised trade association. He called it a cooperative...The National Recovery Act provided that in American industry, each industry should be organized into a federally supervised trade association. It was called a cooperative...it was essentially the same thing...IT WAS FASCISM."[133] (Emphasis added.)

The following quote is from the Italian fascist handbook which was published in 1936. It may just as well have been written by FDR, Hillary Clinton, or Barack Obama:

"Economic initiatives cannot be left to the arbitrary decisions of individual interests. Open competition, if not wisely directed and restricted, actually destroys wealth instead of creating it...More important than the creation of wealth is its right distribution...Private wealth belongs not only to the individual, but in a symbolic sense to the State as well."[134]

MODERN LIBERALS VS INDIVIDUALISM

Individualism is the opposite of collectivism. So if Modern Liberals support collectivism, then they must necessarily oppose individualism. Indeed, Modern Liberal scholars have generally marched right along with the Nazis, fascists and communists in their devaluation of the individual. Herbert Croly was perhaps the most influential Modern Liberal scholar behind the American Progressive movement after the turn of the 20th century. He profoundly influenced an entire generation of post WWI Modern Liberals. Just like all the other Modern Liberal social engineers, Croly denigrated the value of individuals:

"An individual has no meaning apart from the society in which his individuality was formed."[135]

The Modern Liberal disdain for individualism has prompted some people to fabricate entirely new theories about history, without any evidence to support them. For instance, according to Lyman Abbott, the editor of the Modern Liberal journal *Outlook*:

"Individualism is the characteristic of simple barbarianism, not of republican civilization."[136]

Mr. Abbott forgets that our Founding Fathers established a *constitutional republic specifically to protect individual freedom.* Individualism is not barbaric. It is the iron-fisted rule of collectivist leaders that is barbaric, not individualism.

Modern Liberalism's hostility toward individualism began with Saint-Pierre and Rousseau in the 18th century, and it has continued ever since. For example, the famous 19th century socialist Auguste Comte loathed individualism. He claimed that individualism was *"... the revolt of the individual against the species."*[137] This statement by Comte is dangerous for two reasons. First, it implies that each individual must ignore his own interests because of some imaginary obligation to the rest of humanity. Second, it implies that an elite class of rulers (i.e. Comte and his fellow collectivists) can tell everyone else what to do, just because they claim to represent "the species."

Sometimes the Modern Liberal loathing for individualism reaches the absurd. In a bold display of Orwellian double-talk, Walter

Rauschenbusch proclaimed, *"Individualism means tyranny!"*[138] Of course this statement is logically false. In fact, the opposite is true. Individualism is really the opposite of tyranny. After all, if tyranny is the vesting of all power in the state, then individualism means freedom from tyranny. Rauschenbusch was simply lying.

The reason that Modern Liberals hate individual freedom is because it reduces government power. This restriction on government power makes it impossible for them to implement the five main goals of Modern Liberalism, namely: collectivism, authoritarianism, globalism, elitism, and socialism. Remember, government power and individual freedom are inversely related. As government power grows, individual freedom must shrink. The five main goals of Modern Liberalism all require increasing government power. Therefore, Modern Liberalism necessarily seeks to reduce individual freedom.

COLLECTIVISM IN YOUR LIFE

Under our modern collectivist leadership, the government now decides how much money you may keep to live on. This was not true eighty years ago. The government now decides (without even telling you) whether your teen age daughter can have an abortion. This was not true twenty years ago. The federal government is starting to decide what your children will learn in school. This was not true ten years ago. Soon the government will decide which doctor you may see. The government will even decide the type of medical treatment you will receive, and how much care you may have.

This means that with national health care, the government will literally decide how long you will live. The government is becoming as powerful as anything George Orwell could have imagined. In a few more decades, your children will be left with only trivial, mindless choices, such as which holographic movie to rent for the weekend, or which sports team to cheer for.

Collectivism hurts all of us in another way. Because collectivism denies the value of individuals, it demands that *all persons be treated as members of identifiable groups*, instead of treating them as individuals. This demand for group treatment leads to collectivist policies, such as banning guns and drunk driver check-points. You see, under collectivism, if a small percentage of the population abuses a certain right (e.g. the right to drive a car, the right to own a gun, or the right to free speech, etc.) then the government will take away that right from everyone. Of course this approach is heavy handed and authoritarian. Surprisingly, Modern Liberal politicians openly invoke this excuse for collectivism. For example, President Bill Clinton went on national television to declare:

"What's happened in America today is too many people live in areas where there's no family structure, and no work structure. And so there's a lot of irresponsibility. And so a lot of people say there's too much personal freedom. **WHEN PERSONAL FREEDOM IS BEING ABUSED, YOU HAVE TO MOVE TO LIMIT IT**...[And so] we're going to have weapons sweeps and more things like that to try to make people safer in their communities."[139] (Emphasis added.)

This quote is pure collectivism. In this particular case, Mr. Clinton was talking about the right to own guns. Mr. Clinton believes that if a few individuals living in government housing abuse the right to own guns, then the right to own guns should be taken away from everyone living in government housing. By banning guns, the government is treating everyone as potential criminals.

In contrast, an *individualist* society tries to curb gun violence by *punishing the individuals* who use guns to commit crimes. However, a collectivist society will treat all gun owners the same, whether they are criminals or not. This explains why most Modern Liberals actually oppose laws that would add more prison time if a criminal uses a gun. Instead of individual punishment, Modern Liberals prefer to impose group punishment. This collectivist approach to gun ownership can be best understood with an analogy. It is like trying to control drunk drivers by taking away everyone's right to own a car. This may sound ridiculous, but it is exactly the reasoning behind banning guns. This same illogic lies behind all forms of collectivism.

COLLECTIVISM STARTS EARLY

In order to condition our children to accept collectivism, it has become part of the public school curriculum. Nowadays, students are often assigned "group projects." If any one member of the group fails to complete his part of the project, then the entire group receives a lower grade as punishment. All the other members of the group are punished for something that was not their fault. Of course this is grossly unfair. Teachers defend this practice by saying, "It gets kids ready for the real world, to work with other people in teams."

This is a false comparison. In a real job setting, any member of a team who fails to perform is soon fired. The productive members of the team are not punished for his failure to perform. Employers are not as unfair (or as irrational) as school teachers seem to think they are.

In public schools today, if a bully hits a victim, and the victim hits him back, then both students are punished for "fighting." Imagine if a mugger punches you and then you punch him back. Can you imagine the police arresting both the mugger and you for "fighting?" It makes no sense whatsoever, either on the street or on the school grounds. Yet the schools insist that all students be treated collectively. This means that both the attacker and the victim must be treated the same, regardless of their individual guilt or innocence.

Recently my young nephew asked me for a pen, so he could take it to school and write his name on all his books. I handed him a felt tip pen. He promptly told me that such pens were "illegal" at his school. He said that if he was caught carrying such a pen, the school would suspend him. Incredulously I asked him, "Why is that?" He explained that some kids had used felt tip pens to write graffiti on the school walls. As a result, *all children are prohibited from having felt tip pens*. All the students are treated collectively, just for the "crime" of having such a pen. In effect, all of the students are treated as potential criminals.

After several years of such collective treatment our children will gradually learn to accept more restrictions on free speech, more restrictions on gun ownership, more restrictions on their right to own property, and of course more taxes. Our children are well on the road to becoming docile, obedient, collectivists.

CHAPTER FOUR

ECONOMICS 101 (IMPROVED)

The White House, November 3, 1933.

Treasury Secretary Henry Morgenthau felt a chill from the freezing rain that was beginning to soak through his trench coat. As he walked up the private staircase in the rear of the west wing, Morgenthau decided not to take off his coat. He figured that if he took his coat off, the President might want him to stay and chat. FDR was a truly social creature. And Morgenthau was one of FDR's closest friends; a true confidant. But today Henry Morgenthau hoped to escape FDR's convivial instinct. After all, his work load had been crushing lately, and these daily meetings with FDR about the price of gold seemed to be a waste of time.

Every day FDR would arbitrarily pick a new amount for the price of gold. There was no private market to set the price, because FDR had previously banned private individuals from owning gold. Therefore, the government had to set the price of gold, for the benefit of foreign central banks trading in dollars and American firms doing business overseas.

FDR kept raising the price a little bit each day, thinking that an increase in the price of gold would somehow cause an increase in the price of farm commodities. Unfortunately, increasing the price of gold seemed to have no effect on farm prices. For the past few weeks, Morgenthau could sense that FDR was becoming impatient.

After reaching the second floor, Morgenthau walked briskly down the long hall to the President's bedroom. The guard nodded to Mr.

Morgenthau, as he did every day, and knocked on the President's door for him. FDR's voice softly called out *"Enter."*

There lay FDR, half propped up with several pillows, enjoying what appeared to be his first cigarette of the day. The President was still in his baby blue pajamas of course. *"Henry old man, has it been raining all morning? I just woke up. Won't you have some coffee? It's fresh."*

"Thank you Franklin, I've got to get back to a staff meeting as soon as I can," Morgenthau said, purposely not sitting down in the chair that was available to him.

FDR was still cheerful, but he could see that Morgenthau wanted to get down to business. *"Well, my friend, what do you think gold should be today?"*

Morgenthau was glad that FDR asked for his idea first. *"You know, I was thinking at first maybe just a seven cent increase, but if you want to go higher, I think we could responsibly increase it by ten or maybe even fifteen cents."*

FDR looked wistfully at the rain splattering against his window. *"Let's raise it by twenty-one cents,"* he declared.

Morgenthau gave a puzzled look. *"Uh, ok I guess, but why twenty-one cents?"*

"Seven times three is a lucky number," the President chuckled.

"So...twenty one cents?"

"Yes, that'll do nicely, Henry."

"Well, you're the boss." Morgenthau paused awkwardly, hoping to be dismissed. He took a cautious step backward as he said, *"I really should get over to that meeting."*

"Yes Henry, I understand, off you go!"

Morgenthau was relieved to get out so quickly, especially when his friend was in a jovial mood. However, he couldn't help but wonder if it was wise for the two of them to be setting prices based on hunches. *"Or not even hunches,"* he thought to himself, *"Lucky numbers no less!"*

The meeting just described actually took place. Even the words spoken are based upon Morgenthau's recollection of the conversation.[140] This meeting between FDR and Henry Morgenthau illustrates how irrational government managers can be when they try to regulate any part of our complex economy. Important decisions are made without enough information, and often without any reason. A hunch, a gut instinct, or even the flip of a coin have all been used by government officials who lack a private market to guide them.

FDR had earlier abolished the private ownership of gold, so there was no market to determine the price of gold. This same problem plagued the old Soviet Union, except on a larger scale. The Soviets had abolished private markets for all commodities, not just gold. So they had no idea what the price of anything should be. In the absence of markets, the Soviet government decided what items should be produced, and how much should be produced, regardless of consumer demand. This led to a constant roller coaster of under production and over production. Setting prices proved to be yet another nightmare for Soviet bureaucrats.

ECONOMICS: THE DISHONEST SCIENCE

Of all the modern social sciences (economics, sociology, anthropology, and political science) the one subject with the most fraud and chicanery is economics. This is because economics involves questions about money. It determines how much money the government will let us keep and even what the government will do with that money. Such decisions will determine who stays in power and for how long. These important questions cannot be answered with academic disinterest and objectivity. Far from it, economics has become rife with false ideologies and illogic.[141] The purpose of this chapter is to correct the misinformation you were probably fed in college.

HOW IS WEALTH CREATED?

This is the most fundamental question in economics, and yet it is almost never discussed in college classes on economics. This is because most college professors have never even thought about this question. Yet it is impossible to understand economics unless you can answer this threshold question. The Keynesian economists especially seem to have forgotten how wealth is created. I recall asking my college economics professor, "How is new wealth created?" He paused, and offered something like "Economic activity will naturally result in profit, and enough accumulated profit becomes wealth." I was a bit impudent, so I pushed him by saying, "Well, if someone robs me at gunpoint, that's economic activity, but it doesn't generate any new wealth; robbery just shifts it around."

He looked down his patrician nose at me and said something like, "Of course only *voluntary* economic activity can create wealth, because only voluntary activity is motivated by profit. Coerced activity tends to destroy wealth, because it is not profitable."

So according to my professor, voluntary economic activity creates wealth. However, what if Bill Gates spends his money feeding starving Africans? It is voluntary. It is economic activity. Yet there is no generation of profit. So clearly, not all voluntary economic activity creates wealth. Furthermore, even if the profit motive is present, a wasteful business decision will not create wealth; it will destroy wealth. So my professor's explanation was still not satisfactory. Years later, after finally discovering a decent book on economics, the answer became clear:

Wealth is created by transferring assets from a lower valued use to a higher valued use.[142]

Under this principle, an "asset" is anything with a market value, such as a natural resource, a finished product, money, or labor. Here is an illustration: A lumberjack offers his labor to cut trees for a timber company. His labor is an asset. The lumberjack figures that his labor will be put to a higher valued use if he gets paid forty dollars per hour cutting trees, instead of working for ten dollars per hour washing dishes at a restaurant. It is more "profitable" for him to transfer his asset (labor) to the *higher valued use*.

Now let's say the timber company spends one million dollars on labor, equipment and management costs in order to produce a certain amount of wood logs. However, the timber company can sell the wood logs to a lumber mill for two million dollars. This is because the lumber mill *values* the wood logs *more highly* than the timber company does. The lumber mill knows it can turn the logs into finished wood boards. In effect, the timber company and the lumber mill have cooperated to transfer the logs to a *higher valued use*.

Next, the lumber mill sells the wood boards to a furniture manufacturer, for a profit. This profit occurs because the furniture manufacturer *values* the wood boards *more highly* than the lumber mill does. The furniture manufacturer knows he can turn the wood boards into furniture, and sell the furniture for a profit. Once again the furniture maker is transferring the asset (wood boards) to a higher valued use (furniture).

Then the furniture manufacturer will sell the furniture to a retail store owner, for a profit of course. This is because the store owner *values* the furniture *more highly* than the furniture manufacturer does. The store owner knows he can sell the furniture to consumers for their "higher valued use," i.e. for a profit.

Finally, the consumer walks into the retail store and buys the furniture, because the consumer *values* the furniture *more highly* than the retail store does. The consumer decides that buying the furniture is a "higher valued use" for his money than buying something else.

You will notice that all along this chain of events two marvelous things have been created: wealth and jobs. That is why capitalists are so valuable for society. They create both wealth and jobs for other people. The ancient Hebrews understood that honest and efficient businessmen are far more important than government leaders. According to the Book of Proverbs, *"Do you see a man who is diligent in his business? He shall stand before kings."*

It is important to note that in all of the examples above, the assets were transferred *voluntarily*. Obviously, if a transfer creates new wealth, then both parties will enter into that transfer willingly. Both parties are motivated by their desire to make a profit. In contrast, when assets are transferred *involuntarily*, wealth is nearly always destroyed.

HOW IS WEALTH DESTROYED?

Wealth is destroyed in exactly the opposite way from which it is created. This means:

Wealth is destroyed by transferring assets from a higher valued use to a lower valued use.

But how does this happen? The most obvious way is through warfare. Some economists still preach the myth that the destruction of property stimulates the economy. They argue that destruction forces more spending in order to replace damaged infrastructures. They claim this creates new wealth. However, the opposite is true. Bombing buildings and roads destroys wealth. The money used to rebuild *damaged* infrastructure could have been used to build *additional* infrastructure.

Here is an illustration. If a bridge is bombed out, then the nation must spend a billion dollars to replace it. After spending the money, the nation still has a bridge, as it had before the bombing. However, now the nation lacks that same billion dollars. If the bombing had never occurred, then the nation would still have a bridge, and the billion dollars could have been invested in other ways, such as building new factories, office buildings, power plants, or even an additional bridge.

Another way to destroy wealth is by making unprofitable business decisions. Let's use our lumber mill example again. Now, let's assume the lumber mill foolishly decides to take the finished wood boards and shred them into pieces, to create wood pulp for making paper. They will not make the same profit they could have made if they had sold the finished wood boards. In fact, they will even lose money by their decision. They have transferred an asset from a higher valued use to a lower valued use. They have destroyed wealth.

Of course private companies rarely do anything so foolish, because it is obviously counter-productive. If they persist in destroying their wealth in this manner, then they will soon be forced out of business. This explains why in most cases, wealth is destroyed by the government, not by the private sector. The government does not have any profit motive. Also, the government is never forced out of business, even after a series of wasteful decisions. This leads to our next topic.

GOVERNMENT DESTROYS WEALTH; BECAUSE IT WANTS TO

Because the government never has to show a profit, it has no motive to use wealth in a productive manner. It can only be "put out of business" by political revolution. This explains why the government persistently makes economic decisions that destroy wealth. One example of this wanton destruction is our national agricultural policy. The government taxes our money and then gives it to farmers *to pay them not to grow* certain crops. This means those same crops will soon be in short supply, and therefore the price of those crops will rise. That was the government's plan all along. But in the process, the farmer's asset (land) *is transferred to a lower valued use*. It is no longer being used to grow crops; but instead it is just used to grow weeds. This means your tax dollars are being used to destroy wealth.

Even more dramatically, the federal government has actually given your tax dollars to farmers to pay them to destroy valuable assets such as milk, cheese, eggs, and livestock.[143] It's easy to see that pouring wholesome milk down the sewer is clearly transferring the milk *to a lower valued use!* In all of these examples, the government is satisfying the greed of the corporate farm lobby, and hurting the rest of the economy in the process. It hurts the rest of the economy by forcing prices to a higher level than they would be in a free market. This forces consumers to spend their money in a wasteful manner, i.e. on a "lower valued use." The government is causing the destruction of wealth.

There are dozens of examples of government mis-management destroying wealth in the agricultural sector, literally, from apples to zucchini. For example, the government strictly limits who can grow and sell peanuts. If you try to grow and sell peanuts without a federal permit, you will be heavily fined. Yet new permits are rarely granted because the government is trying to keep the supply of peanuts artificially low. In this way the government is keeping the price of peanut butter artificially high. This makes the peanut farmers happy, but it makes every jar of peanut butter cost about a third more than it should. The government's agricultural policy is just the tip of the iceberg. If you examine areas like national defense, social welfare programs, education, Medicare, and corporate welfare, you can find hundreds of more examples. We will examine a few of these examples shortly.

GOVERNMENT DESTROYS WEALTH; THROUGH GOVERNMENT JOBS

A very popular economic fallacy among supporters of big government is the idea that government jobs are just as valuable to the economy as private sector jobs. Nothing could be farther from the truth. All jobs consume some wealth, in the form of the money which is needed to pay the wages of the employee. The crucial difference is that *private sector jobs produce more wealth than they consume.* After all, if a private sector job consumed more wealth than it produced, then that job would quickly be eliminated, because it loses money. In contrast, *government jobs consume more wealth than they produce.* This is because government jobs are not based on any profit motive. The net result is a loss of wealth, i.e. *the destruction of wealth.*

Here is an illustration. A factory owner is in the business of making springs. All of his employees are working in some way to help produce springs. The money earned from selling springs is the "wealth" that sustains the company and pays the employees' salaries. One day the owner decides to hire some landscapers just to keep the outside of the factory looking nice. These employees do not contribute to the creation of springs. They do not contribute to the company's wealth.

Next the owner hires some security guards to patrol the factory. They also do not contribute to the creation of springs. Finally the owner hires a full time staff of counselors in case any employees have personal problems they wish to talk about. These counselors also do not contribute to the creation of springs. Eventually the owner hires so many people who do not create wealth for his company that he no longer makes any profit. Instead he loses money, and eventually the factory goes bankrupt. As a result, everyone loses their job.

Of course it is very nice to have beautiful landscaping and counselors. It might even be necessary to have security guards. However, if a business has too many jobs that do not generate wealth, then the business will go bankrupt. The same thing is true for the national economy. If we have too many jobs that do not create wealth, (i.e. government jobs) then the entire economy can be seriously damaged. This was yet another reason for the collapse of the Soviet Union. The same thing is slowly happening right now in Europe, Canada, and the United States. There are simply not enough private sector jobs to support the burgeoning bureaucracy of government jobs. Yet many politicians still believe they will *help* the economy by creating more government jobs. In fact they are simply destroying more of the nation's wealth.

This is not to say that all government jobs should be eliminated. Police and fire departments, the military, food inspectors, and certain others perform valuable work that is not appropriate for the private sector. However, we must keep in mind that all government jobs destroy wealth to some extent. Therefore, the government bureaucracy must be kept *as small as possible* if we want to maintain a healthy economy.

GOVERNMENT JOB CREATION?

Some economists claim that the damage to the economy is most severe when the government tries to directly create jobs through "make work" programs. This was done on a massive scale during the Great Depression, and to a lesser extent during the 1970's with the federal

CETA program (Comprehensive Training and Employment Act of 1973). In the CETA case, the amount of money spent creating each new job was shocking:

"...the federal government's own General Accounting Office has estimated that some federal jobs programs have provided $14,000 per year jobs at a total cost of more than $100,000 per job, once one accounts for all the administrative expenses."[144]

The government's recent track record of job creation is even more wasteful. In 2009, Barack Obama spent 825 billion dollars in a stimulus bill that he promised would save three million American jobs. However, that means the government spent $275,000 to save each job. Assuming the average salary in 2009 was about forty thousand dollars per year, the government would have done much better just handing out the money to unemployed people, without requiring any work. Of course the best solution of all would have been to leave the 825 billion dollars in the private sector of the economy.

Even if government job programs were more efficiently run, they will never sustain a true recovery. This is because government spending naturally creates only temporary jobs. If there was a natural demand for a certain job, then the private sector would have already filled that position. Therefore, government jobs are necessarily geared toward purposes for which there is no real demand. A sustained recovery can only be achieved by cutting taxes. Cutting taxes will let the private sector have enough money to expand and create new jobs. Remember, only private sector jobs create wealth. As the National Association of Manufacturers explained:

"Pouring public funds into pump-priming projects, no matter how freely, cannot provide permanent jobs and economic stability if private enterprise is not encouraged to proceed and expand. On the other hand, if all possible encouragement is given to private enterprise (i.e. tax cuts) then little if any pump-priming will be necessary."[145]

"SOAK THE RICH"

In a healthy economy, government spending should not be higher than about 19% of GDP. This 19% figure comes from an observation by economist William Kurt Hauser. He noted that ever since 1952, federal revenue from all sources has tended to be about 19% of GDP, regardless of how high the top income tax bracket might be. Federal Revenue normally stays within a narrow range of 17% to 21% of GDP. So when the highest tax-payers were charged 90% back in the early 1950's, the federal government received only about 19% of GDP. Likewise, when the highest tax bracket was reduced to 29% in 1989, the federal government still took in about 19% of GDP. Hauser's observation has proven true during wildly different circumstances. It worked during the recession of the late 1950's, the stagflation of the 1970's, and the dot com boom of the 1990's. This phenomenon has proven so consistent, that it is sometimes called "Hauser's Law."

Furthermore, there were no significant changes in other taxes (such as the estate tax, social security tax, etc.) which could have "made up for" any changes in the top income tax rate.[146] In other words, whenever the government reduced the highest income tax rate, *it did not increase other taxes to "make up the difference."* Likewise, whenever the government increased the top income tax rate, it did not reduce other taxes to compensate. Furthermore, from 1952 to the present, federal income tax has consistently accounted for about 45% of the total federal revenue, *regardless of changes in the top income tax rate.*[147]

There are two good reasons for Hauser's Law. First of all, whenever the government raises taxes to "soak the rich," the government discourages wealthy people from investing for maximum profit. Instead, rich people will protect their income from taxes as much as possible, by investing in tax exempt bonds and other types of "shelter" investments. Rich people are generally not stupid. These tax exempt bonds cannot be easily eliminated because they are the primary means by which counties and cities must pay for desperately needed infrastructural maintenance and improvements.

Unfortunately, this sheltering behavior by rich people makes their assets less productive. This reduces the creation of new wealth and jobs for everyone. This in turn reduces the growth of our GDP. This means the government will receive 19% of a smaller pie. In contrast, tax cuts increase the growth of our GDP. That means the government will receive more revenue, because the government's 19% share will be coming *from a bigger pie.* So lower taxes help everyone, including the government. Hauser's Law clearly casts doubt on the wisdom of a steeply progressive income tax.

The second reason behind Hauser's Law is even more important. Soaking the rich simply doesn't produce nearly as much money as Modern Liberals (socialists) imagine. You see, even if the government eliminated all tax shelters, and taxed 100% of all income earned by wealthy people, the amount collected would still be a drop in the bucket compared to the entire federal budget. As the government's "Grace Commission" concluded back in 1984, the amount of money gained by such confiscatory taxes would only be *enough to run the federal government for seven days*.[148] Finally, if in one year we really did take away all the income of rich people, how much money do you think the rich people will try to earn in the following year? Nothing.

Contrary to popular belief, the tax cuts of both Ronald Reagan George W Bush Jr. actually made the American tax burden more "progressive." These tax cuts encouraged rich people to make more money, so they paid more in taxes. Back in 1980, (just before the Reagan tax cuts) the top 5% of income earners paid 37% of the nation's income tax. However, by 2007, (after the Bush tax cuts) the top 5% income earners were paying a whopping 57% of all federal income taxes.[149]

Recently, Hauser's Law has been criticized, because in 2009 (for the first time in fifty-seven years) federal revenue accounted for only 14.8% of GDP. What happened? During 2009 and 2010, the totals for federal revenue became misleading. Massive federal money creation in 2009 and 2010 have thrown Hauser's Law off balance. In fact, this reckless money creation has thrown our entire economy off balance. This massive creation of new money during 2009 and 2010 allowed the federal government to spend more money *without increasing its "revenue."* Government economists simply did not count this newly created money as "revenue."

But if government economists had included this newly created money in their total for federal revenue, then Hauser's law would still apply. In 2009 America's GDP was 14.1 trillion dollars. Federal revenue from all taxes was 2.1 trillion dollars. However, the amount of new money created by the Fed was 430 billion dollars. Now if we add this 430 billion to the 2.1 trillion in tax revenue, then in 2009, the *grand total for all federal revenue* (tax money plus newly created money) was

2.53 trillion dollars.[150] This amount was 17.9% of our GDP in 2009, well within the range of Hauser's law.

Like every other theory about the social sciences, Hauser's Law does have limitations. It only applies when the lion's share of government revenue comes from income tax. So Hauser's Law does not apply to most state governments, which primarily rely on sales taxes and property taxes for their revenue. Likewise, it does not apply to Europe, where most government revenue is generated by the Value Added Tax (VAT), instead of income tax. A VAT is automatic, like a sales tax, and so it is much harder to avoid than the income tax. For this same reason, if federal "cap and trade" energy taxes are raised, then federal revenue will probably exceed the limits of Hauser's Law. Finally, Hauser's law did not hold true for the US economy before 1952, because both federal revenue and federal spending (in relation to GDP) were much lower between 1945 and 1952.

If the total for federal revenue tends to be about 19% of GDP, then the federal government should only spend 19% of GDP. Maintaining this balance would not only prevent the excessive destruction of wealth; it would also prevent deficit spending. Sadly, federal spending in America for the past three decades has been well beyond this healthy limit of 19% of GDP. During the last year of Republican President George W. Bush Jr. (2008), the US government spent 26% of GDP, and under President Barack Obama, the government spent even more.[151] Partly due to the new money created by the Fed, total federal spending Under Barack Obama for 2010 was a whopping 35% of GDP. During his first two years as President, Obama increased annual federal spending by 28%, which is the greatest peacetime increase in our nation's history.[152]

The only way the government can actually help the economy is to get out of its way. This alone will let the private sector create new wealth and new jobs. The government can only do this by cutting taxes, reducing its own borrowing, and resisting the temptation to print excess money. Of course these are the last things that the government wants to do, because all three of these things will reduce government power. Remember, it is in the nature of government to *constantly expand its power*. And spending money is a source of power. Therefore it is in the nature of government to always spend more money.

GOVERNMENT SPENDING HARMS THE ECONOMY

Perhaps the most popular economic fallacy of all is the belief that government spending stimulates the economy just as much as private sector spending does. According to this myth, the economy is stimulated even if the government just pays men to dig holes and then fill them up again. This idea is false, for two reasons.

The first reason is very simple. In order for the government to spend a million dollars, it must first remove a million dollars from the economy (by taxing or borrowing). The net result is only a neutral effect for the economy. Let's call this phenomenon "switching pockets." Imagine that a senile old man pulls a hundred dollars out of his pocket. Then he puts those same hundred dollars into his other pocket. He does this repeatedly, just so he can feel like he is making himself richer every time he does this. Of course he is not making himself any richer. He is deluding himself. He is merely switching the money from one pocket to the other. This is what the government does when it spends money. It simply takes money from one pocket (via taxes or borrowing) and stuffs it into another pocket.

Of course there is another way for the government to raise money, besides taxing and borrowing. The government can just create more money. It can either have the Treasury Department print more currency, or it can have the Federal Reserve Bank create new money just by making an accounting entry in its books. However, whenever the government finances spending by creating new money, it creates inflation. This inflation damages the economy just as much as taxes and borrowing do. The equivalent damage is done, but in a different manner. Inflation also takes longer to inflict harm upon the economy. We will discuss exactly how inflation damages the economy later in this chapter.

Another reason that government spending harms the economy is because government spending does not generate new wealth. However, private sector spending does generate new wealth. Therefore, *government spending prevents the creation of new wealth that would have been created if the money had been left in the private sector.* Here is a simple illustration. Suppose the government spends a hundred million dollars to build an office building for a government agency. Modern Liberal economists argue that spending money for land, for construction workers, and for construction supplies will all stimulate the economy.

However, like all government spending this government office building will hurt the economy in the long run. After the construction of the office building is completed, the building will not be used for making any profit. It will not be used to create any wealth. This is because the bureaucrats working inside the office building will not be transferring assets from a lower valued use to a higher valued use.

In contrast, if that same money had been left in the private sector, then it might have been used to build a poultry processing plant. The initial construction would have stimulated the economy just as with the government office building. However, that is where the similarity ends. In the case of the poultry processing plant, the employees would be paid for labor that creates new wealth, i.e. transferring an asset from a lower valued use (live chickens) to a higher valued use (packaged meat).

But remember, the government employees will not generate any profit. They will not create any new wealth for the economy. Instead, the government employees will all have to be paid *by taxing the private sector* for many decades to come. So in the long run, the government office building will *destroy wealth,* instead of creating it. This is true whether the government spends money for an office building, a jet bomber, farm subsidies, or for hiring a thousand new bureaucrats or social workers. If that same money had been left in the private sector, new wealth would have been created.

OUT OF SIGHT, OUT OF MIND

This brings up a problem with human perception. Whenever the government builds a road or a building, the supporters of government spending can point to it as a concrete example of how tax money was spent to create something beneficial. However, it is impossible for the opponents of government spending to show how that same money might have benefited the economy much more if it had been left with the tax-payers. The opponents of government spending do not have any new buildings to point to, because they do not exist. The government prevented the new buildings from being built.[153] The money which could have built the new buildings was taken away by the government. Yet even though the missing private buildings do not exist, we should always keep them in mind when evaluating any government spending.

THE MYTH OF THE STIMULUS BILL

The same people who fail to understand that government spending hurts the economy are the same people who foolishly call upon the government to cure recession, by means of government spending. The usual method is to legislate a so-called "stimulus bill" to pump-prime the economy. This means the government will spend a few hundred billion dollars (or even a few trillion dollars) in a quixotic effort to stimulate the economy. If the government borrows money to pay for a stimulus bill, then it artificially shrinks the amount of credit that is available to private business. This makes it harder for private businesses to find money to borrow for expansion.

In a futile attempt to avoid this problem, our elected leaders in Washington financed their 2008 stimulus package by borrowing the money from China. Our leaders thought that by borrowing money from a foreign nation, they would not affect the American credit market. However, they failed to realize that in our inter-connected global economy, a shortage of available credit in any nation will put a brake on all economic activity around the globe. This is especially true for nations like China, England, Japan or Germany. If any of them suffer a credit shortage, the US government will also suffer from a credit shortage, because the US government habitually borrows from them to finance its annual budget deficit.

Our leaders also failed to realize another problem. After Americans received this money from China, Americans went out and spent it on products that were nearly all made in China. Years later those same American tax-payers will have to pay back the debt to China with interest added. So the only nation that really benefited from the so-called "stimulus package" of 2008 was China.[154]

Barack Obama's stimulus bill of 2009 was even more wasteful. For example, it included thirty million dollars to study a cute little rodent called the salt marsh mouse, which just happens to live in the congressional district of House Speaker Nancy Pelosi. It spent eleven million dollars to build a pedestrian bridge to connect two office buildings owned by the Microsoft Corporation. This bridge was built at tax-payer expense so people employed by billionaire Bill Gates could walk to and from each building without crossing the road. Apparently the richest man in America was in need of a government handout. Also as part of this stimulus bill, the government sent out 2.5 million checks *to dead people*.[155]

Yet even if all the waste and abuse were cut out of the federal budget, government spending would still inflict three harmful burdens on the economy:

1. THE BURDEN OF COMPLEXITY

The first burden inherent to all federal spending comes from our extremely complex tax system. Our Byzantine tax system forces citizens and businesses to spend billions of hours and billions of dollars unproductively, just to get our tax money delivered to the government. Tax preparation consumes at least 3.6 billion hours for American businesses, and 1.8 billion hours for individuals.[156] That's a whopping 5.4 billion hours of labor spent on an unproductive activity that does not produce wealth. This amounts to about three million Americans working full time all year long doing nothing but tax preparation. Sadly, all those hours of labor are being transferred from a higher valued use (potentially working at a job that creates new wealth) to a lower valued use (tax preparation). The waste of labor is the waste of an asset, and so it destroys wealth.

To estimate a dollar amount for how much wealth is destroyed by this national waste of time, we can conservatively estimate the value of each hour wasted at fifteen dollars per hour, which is about twice the current minimum wage. So if 5.4 billion hours are wasted by individuals and businesses doing their taxes, this means that roughly 108 billion dollars worth of man hours are wasted each year in tax preparation. Not only is time wasted, but vast amounts of money are spent just to calculate Caesar's share of the wealth. The total spent on paying for tax accountants and tax preparers is conservatively put at 382 billion dollars.[157] However, Keynesian economists would claim that all of the money spent to pay for accountants is put back into the economy. So rather than devoting several pages to refute this claim, we shall simply exclude the costs of hiring tax accountants from our estimate of government waste. We will only use the 108 billion dollar figure.

In 2008, all levels of government (federal, state and local) together collected a grand total of $5,318,000,000 (five trillion, three hundred eighteen billion dollars, or $5,318 billion if you prefer). The 108 billion dollars worth of man hours wasted in tax preparation amounts to *over two percent* of the total revenue taken in by all levels of government. This means that the federal government automatically destroys over two cents out of every dollar it takes in. Therefore, government spending does not merely have a neutral effect upon the economy, as the switching pockets illustration seemed to indicate; it actually has *a negative effect*.

2. THE BURDEN OF BUREAUCRACY

The wealth wasted with tax preparation is only the first of three structural costs connected to government spending. The second cost is the expense of actually running the vast government bureaucracies themselves. This second stage in government spillage occurs within the dispersing agencies, such as the Departments of Defense, Education, Commerce, Health and Human Services, Interior, etc.

The cost of government waste now takes on mammoth proportions. Unfortunately it is impossible to know exactly how much money is spent to run each government bureaucracy. For example, an employee at the Department of Health and Human Services told me that they *did not have any estimates for how much money their agency spends on overhead and administrative costs*. My inquiries to the Department of Defense went completely unanswered.

Fortunately we can extrapolate some fairly precise estimates by using data available from the Government Accounting Office and the Office of Management and Budget. For example, we know that in 2006 the federal government spent 240 billion dollars for the salaries and benefits of 4.1 million permanent employees on the federal payroll, including military personnel. The government also spent an additional 500 billion dollars ($500,000,000,000) to pay the salaries of ten and a half million people who were employed as contractors or grantees under federal programs.[158]

This means that in 2006 the federal government spent a total of 740 billion dollars to employ a total work force of 14.6 million people. In 2006 the total federal budget was almost 2.9 *trillion* dollars ($2,871.9 billion). Therefore, the cost of just paying the salaries and benefits of federal employees eats up almost 26% of the entire federal budget. This amount does not include the other expenses involved in maintaining a bureaucracy, such as office buildings, supplies, energy costs, vehicles, travel expenses, training, etc.

Keynesian economists will claim that the money spent paying federal salaries is not really wasted. The federal employees spend their money on food and shelter like everyone else, and so they put the money back into the economy. Keynesians will argue that *any spending* generates new wealth because of a ripple effect known as "the multiplier effect."

However, economists cannot agree on how much the multiplier effect actually helps the economy, or even if it really exists at all. More importantly, when private sector employees spend their income, they would produce the same alleged multiplier effect, *but without the drawbacks of government spending* which we have just discussed. Once again, private sector spending is superior to government spending.

Keynesian economists also forget that the money being paid to the federal employees is being put to a lower valued use than it would have been put to in the private sector. This occurs because of the artificially high salaries that federal workers normally receive. Remember that wealth is destroyed whenever we transfer an asset from a higher valued use to a lower valued use. Right now, the federal government pays office workers 93% more in total pay and benefits than the private sector pays for the same type of office work.[159] This means that the government is spending almost twice as much money for an asset (office labor) than it should be paying. Therefore, the federal government is transferring an asset (money) to a lower valued use.

When you consider the additional costs of leasing buildings, office supplies, office equipment, furniture, utilities, phone bills, travel expenses and training, then the total cost of running the federal leviathan is staggering. But for now we will disregard all of that potential waste, only because it is impossible to quantify precisely. We will only consider the waste we can calculate with some precision. If federal employee salaries consume 26% of the federal budget, and 46% of this is wasted because of their high salaries, then 12% of the federal budget is wasted. (46% of 26% is 11.96%.)

Recently, spending by the federal government has accounted for about 35% of our GDP. So at first glance, it might appear that the total waste of wealth caused by federal employees is 4.2% of our GDP. (12% of 35% is 4.2%.) However, some of these federal "employees" are serving in the armed forces. Their salaries cannot be compared to civilian pay, because their jobs usually do not have civilian counterparts.

Therefore, to be fair to the government, we shall exclude the 1.5 million members of the armed forces from the permanent federal work force of 4.1 million. This represents a 36% exclusion. (1.5 is 36% of 4.1.) So the total amount wasted by paying federal employees their exorbitantly high wages and benefits is roughly 2.6% of GDP. (64% of 4.2% is 2.68%.) Assuming a GDP of 8.8 trillion dollars then this amounts to 229 billion dollars wasted every year.

Now let's add this to the 108 billion dollars worth of labor hours wasted by tax preparation. Now the cost of government spending amounts to 337 billion dollars wasted every year (108 billion for tax preparation and 229 billion for over-paid federal employees). But wait; there is at least one more source of waste to consider.

3. THE BURDEN OF DEBT

Now we must add the third structural waste that occurs whenever the government spends money; the interest on the national debt. Technically speaking, most economists would say that this is not really a structural (unavoidable) cost. In theory, this cost can be eliminated by paying off the national debt. So in theory, the government could spend money without paying any interest charges. However, the last President to pay off the national debt was Andrew Jackson. That was almost two hundred years ago. In all likelihood, we will probably be paying interest on this debt for another two hundred years.

Currently the government must take ten cents out of every tax dollar, and give it to banks in order to pay the interest (and only the interest) on the national debt. The national debt is not "a debt we owe to ourselves." It is mostly a debt we owe to foreign banks. According to the US Treasury Department, 56% of the national debt is held by foreign governments and foreign banks. This means that only 44% of the national debt is held by American banks and American citizens who hold Treasury notes.[160]

In absolute fairness to the Keynesians, we will assume a best case scenario. We will assume that all these Americans will spend all the interest they earn in our domestic economy. In this case, the loss of wealth is only 56% of 10%, which amounts to 5.6%. However, because we are expressing government waste in relation to GDP, we can only assume that 35% of this 5.6% is actually wasted. (Remember, federal spending accounts for 35% of GDP, not 100%.) So our interest payments on the national debt destroy another 1.96% of our GDP each year. (35% of 5.6% is 1.96%.) This amounts to about 172 billion dollars wasted every year.

THE GRAND TOTAL OF FEDERAL GOVERNMENT WASTE

After you add the interest on the national debt paid to foreigners (172 billion dollars), plus the amount of wealth that is wasted in preparing tax forms (108 billion dollars), plus the cost of paying the high salaries and benefits of government employees (229 billion dollars), we get *a grand total of 509 billion dollars.* Can you imagine if an extra 509 billion dollars were left in the private sector every year, to be reinvested by all sorts of companies to create new jobs and new profits? This amount of new wealth is hard to imagine. It would be like adding ten General Electric Corporations to the economy every year![161] This 509 billion dollars amounts to *almost 6% of our GDP.* If America had an extra positive 6% added to its GDP every year, we would enjoy the most prosperous and growing economy on earth. Alas, the government will not permit this to happen. The beast must be fed.

Recall that the annual federal budget for 2006 was 2.9 trillion dollars (or 2,871.9 billion dollars). Well, if the government wastes 509 billion dollars every year, then this means the federal government wastes (or destroys) *over seventeen cents* out of every dollar that it spends. (509 billion is 17.7% of 2,871.9 billion.)

This is yet another reason that a government "stimulus package" is erroneous. In order for the government to spend one dollar *it must take a dollar and seventeen cents out of the economy,* in taxes or borrowing. That 17% share amounts to wasted wealth. It is money that has been transferred from a higher valued use (private sector investment to create new profit) to a lower valued use (government employees paid to shuffle money around). It is money that will not be spent making our economy more competitive globally. Instead it will be wasted preparing tax forms, paying bureaucrats, and paying interest to foreign banks.

This estimate for government waste (whether it is expressed as just under 6% of GDP, or as 17% of federal spending, or as 509 billion dollars) is actually very low. This estimate does not include the waste created by state and local governments, wasteful military expenditures, or the burden on the economy caused by excessive government regulations. Nor does it include the many individual examples of government waste committed by federal bureaucrats everyday, by purchasing supplies and equipment wastefully, by incurring excessive expenses, and by simply spending money unnecessarily. More comprehensive estimates indicate that the government destroys anywhere from a quarter to a third of all the money it spends.[162]

Conservatives usually focus only on the money wasted by the welfare bureaucracy, forgetting all about the money wasted by our military-industrial complex. However, spending on the military is probably even more wasteful than spending on welfare transfer payments. This is because so much of our military spending goes into military equipment. This equipment is not used to generate any profit. It does not create wealth. After the equipment is worn out, it usually has little or no resale value in the civilian market.

For example, we recently sent billions worth of equipment and material into Iraq, along with thousands of young soldiers. Yet we did not even get free oil in return. At least in the days of old fashioned imperialism, great nations were smart enough to get some natural resources in return for their sacrifice in blood and money. However, under President George W. Bush Jr. the United States embarked on a new form of imperialism, based on nation-building and planting democracy. This altruistic imperialism was disastrous for the US economy. It was simply a waste of our wealth.

BITING THE HAND THAT FEEDS US

Free market capitalism has created all of the wealth which has so greatly improved the quality of life for most people on earth. Yet Modern Liberals generally disparage free market capitalism. Some of them even claim the free market is a dangerous beast, and so we need the government to protect us from it. Some of their fears are so exaggerated as to sound absurd. For example, according to Hillary Clinton:

"The unfettered free market has been the most radically destructive force in American life in the last generation."[163]

First of all, the "unfettered free market" does not even exist. It disappeared over one hundred years ago, when the federal government first began controlling the economy during the Progressive Era of Teddy Roosevelt. More importantly, Mrs. Clinton also forgets that the private sector creates all of the wealth we have in society. Only the private sector transfers assets to a higher valued use. Therefore, only the private sector creates wealth. *So the private sector is productive*, not destructive. Other Modern Liberals have long shared Mrs. Clinton's delusion that the private sector somehow destroys wealth unless it is controlled by the government. Mrs. Clinton's attitude toward the free market agrees perfectly with the fascist handbook of 1936:

"...Open competition, if not wisely directed and restricted, actually destroys wealth instead of creating it..."[164]

These Modern Liberals also forget that the private sector pays all the taxes which make it possible for the government to even exist. The private sector really is the goose that lays the golden eggs. The private sector is even responsible for creating civilization itself. Without private enterprise mankind would never have risen beyond the Stone Age. The only reason that our ancestors worked so hard to first smelt copper was so they could trade it for other commodities they wanted even more.

Almost every major invention we enjoy today (from crop fertilizers to light bulbs) was created by the private sector, motivated by profit. Only recently in human history have governments claimed credit for many inventions that were financed by the government. However, most of these inventions still came from private companies, who happened to be working under government contracts. Furthermore, there is no way of knowing *how many more inventions* might have been created by now, but for the government's removal of money from the private sector through taxes.

Yet despite the phenomenal contributions of the private sector, Mrs. Clinton also proclaimed; *"I think the private sector has failed."*[165] Instead of failing, the private sector has actually managed to carry on surprisingly well, despite government attempts to strangle it to death with taxes and regulations. Of course the private sector would be operating much more efficiently if it did not have to support our bloated government. Yet it has still not failed. Furthermore, if someday the private sector does indeed fail, it will be through no fault of its own. Its death will be due entirely to strangulation by the government.

If the private sector does so many wonderful things for society, then why do many Modern Liberals seem to despise it? One may wonder if perhaps Modern Liberals criticize the private sector for a hidden reason. Perhaps by condemning the private sector they can justify taking more money away from it. Hillary Clinton has so much as admitted this:

"The money has to go to the federal government because the federal government will spend that money better than the private sector will spend it."[166]

Given the fact that private sector spending creates wealth (and government spending destroys wealth) one can only marvel at her lack of understanding.

GOVERNMENT DESTROYS WEALTH THROUGH TAXES

In our discussion of how wealth is created, (transferring assets to a higher valued use) you may have noticed that all such transfers are *voluntary*. This is because both parties to the transfer expect to make a profit. After all, why would a person ever want to transfer his assets to *a lower valued use?* This means he would be destroying wealth and losing money. People are rational creatures, and so they do not want to destroy their own wealth.

In contrast, *involuntary* transfers of assets tend to destroy wealth. This is because involuntary transfers normally transfer assets to a *lower valued* use. Unfortunately, these involuntary transfers happen all the time. The most obvious example is paying taxes. Another example would be robbery committed by a common criminal. In either case (taxation or robbery) the net result is the forced transfer of wealth from a productive individual to a non-productive individual.

There is also an *indirect* way that transfer payments destroy wealth. In our modern semi-socialist economy, government transfer payments are quite high. Therefore, we now require high taxes to pay for them. Unfortunately, high taxes discourage both investment and profit making. As the government raises taxes it takes away more of our profits. This means we have less money to invest. Less money being invested reduces jobs. Fewer jobs mean that more people become unemployed. These people will increase the welfare roles. To pay for them, the government will have to raise taxes again. This becomes a vicious cycle of economic suicide. It is the death-cycle of socialism.

SALES TAX VS CORPORATE TAX

Modern Liberals often decry the sales tax because they claim it is "regressive." They claim that because it falls equally upon the rich and the poor, it is unfair, and "regressive." Modern Liberals argue that poor folks can hardly be expected to pay the same amount of tax as rich people. However, if you look at the historical record of the sales tax, (at least in most states) nearly every increase in the sales tax has been sponsored by Modern Liberal politicians. In reality, the quest for government revenue trumps compassion every time.

Modern Liberals support high corporate taxes because they believe them to be "progressive" instead of regressive. However, they fail to understand that corporate taxes are just as regressive as any sales tax. In order to pay the corporate tax, the corporations simply raise the price of their service or product, thus passing the tax onto consumers. So any Modern Liberal or neo-conservative politician who raises corporate taxes is really taxing the consumer, not the corporations. The federal corporate tax has the same burdensome effect on the economy as a national sales tax.

Conversely, reducing corporate taxes will stimulate the economy and help the common people. For instance, in the early 1990s Ireland had one of the highest rates for corporate tax in the world. It also had a sluggish economy. Then the Irish government reduced corporate taxes to a mere 14%, the lowest of any nation in the industrialized world. The result was dramatic. In 1993, before the tax cut, Ireland suffered from a high unemployment rate of 17%. By the year 2000, it had dropped to below 5%. It remained there through 2007.[167] Ireland enjoyed the fastest growing economy in Europe. For the first time in two hundred years, Ireland saw more people coming back home to live in Ireland than were leaving Ireland. The collapse of the Irish economy after 2007 had nothing to do with these cuts in corporate taxes. Instead, her collapse was caused by reckless government spending and reckless borrowing during the global real estate bubble of 2002-2007.

THE WORST TAX OF ALL

The most unfair tax of all is also the most ancient: property tax. Two hundred years ago, property tax made sense. Before the industrial revolution, all national economies were tied to agriculture. There were only a few rare exceptions, such as fishing, maritime trade, and the trade in rare commodities. All other wealth came from owning land. So if you owned more land than most people, it made sense that you should pay more tax than most people. After all, in the old days you were gaining greater income because of your larger land holdings.

However, this rationale no longer applies when the government taxes a modern family that owns a four bedroom home on a half acre lot. Today, most people use their property as a place to sleep, to prepare meals, and hopefully to raise a family. They do not use their property to generate any profit. Therefore, property tax no longer serves its original purpose at all. In fact, property taxes have degenerated into a tax on accumulated wealth, (i.e. a tax on assets). Any tax on assets is unfair because it taxes an activity that *does not generate any wealth.* In effect, the government is taxing the following non-profit activities: sleeping, preparing meals, and raising families.

A tax on assets is also bad social policy. It punishes people for accumulating wealth. Therefore, it actually discourages people from saving for their retirements. Instead, it encourages them to save nothing at all, and to rely instead on other tax-payers for their support. So any tax on assets naturally encourages parasitism.

Any tax on assets is also a form of "double taxation." The money which the homeowner spent to purchase and maintain his home was already taxed years before, when that money was earned as income. So his home is really a form of savings, like putting his money into the bank. Taxing his home is similar to taxing the principle in his bank account. In effect the government is taxing money that has already been taxed once before, when it was first earned as income.

Even people who use their property for profit-making (e.g. people who own office buildings, factories, and apartment buildings) should be freed from property taxes. After income tax was invented, property taxes became redundant, i.e. double taxation. Remember, *the income earned from the commercial property has already been taxed.* So what is the rationale for taxing the commercial property itself? In other words, the financial benefit from owning the property (income) has already been taxed. To tax the property itself amounts to double taxation.

GOOD RULERS CUT TAXES

The list of rulers who significantly reduced taxes reads like an honor roll of good leaders. These include Augustus Caesar, William Penn, Thomas Jefferson, William Gladstone, John F. Kennedy, Ronald Reagan, and Margaret Thatcher.

Augustus Caesar reduced taxes for both Italy and the Roman provinces.[168] He also reduced government regulation of the economy.[169] As a result of these wise economic reforms, Augustus ushered in the most prosperous era in Roman history.

William Penn created the government for the Pennsylvania colony. He was a product of the Enlightenment, and was a classic liberal. As a classic liberal, Penn supported individualism, limited government, equal rights for all, protection of property rights, freedom of religion, freedom of speech, and a free market economy. Penn kept taxes extremely low and one year he actually suspended all taxes. The resulting economic prosperity in Pennsylvania attracted immigrants from all over Europe, and more than any other colony.

Thomas Jefferson not only cut taxes, but he also eliminated one third of the national debt that had been run up during the previous administration of John Adams.[170] Federal taxes back then consisted almost entirely of tariffs on imported goods. After cutting the tariff, Jefferson's first term was marked by prosperity and growth. Sadly, during his second term, Jefferson imposed an embargo on English goods for political reasons, not economic. As a result of his politically motivated meddling in the economy, Jefferson's second term was marred by economic hardship.

William Gladstone was possibly the *greatest elected leader in English history*. He was also *England's greatest tax cutter*. Gladstone was Prime Minister four times, and also Chancellor of the Exchequer (like our Treasury Secretary) in four other ministries. He abolished 95% of all British tariffs and reduced the income tax from nine percent to a low, flat rate of just over one percent.[171] This stimulated the English economy and made him extremely popular. He also wanted to finance war through taxation alone; as opposed to borrowing money. He knew that the threat of higher taxes would make the public less eager to support going to war.

This would also be a wise lesson for modern leaders to follow. For example, if President Lyndon Johnson had been forced to raise taxes to pay for the Vietnam War, public opinion would probably have forced him to withdraw our troops before the conflict escalated. Fifty-thousand American lives could have been saved. Likewise, if George W. Bush Jr. had been forced to raise taxes to pay for the Iraq War, public opinion would have forced him to simply topple Saddam Hussein and then get out of Iraq in less than one year.

John F. Kennedy ran on a campaign to cut taxes *"Across the board, [from] top to bottom, cut in personal and corporate income taxes."*[172] He kept his promise. As a result, the economic recession he inherited from the Eisenhower administration was rapidly cured, and the economy took off with a rate of growth that was nearly triple the previous administration's.

When Ronald Reagan came to office, the top income tax rate was 70%. In 1981 he persuaded Congress to reduce tax rates *"across the board"* by 25%. Two years later he cut income taxes by another 20%. Most important of all, Reagan made sure that income taxes became "indexed" so that people would not be moved up into a higher tax bracket merely because their income rose with inflation. Reagan's tax cuts were phased in gradually over three years. This explains why they did not help the economy much in the first year they began. In fact, at first the economy hesitated with a small recession in 1981 and 1982, but then it took off, and the nation was prosperous for the remainder of Reagan's eight year administration.

During Reagan's administration, the US economy grew a total of 31%, in real dollars, adjusted for inflation.[173] Reagan also *eliminated over a third of all federal regulations*. This helped businesses operate more efficiently.[174] Contrary to Modern Liberal predictions, this massive de-regulation did not cause any industrial disasters or any deaths to American consumers. Reagan reduced the Treasury Department's printing of money, and so cut inflation to less than a quarter of what it had been during the Carter years.

Reagan's kindred spirit across the Atlantic Ocean was the conservative British Prime Minister, Margaret Thatcher. During the 1980's,

Thatcher served as Prime Minister for almost nine years, during three consecutive terms. Even the Modern Liberal *New Republic* admitted that her big tax cuts helped to create new prosperity for Great Britain:

"She cut the top income tax from 83% to 40%...the basic rate from 33% to 25%, removed the burden of income tax from millions of low-paid workers altogether, and ran a budget surplus at the same time. She quadrupled the number of British shareholders, presided over a doubling of British productivity, and privatized two thirds of state owned companies...Britain's unemployment rate went from the worst of the European economies to the best. The 1980's growth rate was almost double West Germany's."[175]

Another great leader who wisely kept the government from taxing the economy to death was John Cowperthwaite. Cowperthwaite was an English colonial official who was sent to reinvigorate Hong Kong's economy in 1945, after WWII had just ended. Later, between 1961 and 1971, he also served as financial secretary for Hong Kong. During all of his twenty-six years overseeing Hong Kong's economy, he wisely taxed as little as possible, and regulated as little as possible. *Newsweek* described his free market strategy in a nutshell:

"While Britain continued to build the welfare state, Cowperthwaite was saying 'no': no export subsidies, no tariffs, no personal taxes higher than 15%, and red tape so thin that a one-page form can launch a company."[176]

During Cowperthwaite's ten years as financial secretary, Hong Kong's exports grew by an average of 14% per year. Industrial wages doubled, rising much faster than inflation. Most important of all, (and without any social welfare safety net), the number of people living in poverty went from over half the population down to just 16%. Under this free market approach, wealth grew, and poverty shrank, and all the while income taxes were no higher than 15%. Furthermore, Cowperthwaite made sure there was no sales tax, no capital gains tax, and no tax on interest. He understood clearly that taxes reduce economic activity. Therefore, *taxes prevent the creation of new wealth.*

BAD RULERS RAISE TAXES

The list of rulers who significantly increased taxes reads like a rogues' gallery of bad rulers. These include: Emperors Caracalla, Diocletian, and Justinian, Louis XIV, Herbert Hoover, FDR, Fidel Castro, and Mikhail Gorbachev.

The Roman Emperor Caracalla raised taxes. He also declared that all freemen in the Empire were now Roman citizens, so they could be forced to pay inheritance taxes. He de-valued the currency, which caused massive inflation for the rest of his reign. The Roman Emperor Diocletian was one of the earliest rulers to create "stagflation," a combination of monetary inflation and economic recession. He did this by raising taxes (causing recession) and then stamping out large amounts of worthless money (causing inflation).

In the Eastern Roman Empire, Emperor Justinian of Constantinople collected taxes so aggressively that the famous "chariot race revolt" was partly caused by anger over Justinian's confiscatory taxes. Justinian created twenty-six new taxes for his people. His tax collectors were so vicious that they routinely used torture to reveal any hidden wealth that a citizen might have. This would often include raping the tax-payer's daughters. Justinian also forged the wills of dead citizens, making it appear that the deceased persons wanted to give their entire estates to the government.[177]

Yet most historians view the cruel tyrant Justinian as a great ruler. These historians have a childish infatuation for any leader who wins a major war. This childish fascination with "warrior kings" explains why most history professors reflexively include Woodrow Wilson and FDR in their lists of "great presidents." In fact, Justinian's greatest military achievement (uniting the Western and Eastern parts of the Roman Empire) was very short lived. Furthermore, the number of soldiers he lost during his two Italian campaigns was dreadful. His armies also slaughtered the populations of Naples and Milan. It was a great deal of bloodshed without any long term gain.

Louis XIV of France raised taxes with the aid of his avaricious advisor, Cardinal Mazarin. Louis also foolishly started a few European wars, all of which were disastrous for the French economy. France had the richest farmland in Western Europe, the largest population, and broad rivers to facilitate the transport of commerce. However, by the end of his reign, the French people were nearly starving, and the nation was deeply in debt. The crushing taxes that Louis XIV imposed choked off the French economy:

"In every quarter, and at every moment, the hand of the government was felt. Duties (taxes) on importations, and duties on exportations, bounties (subsidies) to raise up a losing trade, and taxes to pull down a profitable one; this branch of industry forbidden, and that branch of industry encouraged…custom-house arrangements of the most vexatious kind…that the duties constantly varied on the same article, and no man could calculate beforehand what he would have to pay. The tolls were so onerous as to double and often quadruple the cost of production."[178]

Louis XVI was no smarter. He too raised taxes, and did such damage to the French economy that revolution was almost inevitable. In some provinces, the peasants were forced to give up 80% of their farm produce to the government. Two bad harvests just before the revolution were simply the final straws. High taxes and mismanagement of the economy had already made revolt almost inevitable.

Herbert Hoover ran the federal government's international food aid program under President Woodrow Wilson, during which time he became enamored with big government. It was during Hoover's administration that the stock market crashed in 1929. Sadly, Hoover failed to treat the stock market crash with free market (conservative) solutions. He failed to let the credit markets adjust, and he failed to encourage new investment of capital.

Instead, Hoover applied Modern Liberal solutions to the Great Depression. He raised taxes, and this reduced the amount of capital available for investment. He also increased government borrowing, which reduced the amount of credit available for investment in the private sector. Hoover also increased government spending. Ironically, during the 1932 presidential campaign, FDR actually criticized Hoover for both high taxes and high government spending.

FDR must also be listed among the ranks of bad rulers who raised taxes. After criticizing Hoover for his failed economic policies, FDR pursued exactly the same policies himself. Both FDR and Hoover raised taxes and used government spending to keep prices and wages artificially high. As a result, what began in 1929 as a simple recession dragged on for at least twelve more years, and became the longest economic depression in American history. We will discuss this "Great Depression" in more detail shortly.

Even communist leaders have made the mistake of raising taxes. The dictator Fidel Castro used a combination of high taxes and socialism to virtually wreck the Cuban economy. After Castro seized power, he raised domestic business taxes above 50%. He also raised the taxes of foreign corporations doing business in Cuba to a ridiculous 95%.[179] Castro even raised taxes on the salaries of every Cuban worker employed by a foreign corporation, also to an astronomical 95% rate. These measures instantly chased foreign investment out of Cuba, even before the US imposed its own trade embargo.

As a result of Castro's tax hikes (and his stranglehold regulation of the economy) the Cuban people are more impoverished now than they were under their previous dictator, Batista. Their poverty has simply become deeper and more widespread. Before Castro seized power, per-capita income was $1,978 in current dollars. Now, under Castro's socialism, per capita income has fallen to $1,200, according to the Bank of Cuba.[180] In truth, it is probably lower than that.

On paper the Cuban people have free education and free medical care. In reality, they have very few books and almost no medicine. The average Cuban family spends over half their income just to buy food.[181] Malnutrition has become a significant problem, with widespread deficiencies in vitamin A and iron. According to foreign visitors traveling to Cuba recently, the biggest industry in the nation appears to be prostitution. The only way for many people to survive is by selling their bodies to tourists.[182]

To prop up the decaying Soviet Union, Mikhail Gorbachev also raised taxes and increased government spending. In a healthy economy, this would only cause a recession. However, because the Soviet Union did not have a market driven private sector, it was already an economic basket case before Gorbachev gained power. To worsen every other economic problem, he also began printing money to meet greater and greater government obligations. This caused runaway inflation. Gorbachev's monetary policies were the last nails in Russia's economic coffin. Modern Liberals in the West tend to idolize Gorbachev. However, most of the Russian people consider him a complete failure as a leader. The nation he led went into bankruptcy and was finally dissolved. Later, it recovered in a much smaller form, and only with massive oil wealth as the basis of its new economy.

WELFARE FOR THE RICH VS WELFARE FOR THE POOR

Welfare for the rich is always much more wasteful and expensive than welfare for the poor. This is because welfare for the rich is very indirect, while welfare for the poor is much more direct. When the government gives welfare to the poor, it hands most of that money directly to the poor people. A relatively small percentage of the money is wasted because it must be used to support the disbursing government bureaucracy. In most cases, the majority of the money spent on poverty welfare goes to the recipients of the program.

However, welfare for the rich is different. The government usually does not give billions of dollars *directly* to rich corporate executives, for their private bank accounts. That would be too obvious, too unseemly. Tax-payers would object. So welfare for the rich has usually been very indirect. When the government gives welfare to the rich, it normally always takes the form of a billion dollar government program. Then the rich parasites who lobbied for the program will receive a few hundred million dollars in profit for themselves. So the rich welfare recipients only receive a small percentage of the total money that is wasted on the huge government program.

For example, the "cap and trade" alternative energy bill that is currently being debated in Congress (June of 2010) is intended to increase gas prices by about seventy cents per gallon (a 23% increase from the current price). It will do this by increasing taxes of course, but also by forcing many domestic oil refineries to shut down. The supply of oil will drop, and so the price will rise even more.

If passed, this energy bill will also force utility costs to increase. Even Barack Obama admitted this. *"Under my plan of cap and trade, electricity rates would necessarily skyrocket."*[183] For the average American household of four people, their household utility bill would "skyrocket" by an additional three thousand dollars each year. The entire program will cost the economy hundreds of billions of dollars in lost wealth every year due to artificially high utility costs, and higher gas prices.

However, as we will see in Chapter Seven, the rich investors who support this program (e.g. Duke Energy, General Electric, and British Petroleum) will only receive a few hundred million dollars in welfare, in the form of government subsidized profits. So the rich welfare recipients will only get a small percentage of the total wealth that is wasted. This illustrates why welfare for the rich is more wasteful than welfare for the poor. Throughout the rest of this book, we will see other examples which demonstrate this.

Welfare is not limited to just the rich and the poor. The middle class has also become addicted to government handouts. The great social welfare complex includes very popular programs, such as Social Security and Medicare. The beneficiaries of these programs claim they are merely getting back the money which they have "already put into the system." But this is a delusion. The money that current beneficiaries receive far outstrips the money they contributed. According to the Social Security Administration, the average person who retired before 1980 will get back all of their SS contributions just three years after they retire. In contrast, anyone who starts working after 1980 will not get paid back until they reach the age of 92. So today's beneficiaries are really living off the contributions of today's workers. Social Security is nothing more than a pyramid scheme. In a pyramid scheme, the only people who benefit are the few who get out early. Everyone else gets cheated.

"THE RICH ARE GETTING RICHER, AND THE POOR ARE GETTING POORER"

This type of news story crops up almost every year, and you will see it several times during an election year if a Republican is the incumbent President. It is nearly always bogus. Yet it makes the gullible reader more willing to accept socialism; in order to correct the perceived injustice of all those rich fat cats getting richer, while poor people are falling deeper into despair.

The Modern Liberal reporters who write these fluff stories forget that "the poor" are a constantly changing group of people, with many formerly poor people moving into the middle class all the time. Also, many rich people move downward into lower economic brackets as well. The two groups are not static. For example, from 1979 to 1988, the American population gained in real income (adjusted for inflation) as follows:

Highest group......Up 18.8 %
Second highest.......Up 11.6 %
Middle group.......Up 10.7 %
Second lowest........Up 10.1 %
Lowest group.......Up 12.2 %.

During the Reagan era, Modern Liberals used this data to complain, "The rich are getting richer." First of all, they failed to mention that poor people also gained more income during those same years. As this table does accurately show, a rising economy tends to help everyone. As both John Kennedy and Ronald Reagan said, "A rising tide lifts all the boats."

More importantly, these critics ignored the economic movement of people from one group to another group. As far as the richest Americans go, by 1988, *35% of them had moved down to a lower income group.* Obviously the rich are not always getting richer, regardless of what "quintile tables" appear to indicate.

Why is this important? Well, after the Millennium, the quintile tables seemed to indicate that the lowest income earners in America were really "getting poorer." However, this group only *appeared* to be growing poorer, because they were increasingly made up of very poor illegal aliens. These newcomers tended to bring down the average income for poor people. After a generation they tend to bring themselves up out of poverty, and into a higher group. But in the meantime, more poor illegal aliens will have moved in. Therefore, the misleading quintile tables will indicate that the poorest people have become poorer. That would be a false conclusion. In reality, *the individuals who make up the lowest group will have substantially changed.*

Yet because of the raw data presented in the quintile tables, journalists keep on imagining that poor people (the lowest quintile) are growing poorer still. They also wrongly conclude that this "fact" proves that the poor are unable to lift themselves out of poverty. This supposedly justifies higher taxes on wealthy people in order to correct the alleged "economic injustice."

Imposing higher taxes on wealthy people is a simple case of the majority exploiting a minority. What if the majority votes for politicians who impose a higher tax on black people? Sound unlikely? Actually we do this sort of thing every year. Imposing a higher tax on black people is not really different from our current practice, where we impose a higher tax on wealthy people.

In both cases a minority group is exploited simply because it can be easily outvoted by the greedy majority. One tax is inspired by racial hatred and ignorance. The other is inspired by class hatred and greed. The race-based tax only sounds worse to us because we have been taught to avoid exploiting black people. However, we have never been taught to avoid exploiting rich people. Racial minorities are preferred over economic minorities, for cultural and emotional reasons. But the end result is identical from the victim's point of view.

This perennial complaint about the gap between the rich and the poor also fails to consider another important fact. In absolute terms, today's poor are much better off than poor people were just half a century ago. Nowadays in America, for the first time in human history, the poor are inordinately fat. They also have televisions, automobiles, cell phones and even air conditioning.

GOVERNMENTS USUALLY CAUSE RECESSIONS

Another stubborn myth that Keynesian professors keep perpetuating is the notion that the free market suffers from *"natural business cycles of boom and bust."* For the past sixty years, economic text books have mindlessly repeated this same drivel, without offering any evidence to back it up. These Keynesian authors suspiciously fail to tell us exactly what mechanism within the free market causes these cycles to occur. This is because there is no such mechanism. It does not exist.

John Maynard Keynes himself feebly suggested one possible mechanism. He claimed that every few years investors go through a cycle of over confidence (bull markets) followed by irrational fear (bear markets). Keynes even named these alternating moods *"animal spirits."* Keynes' idea rests on two faulty assumptions. First it assumes that millions of businessmen across the country somehow all think collectively, as a monolithic group. Second, it assumes that these same businessmen are so irrational that they are given to alternating fits of boldness and fear, as if they all suffered from simultaneous mood swings, or manic-depression. Keynes makes about as much sense as an aboriginal witch doctor, who blames the typhoid epidemic in his village on, *"evil spirits."*

In the absence of government meddling, capitalism naturally tends to encourage *steady growth,* not cycles of ups and downs. You see, a free market consistently encourages greater efficiency and increased productivity. Every company and every businessperson has a strong motive to increase efficiency and productivity. This natural tendency lends itself to the steady creation of new wealth. A few individual mistakes will always be made, but the general trend upwards is undeniable. The process of millions of people working to maximize their own profit creates a general trend towards increased wealth.

The truth is, the so-called "natural business cycle" is not natural at all. These cycles are usually caused by government interference with free markets. Let's look at each recession or "panic" as they were called back in the 19th century. The recession of 1819-1824 was mostly caused by the government. From 1814 to 1818 the government-chartered "Second Bank of the United States" increased the money supply and lowered interest rates, thus creating a temporary boom. Then in the summer of 1818 the national bank feared it had caused both inflation and a real estate bubble. So it reversed policy and restricted the money going into the credit market. The national bank also called in outstanding loans to further curtail the money supply.

The result was a general credit shortage. At the same time, farm prices dropped because European agriculture had finally recovered from the Napoleonic wars, which meant Europe did not need to import as much food from America.[184] Many American farmers needed to borrow to stay solvent, but they found they could not obtain credit. Farmers could not repay their debts, and their foreclosures led to bank failures. This was a serious recession, lasting three years. Andrew Jackson recalled the national bank's incompetence when he vetoed the renewal of its charter in 1832.

Ironically, the next recession to hit America (1837-1843) was caused by the meddlesome policies of Andrew Jackson. He ordered that all purchases of land from the government must be made in gold or silver. This caused less land to be purchased and also led to a shortage of gold and silver reserves in the banks. The lack of gold and silver on hand in the banks led to a general credit shortage, and the fall in land prices led to some bank failures. The lack of gold and silver reserves led some banks to refuse to redeem paper money with gold and silver. This led to a general run on banks, causing a nation-wide recession.

The recession of 1857-1860 was very unusual because it was not caused by any government action. It was the result of huge Russian wheat surpluses which depressed the price of wheat in America. In 1857, Western farmers made very little money because of the low wheat prices, and so farmers purchased fewer items from the factories of New England. Fortunately the surging demand for Southern cotton prevented this from becoming a nation-wide recession. The lesson from this is that *when recessions are caused by market forces, they tend to be brief and regional.*

The recession of 1873-1879 was so bad many historians call it a depression. It was a classic case of corporate welfare hurting the entire economy. It was also long and global in scope. In Europe it was initially sparked by the failure of an English bank, Jay Cooke and Company. However, in the US, it began with the government's reckless decision to pay large subsidies to construct far more railroad lines across the nation than were economically justified. Specifically, the US government over paid the greedy railroad barons for building the transcontinental railroad. The government paid for the track by the mile, and so the railroad barons quickly laid lots of extra track in a circuitous route. Much of the track was of such poor quality it had to be re-laid within a few years.[185] The increased government spending triggered inflation. Then the government raised the tariff tax to help pay for the railroad subsidies. Retaliation by other governments made our exports shrink. Finally, a general panic forced Wall Street to close for ten full days.

The recession of 1893-1896 was caused by many factors, and government negligence was only one of them. The other causes were international. The world-wide economic decline was worsened in America by the dispute over the private coinage of silver. Then the Treasury Department decided to let the US gold reserves dwindle down to dangerously low levels. The final straw was the failure of the Reading Railroad. Together, all of these factors caused a general bank panic. The only way to correct the mess was for the government to borrow money from private bankers such as J.P. Morgan.

Peter W. Hauer

The recession of 1907 was very unusual because it was both created by the private sector and cured by the private sector. J.P. Morgan wanted to destroy a rival Wall Street speculator (and trust owner) named F.A. Heinze. J.P. Morgan succeeded. Heinze went bankrupt, and there was a run on banks that had lent him money. One of these was the Knickerbocker Trust Company, which had numerous dealings with Heinze. When the Knickerbocker Trust (really a chain of banks) closed its doors, a full panic set in. The government spent 35 million dollars trying to shore up the weaker banks, but to no avail. Ironically, J.P. Morgan, who started the whole mess, stepped in and restored banking confidence in three weeks; by pressuring strong banks to loan money to weaker banks, in order to cover deposits.

What lessons can we draw from the seven recessions which occurred before the Fed was created? When recessions are caused by market forces, (as in 1857 and in 1907) they are usually very brief. In fact they generally end in one to three years. However, when recessions are caused by the government, (such as in 1819, 1837, 1873, and 1893), they tend to be longer lasting and more widespread. These four recessions had an average length of five years.

THE FEDERAL RESERVE BANK: "FAILURE INC."

The alleged reason for creating the Federal Reserve Bank (Fed) back in 1913 was to "smooth out" the cycles of boom and bust, i.e. to avoid recessions. However, increased government control over the economy has led to the opposite result. The Fed has greatly increased the number of boom-bust cycles. Let's look at the record. In the hundred years before the Fed was created, the United States suffered a total of *seven* recessions.[186] However, in the hundred years since the Fed was created, the United States has suffered a shocking total of *sixteen* recessions. These occurred as follows:

Aug1918-March1919, Jan1920-July1921, May1923-July1924,
Oct1926-Nov1927, Aug1929-Oct1945, Nov1948-Oct1949,
July1953-May1954, Aug1957-April1958, April1960-Feb1961,
Dec1969-Nov1970, Nov1973-Mar1975, Jan1980-July1980,
July1981-Nov1982, July1990-Mar1991, Mar2001-Nov2001,
Nov2008-present.[187]

But exactly how does the Fed create cycles of boom and bust? Historically speaking, before the creation of central banks, government meddling traditionally took only two forms. First, governments would raise taxes too high, which choked off private investment. This would lead to recession, and the loss of jobs. The second method was for the government to print excess money, which would cause inflation.

However, the creation of central banks in the past two centuries has given government officials yet a third way to wreck the economy. This new method is for the central bank to manipulate interest rates and money supply to artificially stimulate the economy. First, the government expands the money supply and credit via excessive spending and artificially low interest rates. This over stimulates the economy, causing both a false boom, and then inflation. Next, the government panics and contracts both the money supply and investment, which causes recession. This consistent pattern has been demonstrated by the thoroughly researched work of Milton Friedman and Simon Kuznet.[188]

This new method of government meddling is actually a bit complicated, so it requires some detailed explanation. First of all, we must understand that an interest rate is really just a fancy term for the price that banks charge for loaning out money. It is "the price of credit." In a free market economy, the interest rate performs the same function as any other market price. It provides vital information to buyers and sellers about how strong the demand is for any product. The free market brings supply and demand into balance.

In a free market (one without a central bank) interest rates balance the actions of borrowers (the "buyers" of credit) and lenders (the "sellers" of credit). However, in our restricted economy, the Fed works very hard to artificially manipulate interest rates. The Fed routinely forces interest rates either above or below the free market rate. The Fed can *artificially increase the supply of credit* by creating new money which the banks have access to. This is how the Fed forces interest rates to fall below the free market rate. The Fed can also *artificially reduce the supply of credit* by reducing the amount of money that banks have access to. This is how the Fed forces interest rates to rise above the free market rate. Finally, the government can also reduce credit by requiring banks to hold more cash on hand to cover their deposits.

The total supply of credit is not a fixed amount. It is fairly elastic. The supply of credit can be expanded or contracted depending on many factors. The most obvious factors are: 1) the demand for new loans, 2) the willingness of bankers to lend money, and 3) the ability of bankers to raise money either through deposits or by selling bank bonds.

All three of these factors are heavily influenced by short term interest rates, which are mostly controlled by the Fed. (In contrast, long term interest rates tend to be more influenced by free market forces.) The supply of credit is also affected by bank reserve requirements. This factor is exclusively controlled by the government. So in our modern government controlled economy, the supply of credit is heavily influenced by the government.

When the government keeps interest rates artificially low (to stimulate investment and spending), it will encourage more borrowing than bank deposits can possibly support. On the other hand, when interest rates are kept artificially high (to curb inflation), then this will stimulate more savings than investors are willing to borrow. Either way an imbalance is created, which will end up triggering a recession.

In the case where interest rates are kept artificially high, the harm is easy to see. It becomes more expensive for businessmen to borrow money. Therefore, economic expansion (job creation) is reduced, and the economy begins to suffer. The money supply also suffers a contraction, and all economic activity is reduced. A recession is the normal result.

However, in the case where interest rates are kept *artificially low*, the result is a little more complicated.[189] But this situation is vital to understand, because artificially low interest rates have become the usual cause of the "boom-bust cycle." When interest rates are kept artificially low, investors will want to borrow the cheaply acquired new money and spend it to hire more people and purchase more resources. Banks will increase the amount of money they loan out, and this puts more money into circulation. This extra money puts upward pressure on prices. The result is inflation. Of course the Fed's decision to increase the money supply will create an *artificial boom* along with the inflation. However, this temporary boom is unsustainable because of the imbalance between savings and investments. This imbalance will eventually require a market correction.

This market correction will occur when investors (borrowers) discover that the resources available are not enough to pay for all the projects that the investors have foolishly begun. In other words, investors will realize that consumers are unwilling to purchase (at current prices) all of the goods and services that have been created through the borrowers' excessive investments. This discovery will cause prices to fall, as investors realize that they have been sitting on top of an artificial bubble that is about to burst. Therefore, investors will quickly begin to sell their investments in large numbers.

This behavior is perfectly rational, and so it has nothing to do with "the animal spirits" of John Maynard Keynes. Yet most people (out of sheer habit) still call this situation, "a bear market." Corporations lose money as their stock values fall and consumer demand drops, so corporations begin to lay off employees. High unemployment causes more people to default on their mortgages. The increase in mortgage defaults causes a general drop in home values, and this drop in value will encourage still more people to default on their mortgages. This dynamic will trigger bank failures. All of these factors together will normally trigger a recession.

Ironically, this whole chain of events is set in motion whenever the Fed decides to keep interest rates artificially low, in a misguided effort "to help the economy."[190] The recent boom-bust cycle from 2003 to the present (2010) is no exception. It is just one more disaster caused by the government. According to economist Richard Ebeling:

"Between 2003 and 2008, the Federal Reserve increased the money supply by at least 50%. Key interest rates…were either zero or negative for much of the time when adjusted for inflation. The rate on conventional mortgages, when adjusted for inflation, was between two and four percent during this same period. It is no wonder that there emerged the now famous housing, investment, and consumer debt bubbles that have now burst. None of these would have been possible and sustainable for so long as they were if not for the Fed's flood of money creation and the resulting zero or negative interest rates when adjusted for inflation."[191]

Supporters of the Fed claim that politicians cannot be trusted to regulate the nation's money supply, because politicians will try to over-stimulate the economy, in order to get reelected. However, if we went back on the gold standard, we would not have to worry about politicians over-spending. The gold standard effectively prevents over-spending. Furthermore, the Fed has not prevented over spending at all. Nor has it prevented the recessions it was supposed to prevent. The Fed has failed to live up to any of its promises. In fact it has caused more harm than good. The Fed should be abolished.

LESSONS FROM THE GREAT DEPRESSION

The most dramatic example of the federal government mishandling the economy is the Great Depression. The Great Depression of 1930-1941 (some economists say it did not end until 1947) was *not* caused by the stock market crash of 1929. It was caused by the government's wrong-headed *response* to the stock market crash; namely the poor decisions made by the Federal Reserve Board in 1930. Then it was artificially prolonged for over a decade by the incompetent meddling of the Roosevelt administration.

Let's look at the record. Between 1923 and 1929, the Fed aggressively reduced interest rates and raised the money supply by 62%, fueling an artificial (and therefore temporary) period of prosperity, along with some inflation.[192] Fortunately a mass immigration of cheap labor, and increased industrial productivity, both combined to absorb most of the increased money supply. Our production of goods and services increased almost enough to match the increased money supply. This helped to prevent inflation from getting out of control.

What was the Fed's motive for reducing interest rates? Surprisingly, it was not to help the US economy. It was to help Great Britain. During WWI Britain went off the gold standard so it could print money to pay for the war. After the war, Britain wanted to get back on the gold standard at exactly the pre-war rate of exchange. This was nearly impossible because Britain's extra printed money had caused inflation of the pound sterling. Furthermore, both currency and gold were flowing out of Britain and into the USA because of our higher interest rates after WWI. Britain desperately needed gold for two reasons. First, she needed gold to buy up the excess pound notes that were in circulation. Second, Britain needed to build up her national gold reserves before going back on the gold standard.

In a private meeting at the Long Island estate of then Treasury Secretary Ogden Mills, a plan was devised.[193] Attending the meeting were Mr. Mills, Montagu Norman, (head of the Bank of England) and Benjamin Strong, (head of the Federal Reserve Bank of New York). These men made a fateful decision. In order to facilitate the flow of gold back to Britain, Strong agreed to artificially lower interest rates in the US, by reducing the Federal Reserve discount rate. Soon the flow of gold was reversed. Gold started to leave the US and head for Britain, which now had higher interest rates.

Why did Treasury Secretary Mills want to help strengthen the British pound? Most historians say that Mills merely wanted to help Great Britain get back on her feet because she was our biggest trading partner. Conspiracy enthusiasts claim that Mills really supported the pound in order to help the Rothschild banking family. Their argument is that inflation had made the English debt from WWI (owed largely to the Rothschilds) worth less in relation to gold. Inflation generally helps debtors but hurts creditors. So a stronger English pound would make each pound note received by the Rothschilds worth more in gold. Conspiracy advocates claim this was the real reason that the Fed helped to increase the value of the English pound.

Regardless of what Mills' actual motive may have been, the Federal Reserve's reduction of US interest rates caused the already overheated stock market to continue rising even faster. By the end of 1928, the Fed became worried about what it had done, and so it raised the discount rate (a crucial interest rate) back up to 5%. This did not have any *immediate* effect upon the stock market, which continued to rise. In fact, during the eighteen months from March 3 1928 to September 3 1929, most stock prices at least doubled, and many stocks actually tripled in price.[194] Then in August of 1929, the Fed panicked. The Fed raised the discount rate again, this time all the way up to 6%.

The Fed took this drastic step because they did not yet see any immediate effect from their earlier boost to 5%. This was mere impatience. The effect of an interest rate increase on the economy is sometimes delayed for several months, or even one or two years. As Jim Powell observed: *"Fed officials failed to understand, as [Milton] Friedman later documented, that a change in the money supply could take many months, perhaps a couple of years before having a measurable impact on the economy."*[195] In 1929, the Fed refused to wait. Unfortunately the Fed's jump to 6% was over-kill. The stock market crashed within eight weeks of the Fed's decision. This result was far more than the Fed had expected. The Fed had simply panicked and over reacted.

Yet exactly how did the Fed's decision cause the stock market to crash eight weeks later? During the late 1920's, government regulators permitted both banks and stock brokerage firms to loan up to 90% of the purchase price for stocks to their customers wishing to purchase stocks. This practice was called "buying on margin." As long as the stock market kept going up in value (due to the seemingly endless influx of new investors) it was easy for customers to sell their stock later. By the time the stock was sold, the stock's price would have increased enough for the customer to easily pay back his 90% loan, and still have enough left over to make a profit.

Of course this scheme would only keep working so long as more people were buying stocks than were selling stocks. If this sounds like an unsustainable pyramid scheme, then congratulations. You have more common sense than the Treasury Department or the Federal Reserve Board had in 1929. But what does buying on margin have to do with the Fed's decision to jack up interest rates? The Fed's decision caused a sudden and severe credit shortage. This in turn forced banks and brokerage houses (which had lent money to customers "on margin" so they could buy stock) to suddenly begin calling in their marginal loans in large numbers. That forced several hundred thousand investors to all sell their stocks at the same time. This caused prices on the stock market to collapse.

After the stock market crash, the Fed made the situation even worse. The Fed foolishly reduced the money supply by more than a third between 1929 and 1939.[196] This obviously made the credit situation even worse. The best "action" would have been no government action at all. The Depression began as a credit shortage. The best way to recover from a credit shortage is the natural way. Borrowers must repay their debts so the economy can begin to accumulate surplus capital again.[197] However, this is impossible during monetary deflation, which is exactly what the Fed was causing back in 1929. *The Fed prevented the free market from correcting the problem.*

If the previous economic panics are any indicator, then the economy in 1929 would have naturally swung back to equilibrium by 1932 if the government had patiently stood by and done nothing. In the absence of government interference, the economy would have adjusted over a period of one to three years. Prices and wages would have both naturally fallen to match the lower amount of available credit. This is how the economy naturally rebounded in the past after a credit shortage.

Sadly, both Hoover and Roosevelt were under great pressure to *"do something."* Yet the actions they both took made the Depression drag on for at least twelve more painful years. Government interference turned a brief financial downturn into the worst economic ordeal in the nation's history. The problem was that both Hoover and Roosevelt tried to keep prices and wages artificially high. They thought that the reduction in wages and prices was the *cause* of the Depression. They failed to see that the reduction in prices and wages was really just a *symptom* of the Depression. The underlying cause of the Depression was a credit shortage. This occurs when too many people try to convert their assets into cash. In this case it began when too many people suddenly tried to sell their stocks for cash.

The other problem was the method that Hoover and Roosevelt both used to keep wages and prices high. Both men raised taxes. Under Hoover the highest income earners paid 63% to the federal government, and under Roosevelt they paid 75%.[198] Unfortunately these high taxes siphoned money out of the private sector; i.e. that part of the economy that actually creates wealth. At the same time, state and local taxes more than doubled, all of this during a time of money shortage, when people had less money to pay for everything, including taxes. Throughout the Depression, Americans paid more in taxes than at any previous time in her history, including both the Civil War and WWI.[199] The effect upon the US economy was devastating:

"The Revenue Act of 1935 didn't prove to be very effective at raising federal revenue or redistributing the wealth. But it did send a clear signal to employers and investors that they were under attack. Such taxes encouraged them to conclude that they would be foolish to put their money at risk. As if this weren't bad enough, in 1936 FDR signed into law a graduated 'Undistributed Profits Tax.' That penalized companies for building up savings essential for investment."[200]

The increases in Federal spending were so great, that tax hikes alone could not pay for it all. This explains why both Hoover and Roosevelt committed a second mistake, which was almost as damaging as their tax hikes. Both men also borrowed money to help pay for government spending programs. Roosevelt borrowed so heavily that between 1933 and 1939, 57% of all Federal spending was paid for by borrowing.[201] This increased government borrowing only worsened the already serious shortage of available credit. This made it very difficult for the private sector to borrow money to pay for new capital investments and create jobs.

All of the massive taxing, borrowing, and spending by Hoover and Roosevelt did nothing to help the economy. Instead, they delayed the correction in the credit market and also pushed the nation deeper into debt. In 1939, industrial production fell a full 10% in just the first five months of that year. As a result, in May of 1939, unemployment reached 20%. This finally inspired FDR's Treasury Secretary, Henry Morgenthau to confess:

"WE HAVE TRIED SPENDING MONEY. We are spending more than we have ever before AND IT DOES NOT WORK...We have never made good on our promises...I say after eight years of this Administration we have just as much unemployment as when we started...And an enormous debt to boot."[202](Emphasis added.)

Just like the rest of FDR's administration, Morgenthau wasted eight years by not understanding that private sector spending and government spending are very different. Private sector spending creates new wealth, which helps the economy. Government spending destroys wealth, which hurts the economy.

As if a foolish fiscal policy was not enough, the government even damaged the US economy with bad foreign policy as well. In 1930, Hoover signed the Smoot-Hawley tariff. This law raised the import duties on more than 25,000 imported products. In response, more than 60 other nations passed similar laws against American products.[203] American exports dropped immediately, as did the already moribund American stock market.

Despite the overwhelming evidence of government responsibility for the Depression, it is a Modern Liberal article of faith to blame the whole thing on greedy capitalists, or the so-called "Wall Street barons." This myth ignores the fact that most of the Wall Street barons were ruined by the Depression. Whether or not Roosevelt really believed in this myth may never be known, but he certainly encouraged it:

"I know that the present situation is the result of a concerted effort by big business and concentrated wealth to drive the market down just to create a situation unfavorable to me...I have been around the country and know conditions are good...The whole situation is being manufactured in Wall Street."[204]

One reason for Franklin Roosevelt's misunderstanding of the Great Depression was the sheer stupidity of the advice he was receiving from highly educated economists. One of Roosevelt's top economic advisors was Rexford Tugwell, of Columbia University. Tugwell was a closet Marxist. Instead of an economy motivated by self-interest and profit, he actually advocated the same type of centralized planning that was then being wielded by the Soviet Union. Tugwell also failed to understand that wealth can only be created when voluntary economic activity produces a profit. This is just another way of expressing our "transfer of assets to a higher valued use" principle which we discussed earlier. Tugwell did not recognize any merit in profits whatsoever. This means that FDR's top economic advisor did not even know how wealth was created. *He even proclaimed that profits were bad*:

"[profits] create unemployment and hardship...persuade us to speculate [in] dangerous endeavors," and "hinder measurably the advance of [government] planning."[205]

Nearly all economists assume that World War II brought America out of the Great Depression. Yet even this widespread belief is probably a myth. In terms of consumer purchasing power, the average American was actually worse off during WWII than he was during the worst years of the Great Depression (1937-1939).[206] This is because war-time rationing of consumer goods made a wide range of foods and products even less available, and more expensive on the black market.

Conventional wisdom also says that WWII ended chronic unemployment. However, this is also misleading. The millions of men drafted to fight in the war did not hold jobs that created wealth. They represent concealed unemployment. While their military crusade was noble, in economic terms they may as well have been digging holes and filling them up again. Robert Higgs offers persuasive evidence that the US did not escape the Depression until 1947, when the economy was no longer driven by government spending and tax cuts also began taking effect. This means that when FDR became president, he inherited a two year recession and then *he turned it into a fifteen year long depression.*

GOVERNMENT ALWAYS CAUSES INFLATION

Inflation occurs when we have too much money in circulation. If the government prints money faster than we can produce goods and services, then we will have too much money chasing after too few goods and services. This will cause the price of literally everything to go up. This is inflation. Inflation is always caused by the government, because the government controls the supply of money in our modern economy. Creating excess money is very tempting for any government leader. It lets him spend more money without borrowing it and without raising taxes. It seems like "free money" to the average politician.

However, there is no such thing as free money. An over-supply of money destroys the value of the nation's currency. This means that everyone's money becomes worth less. Because of inflation, your dollar can buy fewer goods and services. Your dollar becomes weaker, or diluted. Your savings account gets eaten up, and eventually becomes worthless. This can seriously damage society in many ways. First of all, inflation makes it very difficult for businesses to predict their future costs for raw materials and equipment. Even labor costs become unpredictable. Inflation can literally make it impossible to for a businessman to determine the cost of staying in business. As a result, many companies go out of business completely. Also, inflation tends to wipe out the middle class, because they generally to keep their savings in dollar denominated IRAs or as cash in bank accounts. This means many years of real work, sacrifice, saving, and effort are converted into worthless paper currency.[207] Thomas Sowell nicely explained what inflation does:

"Inflation is a quiet way for the government to transfer resources from the people to itself, without raising taxes. A hundred dollar bill would buy less in 1998 that a $20 bill would buy in 1960. This means that anyone who kept his money in a safe over those years would have lost 80% of its value, because no safe can keep your money 'safe' from politicians who control the printing presses."[208]

Some people mistakenly blame inflation on a sudden price increase on this or that commodity. Petroleum is the classic example. If OPEC drastically raises the price of oil, prices of most retail items would initially rise, because most items are transported to stores on trucks that burn petroleum. However, this would still not cause inflation, *because the total amount of money in the economy would not be increased.* Instead, consumers would be forced to spend less money on all sorts of items, such as food, clothing, shelter, or entertainment. Consumers would be forced to purchase fewer items because so many prices had risen. As overall consumer demand is lowered, market prices would fall back down to a new equilibrium. Therefore, a mere increase in the price of a commodity (even something as vital as oil) does not cause inflation. Inflation is caused by the government artificially increasing the money supply. Inflation is always the fault of short sighted, irresponsible government officials.

The recent expansion of money by governments all over the world is truly frightening. From 1960 to 1995, the total value of all the money in the world went from 15 trillion dollars to 35 trillion dollars. So it took thirty-five years for the world's money supply to more than double. Yet from 1995 to the summer of 2008, the total value of the world's money went from 35 trillion to 80 trillion dollars. This means that governments all over the world more than doubled the money supply in just thirteen years, adjusted for inflation.

From September 2008 through October of 2009, the US Treasury printed a record two trillion dollars, and with help from the Fed, created a grand total of almost three trillion dollars. First the government deliberately paid high prices to commercial banks, in order to purchase worthless "mortgage backed securities." This did nothing to ease the credit shortage, and so then the government bought stock in failing commercial banks. This still did not turn the situation around, and so the government finally just handed money over to commercial banks, to encourage them to lend more freely.

The grand total for all three spending sprees was 2.8 trillion dollars. The stated purpose was to stimulate the economy and keep unemployment low. However, all of this spending failed to accomplish these goals. The economy still faltered, and the unemployment rate rose from 5.5% to 8% during these so-called "bailouts." In November of 2009, unemployment officially reached almost 10%. In reality it was probably around 20%, because government employment statistics exclude people who have given up looking for work.

At the time of this writing (November 2010), the commercial banks are still not putting this money into the economy. Instead, they are investing it in US Treasury bonds, the stock market, and foreign debt. The commercial banks are in no hurry to loan this money out to American companies. Perhaps this is a good thing. If the 2.8 trillion dollars was really injected into the US economy (through domestic loans) this would create terrible inflation. The Treasury Department's various bailout schemes were not only a waste of tax money and a handout for reckless bank executives, they were also inflationary. The money has been wasted, the promised benefit never occurred, and the tax-payer is now stuck with an even greater national debt. The bailouts of 2008 and 2009 are classic examples of why the government should not meddle in the economy.

GOOD AS GOLD?

After almost three thousand years of experience with gold-based money, governments still persist in making the same mistake over and over in regard to inflation. Governments will print as much money as they can get away with. They will recklessly print money until the society is ruined by economic collapse, or revolution, or both.

In ancient times, governments created inflation by stamping out coins that did not contain as much gold or silver as the government claimed. In effect, the governments unofficially "went off" the gold standard. The common people soon caught on, and the money lost value. The money became diluted. This caused inflation.

Today the situation is actually worse. Now the government does not even pretend to back up our money with gold or silver. It is now "fiat" money, i.e. money created by government decree. Therefore, there is no limit on how much money the government may print. This explains why some economists are calling for a return to the gold standard, as a way to prevent inflation and keep the economy stable. Even some Modern Liberal economists are admitting that a lack of confidence in fiat money is causing international traders to begin paying for transactions in gold. According to the Director of International Economics at the Council on Foreign Relations, Benn Steil:

"Gold banks already exist that allow clients to make and receive digital gold payments-a form of electronic money, backed by gold in storage-around the globe."[209]

Political author Jerome Corsi admits why this is happening, *"Globalists are now promoting digital gold as a private bank solution to the potential devaluation of fiat currencies."*[210] So the same type of people who gave us the Breton Woods Accord, and who later took the USA off the gold standard (i.e. Keynesian economists), are now admitting that their best laid plans have failed. Gold must be the basis for money if we are to achieve stability and long term prosperity. Of course it would be hard for a Chinese company to send three billion dollars worth of gold bullion to an American company as payment for jet engines. Shipping gold encourages theft and piracy. That is why private banks have set up "digital gold accounts." With a digital gold account, the gold is held at the bank, and the transfers of gold are completed simply by making entries in the bank's computerized record system, hence the term "digital gold."

The private sector naturally favors digital gold money because it is more stable than fiat money. In a free market, the private sector, which favors gold over fiat money, would naturally win this struggle for monetary supremacy. However, modern governments will probably not let this happen. They have become addicted to fiat money. They enjoy the unrestricted power that comes with fiat money. It is almost impossible for any government to give up a power once it has been acquired. So even if the free market economists demonstrate the benefits of the gold standard, governments will still insist on keeping fiat money instead. To stop the spread of digital gold money in our modern computer age, governments may even ban this new method of payment.

FREE MARKET VS GOVERNMENT MEDDLING

Let's imagine that we live in a free market economy. If the price of oil rose, then this would naturally encourage more oil exploration. This new drilling would cause the supply of oil to rise, and so the price of oil would fall back down again. When the free market experiences a shortage, the free market corrects it by increasing the supply.

However, we do not live in a free market economy. The reason we face an oil crisis every few years is because various governments are meddling with natural forces in the oil market. What government meddling you ask? The first meddling comes from foreign governments. OPEC is an anti-capitalist conspiracy which maintains a cartel in order to artificially reduce the supply of oil. This keeps the price of oil artificially high. OPEC is a multi-government cartel which prevents the free market from working.

Next, our own government's meddling comes into play. The US government has created artificial legal barriers which prevent oil exploration. At the time of this writing, the total area of land that is off limits to oil drilling is larger than Montana and Wyoming combined. In the eleven million acre Alaska National Wildlife Refuge, oil companies only want to drill in two thousand acres of land. The federal government has prevented any such drilling, even though this small area is the equivalent of "a postage stamp on a football field." Worst of all, no other country on earth is restricting oil exploration. Other nations are eagerly seeking new oil fields. So America will achieve no environmental benefits from this misguided policy.

This absurd policy keeps the supply of oil artificially low, and so keeps the price of oil artificially high. As a result, working people in the summer of 2008 could barely afford to drive to work, and our economy paid out almost 700 billion dollars that year to various oil sheikdoms and other petro-hooligans. If the US government would simply remove the artificial restrictions against oil drilling, then we would not even need to import any OPEC oil. The Alaskan Wildlife Preserve and the Gulf of Mexico together contain enough oil to make the USA oil independent for decades.

As with all government meddling, the federal ban against new offshore oil drilling has caused some perverse results. American companies are not allowed to tap rich reserves in US waters between Florida and Cuba. As a result, the Chinese have actually begun to drill into American oil deposits, right on the edge of American territorial waters. So the US government's failure to tap this huge resource *will not* save the planet. The Chinese and Cubans will use the oil for themselves.

Federal meddling goes much farther than making it hard to produce more gas. The government is even controlling what type of gas you can use. For years, the Federal government has used coercive financial pressure to force states to require that all gasoline sold must contain 10% ethanol. This ethanol comes from corn. It should not surprise anyone that food prices have risen sharply because of the government's demand that we must grow corn to produce ethanol. More and more farm fields have been given over to grow corn for ethanol. That means fewer fields are being used to grow soy, wheat, and alfalfa for food.

As a result, everything from pasta to eggs and meat has risen in price well above the average rate of inflation. In fact, the price of corn more than doubled between 2006 and 2008.[211] It went from $2.20 per bushel to $4.50 per bushel. The price of eggs went up by a third in 2007 alone. This is because corn is the most common food for chickens. Because of the artificial demand for ethanol (artificial because the demand is created by federal mandate) fewer fields are used to grow wheat. As a result, the price of wheat nearly doubled in 2007. Wheat went from $4.50 per bushel to $8.50 per bushel.[212]

There is also strong evidence that the government's support of ethanol is not really motivated by concern for the environment, or even by concern about oil prices. For example, the US government maintains a high tariff on all foreign imports of ethanol. At the time of this writing, the US tariff on foreign imports of ethanol is fifty-two cents per gallon. If the government really cared about the environment or gas prices, then it would permit the *free importation* of ethanol from other countries. However, if the government cared more about keeping big American farm corporations happy, then the government would maintain a high tariff on foreign ethanol…which it does!

So the federal mandate to put ethanol into gasoline is another example of welfare for the rich. Consumers are forced to pay billions of dollars more in higher prices for food and gasoline, just so powerful farming corporations such as Archer Daniels Midland and ConAgra can make a few tens of millions in profits. The government often has a perverse incentive to continue a harmful policy, especially if powerful constituents support that policy.

Tragically, the government policy to push ethanol production is not even achieving its stated goal: i.e. to reduce our consumption of oil.

This is because it takes almost one gallon of oil (seven tenths of a gallon to be exact) to produce one gallon of ethanol.[213] When you consider the oil based fertilizers used to grow the corn, the diesel fuel used to harvest and transport the corn, the various fossil fuels used to distill the corn into ethanol, and the diesel fuels consumed by transporting the ethanol to gasoline refineries, then using ethanol has yielded only a trivial reduction in our total use of fossil fuels.

Another factor that our rulers have failed to consider is that ethanol is a less powerful fuel than gasoline. Therefore, adding ethanol to gasoline will naturally reduce the fuel mileage of automobile engines. So adding ethanol results in *more total fuel being burned*. When you consider this mileage factor (along with the amount of fossil fuels needed to produce the ethanol) then using ethanol as a fuel is just as harmful to the environment as using pure gasoline.

Modern Liberals generally understand that a complex eco-system is beyond human comprehension. Modern Liberals understand that the best thing humans can do for an ecosystem is to just leave it alone. Any human meddling will almost certainly cause more harm than good. Yet Modern Liberals fail to apply this same logic to the economy. The economy is also a very complex system. It is also beyond the full comprehension of human beings. The best thing we can do is to leave it alone as much as possible. Beyond child labor laws, safety regulations, and pollution control, the economy should be left to its natural and most profitable course. The collective wisdom of millions of people working and living together is infinitely greater than the knowledge possessed by any government committee.

HOME FORECLOSURES

The tidal wave of home foreclosures in 2008 and 2009 was another example of government meddling in the economy. The cause of the trouble can be traced all the way back to 1977, when President Jimmy Carter signed the Community Reinvestment Act (CRA). This law required any banks with FDIC insurance (all banks and virtually all Savings and Loans) to increase the number of loans they made to people living in minority neighborhoods. Later, President Bill Clinton demanded an increase in these loans, and Clinton even denied permission for banks to open new branches if they failed to meet the new government quotas for minority loans.

President Clinton did not act alone in trying to artificially increase loans for new housing. For example, in the spring of 2000 Federal Reserve chairman Alan Greenspan decided to loosen credit substantially in order to facilitate the creation of new loans, as a way to encourage investment in homes. At first, the banks were slow to follow his prompting, but in 2002 the "sub-prime" lending market was starting to boom. It was an entirely new segment of lending that had been created out of thin air by the government.

Before 2002, banks had generally been very careful about who they lent money to for home purchases. Banks formerly required several paycheck stubs to prove income, a full credit report, copies of income tax returns, several months worth of bank statements, and (most important of all) a hefty down payment. Banks would also rarely ever loan money if the mortgage payment was to be over 30% of household income.

However, in 2002 the banks began to grow quite careless about who they lent money to. The banks were pressured to create risky new home loans for two reasons. First, they were coerced by the racial quotas within the Community Reinvestment Act. Second, they were encouraged by the government chartered corporations Fannie Mae and Freddie Mac, which eagerly bought up the risky mortgages that the banks were creating. The banks were soon lending half million dollar loans to people *based on what they claimed to be earning as income*. No proof of income was required. All too frequently, people borrowed sums they could never hope to repay. But as real estate values continued to rise, the bankers figured that the increasing value of the houses would fully protect their loans.

In other words, if the new home owner found that he could not pay his mortgage, then he could still count on selling the house for a higher price than he had originally paid. In this way he could easily pay off the mortgage and still make a profit. Of course the assumption that housing prices would continue to rise forever was very foolish. It was foolish of the borrower and foolish of the bank. It was the same mistake investors made during the stock market bubble in the late 1920's, right before the Great Depression.

Then in 2006, some lenders that made these risky loans began to have second thoughts about holding such poor quality debt. These bankers put thousands of such loans together in bundles and cleverly sold them, just in case the real estate market might bust. These worthless bundles of mortgages were sold to banks all over the world, under the label of "Mortgage Backed Securities." When the American real estate bubble finally burst the Mortgage Backed Securities could no longer be sold. They could not be sold because no one knew what they were worth. When no one was willing to buy them, they suddenly became completely worthless. A vast amount of wealth was thusly destroyed.

In 2008, the government decided to bail out the irresponsible banks with tax dollars. This was most ironic, because the government was responsible for creating the mess in the first place. If government meddling created this problem, was it really wise to think that further government meddling would fix it?

During the burst of the Japanese real estate bubble in the early 1990's, the Japanese central bank forced interest rates all the way down to zero. You could literally borrow millions of yen for free. This was inflationary enough, but then the Japanese government passed eight "stimulus packages" in less than ten years. The result was even more inflation, along with a huge national debt, and yet none of this helped the Japanese economy. Government meddling in the economy has a truly dismal track record. Sadly, it appears that American leaders refuse to learn from Japan's mistake.

A better solution would be to let borrowers and lenders adjust to the realities of the new credit market. Banks will have to go back to their previous practice of being careful about who they lend money to for homes. Some banks will simply have to fail. Just as with the 1929 stock market crash, the best government policy would have been to let the markets adjust on their own. In 1929 the government ignored this wisdom, and the result was the Great Depression. Currently (2010), if the Federal Reserve Board persists in their scheme to increase the money supply, it will trigger several painful years of rampant inflation.

Some Modern Liberals claim that the financial crisis which occurred in October of 2008 was *caused by a lack of government regulation*. They point to 1999, when Congress repealed the old Glass-Steagall Act of 1933. This law had kept commercial banks from participating in investment banking. American International Group (AIG) lobbied hard to this lift restriction, and then AIG dived recklessly into the investment banking markets. AIG failed nine years later, during the winter of 2008-2009.

However, the failure of AIG was really just the final stage in the financial meltdown of 2008. The collapse really began in the spring of 2007, when mortgage defaults started increasing in alarming numbers. The first big financial institutions to collapse were Lehman Brothers and Bear Stearns, back in the fall of 2008. But these two colossal failures had nothing to do with the old Glass-Steagall law. These two companies were purely investment banks. So even if AIG had never failed, the US financial system still would have collapsed like a house of cards in the fall of 2008, regardless of whether the Glass-Steagall law had still been in effect. Moreover, if the Glass-Steagall law had still been in place in 2008, then it would have prevented J.P. Morgan Chase & Co. from taking over the troubled assets of the failing Bear Stearns. So if the old Glass-Steagall regulation had still been in effect, it might have made the financial meltdown of 2008 even worse.[214]

Gretchen Morgenson (business journalist for the NY Times) has fully documented that government intervention in creating the sub-prime mortgage market was the primary reason for the terrible economic collapse of 2008.[215] The lack of government regulation over financial companies (such as Countrywide, AIG and Goldman Sachs) merely added insult to injury. The lack of government regulation (in addition to the "Bush Bailouts") enabled AIG and Goldman Sachs to profit from the disaster, but this lack of regulation did not actually cause the disaster itself. It was the sub-prime mortgage market which created the deadly housing bubble. When this artificial bubble finally burst, a financial meltdown was unavoidable.

THE CRASH OF 2008: THE OBAMA DEPRESSION?

The autumn of 2008 witnessed three separate but related economic crashes. First, the artificial bubble in the housing market finally burst. Prices dropped and foreclosures soared. Second, the commercial banks that were heavily invested in "mortgage backed securities" started going bankrupt. Third, these bank failures made the remaining banks unwilling to loan money except to only the lowest risk businesses. This created a credit shortage that hurt many corporations. The inability of corporations to get credit inspired a general stock market drop.

We saw something similar to this in 1929, just before the Great Depression. Back in 1929 an incompetent Republican President (Herbert Hoover) over-stimulated the economy and the credit market with government spending. Next, an incompetent Democratic President (Franklin Roosevelt) only increased government spending, which in turn prolonged the economic slump, creating the Great Depression.

In 2008 we were back in the same situation we faced in 1929. In 2008 another incompetent Republican President (George W. Bush Jr.) also over-stimulated the economy and the credit market with government spending. Just as before, an incompetent Democratic President (Barack Obama) has only increased government spending, which will likely turn the current economic slump into either a prolonged stagflation or possibly a depression. History has a stubborn way of being consistent. Even the Modern Liberal Washington Post noted disturbing similarities between Obama's economic plan and FDR's:

"Roosevelt spoke of creating one million new jobs...through his spending packages. At about 850 billion, Obama's stimulus package represents about 5.9 percent of gross domestic product. The spending programs of Roosevelt's National Recovery Administration amounted to almost precisely the same share."[216]

THE TROUBLE WITH KEYNES

The reason that Obama is repeating the mistakes of FDR is that both men were miseducated by the doctrines of the Modern Liberal economist, John Maynard Keynes. Ever since the 1930's, Keynes' theories have been taught as unquestionable dogma at most Western universities. As a result, Keynes has influenced more contemporary government leaders than any other economist. As Richard Nixon said, *"We are all Keynesians now."* This is unfortunate, because most of Keynes' ideas are both mistaken and harmful. By following the theories of Keynes, government leaders have created inflation, recessions, and huge public debts. They have also destroyed vast amounts of wealth.

In his seminal book, *The General Theory of Employment, Interest and Money,* Keynes proposed that during times of recession, the government should spend more money than it takes in, even though this will put the nation in debt. Then later, in times of prosperity, the government should take in (via taxes) more money than it spends. With this surplus of money, the government can pay off the debt it created earlier. In this manner the government can smooth out the ups and downs that supposedly occur in the "natural" business cycle.

Keynes basically told politicians that if they wanted to cure recession, all they had to do was spend more money.[217] Of course, politicians are always happy to hear any excuse to spend more money. Modern Liberal professors in academia support increased government spending on social programs, and so they too embraced this new rationalization for spending more money.

The theoretical flaw within Keynesian economics is the assumption that government spending helps the economy. We have already seen that government spending does not help the economy; it hurts it. Because of the structural wastes that are inherent to government spending, it actually destroys more wealth than it creates. Even in a best case scenario, government spending can only be a neutral factor, i.e. shifting money from one pocket to another.

Yet there is another fatal flaw within Keynesian economics. This flaw is a practical one. Keynes failed to consider the fact that elected politicians who control tax and spending policies are never going to pay off the national debt. Politicians are only willing to follow the first half of Keynes' system. They are eager to borrow and spend money to stimulate the economy. However, they are completely *unwilling to pay off the national debt* during times of prosperity.

There is a simple reason for this. Politicians always listen to the greedy clamor of special interest groups, all of whom demand ever increasing feeding space at the government slop trough. Special interest groups (e.g. big banks, defense contractors, teachers' unions, labor unions, government employee unions, the AARP, agribusiness, and welfare recipients) will never permit politicians to implement the second half of the Keynesian plan. These greedy groups will never permit any surplus tax money to be set aside to pay off the national debt. These groups constantly demand that the government should spend as much money as possible *every year*. By implementing only the first half of Keynesian theory, modern politicians have perverted Keynes' original system into a debt creating monster.

Peter W. Hauer

WHY NATIONAL DEBT IS EVIL

This reliance on half (and only half) of the Keynesian theory has warped the Western economies in our modern era. As a result, the national debts of all the Western nations have grown to crippling levels. Yet the worst part of the national debt is that our generation creates it, but future generations will be forced to pay it back.

Our children, our grandchildren, and our great grandchildren, are *not morally responsible* for this debt. Unfortunately they will be held *financially responsible* for it. Of course if our grandchildren are burdened by our debt, then they will have far less money to spend on social services than we are spending now. This is because our grandchildren will be wasting fifty or sixty cents per tax dollar to pay the interest on the debt. This explains why adding to the national debt is the most selfish thing any generation can do. We are condemning future generations to poverty, just so we can live more comfortably. We are literally stealing money from our grandchildren.

Several State governments appear to be following the federal government's lead into the bottomless pit of debt. New York, New Jersey and California are nearly bankrupt. All three of these State governments are heavily influenced by various public employee unions, especially by the Service Employees International Union (SEIU). These public employee unions have contributed heavily to State politicians. It return, those politicians have given out absurdly generous pension plans to public employees. As a result, in states such as California, private sector workers (who cannot retire until age 65 or 67) are being taxed so that public employees can retire at age 50 or 55.[218] Not only do these public employees retire much earlier, but the majority of them receive at least *three times more money* than private sector workers receive through Social Security.

Many of these privileged public workers receive far more than that. For example, San Francisco's police chief retired in 2011, with an annual pension of $277,656, courtesy of California tax-payers.[219] She has lots of company. In California alone, over nine thousand retired public employees each receive over $100,000 in retirement benefits annually.[220] For comparison, in 2011 the average retiree living on Social Security will receive a grand total of $12,924.[221] Also during 2011, the median household income for working families in the US was only $49,700. By comparison, retiring as a public employee is a great racket!

Giving gold-plated retirements to public employees is yet another example of socialism; i.e. the forced transfer of wealth from one group of citizens to another group. This example shows us that redistributing the wealth does not always help the poor. In theory, socialism was intended to help the poor. However, in practice, socialism helps whatever special interest group has the most influence over politicians. This is because once you allow the government to transfer wealth, you open the door for rampant corruption.

SOCIALISM & HUMAN NATURE: "THE FREE RIDER"

Even if socialism could be limited to only helping the poor, it would still suffer from one fundamental flaw. This fundamental flaw is that socialism can only work in very small social units; such as a family, or perhaps a small clan of people who live together permanently. In such small social units, all members of the group feel a strong emotional bond, due to the fact that they share bonds of kinship. This bond of kinship is enough to motivate individuals to work hard "for the common good."

However, large societies lack this crucial connection of kinship. In large societies the natural human instinct to do as little work as possible takes over. We all have a natural animal instinct to survive while exerting ourselves as little as we can. This natural instinct explains why whenever socialism is attempted on a large scale, it begins to unravel and break down. The following illustration explains why:

"Consider ten workers who share ownership (communally) of the land and who collectively produce 100 bushels of corn, averaging ten bushels each for consumption. Suppose that one worker begins to shirk and cuts his labor effort in half, reducing output by 5 bushels. The shirker's consumption, like the other workers', is now 9.5 (95 divided by 10) bushels thanks to the communal arrangement. Though his effort has fallen by 50 percent, his consumption has only fallen 5 percent. The shirker is free riding on the labor of others. The incentive for each worker, in fact, is to free ride, and this lowers both the total effort and total output."[222] (G. Walton & H. Rockhoff.)

A REVIEW OF SOCIALIST EXPERIMENTS

This "free rider" phenomenon is the basic reason that socialism always fails. In fact, the most perplexing thing about socialism is how many supporters it still attracts after so many decades of continuous failure. Let's review the historical record. In 1824 the famous English socialist, Robert Owen, founded a socialist community in Indiana, called "New Harmony." This socialist experiment died out in a few years. Nearly everyone became infected with *"the disease of laziness."* Individual effort was not rewarded, and so individual effort quickly disappeared. The failure of New Harmony was a perfect example of the "free rider" principle we just discussed.

In 1825 Frances Wright founded a socialist utopia called Nashoba. She also advocated free sex. Despite this promising recruiting inducement, her group failed after just a few years. Because it was socialist, it too fell victim to the "free rider" phenomenon. In 1841 George Ripley and his wife Sophia founded a socialist commune called Brook Farm. All members were paid the same, regardless of what type of work they did. Brook Farm was never financially viable, and the commune folded up seven years later. In 1842, a minister named Adin Ballou founded a similar socialist commune called "Hopedale." It lasted about a decade. The free riders had struck again.

In 1848, John H. Noyes created the Oneida Community in upstate New York. He believed that people could be made perfectly sinless here on earth. All members were considered married to all other members. However, all sexual relations were controlled by the group, and any children born were raised in common. Noyes eventually dropped both socialism and his "complex marriage" idea. Noyes finally became a capitalist, and ended up making high quality silverware. Eventually the business became incorporated.

The only socialist communes that have lasted longer than a dozen years are those that are based firmly upon religion. This explains why communities of religious orders, such as Christian and Buddhist monasteries, have lasted for centuries. The spiritual bond within these institutions seems powerful enough to act as a substitute for the ties of kinship that are normally needed to maintain socialist living practices.

LARGE SCALE SOCIALISM?

If socialism consistently fails in small scale experiments, then what reason do we have to believe that it will ever succeed on a national scale? We have none. When attempted at the national level, socialism leads to economic collapse. Generally speaking, the more socialist an economy is, the more of a failure it becomes. The most socialist nations in the world have created the worst economies in the world. The old Soviet Union, the communist nations of Eastern Europe, Cuba, North Korea and Communist China (before China finally decided to enjoy the benefits of capitalism) were all economic basket cases. This is why Thomas Sewell observed: *"Socialism in general has a record of failure so blatant that only an intellectual could ignore or evade it."*

Socialism is currently not as extensive in Western Europe as it was in the communist nations listed above, but it is still an economic failure. Modern Liberals often point to Sweden as an example of *"socialism that works."* The generous welfare system in Sweden does not require the recipients to do any work. As a result, more and more people are jumping onto the welfare bandwagon for free handouts. This means that fewer people are left working in the private sector to pay for it all. Socialism has turned most Swedes into economic parasites.

Here's proof. Sweden has a total population of about nine million people. Of these, the adult population is seven million. Out of these seven million adults, there are 2.7 million adults who do not work at all. Not surprisingly, nearly all of these people live off social welfare benefits. Another 1.6 million adults work for the government, or for government funded social-service agencies. This leaves only 2.7 million adults who work in the private sector.[223] This means that 2.7 million workers in the private sector are supporting the other 6.3 million people of Sweden, (4.3 million adults who all receive various checks from the government, along with the nation's two million children). This explains why over half of Sweden's GDP is consumed by the government in the form of taxes.[224]

How can one third of the population that works in the private sector support the other two thirds of the population? They cannot. Instead, *the government must keep borrowing money to help pay for it all.* This is yet another reason that socialism is an economic failure. Socialism is forcing Western European nations into bankruptcy, by trying to pay for millions of people who either don't work or who work for the government. Socialist states like Sweden can only survive by borrowing money from future generations.

Let's look at the numbers. The national debt of Sweden is now so large, that just keeping up with the interest payments alone eats up 7% of Sweden's gross domestic product (GDP).[225] In comparison, the interest on the American national debt consumes about 3% of our GDP. In recent years, the annual budget deficit of Sweden has been 12% of GDP. In America it has historically usually been about two to five percent of GDP, (at least before 2009). Sadly, during the second year of Barack Obama's administration, the federal budget deficit shot up to 12% of our GDP, just like Sweden.

In less developed nations, which lack Sweden's highly educated work force and industrial infrastructure (such as Cuba, Venezuela, North Korea, China under Mao, and Chile under Allende), the failures of socialism are simply more obvious. In these less developed nations, it is easier to see that socialism does not produce prosperity. It merely spreads poverty more equally.

Ancient history also provides evidence that socialism on a large scale is doomed to failure. At about the time of Christ, a social reformer in China named Wang Mang became Emperor of the Han Dynasty. Wang Mang confiscated all farmland and redistributed it in equal plots to the peasants. Wang tried to protect consumers by enforcing rigid price controls on most commodities. He also maintained a government monopoly on salt, iron, mining, and wine. Wang even tried to eliminate private banking by offering low interest government loans for business ventures. Sadly but predictably, his "reforms" did not bring prosperity to China. The price controls caused food shortages and riots broke out. The government loan program destroyed wealth because it was plagued by incompetence and corruption. (An unfortunate parallel may be drawn to the American experience in 2009 and 2010, involving Fannie Mae, Freddie Mac, AIG, and Goldman-Sachs.) Finally, barbarian invaders took advantage of the chaos.[226]

A thousand years later China once again experimented with socialism. From 1069-1076 AD, the chief minister for the Sung dynasty was a socialist named Wang An Shih. His beliefs about the role of government make him sound like a thoroughly modern socialist:

"The State should take the entire management of commerce, industry and agriculture into its own hands, with a view to succoring the working classes and preventing them from being ground into the dust by the rich."[227]

Under Wang An Shih's administration, the Chinese government repeated all the same mistakes that Wang Mang had committed earlier. Yet Wang An Shih did not stop there. He went on to create a government sponsored old age pension system, along with government sponsored unemployment compensation. He even established a basic welfare system for the poor. Soon a combination of high taxes, food shortages, and foreign invasions forced Wang An Shih out of office. The Sung dynasty immediately returned to a traditional free market economy. Prosperity was gradually restored.[228]

Both of these ancient Chinese experiments in socialism failed because socialism is not economically sustainable. Socialism is not economically sustainable because socialism destroys wealth. Socialism destroys wealth because socialism requires massive government spending. As we have already seen in this chapter, government spending always destroys wealth. Therefore, socialism always destroys wealth.

This destruction of wealth is the reason for socialism's life-cycle of self-destruction. Under socialism, the benefits keep growing, and the government bureaucracy also keeps growing. In response, the socialist government will normally take the following steps; 1) raise taxes, 2) borrow money, 3) print excess money.

When the government raises taxes, economic activity will shrink due to the increasing tax burden. As economic activity shrinks, the tax base also shrinks. Yet even while the tax base shrinks, government obligations continue to grow. Therefore, the government is forced to borrow money to keep operating. Eventually it falls so deeply into debt that creditors are unwilling to continue lending the government any more money. The government is effectively bankrupt. Finally, to meet its ever growing social welfare obligations, the government will print excess money. Hyper-inflation results. As a result, many businesses are closed, jobs are lost, and cash savings are wiped out. The economy falls into chaos and depression. This same pattern of failure (with some variation of course) eventually overtakes socialism whether it is implemented in ancient China or modern Canada.

Socialism in ancient China never lasted longer than one generation. However, in our modern era we have managed to maintain socialism for several generations in Europe and North America. Does this mean that we modern folk are simply better at running things than the ancient Chinese? Probably not. The most likely reason that socialism has survived longer in our modern era is due to the vast amounts of new wealth created every year by modern industrial technology. In our modern industrial age, socialism is taking a bit longer to fail because technology has given our modern governments larger amounts of wealth to destroy.

So the death-cycle of socialism is being prolonged, but it cannot be prevented. For example, the less industrial socialist states (with lower per capita incomes), such as Greece, Portugal and Ireland, are already teetering on the edge of bankruptcy. In contrast, the more industrialized socialist nations (such as the USA, Canada, England, Germany, France, and Sweden), have higher per capita incomes. Therefore, these more developed nations will probably be able to postpone their collapse for one or two more generations.

Historically speaking, there are only two examples of large scale socialism that worked successfully and lasted more than a few generations. One was the socialist state founded by the Jesuits in colonial Paraguay. It thrived from 1605 until 1750, when it was forcefully abolished by the Portuguese. However, this Jesuit commune was a special case, because it was held together by rigidly enforced religious beliefs. It was a theocracy.

The other example of large scale socialism that worked was the pre-Columbian Incan Empire. It is still a mystery as to how this empire survived under socialism. However, it is entirely possible that this society was also a theocracy. After all, the society was religiously homogenous, with no evidence of any religious dissent. So these two examples are really similar to the socialist societies created by the Christian monks in Europe. All of these socialist societies needed a powerful religious bond to keep the system working.

ECONOMIC IGNORANCE

Many of today's politicians show a depth of ignorance about economics that is truly frightening. For example, Don Perata is one of the two most powerful politicians in California, second only to the Governor. Yet on July 1, 2008 Don Perata was on the radio news in California, explaining to the common people why he needed to raise their sales tax yet again. The reason he gave showed how little he understood about both economics and families:

"The State budget is just like a family budget. If a family cannot balance their budget the first thing they do is find a way to increase their revenue, like taking on an extra job. It's the same with government. We need to increase our revenue."[229]

The first error here is that Mr. Perata fails to understand how most families work. The first thing most families do to balance their budget is *reduce their spending*. Apparently Mr. Perata never even considered reducing government spending. Such a thing is apparently not conceivable to a Modern Liberal politician.

The second error Mr. Perata made was his failure to understand simple economics. He was mistakenly applying a "micro" economic solution, to a "macro" economic problem. You see, a short-fall in a family budget is a micro-economic problem. And if a family increases their revenue by taking on an extra job, they will increase their own wealth, without causing any harm to the general economy. However, the government budget is a macro-economic problem. And if the government increases revenue *by raising taxes*, then the government is *removing wealth* from the general economy. This damages the economy. The family (micro-economic) solution cannot be applied to a government (macro-economic) problem.

Our national leaders are no smarter. While speaking in support of her plan to extend unemployment benefits for a full three years, House Speaker Nancy Pelosi actually said, *"Tax cuts do not create jobs... Unemployment insurance (federal benefits for unemployed people) creates jobs..."*[230] Both of her statements are false. In fact, the opposite is true. Tax cuts do indeed create jobs. Tax cuts leave more money in the private sector, where it is invested to create new wealth and new jobs. However, unemployment benefits do not create any jobs. These are simply transfer payments, which can only shift money from one pocket to another.

The sheer ignorance of our elected leaders is perhaps understandable, given the general level of economic ignorance which pervades our society. Most politicians don't know any more about economics than what they hear from the mainstream news media. Sadly, most journalists share their ignorance of economics. For example, on March 6th 2009, on National Public Radio's program, "Morning Edition," a journalist (who was presented as an expert on economics) told the national radio audience; *"The outlook for the economy looks pretty bleak, except for one bright spot. The government has created several thousand new jobs in the public sector!"* And the band played on…

CHAPTER FIVE

PSYCHOLOGY REVISITED

"Every form of addiction is bad, no matter whether the narcotic be alcohol, morphine, or idealism." (Carl Jung.)

College courses in psychology generally waste a lot of time teaching you about people you will probably never meet, such as sexual deviants, serial killers, psychopaths, neurotics, and schizophrenics. They rarely teach you how to understand the minds of people that you meet everyday, including co-workers, friends, and even family members.

Most important of all, professors of psychology almost never explain how to understand politicians. And politicians will affect your life everyday; by deciding how long you will have to work, how much money you can keep, how many kids you can afford, and even what doctor you can see. This chapter is intended to fill that gap in your education. After reading it, you will understand the motivations lurking inside the minds of the people who want to rule over you. You will also understand the minds of conservatives and Modern Liberals that you meet in everyday life.

The difference between the mental outlook of a conservative and a Modern Liberal is easy to see on a superficial level:

"The liberal looks at the actual and potential power of government, and imagines all the good things that might be accomplished if only wise and benevolent people were in command. The conservative

looks at the same array of power, and envisions all the calamities that might happen if evil people were to gain control."[231]

Yet this only describes the result of conservative and Modern Liberal thinking. It does not describe the root cause of their thinking. Two deeper questions still remain. Exactly *why* do Modern Liberals look upon government power and only see the potential for good results? And *why* do conservatives only view government power as a danger? The difference is not as simple as declaring Modern Liberals to be optimists and conservatives to be pessimists.

Surveys show us that Modern Liberals and conservatives not only think differently about politics and society, they even choose different career paths. Conservatives are generally found in practical occupations such as contractors, independent businessmen, tradesmen, medical doctors, engineers, entrepreneurs, and business managers. In contrast, Modern Liberals are much more often drawn to careers which allow them to influence other people, such as teachers, union leaders, lawyers, and of course, journalists. Modern Liberals also prefer imaginative pursuits such as art, acting, and writing fiction. Why do surveys show that Democrats (Modern Liberals) more often enjoy watching television, shopping, and visiting art museums; while Republicans (conservatives) more often enjoy reading, water skiing, and hunting? Why do Modern Liberals prefer Volvos while conservatives prefer Porsches? Why do most Modern Liberals believe in ghosts while most conservatives do not? Can all of these differences be attributed merely to optimism and pessimism?

DOES AGE BRING WISDOM?

One of the factors that determine whether a person is likely to be a Modern Liberal or a conservative is age. Conservatives like to believe in the old political adage which says, *"If you are not a socialist in your youth, you have no heart. If you are not a conservative by your middle age, then you have no brain."*

Of course in our youth we are naturally idealistic. In our youth, we often think we can solve the great social problems that have bedeviled mankind for generations. After all, our youthful self-confidence assures us that we are smarter than previous generations. We have an innocent faith that the government (if run by people as wise as we) can accomplish great things, if only the people who oppose us would step out of the way.

Later, in our middle age, we often develop the opposite notions. Some of us have witnessed so much government folly and wasteful government spending, that we give up all hope in government. We cynically decide that the best thing the government can do for people is to leave them alone. While this simplistic explanation is a useful starting point, it is not complete. There are other, more important factors at work in the youthful mind besides simple naiveté. And there is more to conservatism than just elderly cynicism.

Conservative pundit James Lewis claims that Modern Liberals support big government because of sub-conscious Freudian motives.[232] He claims that Modern Liberalism is the vestige of a natural childhood fantasy. According to his theory, Modern Liberals never outgrew the childhood fantasy of having the perfect parent. This perfect parent was protective, nurturing, kind, wise, and powerful. This perfect parent would keep you safe from all harm. According to this theory, Modern Liberals are still seeking exactly these same qualities in their government. In effect they are trying to fulfill a childhood dream. Meanwhile, according to Lewis, conservatives are people who have outgrown this childhood fantasy.

The conservative legal scholar Robert Bork offers a different explanation for why young people generally support socialism. His theory is less psychological and more cognitive. According to Bork, young people who are either affluent or middle class see themselves as being born into a prosperous and comfortable lifestyle. However, they also notice that other people are born into poor families. These two observations lead many young people to conclude that the possession of wealth is a matter of accident, i.e. mere luck. Therefore, young people tend to view the possession of great wealth as inherently "unfair." Because these young people believe that the possession of wealth is unfair, they are quick to support socialism as "social justice," to redistribute the unfair inequities of wealth. After all, if the possession of wealth is determined by luck, then it is perfectly fair to use government power to correct the injustice of fate.

What these young people fail to understand is that while their being born into a wealthy family is a matter of luck, *their parents' possession of wealth is NOT a matter of luck*. Young people do not see how hard their parents worked to provide them with their comfortable lifestyles. They also do not understand that poor parents have often made some foolish personal decisions that prevented them from accumulating wealth.

Some of these young liberals will become moderates after working in the real world for a few years, and paying taxes. When they get older, they begin to understand that accumulating wealth takes hard work. Eventually, some of them will realize that it is perfectly fair for some people to have more wealth than others. Later, if they witness enough government waste and misfeasance, they may become strongly conservative in their middle age. However, if they manage to get jobs in the public sector, then they will never object to big government. They will never object to high taxes. The government is their source of support, and so they cannot possibly favor cutting it back.

POLITICAL CONVERSION: A ONE-WAY STREET?

Regardless of whether Lewis' "perfect parent theory" or Bork's "generational theory" is more valid, the fact remains that political conversion tends to be a one-way street. In other words, many young Modern Liberals eventually become conservatives, but conservatives rarely ever become Modern Liberals.

A review of 20th century political thinkers demonstrates this point. For instance, at the turn of the previous century, Sherman Rogers was an ardent socialist and union activist for the Industrial Workers of the World. He began as a union steward, and worked his way up in the union hierarchy. In 1912 Rogers discovered that most of the economic information that his union and other socialist groups were using to justify new labor laws was phony. The socialists were claiming that labor only received a one-fifth share of total corporate compensation, while the other four-fifths was going to management "fat cats." However, the opposite was really true. Labor was actually getting about four-fifths of all compensation, compared to management's one-fifth share. Rogers was sharp enough to discover the fraud.

This great deception originated from a widely publicized study by the socialist demagogue Daniel DeLeon, published in 1905.[233] Unfortunately this fraudulent study by DeLeon strongly influenced the

US government throughout the next three decades, all the way through the Depression. It inspired a series of sharply pro-union laws that were passed as part of FDR's New Deal. This included the famous Wagner Act, which heavily favored the creation of unions. This law also made it very difficult for workers to get rid of their unions. The Wagner Act created the strongly pro-union National Labor Relations Board.

The next important convert to conservatism was Aileen S. Kraditor. Before WWI, Ms. Kraditor made her mark as a Modern Liberal scholar and political commentator. After working for various leftist causes she eventually turned her back on Modern Liberalism and did her best to expose what she decided had become a dangerous movement. Her best work, *The Radical Persuasion,* was just such a warning.[234]

Henry T. Morgenthau was Treasury Secretary for eleven years under the Modern Liberal President, FDR. For the first few years, Morgenthau was a strong supporter of the massive government spending programs that were called "The New Deal." But by 1939, as the Depression only got worse over nine years, Morgenthau decided that government control of the economy was the cause of the problem, not the cure.[235]

Another early "New Dealer" who decided to jump from the Modern Liberal ship was Lewis W. Douglas, FDR's original budget director for the New Deal. He resigned in 1934, because he was appalled at the economic damage caused by FDR's decision to finance government spending with massive debts.[236] Government borrowing was shrinking the supply of credit that could have been used by the private sector, to invest and create new jobs. Douglas understood that this policy was prolonging the Depression.

By 1938, even powerful Democrat insiders such as Joe Kennedy and Harry Hopkins finally went against FDR's plan to keep corporate taxes as high as possible. These otherwise thoroughly Modern Liberal men testified to Congress that high taxes were preventing businesses from making any new capital investments. This was keeping unemployment high. These inveterate Modern Liberals concluded that FDR's tax policies were a big reason that the Depression had dragged on for over a decade. Randolph E. Paul was FDR's chief advisor on tax issues. Mr. Paul eventually admitted that FDR's high corporate taxes made the Depression longer and more severe.[237] The 1928 Democratic candidate for President, Alfred E. Smith, was another early supporter of FDR.

However, over time he too saw the dangers of socialism in FDR's New Deal programs.[238]

Professor Raymond Moley of the Columbia School of Law was a member of FDR's vaunted "brain trust." Throughout the first half of his academic career, he favored government control over the economy. He feared that if the private sector were left alone, then it would inevitably degenerate into monopoly. However, in 1933 Moley decided to oppose big government spending not just because it harmed the economy, but because *it harmed the body politic*. He finally understood that government control over the economy was dangerously close to fascism:

"Planning an economy…is only possible through the discipline of a police state…Economic planning on a national scale in a politically free society involves contradictions that cannot be resolved in practice."[239]

Other Modern Liberals have realized that the idea of a centrally planned economy is doomed to inefficiency and failure. For example, after the collapse of the old Soviet Union, the Modern Liberal scholar Robert Heilbroner admitted:

"…no Central Planning Board could ever gather the enormous amount of information needed to create a workable economic system…Mises (Ludwig Von Mises, the noted free market economist) was right."[240]

The conservative writer Irving Kristol wrote an entire book about his conversion to conservatism. It was called *My Cold War*. Kristol concluded that Modern Liberalism was causing:

"…clear signs of rot and decadence germinating within American society, a rot and decadence that were no longer the consequence of liberalism, but was the actual agenda of contemporary liberalism… IT IS AN ETHOS THAT AIMS SIMULTANEOUSLY AT POLITICAL AND SOCIAL COLLECTIVISM ON THE ONE HAND AND, MORAL ANARCHY ON THE OTHER."[241] (Emphasis added.)

Some Modern Liberals have reluctantly admitted that the anti-communist crusade of Senator Joseph McCarthy was actually justified. According to Nicholas von Hoffman of the Washington Post:

The Big Picture

"[the age of McCarthy] was not the simple witch hunt of the innocent by the malevolent, as two generations of high school and college students have been taught...Ethel and Julius Rosenberg, executed in 1953 for atomic espionage, were guilty; Alger Hiss, a darling of the establishment, was guilty; and that dozens of lesser known persons such as Victor Perlo, Judith Coplon and Harry Gold whose [alleged] innocence of the accusations made against them had been a tenet of leftist faith for decades, were traitors, or, at the very least, ideological vassals of a foreign power."[242]

In the 1950's, Denis Healey was a leading English socialist and a Member of Parliament. In 1957 the middle-aged Healey turned around and shocked his socialist friends by suggesting that government ownership was not as efficient as private ownership of the nation's resources. Even Hugh Gaskill, the leader of the English Labour Party, tried to move away from government ownership of the means of production. In 1959 he tried to persuade the Labour Party to remove the infamous "Clause IV" from his Party's platform. Clause IV demands public ownership of the means of production and distribution.[243]

Other Modern Liberal conversions to conservatism were based on concern for human rights. Eugene D. Genovese was an ardent Marxist for most of his life. Back in 1965, he publicly declared his hope that the communists would conquer all of Vietnam. Yet in his elder years he came to reject socialism, because of all the violence this ideology had caused. He even went back to the Christian faith he had abandoned at the rebellious age of fifteen.

"Having...scoffed at the Ten Commandments...we ended a seventy year experiment with socialism with little more to our credit than tens of millions of corpses."[244]

Perhaps the most important switch to conservatism involved the editor of *Time Magazine*, Whitaker Chambers. Chambers was once so left-wing that he actually worked as a spy for the communist Soviet Union. After the birth of his daughter, Chambers suddenly believed in God. This epiphany led him to conclude that the murders committed by Soviet communists could not be condoned. Socialism, he realized, inevitably leads to totalitarianism and murder. After this realization,

Chambers helped the FBI to investigate his former partners in treason, the most infamous of whom was Alger Hiss.[245]

One of the most strident conservative talk show hosts in America was once a Modern Liberal. After college, Dr. Michael Savage got a job as a welfare case worker. Like so many young Modern Liberals of his generation, he had visions of "changing the world" and "helping the less fortunate." Eventually he realized that most of his clients were capable of working, but they simply preferred to live off other people. Dr. Savage also witnessed the generational dependency created by the welfare system, and how it sapped ambition from the people it was intended to help. Eventually he understood that government programs often cause more harm than good, despite their good intentions. He too grew into conservatism.

Author David Horowitz was a radical Modern Liberal back in the 1960's and 1970's. He made a complete turnaround in his middle age, after he decided that the Modern Liberal agenda was damaging society. Specifically, the expanded welfare system was encouraging out of wedlock births. Racial quotas were encouraging feelings of inferiority among blacks, and resentment among whites. Modern Liberal pacifism was putting the nation at risk from dangerous enemies at home and abroad; from both terrorists and the nations that support them. Horowitz wrote a book about his conversion called *Radical Son,* and a strident pamphlet entitled *"Why I'm Not a Liberal."*

To this long list I must add myself. As the son of an FDR style Democrat I argued passionately in favor of Richard Nixon's impeachment with my grade school teachers and classmates, as a payback for his role in what I saw as McCarthy's "witch hunt." As a Modern Liberal college student I was a member of Amnesty International. I also worked as a volunteer counselor at a crisis intervention center, where we frequently referred our unmarried pregnant clients to the local abortion clinic. During law school I was an active member of a quasi-Marxist group called the Committee in Solidarity with the People of El Salvador. I even joined in several protests against Ronald Reagan's policies in Central America. As a young attorney I did free work for illegal aliens at a free legal clinic in Los Angeles. I got all my news from NPR, the Christian Science Monitor, and the three big TV networks.

However, in my late twenties and early thirties I gradually became conservative. I became an *economic* conservative after I understood how wealth is created by the private sector, and how it is destroyed by government spending. I became a *moral* conservative when I decided that human life is sacred, even if a baby is just waiting to be born. I became a *social* conservative as I realized that the nuclear family is the most stable and effective way to raise children into healthy adults. I became a cultural conservative after I saw that "diversity" inevitably causes divisiveness and conflict. Finally, I became a *political* conservative upon seeing how the people who want to "change the world" always want to take away our freedom.

A TWO-WAY STREET?

In contrast, the political switch from conservative to Modern Liberal is extremely rare. After considerable effort, I could only find two examples of adult conservatives who became Modern Liberals later in life.[246] Furthermore, in one of these cases, the conversion does not seem sincere, but merely feigned in order to gain publicity from a sympathetic Modern Liberal mass media.

The man in question is David Brock. In the mid 1990's Mr. Brock wrote a series of articles for a conservative magazine exposing Bill and Hillary Clinton's record for dishonesty. He also broke the news about the scandal involving Paula Jones. For his punishment the Modern Liberal mainstream news media treated Brock like toxic waste. Brock was only permitted onto the Modern Liberal television news shows twice, once on CNN and once on the Today Show. Both times he was bombarded by hostile questions from Modern Liberal journalists. He did not even get to put in a good word about his book.[247]

After this abuse by the Modern Liberal media, Brock converted to Modern Liberalism. For his penance, Brock wrote a book, in which he claimed he had been deceived by right-wing propagandists for his entire adult life. In this book (*Blinded by the Right*), Brock actually apologized for having caused Bill and Hillary Clinton distress in their marriage. Suddenly, the mainstream Modern Liberal media treated Brock like a folk hero. Brock found himself invited onto all the major television news shows. This time the questions were no longer hostile, but positively affectionate. This introduction for Brock's interview on the Today show was typical:

"His specialty was character assassination, and throughout the 1990s he made a living as a right-wing hatchet man. But after years of lies and some would say, malicious journalism, this Washington insider wants to clear his conscience. In his new Book, Blinded by the Right, best selling author and ex-conservative David Brock exposes how he says the GOP tried to destroy the Clinton presidency through a series of well-plotted smear campaigns."[248]

However, Brock's entire book is notably lacking in specific examples. Brock never says exactly how conservatives lied to him, or to anyone else for that matter. For example, Brock agonizes over whether the Arkansas State Troopers (who said they procured sex partners for Governor Bill Clinton), might possibly have been lying. However, Brock offers no proof that the Troopers lied. All Brock can do is use innuendoes and refer to conservatives' alleged dishonesty. This undermines Brock's entire thesis, that conservatives somehow deceived him for fourteen years. Brock offers no real evidence in support of his claim.

Of course it cannot be conclusively proven that Brock's conversion to Modern Liberalism was insincere. It is very hard to determine another person's true motivation. Still, Brock had strong financial incentives for his "conversion." After all, his new book against conservatives sold well after it received fawning praise in the Modern Liberal news media.

The only other significant case of an adult conservative (that I could find) switching over to Modern Liberalism was Arianna Huffington. Ms. Huffington was married to a Republican politician for many years and even campaigned for him. After losing his campaign to become Senator from California, her husband admitted he was homosexual. The couple divorced. After their divorce, Ms. Huffington embraced Modern Liberal causes with ardor. Unlike the case of David Brock, there is no apparent evidence which would cast doubt upon the sincerity of Ms. Huffington's new-found liberal views.

Still, even Ms. Huffington's conversion is problematic. It is quite possible that Ms. Huffington had always held Modern Liberal views, but that she concealed her liberalism for many years while she was married to a Republican politician. Therefore, her conversion to Modern Liberalism may have really been more of a "coming out."

What can we conclude from the fact that Modern Liberals often change into conservatives later in life, but that conservatives rarely ever change into Modern Liberals? It does not necessarily prove that conservatism is more valid. However, it does indicate that Modern Liberalism is somehow based upon the enthusiasm of our youth. In contrast, conservatism seems to be more often based upon the accumulation of experience that only comes with age.

Modern Liberals are fully aware that their ideology appeals to youthful, idealistic minds. This is why they focus so much effort getting young people registered to vote. According to Democratic Senator Joseph Clark, a prominent leader of the Modern Liberal Americans for Democratic Action:

"...spiritually and economically, youth is conditioned to respond to a liberal program of orderly policing by government..."[249]

In other words, Senator Clark claims that young people are more obedient and less likely to question orders than those grouchy old folks. This explanation for why young people are drawn to Modern Liberalism does not contradict Lewis' perfect parent theory or Bork's generational theory. Clark is merely saying that young people tend to support big government more than old people do. He does not explain *why* this is true. Whatever the true explanation may be, the tendency of young people to support Modern Liberalism is impossible to deny.

SEX AND POLITICS

Age is not the only demographic factor that separates Modern Liberals from conservatives. Gender is also an important factor. As a general rule, American men and women think differently about economic, social, and political issues. Women are more likely to vote for Modern Liberal candidates and are also more likely to support socialism. In Europe the situation is the same. It is no coincidence that the most socialist nation in Europe, Sweden, was also the first nation in Europe to have a majority of women in its national legislature.

Female support for socialism may be due to the fact that women seek to avoid risks more than men do. How often do you see a woman jay-walk by dashing out in front of traffic? Women will rarely ever do this. However, we often see men (risk takers) jay-walking this way. If you watch the X Games on television you will see dozens of young men risk life and limb performing daredevil tricks on skateboards and bicycles. You will see very few women competing. High risk sports such as hang gliding, race car driving, and motocross are all predominantly male activities.

If indeed risk taking and risk avoidance can be traced to gender, then this theory about gender and politics is highly plausible. One interesting fact is that if you exclude the female vote from presidential elections, then the Republican candidate would have won every presidential election from 1968 to 2004, with only one exception. It is likely that the same result would have also been true for the elections from 1924 to 1968, but we do not have sufficient polling data (based on gender) for that time period to say for certain. Several pundits have observed that the social welfare programs created in the 1930s might never have happened if women had not been given the right to vote in 1920.

Surveys have consistently shown that women who are single mothers are the most likely of all people to vote for the Democratic Party. Of course these women are the most insecure financially. Therefore, it makes perfect sense for them to vote for the party that promises them the most social welfare benefits. Perhaps most single mothers instinctively want the same thing in the government that they want in a man; someone who is strong, powerful, and wealthy, i.e. someone who will take care of them. Contrary to what feminists want to believe, generally speaking, women want someone to take care of them, while men want to take care of themselves. This probably explains why women usually vote for Democrats, and men usually vote for Republicans.

The leading female politician of the current era, Hillary Clinton, certainly confirms this suspicion that women want a powerful government to take care of them. On May 5th 2008, while campaigning in Indiana, Mrs. Clinton actually said:

"Americans want a president who will take care of them, who will take care of them and their families."

Of course not all Americans want this. American conservatives certainly do not want a president who will "take care of them," as if they were infant children or sheep. Nor do conservatives want a president who will tax them into servitude, or destroy the nation's wealth through profligate spending. Instead, conservatives want a president who will take his oath of office seriously, and who will protect their freedoms which are listed in the Bill of Rights.

It is significant that no political commentators criticized Mrs. Clinton's remark. Apparently the feminine (and socialist) idea that the government should "take care of us" is now the prevailing American view. Polling data indicates that most Americans really do want Big Mommy Government to take care of them, as if they were little children. Ever since the emotional trauma of the Great Depression of the 1930's, two thirds to three quarters of the US population has consistently supported a federal minimum wage law, Social Security, Medicare, Medicaid, unemployment compensation, and low interest federal loans for housing.[250] It is ironic that the Great Depression frightened the American people into wanting a bigger, more powerful government. As we saw in Chapter Four, the government caused the Great Depression. So the government itself created the crisis which caused Americans to accept bigger government.

A TALE OF TWO HATREDS

Modern Liberals and conservatives dislike each other for different reasons, and on different levels. This is because both sides perceive each other quite differently. Modern Liberals see conservatives as selfish, callous, and even evil. Modern Liberals believe that selfishness is the real reason that conservatives object to paying the high taxes needed to fund social welfare programs. In contrast, conservatives view Modern Liberals as foolish, naïve, and misguided. Conservatives believe that this foolish naiveté renders Modern Liberals unable or unwilling to understand that social welfare programs create many unintended problems for society.

Because Modern Liberals see conservatives as *immoral*, they view conservatives *with more hatred than pity*. Conversely, because conservatives view Modern Liberals as *misguided*, they tend to view Modern Liberals *with more pity than hatred*. This difference in perception explains why Modern Liberals usually dislike conservatives they meet in everyday life. After all, it is easy to hate someone you view as immoral. On the other hand, it's more difficult to hate someone who you see as merely misguided. That is why conservatives generally do not hate Modern Liberals that they meet in everyday life. This dynamic also explains why conservatives are generally willing to maintain friendships with Modern Liberals; while Modern Liberals are generally unwilling to keep friendships with conservatives. It is very difficult to keep a friendship with someone you believe is immoral.

Does this mean conservatives do not hate Modern Liberals? Conservatives are quite capable of red hot political hatred. However, conservatives tend to save their hatred for Modern Liberal *politicians*. This is because conservatives believe that Modern Liberal politicians are personally responsible for causing evil. Conservatives believe that Modern Liberal politicians are continually passing laws that: (1) damage society, (2) take away their civil rights, (3) take away their money, or (4) erode American sovereignty. Conservatives generally hate all of these actions, and so they hate the politicians who do these actions. The following passage from H.L. Mencken is typical of how conservatives feel about the politicians who run the government:

"The government I live under has been my enemy all my active life…When it has not been engaged in silencing me, it has been engaged in robbing me. So far as I can recall, I have not had any contact with it that was not an outrage on my dignity and an attack on my security."[251]

This conservative distrust of big government is not just a modern trend. As early as the 4th century, the Christian church father St. Augustine lamented; *"Absent justice, what is the state then, but one massive act of robbery?"* St. Augustine had biblical support for his anti-government position. According to the Book of Samuel, after the twelve Hebrew tribes settled in the land of Canaan, they lived there for several generations without any central government. The Hebrew tribes were only loosely governed by their own individual tribal chieftains, or "judges." This era of Hebrew history is called, "The Time of Judges."

However, the ancient Hebrews were aware that all the other kingdoms in the Middle East were ruled by kings, who each ruled over a centralized bureaucracy. According to the Bible, the ancient Hebrews felt they could never become a great nation unless they too had a strong monarch. According to the Bible, God warned the Hebrews about the evils of a powerful central government:

"This will be the manner of the King who shall rule over you. He will take your sons and appoint them for himself, for his chariots, and to be his horsemen, and to run before his chariots...And he will take your fields, and your vineyards, and your olive-yards, and even the best of them to give to his officers and give them to his servants. And he will take a tenth of your seed, and of your vineyards, and give them to his officers and to his servants. And he will take your menservants and your maid servants, and your best young men... and put them to his work. He shall take a tenth of your sheep and you shall be his servants. And you will cry out on that day because of your king which you have chosen for yourselves, and the Lord shall not hear you on that day." (Samuel 1:8.)

On the other hand, Modern Liberals' hatred of conservatives is not limited to conservative politicians. Modern Liberals dislike all conservatives on a personal level because they view conservatives as selfish opponents of the Modern Liberal plan to improve the world. Thomas Sewell was perhaps the first to recognize this:

"Cultural wars are so desperate because they are not simply about the merits or demerits of particular policies. They are about the anointeds' (liberals') whole conception of themselves; about whether they are in the heady role of a vanguard, or in the pathetic role of pretentious and self-infatuated people...Because differential rectitude is pivotal to the vision of the [liberal] anointed, opponents (conservatives) must be shown to be not merely mistaken, but MORALLY LACKING...this approach replaces the intellectual discussion of arguments by the moral extermination of persons."[252] (Emphasis added.)

TWO KINDS OF HATE SPEECH

The following examples demonstrate this Modern Liberal tendency to morally condemn conservatives as evil:

"I hate Republicans and everything they stand for!"[253] (Howard Dean, head of the Democrat National Committee.)

"The leading terrorist group in this country right now is the Republican Party." (Keith Olberman, Modern Liberal talk show host.)[254]

"They (Republicans) are reptilian bastards."[255] (American Bar Association President George Bushnell.)

"What they are trying to do is make war on our children."[256] (Bill Clinton, describing conservatives in their attempts to trim the federal budget.)

"What they are trying to do is literally take meals away from kids...run over kids!"[257] (Leon Panetta, a Clinton staffer on the same issue.)

"They'd like to see the [Medicare] program just die and go away. You know, that's probably what they'd like to see happen to seniors too, if you think about it."[258] (Mike McCurry, Clinton staffer.)

"...conservative talk show hosts...are the equivalent of genocidal right-wing militia men in Rwanda."[259] (Dick Gephardt, then Democratic House Minority Leader.)

"Hitler had a minister of propaganda that said tell a lie...a big lie... Republicans are telling the biggest lie in the world...What's next, castration?"[260] (Democratic Congressman Bill Clay, commenting on conservative proposals to reform welfare.)

"When you bring your skills to bear for profit, you (capitalists) are the moral equivalent of Adolf Eichman."[261] (Professor Ward Churchill of the University of Colorado.)

"I hope his wife feeds him lots of eggs and butter and he dies early, like many black men do, of heart disease."[262] (USA Today columnist Julianne Malveaux, describing her death wish for conservative Supreme Court Justice Clarence Thomas.)

"Someone should shoot him with a 44 bulldog."[263] (Spike Lee, movie director, telling how he'd like someone to murder conservative actor Charlton Heston.)

"If we were in another country...we would go down to Washington and we would stone Henry Hyde to death! Wait, shut up! I'm not finished yet. We would stone Henry Hyde to death and we would go to their homes, and we'd kill their wives and their children. We'd kill their families."[264] (Alec Baldwin, Modern Liberal actor, responding to

Senator Henry Hyde's announcement that he intended to investigate Bill Clinton for possible crimes.)

"They ought to have him and shoot him. Put him up against the wall and shoot him."[265] (Democratic Congressman Paul Kanjorski, describing how he would like someone to murder Jack Scott, the Republican candidate for Governor in Florida.)

These last three quotations are most troubling. Here, Modern Liberals are actually advocating the killing of conservatives. Of course conservatives often vent hate speech about liberals, especially on the ultra conservative talk shows such as Michael Savage and Rush Limbaugh. Yet conservative hate speech is usually no more severe than mere name-calling. Conservatives sometimes call Modern Liberals idiots, fools, hypocrites, Marxists, socialists, communists, or even thieves. P.J. O'Rourke once called Modern Liberals "sniveling spoiled children." However, I have never heard any conservative call for the *murder* of any Modern Liberals. Therefore, left-wing hate speech is significantly more hateful than right-wing hate speech. This extreme hatred is inevitable, so long as Modern Liberals continue to view conservatives as morally inferior.

These violent calls to kill conservatives cannot be excused as harmless rhetoric. At least four prominent conservatives have been physically attacked by angry Modern Liberals, as they tried to speak at colleges in the United States. These conservative victims were William Kristol, Pat Buchanan, David Horowitz, and Ann Coulter.[266] In contrast, violent attacks by conservatives upon Modern Liberal speakers are unheard of. The Modern Liberal claim that conservatives are hateful and violent is not merely false. It is also ironic.

CONSERVATIVE MOTIVES

Modern Liberals and conservatives have both identified very different motivations behind conservative thinking. Modern Liberals have often claimed that dark and vile motives lie at the root of conservative thought, including greed, bigotry, hate, and ignorance. On the other hand, conservatives claim they are inspired by only noble and rational motives, such as their desire for freedom, and their sense of justice. We

will now discuss the following five possible motives behind conservatism, to see which are true and which are false:
1) Greed,
2) Bigotry & Hate,
3) Ignorance,
4) Desire for Freedom,
5) Sense of Justice.

1. GREED (FALSE)

Modern Liberals often argue that conservatives do not actually have principled beliefs against big government. Instead, Modern Liberals assert that conservatives simply do not want to pay for government programs with their own money. This is the basis for the popular stereotype that conservatives are selfish. For example, the late John Kenneth Galbraith was one of the leading academic spokespersons for Modern Liberalism. He said that conservatism was simply an effort to make *"greed respectable."* Modern Liberal talk show host Alan Colmes claimed that *"Jesus was a liberal,"* because he gave money to help the poor.[267] A popular T-shirt available on the internet summarizes the prevailing view: *"Liberals love people. Conservatives love money."* As Ben Wattenberg observed:

"The word 'conservative' conjures up images of the miserly Ebenezer Scrooge, while 'liberal' brings to mind kindly Santa Claus."[268]

However, empirical evidence does not support the view that conservatives are more selfish than Modern Liberals. In fact, research on this subject shows the opposite is true. The surveys that have been conducted on this question consistently show that Republicans donate almost one third more to charity than do Democrats.

A Modern Liberal professor named Arthur C. Brooks set out to write a book proving that Modern Liberals are more generous than conservatives. To his surprise, the data he found revealed the exact opposite. Brooks discovered that conservatives give more money to all types of charity (both to church related *and to non-church charities*) than Modern Liberals give.[269] Conservatives give more in both total dollars *and more as a percentage of their income.* Conservatives also give up more of their time for volunteer work than do Modern Liberals. Brooks even found that conservatives give blood more often than Modern Liberals.

The sources for Brooks' conclusions came from data collected by Modern Liberal sources, such as Harvard, Princeton, the University of Michigan, the University of Indiana, the Pew Charitable Trust, the Pew Center for the People and the Press, and the Gallup Company. Brooks admitted that he was surprised by what the data consistently revealed:

"If you had asked me a few years ago to sum up the character of American conservatives, I would have said they were hard-headed pragmatists, who were willing to throw your grandmother out into the snow to preserve some weird idea about self-reliance...The data tell us that the conventional wisdom is dead wrong. In most ways, political conservatives are not personally less charitable than political liberals, they are more so."[270]

For example, according to the Social Capital Community Benchmark Survey, households that were headed by Republicans gave 30% more to charity than households that were headed by Democrats. This was true even though households headed by Democrats had 6% higher incomes than did Republican households. So despite the fact that conservatives earn slightly less income, they still give more to charity both in total dollars and also as a percentage of income. The Social Capital Community Benchmark Survey is not a conservative poll. It is conducted by researchers at various universities in conjunction with the Roper Center for Public Opinion Research and Harvard University's Kennedy School of Government.

These findings are supported by data from the General Social Survey, conducted annually by the National Opinion Research Center. It found that the so-called "red states" (states where the majority voted Republican in the presidential election just before the data was collected) give more to charity (both in money and in volunteer hours) than do the people in Democratic "blue states." For instance, out of the twenty-five states that gave more than the median amount to charity, twenty-four of them cast a majority of votes for the Republican candidate. As Brooks reluctantly points out, *"The electoral map and the charity map are remarkably similar."* The differences in generosity become even more dramatic when you focus on especially liberal cities and counties such as San

Francisco, and then compare them to areas with strongly conservative populations, such as rural North Dakota.[271] As far as charitable giving goes, San Francisco may be the most selfish city in America.

Brooks is obviously uncomfortable with some of his own findings, and so he devotes part of his book trying to explain them away. In this effort Brooks makes some valid points. First of all, Brooks claims that *religion* (not politics) is the main motivation that propels conservatives to generosity.[272] After all, Christianity teaches charity, and many conservatives claim to be religious people. Brooks' research indicates that about 20% of the US population is made up of religious conservatives. However, this same research shows that only about 6% of the American population is comprised of *religious liberals*. Therefore, the argument goes, "conservatives are not really more compassionate than Modern Liberals; conservatives just give more to charity because they are more likely to believe in God." This argument might be true. However, it is also irrelevant. We are not using Brooks' research to prove that conservatives are morally superior to Modern Liberals (more generous, compassionate, altruistic, etc.). We are simply using his data to prove that *conservatives are not any more selfish than Modern Liberals*.

Brooks is more persuasive when he argues that whether or not a person will give money to charity depends largely on whether he considers it to be the role of government to aid the poor. If a person believes it is the government's job to help the poor, then he is *less likely to give to charity*. In fact, Modern Liberals generally believe this is the proper role of government, and so they generally give less money to charity. On the other hand, if a person does not believe the government should be aiding the poor, then he is more likely to step in and fill the need himself. This is largely the conservative approach.

A review of Modern Liberal scholarship shows that Brooks is probably correct in assuming that Modern Liberals believe the government should help the poor, instead of private charities. This explains why many Modern Liberals belittle private charity. According to the archetypal Modern Liberal politician Ralph Nader, "*A society that has more justice is a society that needs less charity.*"[273]

Some Modern Liberal authors go even farther. They are positively hostile to private charity and voluntary giving. When it comes to voluntary giving, Modern Liberal author John Steinbeck sounds a bit like Ebenezer Scrooge himself:

"Perhaps the most overrated virtue in our list of shoddy virtues is that of giving. Giving builds up the ego of the giver, makes him superior and higher and larger than the receiver. Nearly always it is a selfish pleasure, and in many cases it is a downright destructive and evil thing."[274]

It is plainly stupid for Steinbeck to call charitable giving *"a downright destructive and evil thing."* Sadly, this scorn for charity is not limited to Modern Liberal storytellers such as Steinbeck. This uncharitable attitude is also found throughout our college classrooms. According to Modern Liberal scholar David Wagner, charitable giving is *"inadequate to assist those who need help...(and) is tainted historically with visions of control over inferiors."*[275]

The reason all these Modern Liberals loathe charity is because they support socialism. You see, charity is a great threat to socialism. To a socialist, the existence of voluntary charity implies that *poor people are not entitled to support as a matter of right*. Modern Liberals criticize charity because it is the chief rival of socialism. A few Modern Liberals are brazen enough to admit this. David Wagner openly argues that private charity undermines the "right" of poor people to live off others. He even implies (without any evidence) that government welfare programs are more efficient than private charity:

"By harnessing a wealth of volunteer effort and donations, [charity] makes private programs appear cheaper and more cost effective than their public (government) counterparts, thus reinforcing an ideology of volunteerism that obscures the fundamental destruction of rights."[276]

Some conservatives must surely dislike taxes due to simple greed, but these are no doubt a minority. Most conservatives would still oppose big government even if it was funded without high taxes. Most conservatives dislike big government whether it is funded by foreign loans, domestic treasury notes, taxes, or worst of all, by printing more money. The source of government revenue is not what bothers them.

What bothers most conservatives is the loss of freedom that always results from the growth of government.[277]

2. BIGOTRY & HATE (FALSE)

The allegation that conservative thinking stems from bigotry and hate is harder for Status-Quo Conservatives to avoid. Before the Civil War, it was the Status-Quo Conservative social element in the Old South that sought to preserve the tradition of slavery. This is the ugly side of trying to preserve the status quo. Sometimes the tradition being preserved is simply immoral, such as slavery, dueling, debtors' prisons, and laws that demand religious conformity. Furthermore, all the way up until the 1960's, some prominent Status-Quo Conservatives favored separating the races legally with "Jim Crow laws." Thankfully, by the mid 1960's, these people were a small minority within the conservative movement.[278]

Libertarian Conservatives have a much better record of opposing evil traditions. For example, Libertarian Conservatives always believed the government had no business permitting slavery. The government also had no business segregating people by race, whether for school, public transportation, or any other purpose. Therefore, they opposed Jim Crow laws. Libertarian Conservatives also consistently opposed any government intrusion into a person's religious beliefs.

In regard to race relations, it is the Status-Quo Conservatives who owe a debt to Modern Liberals. It is due primarily to the effects of Modern Liberalism that Status-Quo Conservatives have generally reformed themselves and accepted the idea that people of different races should all enjoy the same political, social, and economic opportunities. This debt to Modern Liberalism is not often acknowledged by Status-Quo Conservatives, but it is undeniable. In fact, this particular reform of Status-Quo Conservatism may be the single most positive achievement of Modern Liberalism.

Unfortunately most Modern Liberals today believe that conservatives are still more likely to be racists than Modern Liberals are. They refuse to acknowledge the great turn around that Status-Quo conservatives have made in overcoming racism. For example, if the voting records of politicians are any indication, conservative politicians supported the civil rights movement of the 1960's significantly more than Modern

Liberal politicians did. According to the Congressional Record, it was the Republican members of the Senate and House who overwhelmingly voted in favor of the landmark Civil Rights Act of 1964, not the Democrats. According to the Congressional Quarterly, fully 80% of Republicans in the House of Representatives supported the Civil Rights Act compared to 61% of the Democrats. In the US Senate, 82% of Republicans voted for this act, compared to 69% of the Democrats. So most of the politicians who opposed this reform were Democrats.

These Democratic politicians were clearly Modern Liberals because they supported every aspect of FDR's New Deal agenda for big government. To call these men "conservative" merely because they opposed civil rights legislation would be illogical, and entirely unfair to conservatives. President Johnson happened to be the leader of the Democratic Party at the time, and he signed this bill into law. That is why most people mistakenly give credit to the Democratic Party for the Civil Rights Act of 1964.[279]

Even though most conservatives today are no longer bigoted racially, they still tend to be very bigoted *culturally*. For example, in regard to globalism, this charge of cultural bigotry is especially justified. Conservatives generally look down upon foreign cultures as being inferior to Western culture. This is the reason that conservatives do not appreciate the Modern Liberal effort to promote multiculturalism.

Conservatives are usually quite open about their preference for Western culture. They do not hide this attitude because they do not even see it as bigotry, but instead as common sense. According to conservative provocateur Stephen Klink, it is irrational to think that all cultures are somehow equal to Western Culture:

"Can a liberal really believe that a little band of savages tramping around the savannah is somehow 'equal' to Western culture? Western culture gave us the Renaissance, space travel and the internet. A true multi-culturalist will look at a troop of stone-age bug eaters and declare that they have a culture just as valuable as our own. Well, wake up! Chicken Marsala is superior."[280]

Whether this attitude is due to cultural bigotry or due to simple honesty is in the mind of the beholder. It all depends on your point of view. Suffice it to say that this ethnocentric attitude is widespread among conservatives. It explains the conservative opposition to immigration ("We don't want them in *our* country"), NAFTA ("We don't want to join *their* country"), and globalism ("We don't want to be ruled by *other* countries").

3. IGNORANCE (FALSE)

Another common stereotype that Modern Liberals hold regarding conservatives is that conservatives are less knowledgeable, less educated, and even less intelligent than liberals. It is amazing that Modern Liberals ever came to believe that conservatives are generally ignorant or stupid, especially when the champions of conservatism include intellectual titans such as Adam Smith, Edmund Burke, Thomas Jefferson, John Adams, Winston Churchill, Ludwig Von Mises, Russell Kirk, William Buckley, Thomas Sowell, Robert Higgs, and Robert Bork. Yet this belief is still quite prevalent among Modern Liberals.

For example, Democrat Mario Cuomo boldly asserted that conservatives "*…write their messages in crayons, while liberals use fine point quills.*"[281] After an election defeat, Modern Liberal activist Ted Turner comforted his fellow Modern Liberals by saying: *"People like us may be in the minority, but we're the smart ones."*[282] He even claimed that conservatives who opposed his ideas were *"a whole bunch of dummies."* Even major newspapers have trumpeted this intellectual vanity among Modern Liberals. According to the Seattle Post-Intelligencer:

"Liberals are where the brains are and the brains are where the liberals are. From a historical perspective, conservatives were the folks who clung to the idea that the earth was flat."[283]

When conservative historian John Moser attended a meeting of the Organization of American Historians, he carelessly mentioned that he had voted for George W. Bush Jr. This was a major social blunder in an academic setting. The other members of the organization who heard him were aghast. One of them managed to stammer, *"And yet you write books!"*[284] The obvious implication was that anyone who voted for George W. Bush must be an illiterate oaf. Scholarly journals have published sweeping generalizations about conservative ignorance, and even stupidity, without any objective research to back up such calumny.

For example, without any evidence, the respected journal *American Political Science Review* preached:

"...conservative beliefs are found most frequently among the uninformed, the poorly educated, and, so far as we can determine, the less intelligent."[285]

This is just another way of saying, "Anyone who disagrees with us must be stupid." Yet this bigoted attitude is somewhat understandable. After all, for the past forty years, Hollywood films and television shows have consistently portrayed conservatives with many negative qualities, stupidity being only one of them. In the 1970's the popular television show "All in the Family" portrayed the conservative character Archie Bunker as uneducated, ignorant, racist, and insensitive. The Modern Liberal character named Michael was educated, thoughtful and intelligent. This Modern Liberal character always presented the "civilized" view on current events.

In the 1980's the hit television show "MASH" had a conservative character named Major Frank Burns. Burns was always shown in a negative light, as stupid, bigoted, cowardly, peevish, dishonest, selfish, and insensitive. In contrast, the Modern Liberal character (Hawk-Eye Pierce) was smart, sensitive, brave, wise, witty and kind. In the 1990's television show "West Wing," the hero was a Modern Liberal President, played by Martin Sheen. Of course he was intelligent, educated, compassionate and wise. He was almost daily beset by evil and narrow-minded conservative politicians and diabolical conservative lobbyists.

In the popular cartoon show "The Simpsons" the Modern Liberal character, Lisa Simpson, is intelligent, thoughtful, honest and compassionate. The conservative character, Montgomery Burns, is morally depraved, dishonest, insensitive, greedy and cruel. Television writers consistently portray conservative characters as morally flawed, personally depraved, or just plain stupid.

The movie industry generally marches in lock step with the television industry to perpetuate the stereotype of conservatives as evil and stupid. This smear campaign can be seen in popular films such as: A Face in the Crowd, The Front, Wall Street, American Pie, The Day After Tomorrow, Good Night and Good Luck, Rock the Cradle, Julie and Julia, etc. Likewise, Hollywood consistently glorifies Modern Liberal characters in movies such as: Reds, The People v Larry Flynt, Patch Adams, Dead Man Walking, Malcolm X, Frida, Born on the Fourth of July, Silkwood, Gorillas in the Mist, Norma Rae, and Evita.[286]

The stereotype that conservatives are stupid and ignorant is just as groundless as the stereotype that conservatives are selfish. Once again, empirical evidence shows that conservatives are just as intelligent as Modern Liberals, and just as well informed as Modern Liberals, if not more so. According to the non-partisan General Social Survey, Republicans scored better than Democrats in vocabulary tests and analogy tests. "Strong Republicans" did best of all, out-scoring both independent voters and "strong Democrats" by substantial margins.[287] Other studies conducted by respected institutions indicate that conservatives are also better informed about current events than Modern Liberals are. For example, the National Election Survey conducted in 2000 showed that conservatives were 20% more likely to know the religion of Democratic candidate Joe Lieberman. In the same survey, 12% of Modern Liberals incorrectly believed that Al Gore was Jewish. Only 1% of conservatives made the same mistake.[288]

In 2004, the same survey showed that conservatives were more likely to correctly identify the offices held by William Rehnquist (Chief Justice) and Dick Cheney (Vice President). According to the Social Capital Survey, conservatives were also more likely than Modern Liberals to know the names of both their US Senators. This broad survey also revealed that conservatives were more likely to know how government processes worked, such as which branch of government decides whether a law is constitutional. Other questions included, "How many votes in Congress are needed to override a Presidential veto?" and "How many terms may a President serve?" Conservatives scored higher than Modern Liberals on all of these questions.[289]

In 2006 the Pew Research Center (hardly a right-wing institution) conducted a similar study which found nearly identical results. In the Pew study, conservatives bested Modern Liberals by 20% on their basic knowledge about politics and government. A survey done by professors at both Duke University and the University of North Carolina found similar results. Finally, these findings were again confirmed by a study from George Mason University.[290]

Interestingly, a study done by Princeton University (in conjunction with the Brookings Institution) showed that the more educated a person was, *the more likely he was to support conservative economic policies,* such as lower taxes, free trade, and deregulation.[291] In contrast, support for Modern Liberal economic policies (higher taxes, trade restrictions, and more regulation) was most often found among less educated individuals. Of course this finding does not necessarily prove that conservative economic policies are correct, but it does indicate that conservatives are certainly not ignorant.

Despite all this evidence, most Modern Liberals cling tenaciously to the myth that they are more educated than conservatives. It is always hard to give up a cherished belief, especially when it is flattering. This Modern Liberal myth is accepted as axiomatic by most college professors. Professor Brian Leiter of the University of Texas offered a typical professorial view of Republicans:

"...the Republican Party has gone increasingly bonkers, such that educated and informed people by and large can't stomach it anymore."[292]

Professor Michael Berube of Penn State University is considered a celebrity in American academic circles. He pontificated:

"...conservatism in America becomes more and more associated with the know-nothing, Tom Delay wing of the Republican Party."[293]

However, according to the General Social Survey, Republicans on average have almost one more year of education than Democrats.[294] Republicans are also more likely to hold a higher academic degree than Democrats. This is true despite the fact that college professors themselves are overwhelmingly Modern Liberal. Of course this increased education among conservatives does not prove that conservative ideas are more valid than Modern Liberal ideas. It is very foolish to equate education with either intelligence or wisdom.[295] However it does drive yet another nail into the coffin of this Modern Liberal myth.

In the face of all this research showing that conservatives are, on average, more knowledgeable and better educated than Modern Liberals, a few partisan researchers have made some desperate attempts to "prove" that Modern Liberals are smarter than conservatives. One article published in Vanity Fair claimed that out of the *"ten smartest states,"* eight of them tend to vote for Democrats (i.e. blue states). How did Vanity Fair decide which states were the smartest? The magazine considered certain social welfare factors, such as how much teachers were paid and other social service spending.

Obviously these factors have nothing to do with the intelligence of the general population. For instance, the teachers in Washington D.C., New York, and New Jersey have historically been among the highest paid teachers in the country. Yet their students tend to score far below the national average on most test scores. Utah is usually near the very bottom in regard to teachers' salaries, but it consistently ranks near the top in scholastic achievement. In the most comprehensive survey I was able to locate, nine out of the ten states with the highest student test scores were also in the bottom half of spending per student.[296] So beyond a certain minimal amount, increased spending on education does not yield smarter students. The critical factor is not *how much money* is being spent, but rather *how the money* is being spent. We will discuss this issue in detail in Chapter Eight.

In 2001 the ultra-liberal Lovenstein Institute published a study that claimed conservative politicians were significantly more stupid than Modern Liberal politicians.[297] This study was widely publicized throughout the Modern Liberal news media. It claimed that George Bush Sr. had an IQ of only 98, which is below average. Other Republican politicians were allegedly even dumber, with Presidents Eisenhower, Reagan, and George W. Bush Jr. ranking only slightly above retarded. In contrast, Modern Liberal politicians such as Bill Clinton and Al Gore were said to be near geniuses.

After a little investigation, the whole thing turned out to be a complete fraud. All of the information was made up. One major media outlet (*The Economist* of London) had the courage to admit the truth, and it published a full retraction. Not surprisingly, both of these flawed studies which claimed that Modern Liberals were smarter than conservatives received wide play in the mainstream news media. After all, (as we will see in Chapter Eight) the vast majority of journalists in the mainstream media are Modern Liberals. To Modern Liberal journalists, these studies validated their own cherished belief in their mental superiority over conservatives. However, as we have just seen, the overwhelming weight of research disproves this myth.

4. DESIRE FOR FREEDOM (TRUE)

Modern Liberals prefer to label this an "obsession" with freedom. The term obsession connotes an extremist, even irrational point of view. Indeed, some of the more provocative conservatives have actually admitted that their interest in freedom is obsessive and all-encompassing. It dominates their political, economic, and social thinking. To quote conservative Barry Goldwater, *"Extremism in defense of liberty is no vice."* Of course this extreme attitude has a long history, because it inspired our Founding Fathers, who adopted the radical slogan of Patrick Henry, *"Give me liberty or give me death."* The Founding Fathers in Connecticut picked as their state motto, *"Live Free or Die!"*

The desire for freedom is the core reason for the conservative preference for smaller government. Libertarian Conservatives understand that as government grows in size and power, individual freedom shrinks. Even many Status-Quo Conservatives have an intuitive understanding of this inverse relationship.

The traditional religious beliefs held by many Status-Quo Conservatives also encourage their desire for freedom. All of the truly great teachers of Christianity (e.g. St. Paul, Augustus of Hippo, Thomas Aquinas, and Martin Luther) agreed that free will is necessary to achieve salvation. Therefore, any government which is so powerful that it can control all human behavior would violate God's plan for us to exercise our own free will. It would also be a very repressive police state.

The conservative desire for freedom is also part and parcel with the conservative preference for *individualism*. The opposite view, known as *collectivism*, is favored by Modern Liberals. If we can recall the collectivist statement made by Bill Clinton in 1994:

"...When personal freedom is being abused, you have to move to limit it..."[298]

This approach is the exact opposite of what a conservative would do. A conservative would instead *punish the individual* who abused his freedom. A conservative would never think of abolishing everyone's freedom. His passion for individual freedom would prevent this.

To fully appreciate how thoroughly collectivist America has become, we should compare Mr. Clinton's words to those of the Tory governor of Massachusetts, who, in 1775 stated, "*There must be a restraint on natural liberty.*"[299] Back in 1775 those words caused a tremendous uproar among the colonists. Two hundred years later the President of the USA said basically the same thing, and yet not one journalist in the mainstream news media criticized Mr. Clinton! This failure to object to Mr. Clinton's words indicates that we modern folk are willing to accept collectivism. We are willing to accept the destruction of our liberty so long as the government keeps us safe and well fed. This is yet another sign that true conservatives are just a small minority of our population.

5. SENSE OF JUSTICE (TRUE)

Both types of conservatives are indeed motivated by a sense of justice, especially in their opposition to socialism. As we saw in Chapter One, Libertarian Conservatives believe that forcefully taking money away from people who earned it, and handing it over to people who want it, is nothing more than government sanctioned robbery. So Libertarian Conservatives feel morally justified in fighting against virtually all the social welfare programs proposed by Modern Liberals. The Modern Liberal intent behind a social welfare program may be noble, and perhaps even socially useful. However, to a Libertarian Conservative, redistributing the wealth is still robbery. Therefore, it is an immoral way to achieve any goal.

Status-Quo Conservatives have a more instinctive dislike for welfare transfer payments. The welfare system goes against their upbringing. After all, Western culture has not entirely forgotten the lesson taught by the story of "The Little Red Hen." The little red hen asked the other farm animals to help her make bread. They all refused to help her. So the little red hen did all the work to make bread by herself, which meant harvesting wheat, hulling it, grinding flour, kneading the dough, and baking it. Then all the other animals wanted to eat some of her bread. However, the little red hen refused to share her bread with all the lazy animals, because they had refused to help her in her work. I am summarizing this tale for the benefit of younger readers who attended public school, where socialist teachers have removed this classic from the curriculum.

Some Status-Quo Conservatives are also haunted by the words of St. Paul; *"He who will not work, then he will not eat."* To these religious conservatives, it is sinful to give money to lazy people who simply refuse to work.

MODERN LIBERAL MOTIVES

Conservatives have always been frustrated by the stubborn support that Modern Liberals keep giving to the five major goals of Modern Liberalism, i.e. collectivism, authoritarianism, globalism, elitism, and socialism. Even after socialism failed as an economic system in both the Soviet Union and China, Modern Liberals still defend it. However, if Modern Liberals really know that socialism is bad economic policy, then why do they keep supporting it? Perhaps it is because Modern Liberals are actually committed to the two underlying principles that lurk behind socialism: collectivism and authoritarianism. Ayn Rand recognized this possibility:

"Most people know in a vague, uneasy way, that Marxist economics are screwy. Yet this does not stop them from advocating the same Marxist economics...The root of the whole modern disaster is philosophical and moral. People are not embracing collectivism because they have accepted bad economics. They are accepting bad economics because they have embraced collectivism."[300]

But this fails to answer the deeper question; *why* have Modern Liberals embraced collectivism, (as well as authoritarianism, globalism, elitism, and socialism)? After reviewing both conservative and Modern Liberal views on the subject, it appears that there are five possible motivations which might draw people toward Modern Liberalism:
1) Compassion,
2) Lust for Power,
3) Moral Superiority,
4) Fear of Envy,
5) Self-Delusion.

We will now discuss each of these different motives to see which ones are real and which ones are false.

Peter W. Hauer

1. COMPASSION (PARTLY TRUE, PARTLY FALSE)

Nearly all Modern Liberals believe that their support for social welfare programs proves that they are compassionate. Modern Liberals also believe that the conservative opposition to social welfare programs proves that conservatives are not compassionate. However, as we saw earlier in this chapter, conservatives give more of their time and money to charity than Modern Liberals do.

On the other hand, conservatives would not be justified in assuming that their larger donations to charity somehow prove that they are *more compassionate* than Modern Liberals. After all, the Modern Liberal support for social welfare spending cannot be ignored. Surely their support for socialism indicates that Modern Liberals feel compassion for poor people. Conservatives glibly respond that Modern Liberals are simply, "being generous with other people's money." However, conservatives are forgetting that Modern Liberals pay taxes too. In fact, because Democrats earn 6% more than Republicans, Democrats probably pay more in taxes than Republicans. Therefore, Democrats are certainly not "being generous with other people's money."

Conservatives support voluntary giving more than Modern Liberals do. In contrast, Modern Liberals support the forced transfer of wealth more than conservatives do. Both sides want to help the poor. They simply disagree on which method is more effective and fair. So the difference between the two camps is an *intellectual difference*; not a moral difference. As we saw earlier in this chapter, Modern Liberals think that government action is the best way to reduce poverty. As a result, Modern Liberals support social welfare programs. In contrast, conservatives believe that private charity the best way to reduce poverty. As a result, conservatives give more to private charity than Modern Liberals do. In the end, neither side can really claim to be more compassionate than the other. They simply have different ways of being compassionate.

2. LUST FOR POWER (FALSE)

Back in the 1960s, more than a few professors noticed that the leaders of the radical student movement on college campuses had a strong leaning towards authoritarianism. In effect, the radical student leaders were power hungry. It is natural for power hungry people to support collectivism, authoritarianism, globalism, elitism and socialism, because all of these ideologies tend to give sweeping powers to the government.

S. Robert Lichter (co-director of the Center for Media and Public Affairs) and Stanley Rothman (professor of government at Smith College) studied the radical students of the 1960's, whom they called "the New Left." These researchers concluded what most conservatives suspected all along: "*[We] found a larger number of authoritarians among the student radicals than we found in our comparison groups…We believe these young people exercised an influence far beyond their numbers…*"[301]

This lust for power is the motive most often cited by conservative critics of Modern Liberalism. Conservatives generally believe that Modern Liberals are power hungry. However, the vast majority of Modern Liberals are not motivated by any such lust for power. In fact, just as Modern Liberals are wrong to believe that conservatives are selfish or ignorant, conservatives are wrong to think that Modern Liberals are power hungry.

For example, the lust for power fails to explain why the vast majority of playwrights, poets, novelists, movie script writers, and journalists support Modern Liberalism. None of these creative people stands to gain any power if the government becomes more socialist and collectivist. Yet if you close your eyes and imagine any famous name from the modern literary world, odds are almost any author you think of will be extremely liberal. For example, Arthur Miller, Lillian Hellmen, Gore Vidal, John Steinbeck, Henrik Ibsen, Tennessee Williams, Upton Sinclair, H.G. Wells, Gloria Steinem, Kurt Vonnegut, Norman Mailer, James Joyce, James Thurber, George Bernard Shaw, J.D. Salinger, and Truman Capote are all extremely liberal. All of them favor increasing the power of government as a way to solve social problems. All of them belittle and disparage traditional values, the traditional family unit, and even traditional religion in their works. Yet none of them will actually gain any personal power from Modern Liberal policies.

The same thing is true for Hollywood glitterati. Almost every Hollywood celebrity is an ardent socialist and globalist.[302] Yet no famous Hollywood actor will gain any power if the government expands to control the entire economy, and even controls the rearing of your children. None of them will gain any power through socialist tax policies, or through globalist treaties that take away American sovereignty.

Therefore, most Modern Liberals do not support statism because they are power hungry.

Instead, most Modern Liberals support big government because they know that *massive government power is the surest way to change society*. As we shall see in Chapter Eight, Modern Liberalism must necessarily seek to change society, because the five main goals of Modern Liberalism require drastic changes in our traditional Anglo-Saxon heritage. As Modern Liberals impose collectivism, authoritarianism, globalism, elitism, and socialism, they are indeed changing our society, our Constitution, and our culture.

Politicians are the only people who will gain more personal power as government power grows. Therefore, the lust for power can only explain why *politicians* might favor Modern Liberalism. This means that the vast majority of Modern Liberals must be driven by other motives. In order to discover the true motivations which propel most Modern Liberals, we shall have to keep searching.

3. MORAL SUPERIORITY (FALSE)

Another reason that conservatives frequently give to explain Modern Liberal thinking is moral self-righteousness. Conservatives claim that Modern Liberals support social welfare programs because by supporting such programs, Modern Liberals can appear to be more compassionate and more virtuous than conservatives (who oppose such programs). The most cynical of conservatives argue that Modern Liberals pursue failed social policies merely to inflate their own egos, in order to pump up their self-image of moral superiority. According to this view, the social policies of Modern Liberals are really just sandwich signs to show that they are compassionate, and that they care about their fellow man. The following statement from retired CBS journalist Bernard Goldberg is typical of this cynical conservative view:

"So why then won't more liberals come clean? Why won't they be more honest...and more open, publicly, to the arguments from the other side? What's the payoff [for liberals] in continuing to deny what to many of us is so apparent? Simple, by hanging on to the old party line for dear life...they get to bask in their own moral superiority."[303]

This is a tempting argument because it is simple and plausible. However, for the vast majority of Modern Liberals, this charge is false. It is merely one of the hallowed myths of conservatism. The problem is, these cynical conservatives (such as Thomas Sowell, Mona Charen, and Bernard Goldberg), are confusing cause with effect. It is true that by supporting social service programs, Modern Liberals can indeed appear to be more compassionate than conservatives. However, this does not prove that the desire to appear compassionate is the actual reason for their support for social welfare programs.

Although Modern Liberals do see themselves as morally superior to conservatives, this is only a *side benefit* of their support for social welfare programs. It is not the root cause of their support for socialism. Modern Liberals would still support these same social welfare programs even if there was no conservative opposition to compare themselves to. This is because Modern Liberals really believe that redistributing the wealth is good social policy. That is why Modern Liberals support social welfare programs. The fact that social welfare programs can also be used to make Modern Liberals appear more compassionate than conservatives is just icing on the cake. It is not the root cause of their thinking.

Finally, it is simply not credible that millions of Americans could be so self-absorbed that they would base social policy upon their emotional need for self-affirmation. There are other, more likely explanations for the Modern Liberal motivation to pursue their radical policies, such as racial quotas, open borders, welfare for illegal aliens, government control of the economy, globalism, socialism, collectivism, et cetera. We will now discuss the true motives behind Modern Liberalism.

4. FEAR OF ENVY (TRUE)

Not only does socialism tend to reduce wealth for the entire nation, it also has serious moral flaws as well. It necessarily brings down some people in order to satisfy others. As the old 1960's left-wing protest song said, *"Tax the Rich, Feed the Poor, 'til there are no rich no more."*[304] Robert Bork summarizes the conservative view that socialism is based upon envy:

"The usual strategy for coping with the discomfort of knowing that others are superior in some way is to try to reduce the inequalities by bringing the more fortunate down or by preventing him from being more fortunate. This is the strategy of envy."[305]

As we saw in Chapter Three, the American Founding Fathers recognized the danger of letting envy and greed into the body politic. The Founding Fathers understood that envy would lead one group of citizens to lobby the government to forcefully take money away from another group of citizens. Envy has always had the same corrosive effect upon every society that it has infected. This explains the old Roman adage: *"He who covets is always poor."*

Yet many Modern Liberals boldly admit that socialism is indeed based on the desire to make everyone financially equal. For these people socialism is primarily a way to alleviate feelings of envy. Some Modern Liberals prefer to use noble sounding slogans such as "social justice," but it all boils down to satisfying envy, by forcefully redistributing the wealth. Some Modern Liberals are very candid about this desire. According to the Modern Liberal scholar Martin Maila, the main goal of life is to achieve the equal distribution of wealth:

"The essence of the moral idea of socialism is that human equality is the supreme value in life."[306]

However, this is in sharp contrast to our Founding Fathers, who believed that *liberty* was the supreme value in life. As we saw in Chapter Three, they understood that economic inequality must be accepted if we want to keep our liberty.

The Modern Liberal belief that economic equality is the highest goal in life has been around for a long time. It certainly pre-dates Karl Marx. As early as 1775, the radical Illuminati promoted this passion for material equality. According to the founder of the Illuminati:

"Its (the Illuminati's) object may be said to be checking the tyranny of princes, nobles and priests, and establishing a UNIVERSAL EQUALITY OF CONDITION."[307] (Emphasis added.)

Some Modern Liberal authors have fabricated whole new theories of history in order to justify both envy and socialism. According to Modern Liberal author Christopher Lasch:

"...economic inequality is intrinsically undesirable...Luxury is morally repugnant, and its incompatibility with democratic ideals has been consistently recognized in the traditions that shape our political culture..."[308]

Of course Mr. Lasch fails to tell us exactly which traditions in our political culture condemn luxury or the possession of great wealth. In reality, we have no such political traditions. Lasch is also forgetting that men who create great wealth nearly always create jobs for other people, thereby supporting countless families.

Another prominent Modern Liberal has actually invented a psychological experiment, which he claims justifies both envy and socialism. In his book *Reason: Why Liberals Will Win the Battle for America,* Robert Reich included the following experiment:

"...try this experiment on two people. Here, I'll call them Mike and Ike. In the presence of both, offer Mike $10 but only on condition that he divides it with Ike, and Ike agrees to the division. Ask Mike to write down on a piece of paper how much of the ten dollars he'll part with and hand the paper to Ike. If Ike doesn't agree to the amount on the paper, neither of them gets a penny. (They're not allowed to negotiate...) For years I've done this experiment with my university students...What's the outcome? Interestingly, very few of the Ike's agree to any amount under $4. Quite a few of them won't agree to anything under $5. When I ask them why they were willing to give up any lower amount (remember, their non-agreement means no money for either of them) they say something like 'it just didn't seem fair,' or 'it made make me angry to be offered only $2.'"[309]

According to Mr. Reich, this experiment proves that envy is not only *natural*, it is also based on our human understanding of *fairness*. Therefore (he claims), socialism is morally justified because socialism follows our natural understanding of what is "fair."

However, Mr. Reich's experiment is entirely misleading. It has nothing to do with the real world, where people have a moral claim on their own money, whether they worked for it, traded for it, invested for it, or even if they inherited it from their parents. You see, in this experiment, the money came out of nowhere. It simply fell upon two people (Mike and Ike) just like manna from heaven. Therefore, Ike knew that *Mike had no moral claim on the money.* Ike knew that Mike had not done anything to earn the money. This is why Ike naturally wanted to receive an equal share of the loot.

This is totally different from the real world of economics. In the real world, Mike would have earned the money and would have considered it his own. In the real world, Ike and Mike would never be forced to agree upon a division of the money. Finally, in the real world, Ike would never be given control over the disposition of someone else's money. Remember, in this experiment, if Ike does not agree to the proposed division, then neither of them gets any money. There is no situation in the real world where this would occur. The experiment is completely misleading. It is regrettable that Mr. Reich has been indoctrinating his college students with this specious experiment for many years. To these impressionable young minds, his deceptive "experiment" must seem to justify both envy and socialism.

RELIGION VS ENVY

Religious conservatives have long opposed the Modern Liberal effort to use envy as a justification for socialism. This religious opposition to both envy and socialism goes back to about 1230 BC, when Moses received the Ten Commandments. One of the Commandments was quite explicit on the subject of envy:

"Thou shall not covet (envy) thy neighbor's donkey, nor his goods, nor anything else belonging to thy neighbor."

Twelve hundred years later, Jesus Christ preached exactly the same message when he was confronted by a greedy man who envied his own brother's wealth:

"And the man asked Jesus, 'Master, speak to my brother that he should divide his inheritance with me.' Jesus said to him, 'Man, who made me a judge or divider among you?' And Jesus said to the others, 'Take heed, and beware of covetousness (envy), for a man's life consists not in the abundance of things which he possesses.'" (Luke 12: 13-15.)

Of course Jesus also taught us to be compassionate, and to give aid to the poor. However, Jesus only advocated *voluntary* giving. Jesus never advocated the forced transfer of wealth, which we modern folk call socialism. The New Testament tells us that the Apostles "shared all their possessions in common." However, this was merely a description of how the apostles lived. It was not phrased as a command for us to follow. In his second letter to the Corinthians, Paul says; *"Each of you should give what he has decided in his heart to give, not reluctantly or under compulsion…"*

The Old Testament does contain several verses which tell farmers to leave a small portion of their crop in the field, for poor people to collect. Some Modern Liberals insist that these verses justify socialism. However, the Bible does not list any penalties for failing to leave food for the poor. The only "punishments" are spiritual. Once again, giving to others is meant to be voluntary, not mandatory. It is based on free will, not coercion.

By prohibiting envy, Christianity and Judaism teach us not to be concerned if other people are wealthier than we are. They both teach us to view our material well being *in absolute terms*; i.e. "Do I have enough to live comfortably?" However, Modern Liberalism teaches just the opposite. Modern Liberalism teaches us to view our material well being *in relative terms*, i.e., "Do I have as much stuff as other people?" The Modern Liberal scholar Robert Reich even defines well being in relative terms:

"…well being is a subjective feeling based in part on how others are doing." [310]

This is a bold endorsement of envy as the basis for government policy. In this way, Modern Liberals are openly supporting an idea that the radical Illuminati tried to keep secret. This idea was that people will get along better if the government seizes all property and then redistributes it, so that everyone has the same amount of material goods. However, the Illuminati never imagined that people would ever vote for such a radical socialist plan. The Illuminati assumed that a revolution would be needed to impose radical socialism:

"...there will be a terrible convulsion, and a storm, but this will be succeeded by a calm. The unequal will now be equal—and when the cause of dissention (envy) is thus removed, the world will be in peace."[311]

HOW TO CONTROL ENVY

Envy is certainly a potential problem in any society, large or small. It encourages theft, robbery, and of course socialism. There are only three possible ways to deal with envy. One way is to simply gratify envy. In other words, the government would confiscate all property and then dole it out equally to every person in society. This solution is radical socialism. However, because some people will naturally work harder or smarter than others, eventually some people will once again have more wealth than other people. Therefore, to keep everyone equal, the government would have to repeat the same process over and over again. In fact, we Americans go through a similar exercise every April 15th.

The second possible way to deal with envy is to *eliminate* the feeling of envy through religious indoctrination. Eliminating envy is difficult because it is a natural emotion. Perhaps this is why God used the threat of divine punishment to help us control envy. God included envy as a sin to be punished in his Ten Commandments. Therefore, we might make some progress in reducing envy if we dust off this old commandment and revive the Judeo-Christian teaching that envy is a sin. It would be well worth attempting, because the payoff would be most beneficial for society. By reducing envy, we can reduce the primary motive behind socialism.

The American Founding Fathers certainly considered envy to be a sin. More importantly, they also understood that envy was harmful to society. The Founding Fathers realized that envy would lead to socialism, or as they called it, "leveling." This explains why John Adams and George Washington warned us that a Republic can only be maintained by a *religious* and *virtuous* people. If either religion or virtue is lost, then any free people will naturally give in to their instinct for envy. They will demand that the wealth be redistributed. Therefore, property rights will be violated. Of course redistributing the wealth will require a bigger, more powerful government. This will reduce everyone's freedom. The Founding Fathers understood this dynamic, as we can see from Benjamin Rush:

"The only foundation for a useful education in a republic is to be laid in religion (i.e. Christianity). Without this there can be no virtue, and without virtue there can be no liberty."[312]

The Founding Fathers understood that an immoral people will vote themselves into the mass dependency of socialism. When *all* of the people depend on the state, then the state will be *all* powerful. This is a sobering thought, especially as the federal government is now on the verge of taking control of everyone's access to health care.

Aside from religion, the only other possible way to control envy is to channel it into a socially responsible outlet. In other words, we must take the instinct for envy and re-direct it toward a positive goal. This can be done through education. For example, when a child sees a rich man with an expensive sports car, the child naturally wants the same thing. However, we should teach the child that if he wants a Ferrari he must work hard and productively before he can also enjoy such a car. If envy can be controlled in this way, then it may inspire people to work harder and smarter so they can obtain the material objects they see others enjoying.

This education about envy should also include some basic economics. The child should be taught that the rich man (by owning a Ferrari) does not in any way prevent us from earning enough money to purchase a Ferrari for ourselves. The nation's wealth is not a zero-sum game, where if one person gains wealth then someone else must lose wealth. In most commercial transactions both parties gain wealth. This is why capitalism generally creates new wealth.

"ENVY IS NATURAL"

Envy is a natural human instinct. However, that does not mean we should base social policy on this instinct. Just because envy is natural, that doesn't mean we should gratify it with socialism. After all, we humans also have a natural instinct to do as little work as possible. This means that we humans have a natural instinct to become parasites and live off of other people, if we are permitted to do so. So just because these desires are natural, that does not mean we should give in to these urges.

Our instinct for envy is simply a holdover from our evolutionary past as human beings. When our earliest australopithecine ancestors lived in groups, they probably behaved in a manner similar to baboons. They cooperated enough to share bodily warmth at night, and to fight off common enemies. That was probably the extent of their cooperation. When it came to food (which was the only source of "wealth" that existed back then) there was probably no sharing except between mating pairs or from mother to child. So back then, it made perfect sense for primitive man to envy another man's food supply. Envy motivated him to steal the food for himself. In this way envy helped him to survive in a brutal world. Envy made perfect sense when we were living by "the law of the jungle." Back in those days, envy ensured the survival of the fittest.

Later, as homo-sapiens, we evolved enough mentally and physically (with a larger brain and longer vocal chords) to develop a complex spoken language. This was a great leap forward in communication. With complex language, humans could speak in terms of future events and discuss nouns in general terms. So instead of merely pointing to a deer and saying "deer," early man could talk about where "some deer" (not present) might be grazing. He could also discuss plans for hunting deer in the future.

Our complex human language also caused a huge advance in our ability to cooperate with each other. Complex language gave physically weaker humans (women and smaller men) the ability to reason with the strongest men in the group. Of course reason cannot always overcome brute force, but a complex language at least made this possible for the first time. Language gave humans the ability to advance beyond a hierarchy which was based purely on physical strength.[313]

Our complex language greatly improved our ability to cooperate with each other, and this cooperation helped us to survive in a dangerous world full of carnivores that were ready and willing to kill humans for food. We lacked claws and fangs, but we evolved the intelligence to make spears. Fortunately we also developed the language and cooperative skills needed to organize those spears effectively, to protect the women and children in the group.

With superior intelligence and superior communication, homo-sapiens became the most successful of all hunter-gatherers. Neanderthal man and homo-erectus both had much smaller vocal chords. This handicap prevented them from communicating effectively. They simply

The Big Picture

could not produce enough different sounds to create a sophisticated language. Therefore they could not cooperate with each other as effectively as homo-sapiens could. This explains why we homo-sapiens pushed them both into extinction.[314]

When homo-sapiens lived as nomadic hunter-gatherers, envy still served a useful (but very different) social purpose than it did for the earlier australopithecines. Instead of motivating individuals to steal food and fend for themselves, envy now became useful for the opposite reason, i.e. *to encourage more cooperation and sharing.* About 300,000 B.C., the earliest homo-sapiens lived in tightly knit groups. If any one homo-sapien hunter killed a prey animal, he was under great social pressure to bring it back for the benefit of the entire group. In addition, he too depended on other men to bring back animals to share with the group. Likewise, if a woman found a source of ripe berries, she would share her discovery with the rest of the group, for the very same reasons. The entire group depended on everyone sharing their food.

So during the time period from 300,000 B.C. to 9,000 B.C. (when humans did not yet live in permanent settlements), envy was useful because it encouraged sharing of the group's food supply. Envy made us feel "entitled" to a share of what someone else had obtained. We no longer lived by "the law of the jungle" but instead we voluntarily shared with each other. However, as we saw in Chapter Four, this sense of entitlement (just like socialism) only works well in very small social groups, where all members of the group share bonds of kinship. Indeed, Anthropologists tell us that the first homo-sapiens lived in very small groups. Bonds of kinship among group members enabled this early form of socialism to work quite well.

However, after 9,000 B.C., people slowly started to settle in permanent communities. Eventually these permanent settlements became large enough that many of the residents no longer shared bonds of kinship with each other. As we saw in Chapter One, it was almost certainly at this point in history that religion and custom started to protect private property. Suddenly, envy was no longer useful for any purpose. Envy was now destructive and dangerous. Later, in our modern industrial era, we began to live in larger, more impersonal societies, with even fewer bonds of kinship with the other members of society. Now more than ever, envy no longer serves the useful purpose it did during our hunter-gatherer stage.

Ironically, now that we live in large, impersonal societies, the temptation to stop working and live off other people is much greater than it was in the past. In the past, when we lived together in small groups as hunter-gatherers, other members of the group would have quickly noticed a slothful person. A lazy person would either be pressured to reform, or else be banished from the group. Unfortunately in our modern impersonal society, we lack a social mechanism to persuade lazy people to work. Instead, we have created vast social welfare programs, which only encourage dependency and sloth.

Because we no longer live in small, tightly knit social groups, modern humans are reverting back to the vicious behavior of our earliest primate ancestors. Because we live without close emotional bonds to all the other members of the group, envy is taking us back to the law of the jungle. Two million years ago, a large powerful australopithecine would have taken your food by force. Nowadays, millions of humans band together in large powerful voting blocks, to take away your wealth by force, i.e. through taxes which are collected by force.

Therefore, Modern Liberals are wrong to believe that socialism is the highest evolution of civilization. Socialism is really just a regression back to the most primitive and brutal stage of human development. The modern combination of democracy and socialism has re-imposed the law of the jungle, as many people are once again surviving by the forceful seizure of other people's wealth. Our modern seizure of wealth only appears more civilized because it is better organized and more bureaucratic. David Galland summarizes the role of envy for the past million years:

"The emotion of envy dates back to the earliest human apes and is directly connected to the survival of the species. Simply put, if you and your family did not have food or shelter...you could correct the situation BY CONKING THE OTHER FELLOW OVER THE HEAD... Of course nowadays conking people on the head is largely frowned upon. So the unsuccessful or discontented people simply vote for politicians WHO PROMISE TO DO THE CONKING FOR THEM, i.e. by confiscating and redistributing the wealth of the 'haves.'"[315] (Emphasis added.)

SOCIALISM WITHOUT ENVY?

Some Modern Liberals claim that socialism need not be based upon envy and greed. They reassure us that socialism could be based on something else entirely, something far more noble. However, they never tell us exactly what that "something else" is. According to Lord Alfred Milner, this noble form of socialism combines "genuine sympathy" with an intelligent vision of the national interest:

> "That there is an odious form of socialism, I admit, a Socialism that attacks wealth simply because it is wealth, and lives on the cultivation of class hatred. But that is not the whole story...There is a nobler socialism, which so far from springing from envy, hatred and uncharitableness, is born of genuine sympathy and a lofty and wise conception of what is meant by national life."[316]

Unfortunately Lord Milner never tells us exactly how socialism can be kept "noble." He never tells us exactly how we can maintain socialism based upon "genuine sympathy," especially when more and more people who seek government assistance simply do not want to work for a living. The embarrassing fact remains; no Modern Liberal scholar has ever figured out how to prevent socialism from degenerating into organized plunder, based on sheer envy and greed.

5. SELF-DELUSION (TRUE)

This motivation is true, and it is almost universal among Modern Liberals. Of course, Modern Liberals are unaware that it affects their thinking. If they were aware of it, then they would not really be deluded. Self-delusion gives Modern Liberals the mental freedom to ignore evidence which proves that socialism destroys wealth and breeds tyranny. Self delusion lets Modern Liberals ignore the fact that global government will take away our civil rights.

Conservatives are less likely than Modern Liberals to fall into self-delusion. This is not because conservatives are more intelligent. It is simply because conservatism is not an ideology. Therefore, *conservatism does not offer strong emotional appeal.* This means that conservatives have less motivation to delude themselves into supporting harmful policies, such as racial quotas, open borders, banning guns, and increasing the size and power of government.

Self-delusion explains how very intelligent people can easily fall for the ideology of Modern Liberalism. Modern Liberals are neither stupid nor ignorant. Instead, they are merely self-deluded. Here is an analogy. Imagine that a highly intelligent chemistry professor is raising a troublesome teen-age daughter. Imagine that his rebellious daughter has suddenly started to stay out until well past midnight, her eating habits have changed, her grades are rapidly falling, and she has recently changed her entire circle of friends. Common sense would tell any objective observer that these are all signs of either drug use or serious emotional problems.

Sadly, our professor father cannot accept these possibilities. He tells himself this is just a stage that kids go through, and that things will soon get better. He does this because he has too much emotionally invested in his daughter. He simply does not want to see the truth. Instead he prefers to ignore the evidence, so he can continue believing in his delusion that nothing is seriously wrong with his daughter.

Modern Liberals place themselves into a similar state of delusion. They have so much emotionally invested in their social policies that they refuse to believe any evidence which proves their policies are hurting society. For example, throughout the 1930's Modern Liberal journalists and intellectuals in the West refused to believe the eyewitness accounts about communist abuses in the Ukraine. During the 1930's, Josef Stalin purposely starved about ten million Ukrainians to death. Starving the Ukrainians was cheaper than sending them to concentration camps. All Stalin had to do was to steal their stored food, livestock, and harvests, so that the Ukrainian farmers had nothing left to eat. Then he forbade the Ukrainians from using the roads or railroads. This prevented the starving people from migrating to the cities in search of food. The result was mass murder of an ethnic group, i.e. genocide.

Yet prominent Modern Liberal journalists such as Garrison Villard and Walter Duranty covered up this atrocity, because they did not want to admit the truth about communism and the tyrants who ran the USSR. As Modern Liberals, these self-deluded journalists wanted desperately to maintain their romantic enthusiasm for *"the noble experiment of communism."* So instead of admitting the truth, they preferred to delude themselves, along with the public. Walter Duranty was actually given a Pulitzer Prize for his glorification (and white-washing) of Russian Communism. For example:

"This I repeat is the most stupendous governmental feat ever undertaken—the social, moral, political, industrial, economic emancipation of a people and its reorganization upon the basis of service to society and to the nation, with the profit-making motive suddenly removed from the individual...the minority which controls the destiny of Russia is on its way with extraordinary and completely unselfish devotion..."[317]

The ultra-liberal founder of the American public school movement, John Dewey, was also completely deluded about the USSR. Dewey said that the communist system in Russia was, *"intrinsically religious,"* and that it possessed *"the moving spirit of primitive Christianity."* Mr. Dewey failed to tell us exactly what part of Christ's teachings demanded that ten million Ukrainians should be starved to death. Just a few years later, Modern Liberal journalists such as Edgar Snow performed the same cover up for the Chinese communists, effectively white-washing the horrendous human rights abuses committed by Mao Tse Tung during his quest for power.

Today's Modern Liberals have not changed. They still have the same emotional desire to support collectivism. So they still turn a blind eye to evidence of communist sponsored atrocities. Noam Chomsky is one of the most celebrated intellectuals within Modern Liberalism. He is also one of the most deluded. When Chomsky was confronted with eyewitness reports of genocide in Cambodia under Pol Pot's evil "Khmer Rouge," Chomsky denied that such reports were true. Mr. Chomsky had no factual basis for his denial. He simply refused to believe any accusations of abuse committed by communists. Just like our chemistry professor, Chomsky was deluding himself.

THE GREATEST DELUSION: THE CAUSE OF POVERTY

Other examples of Modern Liberal self-delusion are less dramatic than ignoring genocides. For years conservatives have pointed to studies showing that poverty is the result of several imprudent choices that poor people make in everyday life. If a person decides to take illegal drugs, they will increase their chances of ending up poor. If a woman tries to raise a child out of wedlock, she too increases her likelihood of being poor. If a person fails to complete high school, they also greatly increase their chances of being poor. If a person does all three of these foolish things, then they are virtually guaranteed to live in poverty.[318]

However, Modern Liberals still prefer to believe that poverty is society's fault. Therefore, according to Modern Liberals, the individual bears no personal responsibility for his own poverty. To maintain this delusion, Modern Liberals must turn empirical data upside down. For example, according to the famous Modern Liberal author Robert Reich:

"It's not being single that causes women [with illegitimate children] to be poor. It's being poor that makes it less likely they'll marry."

This statement is clearly delusional. It contradicts the overwhelming research that has been done on the subject of unwed mothers and poverty. It also defies common sense. Being poor does *not* prevent women from getting married. Most men will marry a woman for beauty, kindness, and compatibility. Most men do not marry women for their money. However, having illegitimate babies from other men *does* tend to prevent a woman from getting married. Most men will indeed avoid marrying a woman if she already has a baby from some other man. After all, he would be raising another man's child. It makes little sense biologically, financially, or emotionally.

Furthermore, poverty does not *cause* a woman to have babies out of wedlock. Birth control is widely available and condoms are extremely cheap, even free at most public health clinics and many public high schools. Having a baby without getting married first is simply a foolish personal decision. Illegitimate births are not caused *by* poverty. They *cause* poverty. That's why half of all unwed teenage mothers go on welfare within one year after giving birth. After five years, 77% of these women are on welfare. This also explains why 92% of all the children living on welfare were born out of wedlock.[319] According to sociologist Charles Murray:

"Illegitimacy is the single most important social problem of our time, more important than crime, drugs, poverty, illiteracy, welfare or hopelessness because it drives everything else."

"THE END OF POVERTY"

The belief that poverty is society's fault is only the first Modern Liberal delusion about poverty. This second delusion is that poverty can be eliminated. After all, if poverty is society's fault, then if we properly change society, we can eliminate the cause of poverty. Of course we would all like to live in a world without poverty. So the belief that poverty can be ended has great emotional appeal.

According to this Modern Liberal delusion, all that is needed is enough money directed by wise and benevolent government bureaucrats. The mainstream news media, labor unions, and virtually all American universities have long supported increased money for government-run social welfare programs. All of these institutions have spent the past sixty years promising *"the end of poverty."* This includes the great vanguards of Modern Liberalism: the powerful non-profit foundations. According to the Ford Foundation in 1962:

"...the elimination of poverty is well within the means of federal, state and local governments."[320]

Countless Modern Liberal politicians have also claimed that this or that welfare program *"will end poverty."* In America, this false promise has been given with almost mind-numbing regularity, during every election cycle since 1964. In fact, during the Johnson administration, his chief in the "War on Poverty," Sargent Shriver, confidently predicted that poverty in America would be eliminated by 1976.[321] He was simply following the lead of his boss, President Johnson, who boasted to Congress in 1964:

"I have called for a national war on poverty. Our objective: total victory."[322]

The delusion that poverty can be cured goes all the way back to the Progressive Era in American politics, from about 1870 to 1925. This delusion was not limited to Democrats. In 1921, Republican Herbert Hoover was the Secretary of Commerce. Back then, Hoover thought that he too could end poverty. According to the historian Joan Hoff Wilson, Mr. Hoover thought poverty could be completely eliminated by *"...the transformation of American society."*[323] Politicians are generally not a religious lot, so it is understandable that they may be unaware of the following prediction by Jesus Christ:

"The poor shall always be with you." (John 12:18, See also Matthew 26:11 and Mark 14:7.)

The truth is, social welfare projects which began in the 1960's, such as the "Great Society" program and the "War on Poverty," have failed. These programs have not created a great society, nor have they defeated poverty. Despite the estimated six trillion dollars[324] that has been spent on all of these programs since 1964, the percentage of Americans living in poverty has not changed significantly since these vast social programs were first begun. In the 1960's the poverty rate was about 15%. Fifty years later, the poverty rate still stubbornly hovers at about 15%. Yet Modern Liberals still refuse to admit that such programs are a waste of money. This refusal to admit the truth can only be attributed to self-delusion.

According to Modern Liberals such as Lyndon Johnson, society can never do enough for the poor. According to them, jobs and money are not enough. We must build entire communities for the poor:

"Very often a lack of jobs and money is not the cause of poverty, but the symptom. The cause may lie deeper in our failure to give our fellow citizens a fair chance to develop their own capacities, in a lack of education and training, in a lack of medical care and housing, in a lack of decent communities in which to live and to bring up their children."[325]

Yet what if poverty is not society's fault? What if poverty is caused by the foolish decisions made by poor people themselves? If that is the true cause of poverty, then poverty will never be eliminated, no matter what we do. Poverty will spring back every year like a perennial weed.

In fact, this is exactly what has happened ever since the federal social welfare system was created. Society changed, and money was spent, but poverty was not eliminated or even reduced. Obviously the continued existence of poverty indicates that society is not the cause of poverty. The only other possible cause of poverty is the one offered by conservatives; i.e. the foolish decisions made by poor people themselves, or by their parents.

OTHER DELUSIONS:

The limits of this small book prevent us from discussing all of the recent delusions of Modern Liberalism. However, a few examples are worth mentioning. Modern Liberals believe that government spending is just as beneficial for the economy as private spending. This Keynesian delusion was disproved in Chapter Four. Modern Liberals also believe that America should have "single-payer," (government-run) health care, even though this would mean rationed health care, with lower quality of care for everyone. Apparently Modern Liberals believe that *equality* in health care is more important than *quality* in health care.

Modern Liberals have convinced themselves that diversity in language and diversity in culture is somehow good for America. Of course, history shows us that every time a nation becomes multilingual or multicultural it nearly always leads to civil strife and conflict. Conservatives can point to Northern Ireland, Lebanon, Egypt, Cyprus, Rwanda, Sudan, Congo, Nigeria, Spain, Belgium, and Canada, as proof that diversity leading to divisiveness.

Modern Liberals believe that using racial quotas for hiring and school admissions is fair and necessary, in order to compensate living people for suffering that was endured by dead people 140 years ago. Of course imposing racial quotas to compensate for past evils is neither fair nor necessary. It is another harmful delusion. Modern Liberals also fervently believe in man-made global warming. This delusion will be disproved in Chapter Seven.

Finally, Modern Liberals believe that if we ban guns, (and make everyone defenseless against criminals) this will somehow discourage criminals from committing crimes. Due to a lack of space, we will only discuss this one delusion in detail: banning guns. We will examine the actual results of gun bans in England and in America.

In 1997, in an emotional reaction to a mass shooting tragedy, the English Parliament banned handguns and severely restricted long guns. The supporters of the gun ban promised it would reduce crime. However, the opposite happened. Crime went up sharply, including gun crimes. The result was exactly what conservative civil rights groups (such as the NRA) predicted. According to a December 2001 report in London's Evening Standard:

"In the two years following the 1997 handgun ban, the use of handguns in crime rose by 40%, and the upward trend has only continued. From April to November 2001 the number of people robbed at gunpoint in London rose by 53%."[326]

In just two short years after the British gun ban, the rates for murder and rape also increased dramatically.[327] The rates for robbery and assault actually became *worse than in the United States*. Remember, the law of Parliament now prevents the English people from effectively defending themselves against violent attack on their persons. So it should not be surprising that as of 2002, for the first time in historical memory, a person in England is more likely to be the victim of a robbery or assault than a person in America.[328] In many ways, merry old England is now more dangerous than Main Street USA.

The British gun ban also failed to disarm criminals. This is proven by the fact that gun crimes actually increased after the ban. How could this be, you ask? The truth is, gun bans only disarm honest citizens, not criminals. Therefore, gun bans only make criminals bolder. Yet this is not what the Modern Liberal media tells us. In America, the New York Times (along with the rest of the mainstream news media) simply lied about the results of the 1997 British gun ban:

"In general, crime rates in Britain are much lower than they are in the United States, a phenomenon largely attributed to the strict laws that ban handguns."[329]

Guns make people safer for two main reasons. First, having a gun enables a citizen to chase off a criminal without having to fight with hand to hand combat, (and usually without firing a single shot). This is especially helpful for women and old people who may not fare well in a life and death struggle against a 200 pound felon. Second, gun ownership tends to prevent many home invasion robberies because of the general deterrent effect which occurs when guns are widely dispersed throughout the population.

For example, in America, where gun ownership is widespread, the vast majority of residential break-ins are "cold" burglaries. In these crimes, the burglars purposely *wait until the house is empty*. This is because criminals in armed nations fear getting shot, if an armed family member is at home. This means fewer home invasion robberies in America. In America, only 9% to 13% of all residential break-ins are home invasion robberies.[330] This means that burglars in America only seek out violence about 11% of the time.

In contrast, in England, approximately half of all residential break-ins are home invasion robberies.[331] In these cases, women are often raped, and men are often tortured, in a vile effort to find out where secret valuables may be hidden. Home invasion robberies are usually very brutal. Sadly, English burglars *seek out violence* about 50% of the time. English criminals know that all of their victims are unarmed and helpless. This is why English criminals are much more aggressive than American criminals.

WHAT HAPPENS WHEN CITIZENS CARRY GUNS?

Guns are not only beneficial inside the home. According to the FBI's Uniform Crime Reports, guns are also very beneficial if honest citizens carry them outside the home. In the vast laboratory of America's fifty states, *every time a state permits honest citizens to carry guns*, that state has enjoyed *significant reductions in violent crime as a result.*[332]

According to data from the FBI's Uniform Crime Reports, within just one year after a state permits honest citizens to carry guns, that state enjoys an average reduction in murder of 8.5%, a reduction in rape of 5%, and a reduction of felonious assault of 7%.[333] After a number of years, the long-term benefits continue to accrue. Interestingly, not only are all crimes of violence reduced (e.g. robbery, rape, felonious assault, murder) but even the amount of gun violence is reduced.

To Modern Liberals this information must seem counter-intuitive. Most Modern Liberals believe that guns are only used to kill people; not for self defense or preventing crimes. This belief is based on Hollywood movies, television shows, and articles from news journalists, who are generally anti-gun. But national polls consistently show that guns are used defensively (to prevent crime) roughly anywhere from one to three million times each year in the USA. However, guns are used to commit crime far less often, usually less than one million times per year. Obviously guns are a net benefit for American society.[334]

Some Modern Liberals actually believe that guns are intrinsically evil. In contrast, most conservatives believe that guns are powerful tools, which can be used for either good or evil, *depending on who possesses them*. The most reliable data about crime and gun ownership confirms the conservative belief. Using data from the FBI's Uniform Crime Reports, let's compare how two different states have been affected by changes in gun laws. In 1987 Florida started to permit honest citizens to carry guns for self-defense. The new Florida law caused an immediate and lasting *reduction in crime*. According to a 1995 review of FBI data, in the first eight years under the new law, Florida's murder rate dropped by 22%. *This was not part of a national trend.* In fact, the national murder rate during that same time period went up 15%.

Furthermore, almost no one who had a permit to carry a gun abused this right. According to the State of Florida's last report on this issue, of the 266,700 gun permits that were issued, only 19 had been revoked.[335] Surprisingly, a police officer is statistically more likely to shoot the wrong person than a regular citizen who legally carries a gun.[336] This is because when the police arrive at the scene of a crime they are not certain who the "bad guy" is. A citizen who is being victimized knows for certain who the "bad guy" is.

However, the state of Massachusetts went the opposite direction. Following England's example, Massachusetts passed a comprehensive anti-gun law in 1998. Not only was the right to carry guns severely restricted, but even the right to own guns was severely limited. As a result, almost 75% of all the legally owned guns in the state were confiscated. The results of these two different laws were striking.

As a result of this general ban on guns, Massachusetts suffered an immediate crime wave which has persisted to this day. According to a 2006 review of FBI data, in the eight years after the gun ban became law, the murder rate in Massachusetts rose a shocking 49%.[337] This was not part of a national trend. In fact, during those same years, the national murder rate dropped 16%.[338] Unfortunately this gun ban is still in effect. As a result, the people of Massachusetts still suffer from the worst overall crime rates of New England.

and authoritarianism. This means that Christianity is an obstacle for any Modern Liberal who seeks to increase the power and scope of government.

Christianity has additional qualities that stand in the way of Modern Liberalism's social agenda. Christianity holds that God's laws are a higher moral authority than man's laws. Where the two conflict, God's law must be obeyed. Jesus told his followers to pay their taxes, but not to obey unjust laws. The New Testament teaches us that *"We must obey God, not man."* (Acts 5:29) This idea gets in the way of Modern Liberal politicians, who want to impose policies that violate Christian morals. Such policies include homosexual marriage, sex education taught in schools, welfare programs that do not require any work, and legalized prostitution. Most important of all, Christianity's belief that innocent human life is sacred gets in the way of social engineers who support abortion or euthanasia. It should not surprise anyone that so many feminists have abandoned Christianity in favor of yoga, Gaia worship, Wicca, or crystal gazing.

Not only have many Modern Liberals rejected Christianity for themselves, but they are also trying to eliminate it from Western culture in general. Incidents of Modern Liberals persecuting Christianity are so common place that they cannot all be listed here. A few examples will have to do.[341] In Bremerton, Washington, the children in a kindergarten class were asked to sing their favorite songs. When one little girl began to sing "Jesus Loves Me" the teacher cut her off and told her such songs were not allowed in school. In Selkirk, New York, a third grade girl was told to bring any book she liked to school for free reading time. When the teacher noticed the little girl was reading a Bible, she scolded the child and told her to never bring it back to school again.

In Chicago, a Christian group set up a nativity scene in the city's Daly Plaza. They were ordered to tear it down. The Chairman of the Christian group said it would be easier to display a Christian nativity scene in Red Square in Moscow. To prove his point, he actually did so. He was allowed to display his Christian nativity scene for two weeks in the land of Lenin, but not in the land of Lincoln.

In December of 2009, eight year old Mariah Jordat was reading her Bible during quiet time at Madison Park Elementary School in Oldbridge, New Jersey. When her teacher saw the Bible, she told the child to put the book away. Mariah put her Bible under her desk, but that wasn't good enough. The teacher told her to hide the Bible in her backpack.[342]

"THE POLITICS OF MEANING"

Most Modern Liberals do not worship the moon or the stars, or Wicca or Isis for that matter. Yet if they do not obtain their spiritual fulfillment from either paganism or Christianity, then how do they obtain it? The answer is politics. As an outspoken Modern Liberal professor from Harvard University named Daniel Bell wrote:

"My final essay is a reaffirmation of liberalism as a political creed."[343]

Modern Liberals pursue politics *to add meaning to their lives*. This is the most important motivation among Modern Liberals. It is by far the most fundamental and pervasive. It explains why Modern Liberals willingly delude themselves into pursuing social policies that cause more harm than good. As we saw in Chapter One, an ideology has three defining properties. One of these is that the person who follows the ideology *will dismiss or ignore any evidence which disproves the ideology*. Self-delusion is the reason this happens. Self-delusion prevents the ideologue from having to objectively evaluate the actual results of her ideology. It helps the true believer to avoid facing reality.

For most Modern Liberals, the 18th century intellectual movement called the Enlightenment killed off their religious beliefs. The Enlightenment firmly established observation and reason as the only sources of knowledge. Observation and reason have become the foundations of all human understanding, for everything from physics to ethics. There is no place in this intellectual framework for God. After all, our powers of observation and reason tell us that we were created by the natural process of evolution. If so, then why should we worship any god at all?

The human spirit, if left in the vacuum of disbelief, will see no purpose to life. If there is no afterlife, then we are no better than any other mammals. We spend our lives collecting food, mating, rearing our young, and then dying. Our life has no more purpose than the life of a gerbil. Only if there is an afterlife does human existence have any

CHAPTER SIX

POLITICS FOR THE SOUL

Beijing, September 5th 1995, at the fourth annual United Nations Conference of Women.

Bella Abzug paused and carefully estimated her distance from the microphone. Then she smiled warmly at the colorful crowd of about eight hundred eager and attentive women. They had come from all over the world. Most of them were middle-aged, and many of them were dressed in colorful ethnic costumes, honoring various native cultures. Her first words to the crowd were clear, deliberate, and forceful.
"Welcome, sisters of the Earth!"
A communal squeal of delight filled the small auditorium, along with frantic applause. Abzug waited for the crowd to quiet down, and then she announced, *"Let us all take a moment to quietly pay devotion to our goddesses and also to the great goddess within ourselves."*
Most of the assembled women bowed their heads, some murmured almost silently. After about a half minute of this self-homage, Ms. Abzug called upon her pagan sisters once again.
"It is time to place our goddesses in their proper place of honor."
With that signal, the women in the first two rows slowly stood up. In single file, they reverently walked up a few steps onto the stage, and over to a large tree that had been set up on the stage to the left of Ms. Abzug. One by one, the women began hanging small

female figurines onto the tree, like so many Christmas ornaments. But unlike children hanging Christmas ornaments, these women hung their totems in somber reverence. As each woman hung her own special idol on the tree, she would proudly call out the name of her chosen goddess. "Tara," "Sonji," "Athena," "Aditi," "Pasowee," "Ishtar," "Nanshe," "Ixmucane," the exotic names kept rolling on. Finally, almost fifty goddesses later, the procession was finished.

"Thank you ladies. Oh, now before I forget, I want to announce a special seminar that did not make it onto your program. Tomorrow at four PM there will be a wonderful presentation called 'Religion and Culture.' It's about a brave woman who left the patriarchy of Christianity and found peace, justice, harmony, and joy as a Wiccan. I highly recommend it. I know you'll be there."[340]

THE NEW PAGANISM VS CHRISTIANITY

The meeting just described really took place. It illustrates the extreme degree to which some people are willing to delude themselves in order to add spiritual meaning to their lives. There is absolutely no plausible reason to believe that any of these ancient pagan goddesses are real. It is even more improbable to believe that somehow all of them are real. These women are obviously just rebelling against the religion that was taught to them by their parents. The only reason they believe in their talismans is because *they want to believe in them.*

The new religions of the 19th and 20th centuries (paganism, Gaia worship, humanism, and Wicca) are all attempts to find spiritual meaning outside of traditional Christianity. Why have some Modern Liberals abandoned Christianity for such spiritually anemic substitutes? It would appear that two things are at work here. One reason is that multiculturalism has taught Modern Liberals to disparage anything having to do with Western culture. Because Christianity took root and flourished in Europe, Modern Liberals tend to view Christianity as the religion of the "white male establishment."

The second reason that some Modern Liberals reject Christianity is practical. Christianity is an obstacle to the creation of an all powerful state. Remember, Christianity (heavily influenced by Judaism) reinforces the three foundations of Anglo-Saxon liberty, namely: government by consent, the law of the land, and property rights. These three traditions stand in the way of Modern Liberal goals such as socialism, collectivism, deeper meaning. Only our belief in God and Heaven separates us from the spiritual wasteland of animal existence. Only humans contemplate the fates of their immortal souls. When homo-sapiens first began to bury their dead with treasured personal possessions, they demonstrated their separation from the animal kingdom.

As we saw earlier, life without religion naturally leads to nihilism. To a nihilist, human life has no purpose and so it has no value. To a nihilist, the most rational act a human being can do is to commit suicide. Of course most atheists want to avoid both depression and suicide. The only effective way for atheists to escape the brooding cycle of nihilism is to devote themselves whole-heartedly to a *secular ideology, or to a meaningful social cause.*

By working for a great social movement to perfect society, Modern Liberals can feel as if they are part of a great movement that will continue long after they die. In this way these crusading non-believers can partially satisfy their craving for immortality. This quest for spiritual meaning is the strongest motivation behind Modern Liberalism. Among the earliest Modern Liberals were the Illuminati we discussed in Chapter Two. It is no coincidence that the Illuminati also denied the existence of an individual afterlife:

"...so the Soul of Man, after performing its office, and exhibiting all that train of intellectual phenomena that we call human life, is at last swallowed up in the great ocean of intelligence."[344]

Lest anyone think that Modern Liberalism is not a substitute for religion, one should consider the words of John Dewey, arguably the intellectual patriarch of Modern Liberalism in the 20th century. In his 1935 tract, *Liberalism and Social Action*, Dewey said that government assistance to the poor and social re-construction had together *"virtually come to define the meaning of THE LIBERAL FAITH."*[345] (Emphasis added.) The noted Modern Liberal scholar Alan Brinkley also admitted that the technocrats who created the New Deal policies of FDR approached government planning *"with almost religious veneration."*[346] The Modern Liberal author, Christopher Walton, proudly wrote; *"The Spiritual Left...is extra-ecclesial; its institutions are retreat centers, college classrooms, and bookstores—never congregations or denominations..."*[347]

Many of today's Modern Liberals find so much of their personal meaning in politics that some of them openly call their motivation *"The Politics of Meaning."* This interesting phrase first appeared in the writings of radical Modern Liberal activist Michael Lerner. It was later officially adopted at a conference of radical student leaders who met at the AFL-CIO facility in Port Huron Michigan, in June of 1962. This conference spawned the SDS (Students for a Democratic Society). Robert Bork offers the conservative view of this conference:

"Starting with a draft by Tom Hayden, the conference wrangled out the 'Port Huron Statement'... setting forth the SDS agenda for changing human beings, the nation, and the world. Like the wider student radicalism that ensued, the document displayed the ignorance and arrogance proper to adolescents. These youths were in a state of euphoria about their own wisdom, moral purity, and power to change everything...The religious impulse is obvious, but it is only an impulse, a religious feeling without structure."[348]

Among other things, these radical Modern Liberals all agreed on the following crucial statement:

"POLITICS [IS A] MEANS OF FINDING MEANING IN PERSONAL LIFE."[349]

The "politics of meaning" is a passionate desire for political power. It is based on the individual's lack of traditional spiritual fulfillment. The "politics of meaning" occurs when a person believes that *he can only find personal meaning in politics*. Politics literally defines their entire existence.

The perceptive Modern Liberal writer Terry H. Anderson admits that this "politics of meaning" from the Port Huron Statement has influenced nearly all Modern Liberal politicians ever since.[350] Some of these Modern Liberal politicians readily admit their need to find personal meaning in politics. For example, first lady Hillary Clinton openly referred to her devotion to *"the politics of meaning"* in a speech she gave to the graduating class at the University of Texas. Ironically, she even implied that Americans who did not share her devotion to politics were shallow pragmatists, without a well-developed spiritual side.[351] For Mrs. Clinton, her need to find personal meaning in politics has been a life-long craving. For example, several decades earlier, as a college student herself, she also referred to *"the politics of meaning"* in her own college graduation speech, when she addressed her classmates, parents, and faculty.

After conservatives began pointing out the spiritual emptiness that lurks behind "the politics of meaning," other Modern Liberals jumped to Hillary Clinton's defense. Norman Lear, head of the aggressively atheistic group, People for the American Way, said that what Ms. Clinton really meant was that devotion to social reform would lead Americans to renew their reverence for, *"the unquantifiable and the eternal."* Mr. Lear called on the American people to re-discover:

"...our capacity for awe, wonder and mystery, that place where acts of faith in something other than ourselves [will] prove ultimately satisfying in the fullness of time." [352] **(Emphasis added.)**

As conservative critics Charles Krauthammer and Pat Robertson pointed out, conservatives in general (and Christian conservatives in particular) do not need to "re-discover" spiritual values. Pat Robertson observed, *"We never lost them in the first place."* According to Mr. Krauthammer, the Modern Liberal *"secular religion of politics"* is a poor substitute for the spiritual comforts of traditional religion:

"Conservatives are not against spirituality in public life. But they see such stabs at it as Mr. Lear's vapid call for public discussion of our common spirituality as limp substitutes for the real thing."[353]

By now it should be no surprise that the most socialist nations on earth are also the most atheistic. In nations where the majority of people have adopted Modern Liberalism as their new secular religion, socialism has absolutely triumphed. For example, in the most socialist nation of all, Sweden, only 5% of the population still attends church.[354] Similar statistics can be found for England, Germany, and France. Sweden and England officially still have state churches, but these are just historical relics.

Peter W. Hauer

THE MODERN LIBERAL GOAL: "HEAVEN ON EARTH"

The religious motivation behind the Modern Liberal goal of creating heaven on earth (using the power of government to change society) is directly connected to the "politics of meaning." In fact, this desire to create heaven on earth is the logical end goal of anyone who pursues the politics of meaning. This would include nearly every Modern Liberal politician in the world today.

The radical Illuminati and the Jacobins were the first Modern Liberals to call for creating heaven on earth. As atheists, they rejected traditional Christian beliefs. However, they cleverly borrowed some vocabulary from Christianity in an effort to change Christianity into a secular ideology that they could exploit. According to the founder of the Illuminati:

"...everything in the New Testament will be comprehensible; and Jesus will appear as the redeemer of the slaves. Man is fallen from the condition of Liberty and Equality, the state of PURE NATURE. He is under subordination and civil bondage, arising from the vices of man. This is the FALL, and Original Sin...The KINGDOM OF GRACE is that restoration which may be brought about by Illumination and a just Morality. This is the NEW BIRTH...This is the redemption of men—this is accomplished by Morality; and when this is spread over the world, we [will] have the KINGDOM OF THE JUST."[355] (Emphasis in the original.)

These ideas can be traced directly back to Rousseau. According to Rousseau, man's natural condition is a perfectly moral state of *"Liberty and Equality."* Rousseau tells us that man has only become evil because he has grown away from these two natural conditions. Furthermore, the only way to redeem mankind is to change human beings into perfectly moral creatures again. After we have perfected mankind, then we will enjoy heaven on earth, or as the Illuminati called it: *"the kingdom of the just."*

This burning religious desire to create heaven on earth (by changing other people) did not die off with the illuminati. During the upheavals and mass murders of Stalin and Mao, Modern Liberals gushed that all you needed to create heaven on earth was:

"...no further incentive but the burning zeal TO CREATE A NEW HEAVEN and a new earth, which flames in the breast of every good communist. It is something—this flame—that one has to see to appreciate. There is nothing like it in the world today."[356] (Stuart Chase, emphasis added.)

Modern Liberals want to create paradise on earth because they have no spiritual faith in an afterlife for themselves. Remember that Alan Brinkley (a very leftist historian), admitted that the Modern Liberals who created the New Deal policies of FDR approached government planning *"with almost religious veneration."* So it should be no surprise that the Modern Liberals who created FDR's New Deal programs shared the religious enthusiasm of their Soviet Communist friends. After all, they shared the same underlying goals. According to Professor Lewis Feuer of UC Berkeley:

"The whole conception of a 'social experiment,' the whole notion of planned human intervention...to raise the welfare of the people, had become linked in the minds of America's intellectual and social leaders with the practice of the Soviet Union. This transformation in American thought was largely the work of a small number of several hundreds of travelers to the Soviet Union during the previous decade...the reports they published affected the American political consciousness more deeply...than any other foreign influence in its history."[357]

THE UGLY SIDE OF UTOPIA: ELITISM

What do Modern Liberals mean when they say they want, "to change the world?" They cannot mean changing our physical world. They cannot be referring to changes in our coastlines or topography. Modern Liberals are obviously referring *to changing society*. This means they want to change the way other people live, and how they interact with each other. They want to change the way other people work, educate their children, and treat each other. They also want to change the way other people think about social issues, such as abortion, gun control, gay marriage, globalism, etc. This all means they *want to change other people*.

There is no escaping the fact that every person who wants "to change the world" is dangerously delusional about their relationship with their fellow man. They are also delusional about their proper role on earth.

Such people are invariably Modern Liberals. For example, Stuart Chase was one of the Modern Liberal architects for FDR's New Deal. Mr. Chase was positively giddy about the prospect that he might be given power to change the world. Mr. Chase referred with envy to the lucky Bolsheviks who were busy changing the world around them: *"Why should the Russians have all the fun of re-making a world?"*[358]

The Modern Liberal passion to "change the world" carries along with it a powerful sense of elitism, on the part of the people who think they know what's best for other human beings. This elitism originated with men like Plato and Pythagoras, but it finds new energy with every generation of Modern Liberal technocrats and politicians. John Stuart Mill was a highly influential Modern Liberal thinker. He argued that men of superior intelligence could re-arrange society to eliminate all of mankind's suffering, *"if the superior spirits would but join with each other."* Mill called upon the universities to, *"send forth into society a succession of minds, not the creatures of their age, but capable of being its improvers and re-generators."*[359]

This elitism has led many Modern Liberals to some bizarre delusions about themselves. Many of them have dreamed of creating a new race of men. Fully two centuries ago, the great Modern Liberal ideologue William Godwin referred to *"men as they may hereafter be made."*[360] The first Modern Liberal to gain political power was the French Revolutionary Robespierre. He too sought to change human nature to satisfy his own elitist delusions:

"I am convinced of the necessity of bringing about a complete re-generation…of creating a new people."[361]

President Woodrow Wilson was the first true Modern Liberal to hold power in the United States.[362] It's no surprise that Wilson (just like Rousseau and Robespierre), wanted to change other people to his own liking:

"Our problem is not merely to help students to adjust themselves to world life…[but] to make them as unlike their fathers as we can."[363]

Modern Liberal historians like to portray Woodrow Wilson as a humanitarian, and as a kindly intellectual. In fact Wilson was probably the most dictatorial and high-handed of all American Presidents. Using WWI as his pretext, Wilson denied habeas corpus, conducted warrantless searches, and appointed thousands of citizen vigilantes, who arrested people merely for speaking out against the draft (the infamous "Palmer Raids"). Wilson even created the world's first ministry of propaganda.[364] Only Lincoln was perhaps more autocratic (denying habeas corpus, shutting down newspapers, etc.) However, Mr. Lincoln was fighting a war on his own soil. The very nation was in peril. In contrast, Wilson was merely fighting to keep Paris safe from the Kaiser. There was no excuse for Wilson's authoritarianism.

Like most Modern Liberal politicians, Wilson was enthralled by the idea of changing mankind into better creatures. This naturally gave Wilson an outlook that was arrogant, elitist, and authoritarian. Wilson believed that government leaders had the right to mold other people into whatever shape the elite thought best. Here are Wilson's own frightening words:

"The competent leader of men cares little for the internal niceties of other people's characters: he cares much—everything—for the external uses to which they may be put…He [the competent ruler] supplies the power; others supply only the materials upon which that power operates…It is the power which dictates, dominates; the materials yield. MEN ARE AS CLAY IN THE HANDS OF THE CONSUMMATE LEADER."[365] (Emphasis added.)

Next it was the turn of the Bolsheviks and the Nazis to change mankind into something better. As Jim Marrs points out in his book, *The Rise of the Fourth Reich*, "*Anyone who interprets National Socialism merely as a political movement knows nothing about it… it is the determination to create a new man.*"[366] Likewise the Russian communist ideologue, Nikolay Chernishevsky, called upon his fellow communists to create "*men of the new age.*"[367] Trotsky and Stalin variously referred to the new race of mankind they wanted to create as "*the man of the future,*" "*communist man,*" and "*Soviet man.*"

Today's Modern Liberals have not changed. For example, as early as 1969 (in her college speech that we mentioned earlier), Hillary Clinton boldly declared:

"...the challenge now is to practice politics as the art of making what appears to be impossible, possible...We're not interested in social reconstruction, IT'S HUMAN RECONSTRUCTION."[368] (Emphasis added.)

You may shudder at the thought of a twenty-one year old college girl boasting about how she will reconstruct your human character. Remember, this was not just a fit of youthful braggadocio. As we just discussed, 24 years later, in her speech to the University of Texas, first lady Hillary Clinton repeated the same adolescent impudence. She boldly repeated her earlier call for *"a new politics of meaning."*[369]

If a person wants to reconstruct the rest of humanity, (presumably in her own image) what can this be but playing God? Modern Liberals who pursue the politics of meaning actually see themselves as the saviors of mankind. This messianic egotism is widespread among Modern Liberal politicians. Hillary Clinton's opponent for the 2008 Democratic Party nomination, Barack Obama, shared this same messianic delusion about himself. Throughout 2008, Barack Obama frequently proclaimed to his followers, *"We are the ones we've been waiting for!"*

Obama borrowed this phrase from a poem by the Modern Liberal poet, Alice Walker. According to Walker, this sentence simply means *"We, the modern young generation of Americans are wiser than earlier generations, more perceptive, and better able to solve the world's problems."* However, according to conservatives it really means, "We are young and naïve, so we foolishly assume that we are smarter than our parents." This impertinent attitude is brimming with inflated self-confidence and unjustified self-esteem.

The cleverest of Modern Liberals know that the most effective way to change society is to change the very traditions upon which society is based. The early English socialist Robert Owen understood this. Owen claimed that there were three "mortal enemies" of civilization. These terrible evils were: Christianity, marriage, and property rights. Of course these three traditions are not the enemies of civilization. They are actually three important *foundations of civilization.*

ELITISM BREEDS ARROGANCE

The idea that Modern Liberals may properly tell other people how to live and how to think rests on a dangerous assumption. It assumes that these same Modern Liberals are mentally and morally superior to the common masses that they are trying to change. This means that Modern Liberals must necessarily look down upon the brutish dullards that they are so generously stooping to help.

This unbridled arrogance is openly admitted by many of the greatest Modern Liberal authors. For example, the greatest theorist of Modern Liberalism was Rousseau. He looked upon the common man as mentally handicapped. Rousseau wrote that the intellectual ability of the average working man was that of *"a stupid pusillanimous invalid."*

Voltaire was another highly influential philosophe. Voltaire called the common man *"rabble, scum."*[370] The philosophe Condorcet said that the common mass of humanity nauseated him.[371] The early English Modern Liberal William Godwin believed that the common man had all the *"contemptible insensitivity of an oyster."* [372] One of the most influential Modern Liberal writers of the 20th century, George Bernard Shaw, said he found the working classes *"detestable."* Shaw even declared that working class people, *"have no right to live."*[373]

Modern Liberal politicians in America have long shared this arrogant attitude toward the common people. On this topic, it is useful to look once again at the first Modern Liberal to gain power in the United States, Woodrow Wilson. Wilson felt justified in playing God, because he believed that he was vastly more intelligent than the average American. This egotistical delusion made Wilson think that he was morally justified in lying to the American people, who he called "the masses."

"Only a very gross substance of concrete conception can make any impression on the minds of the masses...They must get their ideas very absolutely put, and are much readier to receive a half truth which they can promptly understand than a whole truth which has too many sides to be seen all at once."[374]

ARROGANCE & BIGOTRY: BARACK OBAMA

This statement by Woodrow Wilson might just as well have been made by Nietzsche, Hegel, Hitler, Pol Pot, or any other megalomaniac. Recently, President Barack Obama proved that this same disdain for the common man is still very much alive within Modern Liberalism. Almost a hundred years after Woodrow Wilson, Obama also sees himself as vastly more intelligent than the average American. And just like Wilson, Obama sees the average American as stupid, irrational, and even bigoted. For example, while speaking at a fund raising event in San Francisco on April 6th, 2008, Obama gave his opinion about one large demographic group that was not supporting him; working-class white people who live in small towns (i.e. conservatives):

"So it's not surprising that when they get bitter, they cling to guns or religion or antipathy to people who aren't like them, or anti-immigrant sentiment, or anti-trade sentiment as a way to explain their frustrations."

So according to Barack Obama, working-class white people own guns because they are bitter and frustrated. The truth is, most people who own guns (white or non-white) keep them for self-defense, and to protect their homes from criminals. A secondary reason for some people is hunting. However, Barack Obama presumes that the real reason working-class white people keep guns is their emotional inability to deal with their own "frustrations." This is not merely arrogant and simple-minded. It is also racist.

Obama says that working-class white people cling to religion for the same irrational reason. Obama's sweeping generalization forgets that these common people are all individuals; with millions of unique life experiences that make each of them seek God for different reasons. Obama also assumes that their faith is not based on reason, revelation, or prayer. Obama assumes that their faith cannot be the result of God actually giving them the gift of faith. Instead, Obama says their Christian religion is, *"a way to explain their frustrations."*

Finally, Obama attributes the "anti-immigrant sentiment" of working-class white people to these same alleged frustrations. It may surprise Obama to know that many working-class white people oppose illegal immigration because it is creating a surplus of labor. This surplus of labor is forcing wages down lower than they would be otherwise, according to the law of supply and demand. As the supply of labor rises, then the price of labor (wages) goes down. It might surprise Obama to realize that these working-class white people are smart enough to understand a basic economic principle like supply and demand. Ironically, it is the Harvard educated Obama who seems unable to understand this principle.[375]

These same working-class white people are also smart enough to worry about the costs of educating the children of illegal aliens, and the cost of paying for their medical care and social welfare needs. However, according to Obama, working-class white people do not think about these complex ideas. Instead, Obama says working-class white people reflexively oppose immigration because they are *"frustrated"* and *"bitter."* Apparently Obama believes that working-class white people are just a bunch of irrational, slack-jawed bigots. Sadly, most Modern Liberal politicians share Obama's condescending view of the common man.

Remember, it is not a mere coincidence that Modern Liberals look down upon the common people. Modern Liberals *must* look down on the common people, in order to justify seizing power over their lives.[376] If Modern Liberals do not see themselves as superior to "the masses" (mentally and morally) then how can they justify their assumption of power over the masses? Their belief in their own superiority is a self-serving delusion, and a very dangerous one at that. F.A. Hayek warned us that as modern governments grow more powerful, they tend to attract more arrogant and belligerent persons to positions of power. Then what are we to think of these Modern Liberal politicians who want to control our lives and "change the world?" The libertarian scholar Robert Higgs answered this question:

"Decent people, virtually by definition, do not seek to exercise political power over their fellows. The mystery is [why] so many citizens continue to admire and defer to the reptilian wretches who rule them."

VOTING RIGHTS

Most of the classic liberals who dominated England and America in the 19th century did not look down upon the common man. That is why classic liberals generally favored giving the common people widespread voting rights. However, during the "Progressive Era" at the turn of the 20th century, most Modern Liberals went back to the elitism originally envisioned by Plato. These Modern Liberals favored the Platonic idea that elite technocrats and social engineers should run other peoples' lives. This elitism explains why Modern Liberals are currently using activist judges to change society faster than voters are willing to tolerate. These rogue judges are now enforcing Modern Liberal causes, such as abortion, gay marriage, racial quotas, and separation of church and state, regardless of the wishes of the voters.

On the other hand, today's Modern Liberals also favor widening the voting franchise by granting citizenship to illegal aliens via amnesty programs. However, this support for wider voting rights does not mean Modern Liberals have given up on elitism. In fact, their support for amnesty programs is really a play for more power. Modern Liberals know that illegal immigrants will generally vote to support socialist candidates. Besides, Modern Liberals are appointing activist judges, who will eventually render those same voting rights meaningless.

In fact, Modern Liberals are happy to take away voting rights from conservatives. During the controversial vote count for the razor thin presidential election of 2000, Modern Liberals in the Democratic Party worked hard to invalidate thousands of absentee ballots that were cast by military service members, all on a mere technicality.[377] These Modern Liberal activists and their lawyers knew that military voters tend to vote Republican.

In a similar move, in May of 2010, the US Department of Justice under Barack Obama decided it would only enforce the Voting Rights Act against white people who tried to intimidate blacks from voting. *The USDOJ would no longer do anything to protect white voters from being intimidated by blacks.*[378] The political motive behind this decision is obvious. Black people tend to vote overwhelmingly for Democrats. Therefore, their right to vote must be protected. White people tend to vote more often for Republicans. Therefore, their right to vote may be violated.

THE DARK SIDE OF THE ENLIGHTENMENT

The Enlightenment spurred Western culture to adopt secular government, i.e. the separation of church and state. Modern Liberals firmly believe that the Enlightenment was a liberating movement because it freed the individual *from the intellectual oppression of the Catholic Church*. However, what Modern Liberals fail to realize is that the Enlightenment also opened the door for *the political oppression of the individual by the state*. You see, when the Enlightenment took away the church's influence over government, it also took away an important safeguard against tyranny. So while the Enlightenment *prevented oppression by the Church*, it actually *encouraged oppression by the state*.

Before the Enlightenment, the Christian Church in England and North America had often acted as a check against the growth of government power. As we saw in Chapter One, Christianity tended to protect individual rights against an over-reaching monarch. For better or for worse, the Enlightenment eliminated the Church's role in Western politics, possibly forever. Of course this led to more intellectual freedom for scientists who wanted to teach things like evolution. However, secular government also led to the growth of government power, and the consequent reduction of individual rights. For example, the growth of the social welfare state and the military industrial complex have reduced property rights for people who want to keep their own income to support their own families. The growth of the nanny state has reduced rights for people who want to choose their own doctor and their own options for medical treatment.

The growth of Big Brother government has even reduced the rights of people who want to exercise free speech, (e.g. the McCain-Feingold Campaign Finance law). Modern Liberalism is leading us toward laws that will prohibit anyone from speaking critically about another person's religion, culture or sexual practices. The definition of hate speech will be expanded to include anything that another person might not like. In the European Union, it is already illegal to criticize Islam on several issues. For instance, retired actress Bridget Bardot is an animal rights activist. Mrs. Bardot has been fined to the tune of forty thousand dollars by the French government for criticizing the manner in which Muslims slaughter animals for food. Other less notable Europeans have been fined for daring to criticize the Muslim oppression of women. America is headed toward the same repressive state of affairs.

STATISM VS CHRISTIANITY

If Modern Liberals in general shun Christianity, then the most extreme of Modern Liberals would likely have the most extreme hatred for Christianity. The most extreme of the Modern Liberals were the Jacobins, Nazis, and communists. Indeed, all of these groups detested Christianity.

There is a logical reason for this. Every one of these Modern Liberal ideologies is authoritarian. All of these ideologies demand absolute and unquestioning obedience to the authority of the state. All of these ideologies place no value on an individual's life, but instead place all value in the survival of the state. Any rival belief system which contains its own moral code might inspire disobedience against the state. This is why extreme Modern Liberals have tried to eliminate Christianity. According to former communist Lev Alburt:

"Religious people believe in God, in a life hereafter, in certain religious and moral values. And a religious person, when pressed too far by Communist authorities, is likely to say, 'I won't do it. I draw the line. I won't cross this line, no matter what you are going to do to me or my family. I won't do it because it is immoral…I would rather die, but I won't commit this act of betrayal against morality.' And therefore, for Communist rulers, religion is a dangerous phenomenon. And they are doing everything they can to discredit, and destroy religion."[379]

The Jacobins of the French Revolution were the first Modern Liberals who tried to destroy Christianity, because it was an obstacle to their goal of creating an all powerful government. The Jacobins persecuted Christianity with a vengeance. For example, the Prussian Baron Anacharsis Clootz was an active member of the Illuminati who joined the Jacobins during the French Revolution. Robespierre (the Jacobin leader of the French Revolution during the Reign of Terror) used Clootz as his sword to slaughter Christians in France. Clootz was happy to oblige, because he hated Christians. In one notorious incident, Clootz used mounted cavalry troops to trample hundreds of Christian children to death. Ironically, after committing this beastly act of savagery, Clootz said:

"Religion is a social disease which cannot be too quickly cured. A religious man is a depraved animal."[380]

The most influential communist of them all, Karl Marx, shared this loathing for traditional religion. Marx also thought of religion as a social pathology, similar to drug addiction. Marx called religion *"the opium of the people."* Of course he was referring to Christianity. Perhaps the greatest statists of the 20th century, the Bolsheviks, shared this anti-Christian bigotry for exactly the same reasons mentioned earlier by Lev Alburt. Lenin was almost hysterical in his hatred of the Russian Orthodox Church:

"Every religious idea, every idea of a god, even flirting with the idea of god, is unspeakable vileness of the most dangerous kind, a disease of the most abominable kind... Millions of sins, filthy deeds, acts of violence...are far less dangerous than the subtle, spiritual idea of a god decked out in the smartest ideological costumes."[381]

The other great statists of the 20th century, Hitler and Mussolini, also detested Christianity. According to Hitler, *"With the appearance of Christianity, the first spiritual terror has been brought into the much freer old (pagan) world."* Hitler boasted that he would *"...eradicate Christianity in Germany root and branch."*[382]

Mussolini made a treaty of necessity with the Catholic Church, but like all statists, he was deep down an atheist, and therefore also a materialist: *"...for the fascist, everything is in the state, and nothing human or spiritual exists, much less has value, outside the state..."*[383]

Even the great humanitarians of Modern Liberalism disliked religion. For example, according to the first great English socialist, Robert Owen, all religions are, *"based on the same absurd imagination."* He also believed that Christianity only damaged the human character, turning a man into *"a weak imbecile (sic) animal; a furious bigot and fanatic; or a miserable hypocrite."*[384]

The campaign against Christianity can also be seen today in our universities, where Modern Liberal professors refuse to date historical events with the very logical and simple "B.C." and "A.D." method. Instead they resort to an awkward artifice called "B.C.E." ("Before the Common Era"). The first problem with this measurement is its ambiguity. There is no universally recognized date for the start of "the common era." At first the petulant professors tried to use 1956 as their "year one," but this caused great confusion. Finally, these impudent scholars reluctantly went back to using the year of Christ's birth for the year one. However, they still refused to mention Christ in any way. Instead, they insisted on labeling any year before Christ's birth as "BCE," instead of BC. Of course, if the start of "the common era" is really just the year of Christ's birth, then why not refer to it that way?

GLOBALISM AND GAIA WORSHIP

In the late 20th century, globalists wanted a religion that could be molded to support global government. They were naturally drawn toward Gaia worship. (Pronounced "jee-uh.") So it is no coincidence that the most ardent globalists also support Gaia worship. The reverse is even more true. Virtually all Gaia worshippers support global government. The two concepts have become wedded together. Just listen to what a few of these earth-worshipping globalists have to say:

"We have now a new spirituality...the New Age movement...beginning to influence concepts of politics and community in ecology... This is Gaia politique...planetary culture."[385] (William I. Thompson, founder of the UN sponsored Lindisfarne Association.)

"I believe the appropriate symbol of the Cosmic Christ...is that of Jesus as Mother Earth crucified yet rising daily..."[386] (Matthew Fox, globalist and self-styled New Age theologian.)

"Each person must learn to think like Earth, to act like Earth, to be Earth..."[387] (Gerald Barney, founder of the Millennium Institute.)

Interestingly, the religious beliefs of the Illuminati are strikingly similar to Gaia worship. According to the Illuminati, God was merely, "...*the Soul of the World. It is this substance, the natural object of wonder and respect that men have called God...*"[388] Why would the Illuminati and modern Gaia worshippers both independently choose the earth as their object of worship? Well, if you wanted to invent your own religion, and you needed something for your followers to worship, what would you pick? The sun? The moon? Zeus? Baal? The most likely choice would be the earth itself. It sustains life, and it is literally "everywhere," (at least in our everyday perception).

These are at least two of the attributes of God, i.e. he sustains life, and he is omnipresent. Trotting out old pagan gods from the past would never work. The old gods have too long been seen for what they really are; the fairy tale legends of our imaginative ancestors. The dead gods of mythology had only one brief encore performance in a very peculiar society, namely Nazi Germany. Worshipping the earth is no better than worshipping Thor or Odin. The earth is a large rock. Of course it is a very nice rock, with many fine qualities we can all appreciate. However, it is still a rock. Gaia worship is just as primitive as any other form of animism. It is worshipping the creation, rather than the Creator.

The Big Picture

Gaia worship is also politically dangerous, because it treats human beings as no better than any other animal. If people are not special, then why should a man have any more rights than a spiny anteater? M. Stanton Evans posed the question more eloquently:

"If people are really no different from objects in the natural order, why not treat them accordingly? If human beings are mere phenomena… why should they enjoy freedom?"[389]

The Modern Liberal psychologist B.F. Skinner actually wanted to abolish freedom, so that he could use his scientific method to re-make humanity into better creatures. Sadly, Skinner's method (reflexive conditioning) is exactly the same technique commonly used by animal trainers. Dr. Skinner boldly admitted that his training would be impossible to conduct if the common man was left free from government control. So according to the people who want to re-make humanity, freedom is a very bad thing indeed. Dr. Skinner said: *"…the hypothesis that MAN IS NOT FREE is essential to the application of scientific method to human nature."*[390] (Emphasis added.) His seminal book on this subject is chillingly entitled *"Beyond Freedom and Dignity."*

Skinner was not proposing a new idea. He was merely echoing an old idea from the very first Modern Liberals of all, the French philosophes of the 18th century. Voltaire himself declared:

"We are a species of monkey that can be taught to act reasonably or unreasonably."[391]

The human soul, free will, and human dignity are all meaningless words to these men, who would happily train the rest of us like circus animals!

THE CONSERVATIVE GOAL: A CHRISTIAN NATION

Technology has changed, and society has changed, but our need for traditional religion has not. In past centuries, man was told why he was living so that he might know how to live. This was the gift of Christianity. Nowadays, man is told how to live without ever being told why. This is the curse of Neo-paganism.[392] It can only have a corrosive effect upon our social fabric and upon individual morality.

The corruption and veniality of modern politicians is partly caused by our general loss of religious faith. Politicians come from the general population. If we ourselves are not religious, then we will not elect religious persons to office. If we elect politicians who are neither religious nor moral, then our government will certainly become oppressive. The father of our country, George Washington, warned us of this danger:

"Of all the dispositions and habits which lead to political prosperity, religion and morality are indispensable supports. In vain would that man claim the tribute of patriotism who should labor to subvert these great pillars of human happiness..."[393]

The Founding Fathers assumed that a nation of Christians would continue to elect Christians to public office. For the first 200 years of our history as a nation, this was generally true. Sadly, in the twilight of the 20th century, Christianity lost its grip on our national character. This decline of Christianity in America at least partly explains why Americans have recently elected men such as Bill Clinton and Barack Obama: men who are neither religious nor patriotic. Regardless of what their supporters may claim, these men are "Christian" in name only. Mr. Obama spent 18 years attending a racist congregation which was run by a militant black bigot named Jeremiah Wright. Obama has also never indicated how the Christian religion has influenced either his personal life or his political life in any way. While Obama lived in Indonesia as a child, he was taught to be a Muslim. As an adult, he astonished a BBC journalist by singing Muslim prayers from memory, with perfect Arabic inflection.

President Bill Clinton's record for both sexual immorality and sheer dishonesty is legendary. One example will have to suffice. As President, Bill Clinton regularly scheduled his weekly oral sex with Monica Lewinsky to begin immediately after attending church every Sunday. One can only imagine what Clinton was thinking about with lurid anticipation during the church services.

But are Obama and Clinton unpatriotic? Well, both men are zealous globalists. They have long supported the surrender of US sovereignty to the United Nations. By supporting various UN treaties, (The Convention on the Rights of the Child, the International Arms Trade Treaty, the Convention on the Elimination of Discrimination Against Women, the Law of the Sea Treaty, etc.) these men are aiding and abetting the surrender of American sovereignty.

For example, the International Arms Trade Treaty would take away many of our rights under the Second Amendment to the US Constitution, which is part of our Bill of Rights. Any man who wants our Bill of Rights to be subordinate to a foreign organization can hardly be called "patriotic." It would be more accurate to call such a man a "traitor." Unlike Alger Hiss, Mr. Obama and Mr. Clinton are not spies in the pay of a foreign power. However, just like Alger Hiss, Obama and Clinton are committed globalists, which means they seek to destroy American sovereignty.

As they destroy our sovereignty, they will also destroy our liberty. Therefore, these men are indeed working against the interests of their own nation. This means they are traitors. They are not alone. Any president who gives up American sovereignty to a global government is a traitor. This means that Presidents Woodrow Wilson, Dwight Eisenhower, and George Bush Sr. were also traitors. "The big picture" can be rather ugly.

In regard to religion and morality being the foundations of patriotism, the other Founding Fathers agreed with George Washington. According to John Adams, the US Constitution was, *"…made only for a moral and religious people [and] wholly inadequate for the government of any other [type of people]."*[394] By *"religious"* Adams certainly meant Christian. The greatest journalist and educator among the Founding Fathers was Noah Webster. He too understood that instruction in Christianity was vital to protect our republican form of government:

"In my view, the Christian religion is the most important of…things in which all children, under a free government, ought to be instructed… The Christian religion must be the basis of any government intended to secure the rights and privileges of a free people."[395]

THE BIG LIE: "SEPARATION OF CHURCH AND STATE"

Modern Liberals often cite one letter by Thomas Jefferson, in which he said that the First Amendment created a *"wall of separation between church and state."* Unfortunately Modern Liberals are quoting this letter completely out of context. Jefferson's letter of 1802 was addressed to a group of Anabaptists. These religious dissenters had complained to Jefferson about their second-class status in Massachusetts. Jefferson was merely explaining to them why the federal government could not protect them. Jefferson told them that the First Amendment prevented the federal government from telling the States how to regulate religion. Jefferson was only referring to the *federal* government being separated from religious disputes. Jefferson's letter clearly avoided enforcing the First Amendment against the states.

Therefore, the modern Supreme Court is grossly mistaken when it invokes Jefferson's expression about "separation between church and state" as an excuse to ban Christian prayer from *state-run* public schools. Jefferson never intended his theory to be applied against state governments. When Jefferson used the word "state" he was simply referring to the federal government as "the state" in the generic sense of the word, in which "state" means the nation's government. Jefferson was not referring to the individual sates of the Union. So by quoting Thomas Jefferson out of context on this issue, the US Supreme Court has been running a gigantic fraud for half a century.

The modern Supreme Court rationalizes their deception by claiming that the 14th Amendment somehow "incorporates" the Bill of Rights against the states. However, this misguided legal theory gives a radical new power to the federal government; the ability to nullify virtually any State law that the Supreme Court does not like! This was never intended by the drafters of the 14th Amendment, or by the state representatives who ratified it. The 14th Amendment was only intended to prevent the States from discriminating against people *due to their race*. Yet the modern Supreme Court has used this "incorporation theory" to create a whole new body of court made law, amounting to a sort of federal common law. It is a bastard body of law which should not exist. It is based on a false interpretation of the 14th Amendment. This false legal theory has spawned a whole series of decisions that are hostile to Christianity.

The truth is, the men who wrote the Constitution assumed that America would be a Christian nation. They only intended the First Amendment to prevent the federal government from establishing one particular Christian sect over all the others. When the Founding Fathers wrote the First Amendment, they did not use the word "religion" in the same sense that we do today. The Founding Fathers considered Presbyterianism and Anglicanism to be *totally different religions*.[396] Today, we consider all forms of Christianity to be basically the same religion. But when the Founding Fathers used the word "religion" in the First Amendment, they were only thinking about the rival *Christian faiths* that existed throughout the country. They were certainly not thinking about non-Christian faiths, such as Buddhism, Hinduism, Islam, or even Judaism.

Why was the first US Congress so afraid that one type of Christianity might be established as superior to all the others? At the time our nation was founded, there was a great deal of rivalry among the different Christian denominations in the new states. Nine of the original thirteen states had official state religions. Some of these states would not let men vote unless they belonged to a congregation of the official state religion. A few of the new states even maintained these voting bans against "godless dissenters" (e.g. Quakers, Anabaptists and Congregationalists) for almost two decades *after* the US Constitution was ratified. So the First Amendment was never intended to separate religion from state and local government, as Modern Liberals pretend.

We should also remember that Thomas Jefferson selected the Bible as the basic text for English instruction when he helped to set up the first schools in the District of Columbia. Obviously Jefferson did not intend to separate Christianity from the state. Jefferson clearly understood that the First Amendment only prevented the federal government from establishing one type of Christianity above all the others. It did not prevent the federal government from aiding Christianity in general. This widespread assumption that the Christian religion would be taught to the nation's school children was even put into law with the Northwest Ordinance of 1787. It required that "religion" must be taught to all children in the new territories. By "religion" the Founding Fathers obviously meant Christianity. America's greatest Chief Justice, John Marshall, spelled it out:

"The American population is entirely Christian, and with us Christianity and religion are identified (identical). It would be strange indeed if

with such a people our institutions did not presuppose Christianity... and exhibit relations with it."[397]

So according to John Marshall, the modern Supreme Court's theory about the separation of church and state is *"strange indeed."* On this question, nearly all the other Founding Fathers agreed that America was founded as a Christian nation. They never supported Modern Liberalism's radical interpretation of Jefferson's letter:

"The general principles upon which the [Founding] Fathers achieved independence were...the general principles of Christianity...those principles of Christianity are as eternal and immutable as the existence and attributes of God."[398] (John Adams)

"Providence has given to our people the choice of their rulers, and it is the duty...OF A CHRISTIAN NATION to select and prefer Christians for their rulers."[399] (John Jay, America's first Chief Justice. Emphasis added.)

In fact, if you examine the Constitution itself, it is obvious that we were founded as a Christian nation. The Constitution permits a seven day time period for the President to veto a bill, but it explicitly excludes Sundays. The Founding Fathers believed that the Christian Sabbath day should be a day of rest, as required in the Bible. So the Constitution was written to prevent the President from working on Sunday. Numerous local laws also prevented federal officials from working on the Christian Sabbath day as well.

For example, one Sunday in 1789, George Washington and a few companions were stopped and fined in Connecticut, for the crime of riding horses on Sunday. The fact that President Washington was on government business was considered irrelevant. He was in violation of the law because he was working on the Lord's Day. Back in 1789 no one dreamed of running to the Supreme Court to have such laws declared "unconstitutional." Such a thing would have been irrational. Of course this is exactly what we do in our modern world. It is still irrational, regardless of what the modern Supreme Court says.

The national motto, "In God We Trust" has been on our currency for almost two centuries.[400] If you read the writings of the Founding

The Big Picture

Fathers, it is obvious that they were referring exclusively to the Judeo-Christian God. The Founding Fathers were *certainly not referring to* Shiva, Allah, Isis or Gaia. The Great Seal of the United States contains the all-seeing eye of God, a Masonic symbol which represents the omniscience of the Christian God. Ben Franklin wanted the Great Seal to show Moses parting the Red Sea for the Hebrews. Thomas Jefferson favored an image of the Hebrews following God's pillar of Light through the desert. However, George Washington was an enthusiastic Mason, and he simply preferred Masonic imagery.

Finally, the first US Congress spent federal money for 10,000 Bibles to be printed and distributed to the nation's schools, in order to help preserve Christianity as the foundation for the new nation. This was the same Congress that passed the Bill of Rights, which included the First Amendment. These Founding Fathers obviously did not intend to separate Christianity from the government.

In light of all this evidence, the idea that the US Supreme Court can ban Christian prayers in public schools and public buildings is not only false, it is absurd. The Founding Fathers clearly intended America to be a Christian nation, with Christianity permeating both our private and public institutions. This is true regardless of what five lying radicals on the Supreme Court claim today. The Founding Fathers intended for us to be a Christian nation, with exclusively Christian prayers permitted in public schools and public buildings. Nowadays this idea only sounds "extreme" and "intolerant" because we have been brainwashed for sixty years to accept the big lie about "separation of church and state."

CONCLUSION

Being part of a great political movement to create heaven on earth provides Modern Liberals with a feeling of immortality. This gives meaning to their lives. Unfortunately, the goal of perfecting society carries along with it the assumption that certain people are so full of wisdom that they should tell the rest of us how to live. This assumption breeds arrogance, and eventually it leads to tyranny. The great question for us today is, "How can we avoid tyranny?"

CHAPTER SEVEN

HOW TO AVOID TYRANNY

Greg Dusky was a junior in high school. He had been in Mr. Filbert's history class for almost an entire semester. Greg noticed that everyday, Mr. Filbert always wore the same belt. It had a very large buckle, which displayed the face of Che Guevara. It was the famous image, with the communist beret and the partial beard.

Greg had never really given the belt buckle much thought, until about a week ago, when a television show about politics flashed the same image of Che Guevara on the screen for a few seconds. At the time, Greg was sitting on the couch next to his elderly Uncle. Greg innocently asked his Uncle, *"Why was Che Guevara so great?"*

To Greg's surprise, his Uncle (an amateur historian) reacted like a volcano. *"He wasn't great! He was a son of a bitch. He killed thousands of people, political prisoners, in cold blood. He took them out and shot 'em. Shot 'em like dogs. Guevara was a cold blooded killer!"*

Greg was surprised at this outburst, and instinctively he knew that he had better not say anything about his teacher's belt buckle to his Uncle. His volatile Uncle might go to the school and make an ugly scene. He had already done that several years ago, when one of Greg's teachers told him that he could not bring a Bible to school.

Later that night, Greg quietly used his computer to research Che Guevara. He was a little disturbed to see that his Uncle had not been exaggerating at all. He quickly took a piece of paper and wrote down some of the awful things that Che Guevara had done to people.

The next day, during Mr. Filbert's class, Greg couldn't help thinking about what he had read on the Internet. Greg decided not to

The Big Picture

challenge Mr. Filbert during class, but instead to wait until the bell rang. He wanted to question Mr. Filbert, but not to embarrass him in public. Just before the class ended, Greg instinctively reached into his shirt pocket and touched the piece of paper on which he had written down all the bad information about Che Guevara from the internet. Suddenly the bell rang. Greg thought it sounded louder than usual.

As the kids were shuffling out of class, Greg pivoted and stepped over to Mr. Filbert, who was still sitting at his desk.

"Can I ask you something?" Greg said tentatively.

"Of course," smiled Mr. Filbert.

"Why do you always have that Che Guevara belt buckle?"

"Well, he's one of my heroes I guess."

Greg knew this was his moment of truth. Life was calling him out. Life was daring him to challenge his superior. *"I read on the internet last night that he killed a lot of people who were just political prisoners, over two thousand of them."*

Mr. Filbert winced just a little, and an uncomfortable look took over his face. *"Well, of course some people had to be killed. It was a revolution. Some people were still trying to fight back against the revolution."*

Greg surprised himself as he blurted out, *"But these guys weren't fighting back. They were all in jail. They were just tied up and shot. Some of them were even journalists and newspaper editors who spoke out against Castro. They were no danger to anyone. Sometimes Che even made the families witness the killings. "*

Mr. Filbert paused, but not awkwardly. He kept his poise and coolly said, *"It's impossible for us today to sit back and judge what Che and Castro did back then. Cuba was in the middle of revolution, chaos…and order had to be restored."*

Greg thought for a moment. His eyebrows twisted. Something didn't sound right. He looked back at Mr. Filbert and asked, *"So does that mean we can never criticize a revolutionary? We can't criticize Mussolini or Lenin? Guevara killed people just for speaking out against him. That means he was a fascist, just like Mussolini. You may as well have Mussolini or Hitler on your belt buckle."*

That made Mr. Filbert lose his patience, but not his composure. He calmly opened his binder as a signal that he was preparing for his next group of students. His next class was starting to enter the room right then anyway. He told Greg dismissively, *"You're still young. You don't understand. It's different when people are trying to change the world. Now hurry up or you'll be late."*

GOVERNMENT POWER MUST BE LIMITED

This story illustrates how intelligent, educated people often delude themselves into supporting leaders who are in fact morally depraved mass murderers. It does not matter what banner a tyrant flies over his palace. It does not matter what ideological label he claims for his rule. It does not even matter whether his intentions are good or evil. The only thing that matters is *whether he wants to control the lives of other people.* The great 20th century historian Clarence B. Carson warned us:

"The horrors of communism and Nazism were not simply the consequences of evil men coming to power; they were the precise results that followed naturally from the concentration of power to impose collectivist ideas."[401]

As we will see in this chapter, all governments (even democratic republics) naturally gravitate toward tyranny. Yet why is this so? The reason is simple. Human beings will naturally try to gather as much power for themselves as they possibly can. Governments are made up of human beings. Therefore, governments also tend to gather more and more power for themselves. As government power grows, the people who run the government become more abusive (tyrannical) with their power. Lord Acton gave us perhaps the most astute observation about government; *"Power tends to corrupt and absolute power corrupts absolutely."* So how can we prevent any government from developing into a tyranny? The only way to prevent tyranny is to put an iron chain upon the government, in the form of a constitution.

THE GREAT CHAIN: THE CONSTITUTION

The Constitution was originally intended to strictly limit the power of the federal government, in order to protect individual liberty. To preserve this intent behind the Constitution, conservatives look to the original intentions of the federal representatives who passed the Constitution, as well as to the intentions of the state legislatures who ratified it. Their original intent can be easily found in the recorded legislative debates, published letters, and newspaper articles that were printed at the time (e.g. the federalist papers). This same method can be used to interpret the various amendments which were later passed by Congress and ratified by the states. With a little research and careful reading, the original intent behind the Constitution (and the amendments) is readily apparent for anyone who cares to see the truth.

However, Modern Liberal politicians and derelict judges on the Supreme Court interpret the Constitution in a radically different way. Instead of following the "originalist" method, Modern Liberals follow the *"revisionist"* method, which lets them revise the Constitution to mean whatever they want. Modern Liberals rationalize this interpretation by claiming they want a "living constitution." Modern Liberals say they merely want the Constitution to "evolve with the times." Conservatives have rightly called this method *"the Silly Putty Constitution,"* because it can be twisted and stretched into whatever shape our rulers want it to be.

You see, the whole purpose for having a constitution is to put strict limits on government power. But the Silly Putty interpretation removes the strict limits on government power. So the Silly Putty approach defeats the whole purpose for having a constitution. It's like having no constitution at all. This is exactly why the supporters of big government want the Silly Putty Constitution. Modern Liberals want a document that they can basically ignore, in order to create new government powers for whatever social program they wish to impose. For the Constitution to be of any use, it must be strictly enforced. Otherwise there is no limit on government power. Without this restraint, the beast will grow, and the beast must be fed.

How fast can the beast grow? Well, back in 1961 the US government controlled only about 10% of our nation's economy.[402] Now, in 2010, the government controls over 35% of our economy. If the federal government takes over the nation's health care system, then it will control approximately 52% of the economy. Yet if the Constitution were followed strictly, then the federal government would not be permitted to take over health care. The beast would not grow. The beast would be chained.

For example, the Tenth Amendment strictly limits the federal government to only those powers that are specifically listed in the Constitution. All other powers should stay with the states or with the people themselves. If we had strictly followed the original intent behind the Tenth Amendment, the Federal government would be a fraction of its current size. It would be scaled back to far less than 10% of our GDP. Most of today's federal agencies would not even exist. Whatever would we do without the departments of Commerce, Education, Health and Human Services, the National Endowment for the Arts, the Corporation for Public Broadcasting, the Federal Reserve Bank, Fanny Mae, and the Tennessee Valley Authority? We would be far better off without them, both economically and politically.

How do Modern Liberals get around the limits of the Tenth Amendment? They use the Silly Putty method to stretch the meaning of the Constitution into whatever they want it to be. Let's take the *"general welfare"* clause, for example. According to Article One, Section Eight of the Constitution, Congress can only spend money in order to *"provide for the common defense and general Welfare of the United States."* This means that Congress should never spend any money that benefits any particular set of individuals, such as corporations, unions, welfare recipients, or people over sixty-five. Any federal spending must benefit *everyone* in the entire nation. Examples of proper federal spending are military defense, postal services, and customs inspections, because these things benefit the entire nation.

James Madison (who, more than any other single person, wrote our Constitution) understood that the general welfare clause was meant *to restrict the power of Congress*, not expand it. That is why President Madison vetoed a big federal spending bill in 1817. Some of the money would have been spent on special interest groups. Madison understood that any federal spending that did not benefit *everyone* would violate the general welfare clause.

President James Monroe also understood the original intent behind the general welfare clause. This was the reason that he vetoed federal spending for the Erie Canal. He knew the canal would benefit the merchants of New York much more than it would benefit anyone else. President Monroe figured that if New York wanted the canal so badly, then the people of New York should pay for it, which in fact they did.

So the Founding Fathers used the term "general welfare" to mean *universal*. Sadly, under FDR in the late 1930's, politicians and a majority of Supreme Court judges began to reinterpret the words "general welfare" to mean any vague benefit to society, *"in general."* This Silly Putty interpretation completely changed the meaning of the "general welfare" clause. Suddenly it became a *grant of power*, instead of a restriction on power. With this radical new view, nearly any federal spending might be justified because it could somehow benefit society "in general."

The other vital part of the Constitution which Modern Liberals have stretched beyond recognition is the "commerce clause" of Article One, Section Eight. It gives Congress the power, *"To regulate commerce with foreign nations, and among the several States, and with the Indian Tribes."* In Federalist Paper #22, Alexander Hamilton explained that the "commerce clause" was intended for only one reason: *to prevent individual states from imposing their own tariff barriers,* whether against each other or against foreign countries. That is all. Yet Modern Liberals routinely invoke the commerce clause as an excuse for all sorts of new and illegitimate federal powers. This includes federal control of education, agriculture, and most recently, health care.

Modern Liberals claim (without any historical evidence) that the commerce clause gives the federal government power to control any activity that might remotely have any "effect" on interstate commerce. For example, at one point during the Great Depression, the federal Department of Agriculture declared that no farmer could produce more than 20 bushels of wheat per acre. The government wanted to keep the supply of wheat low, so the price would stay high. One chicken farmer refused to follow the limit. He was not selling any of his wheat. Instead, he used all of his wheat to feed his own chickens. His wheat was not being placed into the stream of interstate commerce. So the farmer figured that the federal government had no authority over him.

The federal government quickly tried to punish this poor farmer with fines, and took him all the way to the Supreme Court, in a case called Wickard v Filburn. The government claimed that if the farmer produced his own wheat, he would not be buying wheat from other farmers. So his personal wheat production might have an "effect" on the price of bread. Unfortunately, the court upheld this new expansion of federal power. Conservatives point out that nearly any human activity can be argued to have some microscopic "effect" on interstate commerce. Therefore, under this Modern Liberal interpretation, the federal government might control any person's economic decisions.

After all, every economic decision you make can arguably have some vague "effect" on interstate commerce, whether it's how many socks you buy, or your preference in restaurants.

This Modern Liberal passion for creating massive new powers for the government did not begin in the 20th century. The most influential Modern Liberal thinker of all time was the 18th century philosophe Rousseau. He too had no use for constitutions, precisely because they limit the power of government. Remember, as we saw in Chapter Two, Rousseau believed the government should have absolute power, unrestricted by anything or anyone. It is worthwhile to quote Rousseau once more: *"The social compact…gives the body politic ABSOLUTE POWER over all its members."*[403] (Emphasis added.) Of course any government with absolute power will eventually impose either fascism or socialism. If Rousseau were alive today, he would certainly support the "Silly Putty" Constitution.

Modern Liberals view the Constitution as an inconvenient obstacle, because it gets in their way. In contrast, conservatives view the Constitution as sacred, because it represents the rule of law. To Modern Liberals, the rule of law not important. Instead, Modern Liberals prefer to follow Jeremy Bentham's utilitarian goal of "the greatest good for the greatest number of people." Unfortunately, following this goal leads to the immoral conclusion: "The ends justify the means." This attitude leads Modern Liberals to disregard the rule of law, and treat the Constitution with scorn.

For instance, on October 23rd 2009, House Speaker Nancy Pelosi held a press conference to support the proposed federal takeover of the health care industry. A conservative journalist (a rare bird indeed) asked her to identify which part of the Constitution gave Congress the power to control health care. Pelosi's arrogant response was revealing; *"Are you serious? Are you serious?!"*[404] Then she quickly turned away from him and took another question. No one in the room asked Ms. Pelosi if *she* was serious, because everyone knew she was deadly serious. Pelosi did not give a damn about the US Constitution. She thought federal health care was good for society, and that's all that mattered to her. Obviously to Ms. Pelosi, "The ends justify the means."

Unfortunately, since 1938 the majority of judges on the US Supreme Court has generally played along with these politicians, and supported the "Silly Putty" Constitution. One reason for this is because the judges personally favor bigger government. After all, they too are mostly Modern Liberals. Yet another reason is because the Silly Putty Constitution *gives the judges more personal power.* If the judges can interpret the Constitution using their own personal ideas about how society ought to be run, then the judges can wield great personal power. This means they too can play God. Some of them have come close to admitting this divine status. The Modern Liberal (Silly Putty) judge William O. Douglas bragged about his absolute power over society:

"We who have the final word can speak softly or angrily. We can seek to challenge and annoy, as we need not stay docile and quiet."[405]

The Modern Liberal judge William Brennan boasted that his god-like powers justified him in changing the Constitution however he wanted:

"...because WE ARE THE LAST WORD on the meaning of the Constitution, our views must be subject to revisions over time, or else the Constitution falls captive...to the anachronistic views of long-gone generations." [406](Emphasis added.)

Judge Brennan is conveniently forgetting one important fact. The Constitution contains within itself a mechanism for evolution and change. The Constitution permits amendments, which can be adopted to change the Constitution. The process can take a few years, but it is a very democratic way to alter the Constitution, because it requires two thirds of Congress and three quarters of the state legislatures to approve an amendment. However, the Modern Liberal judges on the Supreme Court prefer to change the Constitution all by themselves, and treat it like Silly Putty, in a power grab that is anything but democratic. This is a regression back to lex regia, i.e. *the law is whatever the people in power say it is*. It is further evidence of elitism within the Modern Liberal movement.

Brennan's lex regia attitude is in stark contrast to the conservative Founding Fathers. These men understood that a strictly enforced constitution is the only way to prevent the central government from growing oppressive:

"In all free states, the Constitution is fixed."[407] (Samuel Adams)

"In questions of power, let no more be heard of confidence in man, but bind him down from mischief by the chains of the Constitution."[408] (Thomas Jefferson)

"Do not separate the text from the historical background. If you do, you will have subverted the Constitution, which can only end in a distorted, bastardized form of illegitimate government."[409] (James Madison)

"On every question of construction, carry ourselves back to the time when the Constitution was adopted. Recollect the spirit manifested in the debates, and instead of trying whatever meaning may be squeezed out of the text, or invented against it, conform to the probable one in which it was passed."[410] (Thomas Jefferson)

In years past, the Supreme Court understood this principle, and honored it as the only sure safeguard of liberty. Back in 1905 the Supreme Court stated:

"The Constitution is a written document. As such, its meaning does not alter. That which it meant when it was adopted, it means now."[411]

The Silly Putty Constitution also violates our legal concept of the separation of powers. The judges who sit on the Supreme Court are not elected. These judges hold their power for life. The common people cannot vote them out of office. Therefore, their power should not be as expansive as the power of the legislature. In contrast, the legislature can be voted out of office. Therefore, only the legislature should have the power to make new law, not the Supreme Court. And even the legislature must be limited by a fixed Constitution. So when the Supreme Court makes a new law (or creates a new right, such as abortion or homosexual marriage) the judges are usurping the role of the legislature. Abraham Lincoln warned us of this danger:

"...if the policy of the government...is to be irrevocably fixed by decisions of the Supreme Court...the people will have ceased to be their own rulers..."[412]

The scholar M. Stanton Evans explains how modern Supreme Court judges are no better than tyrants from Alice in Wonderland:

"If the Constitution is merely whatever five justices can agree on at any given time, then the question is simply, as Humpty Dumpty put it, 'Who shall be master?'...This is a recipe for arbitrary power."

BARACK OBAMA'S ABUSE OF POWER

As we learned in Chapter One, the "law of the land" is the sum total of our ancient Anglo-Saxon liberties, as they were developed and augmented through centuries of English common law. This law of the land was eventually codified in our Bill of Rights. Whenever the Supreme Court "makes a law" then America is no longer ruled by the law of the land. Instead we are ruled by lex regia, which means the law is whatever five fatuous judges say it is. This is why the election of Barack Obama was such a devastating blow to liberty. In a stunning 2001 interview on an Illinois Public Radio station, Mr. Obama implied that he wanted to change the structure and purpose of our government, by changing our interpretation of the Constitution:

"As radical as I think people tried to characterize the Warren court, it wasn't that radical...It didn't break free from the essential constraints that were placed by the Founding Fathers in the Constitution... Generally the Constitution is a charter of negative liberties. It says what the states can't do to you, says what the federal government can't do to you. But it doesn't say what the federal or state government must do on your behalf."[413]

Apparently Mr. Obama wants to "break free" from two and a half centuries of Constitutional law. He no longer wants the Constitution to be a chain that restricts the government. In other words, Obama no longer wants to interpret the Constitution as a *negative* document. Instead, Obama wants to re-interpret the Constitution as a *positive* document, in order to justify creating new powers for the government.

This is almost certainly what Obama meant just before his 2008 election, when he said; *"We are five days away from fundamentally transforming the United States of America."* Apparently not many people took his statement seriously. That was a grave mistake. Obama's method for transforming America is proving to be simple, effective, and very dangerous. At the time of this writing, Obama has already appointed two radical Modern Liberals to the Supreme Court; women who share his authoritarian interpretation of the Constitution as a "positive" document, instead of a negative one. Under this new interpretation, the government will assume new powers to act *"on your behalf."* Obama's activist judges will create new "duties" for the government to take care of us, as if we were infant children or sheep, who need big Daddy government to nurture us.

Here's proof. In his 2008 campaign, Obama repeatedly said that his chief criteria for selecting Supreme Court judges would be, *"how much sympathy they have for poor people in our country."* Obama did not say anything about honesty or scholarship. He did not mention how seriously his nominee would take her oath of office. Obviously Obama is appointing judges who will decide cases based on their own personal feelings of "social justice," instead of applying the law impartially. Read Obama's own words:

"We need somebody who's got the heart, the empathy to recognize what it's like to be a young teen-age mom, the empathy to understand what it's like to be poor, or African-American, or gay, or disabled or old. AND THAT'S THE CRITERIA BY WHICH I'M GOING TO BE SELECTING MY JUDGES."[414] (Emphasis added.)

This explains why Obama is appointing judges who will create what Modern Liberals have long dreamed of: *a constitutional right to welfare.* Unfortunately this will impose a commensurate "duty" on working people to support the newly enshrined class of parasites (and also pay for the army of bureaucrats who will attend to their needs).

It is very tempting for undisciplined minds to use government power to "change the world." Lots of other men throughout history shared Obama's grandiose dream of expanding government power to change society. Similar men throughout history included: Lycurgus, Julius Caesar, Oliver Cromwell, Pol Pot, Mussolini, Stalin, Hitler, Mao

Tse Tung, Bela Kuhn, Fidel Castro, Che Guevara, Kim Il Soon, etc. Of course Obama does not have the same evil intent as these other notorious social engineers. Obama may even have noble motives, such as helping the poor. However, he will still impose new burdens on the tax-payers. He will still pervert the Constitution to legitimize socialism. He will still create massive new government powers. He will still destroy individual freedom.

So while Obama does not have the same evil intent as Stalin, the end result of his expansion of government power could easily be the same, after a few generations have come and gone. Daniel Webster once pointed out that it is irrelevant whether a leader has good or bad intentions. If any leader increases government power beyond the Constitution, then he is a danger to liberty:

"Good intentions will always be pleaded for every assumption of authority. The Constitution was made to guard the people against the dangers of good intentions. There are men in all ages who mean to govern well, but they mean to govern. They promise to be good masters, but they mean to be masters."

WELFARE AS A "RIGHT"

Like most Modern Liberals, Obama believes that poor people have a "right" to welfare payments. However, this idea is a gross distortion of the word "right." It turns the definition of a "right" upside down. According to the past 500 years of English common law, *a right is anything you may do which does not infringe upon other people.* John Stuart Mill entertained many Modern Liberal ideas. However, even he admitted that one man's "right" cannot infringe on another man's freedom:

"The only freedom…is that of pursuing your own good in your own way, SO LONG AS YOU DO NOT ATTEMPT TO DEPRIVE OTHERS OF THEIR'S." (Emphasis added.)

So for example, Bill has the right to free speech. However, that does not mean Tommy has any obligation to listen to Bill's speech. Tommy is free to ignore Bill and walk away from him. So Bill's right to free speech does not infringe on anyone. His right to free speech does not impose any obligations on anyone else.

However, so-called "welfare rights" do indeed infringe upon other people. For example, if Bill has a right to welfare, then Tommy must pay more in taxes to support Bill and millions more people like him. This burden on Tommy to pay more in taxes is an infringement on Tommy's right to keep his own property. It will also force Tommy to work longer hours, and so cause him to spend less time with his own family.

Things like welfare payments, government health care, subsidized housing, and corporate welfare, *impose a financial burden upon tax-payers*, by forcing them to give up their wealth in order to pay for it all. The "right" to welfare is really an infringement on the property rights of tax-payers. Therefore, "welfare rights" are not really rights at all. "Welfare rights" are really just *impositions* masquerading as rights.

THE ENGLISH EXPERIMENT

As bad as big government is becoming in America, the situation is worse in England. The people of England are living under an even more oppressive version of lex regia. However, in England, this usurpation of power is not being committed by a grasping group of judges. In England, lex regia is being imposed by a grasping group of legislators, better known as Parliament.

The 17th century tyranny of Oliver Cromwell destroyed the checks and balances in the old English legal system. Before Cromwell, legal scholars such as the great Edward Coke (pronounced "Cook") boasted that the English people enjoyed permanent liberties that could never be taken away by either King or Parliament. The English courts would strike down laws that violated the law of the land, (just as the US Supreme Court still occasionally strikes down laws that violate the Constitution). In 1610 the venerable Coke overruled Parliament, saying; *"...when an Act of Parliament is against common right and reason, or repugnant or impossible to be performed, THE COMMON LAW will control it and ajudge such Act to be void."*[415] (Emphasis added.)

Edward Coke was equally willing to overrule the King. Coke bravely went against James I, ruling that King James had violated the law of the land when he granted royal monopolies to certain businessmen: *"...all monopolies are against the Great Charter, because they are against the liberty and freedom of the subject, and against THE LAW OF THE LAND."*[416] (Emphasis added.)

Oliver Cromwell changed all this, forever. Under Cromwell's iron rule, Parliament assumed absolute power. This explains why, barely a century after the great jurist Coke passed away, the next famous English legal scholar, Blackstone, starkly described the new relationship between Parliament and the courts:

"No court has power to defeat the intent of the legislature, when couched in such evident and express words, as to leave no doubt concerning its intention."

This was a radical change in English law. Under Cromwell, Parliament first tasted absolute power, and it has remained addicted to absolute power ever since. This explains why, after Cromwell, no English court has successfully overturned an act of Parliament.[417] The law in England now is truly whatever comes out of parliament's collective mouth.

You may recall from Chapter One, that five centuries earlier King Richard II claimed the law was whatever came out of his mouth. He was deposed for his arrogance. Yet Parliament has successfully usurped this same absolute power for itself. Parliament now enjoys a level of despotism that King Richard could only dream of. England, like America, now lives under the rule of lex regia, and not the law of the land.

TYRANNY BY COMMITTEE

As a result of Cromwell's dictatorship, there is no more law of the land in England. There is now only the law that is decreed by Parliament. Legally speaking, the people of England now live under a tyranny by committee. The tyrants who rule England (the members of Parliament) are elected and therefore frequently replaced, but they are tyrants nonetheless. Whether or not a leader is elected does not determine whether he is a tyrant. In Federalist Paper #47, James Madison explained that *tyranny can come from elected politicians just as easily as from a military dictator:*

"The accumulation of all powers, the legislative, executive and judiciary, in the same hands, whether of one, a few, or many, and whether

hereditary, self appointed or elective, may justly be pronounced the very definition of tyranny."

Charles James Fox was England's greatest advocate for civil rights during the 18th century. Fox also understood that any government with unrestricted power was a danger to society. He proclaimed himself to be; *"the enemy of all absolute forms of government, whether an absolute monarchy or an absolute democracy."* So a tyranny is any type of government which has no limits on its power. Unfortunately, the English Parliament has no limits on its power.[418] As historian James Bovard noted:

"A democratic government that respects no limits on its power is a ticking time bomb, waiting to destroy the rights it was created to protect."

Modern Liberals believe that a legislature (such as Parliament) with absolute power is still better than a monarch with absolute power. First of all, this claim is probably doubtful. But more importantly, it is also irrelevant. You see, even if tyrannical legislatures are slightly "better" than tyrannical monarchs, *they are still very bad*. It is much better to have a government *with limited powers*. This can only be achieved with a written constitution, which incorporates the ancient law of the land.

Furthermore, a legislature with absolute power can be even worse than a cruel monarch. An evil monarch may well be replaced by an enlightened heir. However, once an assembly of men (such as a Parliament) obtains absolute power, the enjoyment of this power becomes institutionalized within the assembly itself. Older members preserve it and new members quickly learn to enjoy it. Therefore, the collective exercise of absolute power tends to become permanent.

To reform an abusive king, you only need to convince one man (the king) to reform. To reform an abusive legislature, you can only replace a majority of them in an election, and simply hope for the best. Sadly, as we will see in the next chapter, voting in a new majority is not really a solution in England or the United States. This is because the candidates offered by the two main political parties in both nations are nearly identical. When the candidates are so similar, elections become useless.

Even back in the 19th century, the libertarian Lysander Spooner noticed that the right to vote does not protect individual liberty:

"The second body of legislators are liable to be just as tyrannical as the first. If it be said that the second body was chosen for their integrity, the answer is, that the first were also chosen for that very reason, and yet proved to be tyrants."[419]

Finally, even if the tyrannical legislature has good intentions, it can still be highly oppressive with its power. As C.S. Lewis observed:

"Of all tyrannies, a tyranny exercised for the good of its victims may be the most oppressive. It may be better to live under robber barons than under omnipotent moral busy-bodies. The robber baron's cruelty may sometimes sleep, his cupidity may sometimes be satiated. But those who torment us for our own good will torment us without end, for they do so with the approval of their own conscience."

Parliament's effort to ban guns is a perfect example of this well-intentioned tyranny. In an attempt to make people safer, the government outlawed guns. As we saw in Chapter Five, the gun ban made crime much worse. Now Parliament refuses to re-consider the gun ban, because of the Modern Liberal delusion that banning guns will reduce crime. This means a freely elected Parliament is violating our most basic human right (the right to self-defense) "with the approval of their own conscience."

So the vital issue is not what form of government we have. The truly vital issue is "how much power does the government have over our lives?" This is the crucial question, regardless of whether we live under monarchy, oligarchy, democracy or a republic. If the government's power is not limited by a strictly enforced constitution, then it will eventually become tyrannical, and crush individual freedom.

DEMOCRACIES ARE TEMPORARY

An 18th century Scotsman named Alexander Tyler Fraser observed that democracies are temporary and only last about two hundred years. He argued that democracies are doomed to collapse because of economic cannibalization. Fraser observed that when enough voters realize that they can elect leaders who will give them money from the public treasury, then the nation's leaders go on wild spending sprees. The politicians will simply spend public money in a manner that pays back their political supporters. In fact, the US government has been on this same self-destructive path ever since the administration of FDR. After the administration of Lyndon Johnson, this process has only accelerated.

Eventually the democracy is plunged deeper and deeper into debt. Soon international banks will decide that the democracy is not credit worthy. Suddenly the democracy cannot borrow money to meet its obligations to creditors. Next (as we saw in Chapter Four) the government panics and prints excess money so it can pay its obligations. Inflation explodes. People lose their life savings through no fault of their own. This causes economic chaos. This chaos provides the opportunity for a dictator to take over. As John Adams observed:

"Democracy never lasts long. It soon wastes, exhausts and murders itself. There never was a democracy that didn't commit suicide."[420]

This theory very accurately describes the fall of the Roman Republic. Sadly, it also describes the United States today. Just like Rome, the number of people living off public assistance has grown overwhelming. Like Rome, our trade deficit is bleeding wealth out of our nation, and our government is deeply in debt. And like Rome, our leaders routinely violate the Constitution, by creating new powers for themselves, while they buy votes with government spending.

Both political parties in America are to blame for our modern crisis. Republican politicians have preached the virtues of a balanced budget for many decades. Yet they proved to be hypocrites when they ruled Congress from 1994 to 2006. In that time they frequently increased government spending at alarming rates. The Democrats took over Congress with the election of 2006, and predictably, the Democrats only made a bad situation worse. When the incoming Democratic Speaker of the House, Nancy Pelosi, took office in January of 2007, she promised there would be, *"No new deficit spending."* At that time the national debt stood at 8.6 trillion dollars. However, by October 24th, 2010, the national debt had risen to 13.5 trillion dollars.[421] So in less than three years, the Democrats used deficit spending to add another 4.9 trillion dollars to the national debt.

This massive spending brings us back to the mortgage meltdown and stock market crash of 2008, and the trillion dollar bailouts that both parties forced upon the backs of American tax-payers.[422] The worst part of their 2008-2009 spending spree was that it rewarded irresponsible people, and punished responsible people. Socialism always causes this perverse result. For example, if you were an *irresponsible* local banker who made risky loans (on the foolish assumption that home prices would continue to rise forever) then the bailouts helped you. If you were an *irresponsible* international banker who dishonestly sold thousands of these risky loans, calling them "mortgage backed securities," then the bailouts helped you. If you were an *irresponsible* foreign banker who foolishly purchased these securities without knowing what they were really worth, then the bailouts helped you.

However, if you were a *responsible* person who did not borrow more money than you could pay back, then *the bailouts will hurt you*. You will be paying higher taxes for decades to come. Your children will be hurt in the same way, when they start paying taxes. Ironically, the politicians of both parties told us that we needed the great Wall Street bailouts because otherwise, foreign banks would no longer issue new loans to the federal government, to finance our annual budget deficit.

This is ironic because scaring foreign bankers is actually the best argument *against* the bailouts. If foreign banks become so frightened that they will no longer finance our budget deficits, then our own government would be forced to maintain balanced budgets every year. The federal government would be forced to behave responsibly, and this might prevent the economic chaos that usually destroys democracy. Unfortunately, we appear to be in the final stage of democracy, just a decade or two before economic collapse. It seems Alexander Tyler Fraser was right after all.

As with most problems we face, if the Constitution had been strictly followed, this whole mess would never have happened. If we had followed the Constitution, the Federal Reserve Bank would never have been created. This would have prevented the Fed from keeping interest rates artificially low. Therefore, the risky sub-prime mortgage market would never have been created. Also, if we had followed the original intent of the Constitution, then Fannie Mae would never have been created either. Without Fannie Mae, the banks would have been more careful about who they lent money to. Instead, Fannie Mae encouraged reckless lending when they assured banks that the government would purchase their sub-prime mortgages. This further inflated the real estate bubble and made the inevitable collapse far worse. The beast always needs chains.

THE SHADOW GOVERNMENT: THE FEDERAL RESERVE BANK

The official web site operated by the Federal Reserve Board says flatly, *"No one owns the Federal Reserve Bank."*[423] This is a naked lie. The ownership of the Fed has simply been concealed from the public with a clever shell game. The Fed is made up of twelve "Regional" Reserve Banks. These twelve regional banks have all issued shares of stock as ownership. *These shares are owned by very powerful private banks.* These private banks are in turn owned by the wealthy men who own the majority of the shares of these same private banks. So indirectly at least, the Federal Reserve Bank is owned by some of the wealthiest and best connected men in America.

The Fed can also create money out of thin air. The Fed can create money just by making an accounting entry in a ledger it maintains with the Treasury Department. Yet the Fed charges interest on these "loans" to the Treasury Department. This means that the Fed automatically creates a profit for itself. (Congress currently limits this profit to 6%.) The Fed can also create new money by merely typing ledger entries that show loans going out to its member banks at the low "discount window" rate. The member banks then loan that same money to the Treasury Department. These member banks also charge interest, which the Treasury Department (i.e. the tax-payer) must pay.

Not only can the Fed create money out of thin air, but it also controls the pace of our economy through its influence over interest rates. These two powers have given the Fed so much influence that it has quietly become even more powerful than the Congress which created it.[424] However, unlike the other three branches of government, there are no effective checks or balances against the Fed's power. According to Federal law, (31 USC 714(b)) no other branch of the government is

The Big Picture

allowed to examine the Fed's books. No one outside the Fed knows what they have done with the *three trillion dollars* the Fed created (and spent) from July of 2007 through December of 2009. This money was above and beyond the so-called "TARP" (Troubled Assets Relief Program) money that the media focused its attention on in the fall of 2008. The Fed's creation of money dwarfed anything done by either Congress or the Treasury Department, yet it received virtually no news coverage. Senator Bernie Sanders was suitably appalled:

"We spend hours and hours arguing over ten million dollar amendments on the floor of the Senate, but there has been no discussion about who has been receiving this three trillion dollars…It's beyond comprehension."[425]

The Fed has only told Congress that the money was handed over to *"qualified lending institutions."* During Congressional testimony, Representative Alan Grayson pressed the Fed's Vice Chairman, Donald Khon, by asking him exactly where the trillions of dollars had gone. The Congressman wanted to know the names of the banks which had received this welfare, i.e. huge sums of government money in exchange for the banks' worthless "derivative debts." Kohn refused to budge an inch. He refused to tell Congress where the money went. The tax-payers were simply going to be billed for money that the Fed had given away to unknown banks.

Why did this happen? Because a few very large banks and insurance companies (e.g. AIG and Goldman Sachs) had gone wild by placing wagers on strange new financial instruments they had created. They deliberately concocted these weird new financial instruments in order to avoid traditional securities regulations. They made bets on whether the underlying mortgages behind Mortgage Backed Securities would go into default. They even bet on mortgages they had no financial interest in. Goldman-Sachs actually placed multiple bets on these dubious financial products, which they called "derivatives," and "credit default swaps."[426]

This was no different than going to Las Vegas and placing multiple bets on a college football game. If the commercial bankers won their risky bets, they would make millions in bonuses. If they lost these bets, they were counting on their friends in the government to bail them out.

The only sucker in this rigged game was the poor tax-payer. In the 19th century, the Governor of the Bank of England, Thompson Hankey, warned how foolish it would be to assure bankers that their reckless investments would be covered by the government. When approached about such a plan (under the theory that some banks were "too big to fail"), he replied, *"I cannot think of anything more likely to encourage rash and imprudent speculation."*[427]

Sure enough, in the second half of 2007, the reckless bets placed by these greedy bankers finally started to go bad. The "rash and imprudent" bankers did not have nearly enough money to cover the bets they had made. Therefore, AIG and Goldman Sachs went to the government for some corporate welfare. First the Fed came to their rescue. But the corruption of our government did not stop there. The Treasury secretaries under Bush Jr. (Secretary Paulson) and Obama (Secretary Geithner) were also both happy to oblige. Both of these bureaucrats had professional and personal connections with Goldman Sachs. Goldman Sachs was the single biggest purchaser of delinquent "bets" that were sold by AIG. So the bailout of AIG enabled AIG to pay off Goldman Sachs.

This means the AIG bailout was really a bailout for Goldman Sachs. According to the New York Times, the US government bailout of AIG saved Goldman Sachs from suffering a 12.9 billion dollar loss in 2009. Then the CEO of Goldman Sachs, Lloyd Blankfein, took a nine million dollar bonus for 2009. Why not? After all, the bailout made 2009 an awfully good year for Goldman Sachs. Remember, welfare for the rich is far more wasteful than welfare for the poor, because it is less direct. The federal government spent billions so Goldman Sachs executives could skim off mere millions for themselves.

The arrogant behavior of the Fed in 2008 and 2009 was not just welfare for the rich. It was also a dangerous transfer of power from an elected Congress to the bankers on the Federal Reserve Board. Thomas Jefferson and Andrew Jackson both warned us about the dangers of a central bank long ago. They knew that a central bank would have control over both the money supply and interest rates. They warned us that these central bankers would manipulate the money supply and interest rates for the benefit of themselves and their cronies in the private banking industry.

We modern folk have ignored the warnings of Jefferson and Jackson. As a result, the most powerful banking executives in America (the men who run Goldman Sachs, Chase, and Morgan Stanley) have quietly gained control over our money supply. Along with this power they have also gained de facto control over the US Treasury Department. Political analyst Matt Taibbi, describes the terrible damage that Wall Street and the Fed have jointly inflicted upon America:

"...a kind of revolution, a coup d'etat. They cemented and formalized...the gradual takeover of the government by a small class of connected insiders, who used money to control elections, buy influence, and systematically weaken the financial system."[428]

MODERN LIBERALISM VS CIVIL RIGHTS

Hopefully by now you realize that Modern Liberals are a much greater threat to individual freedom than conservatives are. A conservative may seek to screen your cell phone calls to see if you are speaking in Arabic. He may want to know if you are visiting the public library to borrow books on how to make bombs. However, for the past eighty years, Modern Liberals have tried to take away your right to free speech, your right to property, your right to free exercise of religion, and even your basic human right to self-defense.

Let's look at the historical record. In regard to free speech, it was the Modern Liberal Clinton administration that obtained court orders to prevent citizens from protesting against new welfare housing ("Section Eight" housing) in their neighborhoods. The Clinton administration argued that the right of poor people to obtain subsidized housing was *more important than the neighbors' free speech rights* to protest against such housing. Fortunately the Supreme Court back then was more concerned with the traditional civil right of free speech, and less concerned about the socialist "right" to free housing. The court ruled against the Clinton administration, and the protests were permitted.

The McCain-Feingold Campaign Gag Law (officially called the Campaign Finance Reform Act of 2002) was another Modern Liberal effort to restrict free speech. Shockingly, for eight long years the Supreme Court accepted most of this brazen restriction on free political speech. Modern Liberals claim this law only prevented "corporations" from making political donations. In reality, it restricted the free speech of any 527(c) organization. As a result, conservative political groups such as the NRA and Right to Life were prevented from running any campaign advertisements that criticized a candidate by name within two months of a general election. Modern Liberal views were still presented overwhelmingly on the three major television networks, most cable news programs, and on National Public Radio. So this law effectively eliminated only conservative opinions. That is why so many Modern Liberals supported the Campaign Gag Law. Fortunately, this pernicious law was finally struck down by the Supreme Court in 2010.

In regard to taking away our property rights, it was Modern Liberal politicians at the city government level who began aggressively seizing private homes in the 1990s, and forcing home owners to sell their houses to local governments. The local governments then turned around and sold the properties to commercial developers. Why did local Modern Liberal politicians force these sales? The new store owners would pay more in taxes than the home owners could. Modern Liberals claimed that increasing tax revenue was a "public use," under the Constitution.

Unfortunately, in 2005, the Modern Liberal judges on the Supreme Court agreed with these greedy local politicians.[429] For the previous 230 years, a "public use" had been limited to seizing land for a public road, a public school, a public library or a public hospital. But the court created a new definition of "public use," turning a blind eye to individual liberty. Public use now means anything that will increase government revenue. This new seizure policy was enshrined as constitutional law. Only the conservative judges disagreed, but of course they were the minority.

In regard to freedom of religion, we already discussed in Chapter Six several examples of Modern Liberal pressure groups trying to prevent Christians from praying in public, in school, or at any government function. These efforts invariably come from Modern Liberal groups such as the ACLU and People for the American Way. It is only Modern Liberals (not conservatives) who impose racial quotas for education, employment, and government contracts. Racial quotas violate our right to equal protection under the 14th Amendment.

Finally, it is nearly always Modern Liberals who want to take away the basic human right of self-defense. It is a Modern Liberal article of faith that private ownership of guns should be abolished. If this is ever enacted, then women, old people, the weak, and the handicapped, will all be completely vulnerable to being robbed, raped, or murdered. Common sense tells us that the right to self-defense is the most basic human right of all. Only Modern Liberals want to take away this right.

In response to all this evidence of Modern Liberal opposition to civil rights, Modern Liberals claim that the conservative opposition to abortion is an effort to take away a civil right from women. However, this argument is highly problematic. After all, opposing abortion can also be seen as a conservative effort *to protect the civil rights of unborn babies.*

MODERN LIBERAL CONFESSIONS

The fact that Modern Liberals are a greater threat to freedom than conservatives will no doubt surprise many readers. History professors rarely admit that Modern Liberals favor burgeoning government power at the expense of individual liberty. However, not only does the historical record support this conclusion, but the most influential Modern Liberals of all time have openly admitted that *the essence of liberalism is the pursuit of sheer power*; wielded by an omnipotent government. For example, Democratic Senator Joseph Clark, former head of the Americans for Democratic Action, defined a "liberal" as:

"...one who believes in USING THE FULL FORCE OF GOVERNMENT for the advancement of social, political, and economic justice at the municipal, state, national, and international levels...subject to the popular will, in the interests of social justice."[430] (Emphasis added.)

This quote does not show any concern for individual liberty, civil rights, or the Constitution. According to Senator Clark, nothing should limit the power of government except "the popular will." Ever since Modern Liberals embraced the philosophy of Rousseau, they accepted his dream of a government with absolute power. This is why Modern Liberals prefer to have no limitations on government power.

One of the most influential Modern Liberals in the first half of the 20th century was Herbert Croly. He ran the Modern Liberal publication *New Republic* during the 1920's and 1930's, and he greatly influenced the men who ran FDR's administration. In the 1930's, conservative critics challenged Croly to identify any real differences between FDR's New

Deal programs and the nearly identical programs created by Mussolini's fascist state. Conservatives also challenged Croly to define liberalism so it could be distinguished from fascism. Mr. Croly refused.[431] Croly even denied the existence of any "liberal principles." Instead he said, *"Liberalism is an activity."* This is disturbingly similar to Mussolini's famous shorthand definition for fascism; *"Fascism is action!"* Yet without any limiting principles, then liberalism is simply whatever liberals choose to do with government power.

Some Modern Liberals are positively brazen about their preference for authoritarian rule. The Modern Liberal film director Woody Allen recently said: *"It would be good…if he (Obama) could be dictator for a few years, because he could do a lot of good things quickly."*[432] While most Modern Liberals in America do not support dictatorship, still, the impetus for authoritarianism only comes from among Modern Liberals. No significant conservative in America has ever wished for dictatorship.

This preference for authoritarianism can be found in nearly all of the famous champions of Modern Liberalism, such as Saint-Pierre, Rousseau, Comte, Marx, John Dewey, George Bernard Shaw, H.G. Wells, Herbert Croly, and Herbert Marcuse. In contrast, the famous philosophers of conservatism seek the opposite. They seek limited government which permits the most freedom possible. This is true for all the great conservative scholars, including Edmund Burke, Thomas Jefferson, Algernon Sydney, Frederic Bastiat, Ludwig Von Mises, Russell Kirk, Ayn Rand, William Buckley, Thomas Sowell, and Robert Higgs.

"THE POPULAR WILL"

As we discussed earlier, without a strictly enforced Constitution, democracy is nothing more than mob rule. This means that *democracy can be just as oppressive as dictatorship*. Even the French socialist Pierre-Paul Prudhon admitted that majority rule without any restrictions can be very dangerous:

"Democracy is nothing but the Tyranny of Majorities, the most abominable tyranny of all, for it is not based on the authority of a religion, not upon the nobility of a race, not on the merits of talents and of riches. It merely rests upon numbers and hides behind the name of the people."[433]

This problem was evident in ancient Athens. Their democratic government did not have any guarantees of personal freedom. This was because ancient Athens did not place any limits on government power. Therefore, if the majority voted to execute someone because of the color of his hair, nothing could stop them. Socrates found this out the hard way, when a majority of the people voted to execute him simply because of his ideas. This explains why it is no comfort at all when a Modern Liberal politician such as Senator Joseph Clark promises us that government power will be *"subject to the popular will."*

This Modern Liberal delusion that the popular will can protect individual liberty is not just some accidental development. This delusion is actually central to the ideology of Modern Liberalism. In order to give new powers to the government, Modern Liberals must ignore the Constitution, and treat it like Silly Putty. However, if the Constitution no longer protects us from oppression, what does? Even Modern Liberals know that we need *something* to protect individual freedom. But remember, they have turned the Constitution into Silly Putty. This is why Modern Liberals pretend that "the popular will" can protect us. It is their feeble substitute for Constitutional protection.

History shows us that "the popular will" is no protection at all. For example, in the 19th century, President Jackson illegally forced the Cherokee Indians off their land in Georgia. This terrible injustice was very popular among Southern voters. Therefore, this evil act was perfectly consistent with *"the popular will."* In the 20th century, FDR forced innocent Japanese Americans to leave their homes, and to live behind barbed wire at internment camps that were no better than prisons. This cruel deed was politically popular in America, so once again "the popular will" was worthless as a protection against tyranny and injustice. Furthermore, the Jim Crow laws that discriminated against black people were very popular among the majority (white) population. By following "the popular will" we treated blacks as second class citizens for a hundred years.

In all three of these cases, if the Constitution had been followed, these crimes would never have occurred. It is the Constitution that protects us from tyranny, not the popular will. The problems only occur when we fail to strictly follow the Constitution. When we fail to obey it, tyranny and injustice result. Any type of government (democracy, republic, or dictatorship) will eventually violate our civil rights, unless it is restricted by a fixed constitution.

Modern Liberals usually respond to these charges with something like this; "We are more civilized today than in previous generations, and today's population will not tolerate injustice." This plea is so naïve as to be pathetic. The government is committing new cruelty and new injustice everyday. Right now, in many states, a terrible injustice is being inflicted on men who are falsely accused in state court paternity actions. In California for example, if a woman falsely tells the county welfare office that you are the father of her newborn baby, the county will send you a legal notice (by regular mail) to the address the woman gives them. This legal notice tells you the court date on which you may appear to dispute your paternity.

Here is the problem. If the letter miscarries, or if the address is incorrect, then the court will enter a default judgment against you.[434] The court will simply declare you to be the father, *and you cannot appeal this ruling*. The state will then garnish your wages and your bank account to get support money for "your" child. Even if you later obtain DNA evidence proving that you are not the father, it is irrelevant under California law. The default judgment cannot be overturned. This injustice has trapped thousands of innocent men. Most of them have their own families to support. Yet no one seems to care. The will of the people is very apathetic to this injustice.[435]

The federal government is no better. Right now the federal government is sponsoring an epidemic of racial quotas that are discriminating against white people and Asian people who seek contracts with the federal government. Ironically, polls consistently show that the vast majority of Americans *of all ethnic groups* are opposed to racial quotas.[436] So the will of the people is simply being ignored by Supreme Court judges, who are also happy to ignore the Constitution. Obviously the will of the people is no protection from anything. Yet if we had strictly followed the Constitution (i.e. the equal protection clause of the 14th Amendment), then we would have prevented this terrible injustice. Once again we ignore the Constitution at our peril.

GLOBALISM: OPPRESSION WITHOUT LIMITS

We already discussed the failings of the UN Declaration on Human Rights back in Chapter Three. But another danger of world government is that it is not limited by any kind of "law of the land." The global government determines for itself the reach of its own powers. This is a recipe for abuse of power. John Foster Dulles was one of the most well connected men in the international globalist network. Dulles realized that the UN would have no limits on its power, and he was honest enough to admit this was a potential problem:

"The Security Council is not a body that merely enforces agreed law. IT IS A LAW UNTO ITSELF. If it considers any situation as a threat to the peace, it may decide what measures shall be taken. No principles of law are laid down to guide it: it can decide in accordance with what it thinks expedient."[437] (Emphasis added.)

The recently created International Criminal Court (ICC) may be just as dangerous as the United Nations itself. First of all, this court (sometimes called "The World Court") is not obligated to follow any written constitution or law of the land. Therefore, it can trample on individual liberty as much as it likes. The second problem with the ICC is that *this court controls its own jurisdiction*. Any time a high court is created, an independent body (not connected to the court) should also be created, to put limits on the court's jurisdiction. Our Founding Fathers understood this. When they wrote the Constitution they restricted the Supreme Court's jurisdiction. The US Supreme Court cannot take on any cases unless the Constitution permits it. Furthermore, according to the Constitution, Congress can further restrict the types of cases that the Supreme Court may consider.

However, the statists and globalists who operate the World Court do not appreciate the concept of limited jurisdiction. Superficially, Article Seventeen of the Rome Statute (which created the ICC in 2002) would seem to set some limits on the ICC's jurisdiction. But in practice, the ICC has ignored Article Seventeen whenever they feel the urge to improperly take over a case. In these cases, the ICC slyly invokes Article Nine of the Rome Statute, which reads as follows: *"The court shall satisfy itself that it has jurisdiction in any case brought before it."*

Because the World Court controls the scope of its own power, we should not be surprised that the ICC has declared itself to have power over every nation on earth, including nations that have not even ratified the Rome Statute.[438] So the World Court is arrogantly *claiming authority over countries that never agreed to accept its authority*. This is nothing but a naked usurpation of power.

The ICC is not the only court that goes by the name "World Court." The other World Court is called the International Court of Justice, or ICJ. It has also seen fit to meddle in the internal affairs of sovereign nations. For example, the ICJ has tried to stop American state courts from executing Mexican citizens who have committed murder in the United States. Fortunately the US Supreme Court recently blocked the ICJ from enforcing its will upon the United States. However, the Supreme Court did so by a bare five judge majority. If just one more Modern Liberal (globalist) judge is appointed to the US Supreme Court, then America will give up its sovereignty over criminal justice.

GLOBAL WARMING AND GLOBAL GOVERNMENT

For three hundred years, the supporters of global government had only one justification for their dream: the prevention of war. Recently however, they have begun to exploit another rationalization for global government: global warming. This means that the recent scare campaign about global warming is dangerous in a political sense. It is dangerous because global warming is being used as a pretext to increase the power of the United Nations to impose global government. The following pages will expose the shoddy science behind the global warming movement, as well as the hidden motives that lie behind this new ideology.

First, let's look at how the news media have created climate scares in the past. Over a hundred years ago, the major newspapers (led by the New York Times) launched a thirty year campaign (from 1895-1926) to frighten us about global *cooling*.[439] Then from 1933 to the early 1950's, the NY Times changed gears and began warning us about global *warming*. Next, from 1958 to 1993, the NY Times switched back to scaring us about global *cooling* again. Now, and ever since the mid 1990's, the NY Times and the rest of the media have been trying to get us worried about global warming all over again.

In the past, every time the news media warned us about global cooling they always trotted out lots of "experts" to give us alarmist predictions. Of course the news media is doing exactly the same thing now with global warming. Here are just a few examples of the hysterical warnings we heard from the news media during the last climate scare of 1958-1993:

"The advent of a NEW ICE AGE, scientists say, appears to be guaranteed. The devastation will be astonishing."[440] (Gregg Easterbrook, *Newsweek*, November 23 1993, emphasis added.)

"Certain signs, some of them visible to the layman as well as to scientists, indicate that we have been watching an ICE AGE approach for some time…Scientists predict that it will cause great snows that the world has not seen since the last ice age."[441] ("The Coming Ice Age" *Harper's*, September 1958, emphasis added.)

"The threat of a new ice age must stand alongside nuclear war as a likely source of wholesale death and destruction."[442] (Nigel Calder, *International Wildlife*, June 1975.)

The New York Times has promoted the current climate scare about global warming more than any other media outlet. Sadly, nearly all the other big American newspapers and the big three television networks reflexively follow the NY Times for their national and international news stories, regardless of what the current scare story might be.[443] So the mere fact that all the other newspapers and talking heads are repeating the same claims about global warming is not persuasive. As Mark Twain said, *"If a hundred newspapers call a dog a cow, it's still a dog."*

As if to admit their mistake, the NY Times and the other papers are no longer calling it "global warming." Just to hedge their bets, the big media outlets are now calling it "climate change," because deep down they know that they have no idea what will happen to our climate in the future. There seems to be a twenty to thirty year cycle for these climate scare stories. If history is an indicator, then the current scare story about global warming should fizzle out by about 2018. In the meantime, it appears that our gullible political leaders will damage the economy by following the advice of fanatical people.

ERRORS BY AL GORE

Al Gore is the best known spokesman for the theory that man-made CO2 is causing significant global warming. His movie "An Inconvenient Truth" contained at least thirty-five important factual errors.[444] Gore's errors are so serious that the High Court of London decided his film could not be shown to school children unless equal time was also given for instruction pointing out Gore's factual errors.

Limitations of space permit us to look at only a few of Mr. Gore's mistakes. The Atlantic Gulf Stream is a strong current which warms northern Europe. Al Gore claims that the Gulf Stream is faltering because of global warming. It is not. The Gulf Stream current is just as strong as when it was first discovered and measured by Benjamin Franklin.[445] The Gulf Stream probably won't stop until the continents all come together again through plate tectonics. That event will be far in the future, and it will have nothing to do with global warming.

An even more glaring error is the false information Gore gives about the expected rise in sea levels. When Al Gore pulled this data from a legitimate report on sea levels, he somehow managed to misalign the decimal points, accidentally changing his numbers from centimeters to meters. As a result, Gore exaggerated the expected rise in sea level by a factor of ten.[446] So the sea level in New York City might rise by six centimeters, but not by six meters!

This brings up the most serious error committed by Mr. Gore. Even if the earth is warming, that does not mean humans are responsible for it. Al Gore failed to honestly consider how increased solar radiation has warmed the earth. Gore claims that man-made CO2 alone has caused the Arctic temperature to rise. However, if you look at a graph which shows both Arctic temperature and solar activity, you will find a very dramatic correlation. Arctic temperature consistently rises and falls with solar activity. Therefore, solar activity is probably causing the Arctic warming that so frightens Al Gore. In his movie, Al Gore conveniently fails to show these two graphs together. Early in his movie, he shows a graph of Arctic temperature, and later on he shows a graph of solar activity, but *Gore never shows the two graphs together*. In fact he cannot. It would undercut his whole message.

The planet Mars has experienced several decades of slightly increased surface temperature, virtually identical to earth's increase. Yet the CO2 levels on Mars are perfectly constant. They don't have any automobiles on Mars. They don't have any active volcanoes on Mars. *But Mars is affected by the sun.* Obviously these solar flares are warming up Mars. So how can Al Gore claim that solar flares are not warming up our own planet as well?

In fact, solar flares have been extremely active for the past seven decades. According to one of the most renowned solar scientists, Sami Solanki, (Director of the Sun-Heliosphere Department at the Max Planck Institute for Solar System Research); *"The level of solar activity in the past seventy years is exceptional, and the previous period of equally high activity occurred more than 8,000 years ago."* In fact, solar flares probably account for any global warming that has occurred for the past seventy years.

"SCIENTIFIC CONSENSUS"

For years, the global fear mongers cited a letter signed *"by 2,600 scientists"* which supposedly backed up their claim about man-made global warming. The press kept on citing that letter as proof of "scientific consensus." However, the press finally stopped citing this letter after conservative critics pointed out that it contained the signatures of very few real scientists. Instead, it was signed by several chiropractors, some entomologists, medical doctors, dentists, a hotel manager, seven linguists, two landscape architects, and one person who claimed to be certified to practice Chinese medicine. The letter was signed by only one qualified climatologist.[447] Immediately after conservative websites exposed this fraud, the mass media suddenly stopped referring to this bogus letter. It just disappeared from their news stories. No corrections or retractions were published.

The truth is, *there is no consensus* among true climate scientists (PhD climatologists) about the cause of global warming. Here's proof:

"The most recent survey of climate scientists, following the same methodology as a study published in 1996, found that…only 9.4% of respondents 'strongly agree' that climate change is mostly the result of anthropogenic (man-made) sources. A similar proportion 'strongly disagree.' Furthermore, only 22.8 % 'strongly agreed' that the IPCC reports accurately reflect a consensus within climate science." (Professor Dennis Bray, GKSS Forschungszentrum, Geesthacht

Germany, in an open letter to *Science Magazine*, which they refused to publish.)[448]

In 2006, sixty Canadian climatologists sent an open letter to the Canadian government, asking it to "re-open" the Kyoto treaty for debate, because it had not been objectively and honestly discussed. The letter read:

"When the public comes to understand that THERE IS NO 'CONSENSUS' among climate scientists about the relative importance of the various causes of global climate change, the government will be in a far better position to develop plans that reflect reality and so benefit both the environment and the economy."[449] (Emphasis added.)

FRAUD BY THE IPCC: "CENSORED DATA"

The first problem with the UN's Intergovernmental Panel on Climate Change (IPCC) is the way it produces its reports. This has been misunderstood for years. The IPCC really puts out *two* reports. The first report is a long document written by *real scientists*. The second report is called the "Summary for Policy Makers." This is the part the press always uses for their news stories. It is written by bureaucrats who want to keep their jobs in the global warming media complex. It is a *heavily edited summary* of the original scientific report.

The people who write this summary are bureaucrats who are appointed by politicians. Like any other government agency, the IPCC wants to justify its existence, in the hope of getting continued funding. In fact, these bureaucrats will only keep receiving money so long as they keep scaring people about global warming. This fact probably explains why their summaries have consistently been slanted, distorted, and deceptive. They invariably exaggerate the evidence in favor of man-made global warming, and they delete all the evidence against it.

This is not surprising. After all, the first chairman of the IPCC (Sir John Houghton) set the standard for the IPCC when he said, *"Unless we announce disasters no one is going to listen to us."*[450] Space limitations only permit us to look at two examples of their fraud. First of all, in the rough draft of the 1995 IPCC scientific report (which had been approved by the scientific committee of the IPCC), two important statements revealed that the IPCC's own scientists did not believe that man-made CO2 was causing global warming. The IPCC scientists stated:

"No study to date has positively attributed all or part of observed climate change to anthropogenic (man-made) causes."[451]

"None of the studies cited above has shown clear evidence that we can attribute the observed [climate] changes to the specific cause of increases in greenhouse gasses."[452]

However, in the final version of the 1995 report, these two sentences were somehow deleted. Instead, the following very unscientific statement was inserted by the IPCC bureaucrats:

"The balance of evidence suggests a discernable human influence on global climate."[453]

Sadly, the staff at the IPCC (including some of the scientists) has become so politicized that they have fraudulently altered some of their own data. Back in 1990, the IPCC published an accurate graph of the earth's surface temperature. This graph showed that it has been going up and down since 1000 AD. However, in the IPCC 2001 report, the same graph was altered to eliminate the "medieval warm period." As a result, the graph looked completely different. It now showed a steady earth temperature until 1900, when it suddenly surged higher. This act of fraud created the famous "hockey stick" graph that Al Gore loves to show people. It is false.[454] As if to drive home this false propaganda, the dubious graph was printed six times throughout the 2001 IPCC report, each time in full color.

Eventually the IPCC gave two Canadian scientists access to all of the scientific data which was used to produce the 2001 report. These two Canadians stumbled upon the missing data which showed there was indeed a severe global warming during the medieval warm period. The IPCC scientists had hidden this missing data in a computer file which they had appropriately named *"Censored Data."*[455] What can we conclude about a scientific organization that censors its own data? We must conclude that it is not really a scientific organization, but rather an advocacy group.

WHAT DO REAL EARTH SCIENTISTS SAY?

The most respected earth scientists are the ones who have already established their reputations. They already have tenure, and so they are less likely to let ambition and grant money influence their research. In contrast, the younger, less established scientists know that they will never get any grant money unless they support the man-made global warming orthodoxy. The global warming activists are well aware that the older scientists are the ones who doubt that man-made CO2 is causing global warming. The well known global warming zealot James Hansen remarked, *"Some of this noise (skepticism) won't stop until some of these scientists are dead."*[456] Let's see exactly what kind of "noise" these older men of science are making:

"Alarm rather than genuine scientific curiosity is essential to maintaining funding. And only the most senior scientists can stand up against this alarmist gale, and defy the iron triangle of climate scientists, advocates, and policy makers."[457] (MIT Professor Dr. Richard Lindzen.)

"The Greenhouse effect must play some role. But those who are absolutely certain that the rise in earth temperature is due solely to carbon dioxide have NO SCIENTIFIC JUSTIFICATION. It's just guess work."[458] (Henrik Svensmark, director of the Center for Sun-Climate Research, Danish National Space Center, emphasis added.)

"Scientists who want to attract…great funding for themselves have to find a way to scare the public…and this you can achieve only by making things bigger and more dangerous than they really are."[459] (Petr Chylek, professor of Physics and Atmospheric Science, Dalhousie University, Halifax, Canada.)

"Gore's circumstantial arguments are so weak that they are pathetic. It is simply incredible that they, and his film, are commanding public attention."[460] (Professor Bob Carter, Marine Geophysical Laboratory, James Cook University, Australia.)

In contrast to these qualified earth scientists, Al Gore is a politician. Even worse, Al Gore has a strong financial motive to support new laws against CO2 emissions. Al Gore and four other partners have formed a venture capital fund designed to make huge profits from global warming. These clever robber barons have shrewdly invested 75 million dollars into various "green" industries, but mostly into the CO2 "cap and trade" futures market. Al Gore has made himself the high priest of global warming, because he is hoping to make a fortune by exploiting federal legislation on global warming. He is well on his way to becoming the world's first "cap and trade billionaire."[461]

Several major corporations, such as British Petroleum, General Electric, and Cinergy, have also positioned themselves to gain billions in government money through new federal policies on global warming.[462] If the "cap and trade" bill that is currently before Congress passes, it will create the greatest tax increase in American history. Hundreds of billions will be wasted so that a mere few billions may be skimmed off by the rich. Again we see that welfare for the rich is the most wasteful welfare of all.

DARK MOTIVES BEHIND THE SCARE TACTICS

If the evidence to support man-made global warming is so pitifully weak, then why do Modern Liberals passionately believe in it? Like all the other self-delusions of Modern Liberalism, it is because *they want to believe in it*. They want to believe in it because man-made global warming pushes forward the two main goals of Modern Liberalism: globalism and socialism.

In regard to globalism, global warming is a perfect pretext for the United Nations to regulate the economies of the Western world, deciding how much industrial activity they may enjoy. This means the United Nations would determine the fate of every industrialized economy on earth. The global warming crusade is really an excuse to increase government control over the lives of the common people. So the real motive is authoritarianism, through a global government. For instance, French socialist (and ardent globalist) Jacques Chirac applauded the Kyoto protocol on global warming, calling it; *"...the first component of an authentic global governance."*[463]

In regard to socialism, the UN Copenhagen Summit on Climate Change requires the developed nations (rich people) to give trillions of dollars to undeveloped nations (poor people). Global warming activists sometimes admit that this redistribution of wealth lies at the heart of their cause:

"This is not a simple environmental issue where you can say it is an issue where scientists are not unanimous. This is about international relations, this is about the economy, about trying to create a level playing field for big business throughout the world."[464] (Margaret Wallstrom, EU Minister for the Environment.)

"Climate change [provides] the greatest chance to bring about justice and equality in the world."[465] (Christine Stewart, Canada's Minister for the Environment.)

If socialism is the real motive behind the global warming campaign, then it follows that the global warming activists must also oppose capitalism. Indeed, one UN aide actually admitted that the UN's "Global Compact" was an effort *"to end capitalism."*[466] Maurice Strong is one of the most powerful men behind the Green movement. Mr. Strong is the founder of the UN Eco-Summit and an undersecretary general of the UN. He is one of many radical environmentalists who hate all the conveniences we enjoy through industrial capitalism.

"Isn't the only hope for the planet that the industrialized civilizations collapse? Isn't it our responsibility to bring about?"[467]

Of course without industrialization we will all be forced to live like medieval peasants. Rational people are appalled at the prospect of enduring a medieval lifestyle. Yet some global warming fanatics are enchanted by romantic visions about how wonderful life will be without light bulbs, cars, grocery stores, refrigerators, heating, air conditioning, or even bathing.

"In short, if we can rise to the challenge, the permanent abolition of the wheel would have the marvelously synergistic effect of creating thousands of new jobs, as blacksmiths, farriers, grooms and so on, at the same time as it conserved energy and saved the planet from otherwise inevitable devastation."[468] (Catherine Bennett, The Guardian, UK.)

ACTIVISTS ADMIT LYING ABOUT GLOBAL WARMING:

Even Al Gore said it's perfectly all right to lie and exaggerate about global warming, because this will get people's attention. Of course being a politician, he did not use the words lie or exaggerate. Here are Al Gore's exact words; *"I believe it is appropriate to have an over-representation of factual presentations on how dangerous it is, as a predicate for opening up the audience to listen to what the solutions are, and how hopeful it is that we are going to solve this."*[469]

Other proselytes for the church of global warming are more blunt. Some of these alarmists openly claim they are morally justified to lie about global warming:

"NO MATTER IF THE SCIENCE IS ALL PHONY, there are still collateral environmental benefits to global warming policies" [470] (Christine Stewart, Canada's Minister for the Environment, emphasis added.)

"To capture the public imagination, we have to offer up some scary scenarios, to make simplified dramatic statements and little mention of any doubt one might have. EACH ONE OF US HAS TO DECIDE THE RIGHT BALANCE BETWEEN BEING EFFECTIVE AND BEING HONEST."[471] (Global warming activist Stephen Schneider, Discovery Magazine, October 1989, emphasis added.)

CONSERVATIVE TYRANNY?

The global warming crusade demonstrates that Modern Liberals can exploit almost any problem (even a non-existent problem) to encourage both globalism and socialism. In the process, they encourage tyranny. But what about conservative tyranny? Some conservatives have proven that they too can establish brutal and repressive regimes. For example, Francisco Franco in Spain and Augusto Pinochet in Chile were both conservative, and they were also tyrannical. However, it is crucial to remember that these two dictators had nothing to do with the *Status-Quo Conservatism of Anglo-Saxon culture.*

Conservative Latin dictators, such as Franco and Pinochet, had little more to do with Anglo-Saxon political traditions than did the conservative Chinese emperors or the conservative Iranian ayatollahs. Conservatism in Asian, African, Latino, Middle Eastern, and

Mediterranean cultures frequently leads to tyranny. However, conservatism *in Anglo-Saxon culture* consistently leads to limited government and greater individual freedom. This trend is no accident. It occurs because of the three foundations of liberty contained within the Anglo-Saxon legal tradition: government by consent, the law of the land, and property rights.

SOCIALISM AND SLAVERY

Everyone knows that socialism requires high taxes. What most people do not know is that high taxes are a form of oppression, much akin to slavery. After all, what is the essence of slavery? Slavery is forcing one person to work for the benefit of someone else. This is exactly what happens when a tax-payer is forced to pay his money to the government, in order to support people living on welfare. This is true whether the people living on welfare are sitting at home watching television, or sitting on the board of Archer-Daniels-Midland Inc.

Our wages represent our precious time on earth. We would much rather spend that time enjoying the company of family and friends than working. Yet the modern tax system makes us work twice as long as we would otherwise. Remember, the total burden of government consumes nearly half of the average income, through Social Security tax, Medicare tax, federal income tax, property tax, gasoline tax, car registration fees, state income tax, sales tax, excise taxes, phone taxes, utility taxes, etc. This means we must *work twice as long* to make up the loss. So when the government raises our taxes, the government forces us to spend more of our lives at work. Taxes take away more of our lives.

Comparing high taxes to slavery will no doubt surprise some people. After all, slavery was barbaric, and modern tax-payers don't suffer nearly the same torment that slaves did. However, the central element of slavery is still present in our modern tax system. For six months out of the year we are forced to work for someone else's benefit. Furthermore, our modern government treats delinquent tax-payers almost the same as disobedient slaves were treated in the Old South. In the Old South, if a slave refused to work for his master, the overseer would take the slave out of his shack (at gun-point), and have him flogged. Today, if you refuse to pay your taxes, federal agents will take you out of your house (at gun-point), and throw you in jail. The only real difference is the type of punishment inflicted.

Modern Liberals usually defend high taxes on businessmen and corporations by claiming that every business should "give back to the community." First of all, Modern Liberals forget that capitalists are already giving back to the community. Capitalists create jobs for other people, so these workers can support their own families. Capitalists also provide a product or service that people want to have. The capitalist can only make a profit if he provides something that other people want. Generally, the more people he satisfies the more money he makes. So the capitalist has already "paid back" society long before the tax collector knocks on his door.

This Modern Liberal appeal to "pay back society" is also based on a false assumption. It assumes that giving large amounts of money to the government will somehow help society. But as we saw in Chapter Four, government spending can only harm the economy, by destroying wealth. Increasing government spending with more tax dollars will only destroy more wealth. Furthermore, giving more tax money to the government may also cause political damage to the nation. Currently our leaders in Washington D.C. are plotting to merge the United States with Mexico and Canada to form one nation called "The North American Union." How exactly are we helping society if we give more money to these mad men?

DEBTORS' PRISON

Perhaps the most troubling aspect of our modern tax system is the ugly part, the part no one ever talks about: *enforcement*. In previous centuries, if you could not pay your debts, you were sent to debtors' prison. Eventually, Western society realized that debtors' prisons were bad for two reasons. First, they were counter-productive. A person who was put into debtors' prison could not possibly pay off his debt. This is because the debtor could not earn any money while in jail. Second, it was considered cruel to punish someone merely for not paying a debt. Perhaps the debtor was foolish to borrow the money, or perhaps misfortune prevented him from paying it back. Either way, it hardly justified a criminal punishment such as a prison sentence.

We ought to apply this same logic to people who fail to pay their debt to the government. If it is wrong to imprison a person for not paying a debt to the bank, then it is also wrong to imprison a person for not paying a debt to the government. Tax evaders should not be treated as criminals, and thrown into jail. In fact the tax debt is not even a real debt, not in the traditional sense of the word "debt." A true debt is an obligation you *voluntarily assume*. A true debt means you must pay back money that you have borrowed.

However, the delinquent tax-payer never borrowed any money from the government. Nor did he ever promise to pay any money to the government. The tax debt was imposed upon him without his consent. It was simply thrust upon him by the rulers who wrote the tax code. The tax debt was created out of thin air.

The fact that taxes are authorized by elected officials is not relevant here. That fact is only relevant when you are questioning the *legitimacy of a tax*. The question here is *the method of enforcement*. So even if federal income tax is a legitimate debt, this does not mean that prison time is a legitimate way to enforce that debt. The only legally accepted methods for enforcing a private debt are seizing assets and garnishing wages. These same methods should be the only methods used to enforce the payment of a tax debt.

THE GREAT CONFLICT: VOTING RIGHTS VS PROPERTY RIGHTS

High taxes are the result of one of the greatest conflicts in history: voting rights vs. property rights. As the majority of the people realize that they can vote to take money away from other people, this temptation becomes irresistible. More and more voters will elect leaders who promise to give them more money and benefits from the public purse. This is why democracy naturally leads to socialism. Eventually each new election becomes yet another feeding frenzy, where everyone tries to live off everyone else. This explains James Bovard's famous observation, *"Democracy must be something more than two wolves and a lamb voting on what to have for dinner."*

This tendency of democracy to breed parasitism and class warfare has inspired some conservatives to call for restrictions on voting rights. They point out that the American Revolution was mostly based on the principle, "Taxation without representation is tyranny." These conservatives argue that the opposite is also true. "Representation without taxation" is also tyranny. What do they mean by "representation without taxation?" This occurs when someone who does not pay any income tax is allowed to vote for politicians who promise to increase the income tax. In effect, these voters are voting for tax increases that they will never have to pay. They are voting to sponge off other people.

This injustice occurs every time a welfare recipient is allowed to vote. It is undeniable that welfare recipients have a strong financial motive to vote for whichever politician will increase their welfare benefits the most. After all, the government is their sole source of income. Sadly, politicians are quite eager to pander to this base motive. The English conservative Edmund Burke saw the danger of people voting to receive money from the public purse. This was why he warned us that *"an excess of democracy"* was just as dangerous as absolute monarchy.

Conservatives are quick to apply this logic to welfare recipients, but they fail to apply it to the beneficiaries of the military-industrial complex. Although these people do pay income tax, the argument can be made that anyone who works for a company that supplies military equipment or services to the Defense Department should also not be allowed to vote. After all, they too have a strong financial motive to vote for whichever politician will increase military spending. Just like the welfare recipient, they too are beneficiaries of other people's money. So their vote is also corrupted by their financial interest in the election.

The same is true for farmers who receive government subsidies. Under this reasoning, they also should not be allowed to vote. Their financial interest in the government purse naturally corrupts their vote. The same logic applies to anyone living on government checks, including fire fighters, police, judges, politicians, teachers, and in fact anyone living on Social Security.

Will this type of reform ever be adopted? Probably not. Will people keep on voting to plunder money from each other? Absolutely! Recently it has become fashionable for politicians to speak of "quintiles" of the population. This simply means separating the population into five groups based on income. Using this clever method, a politician can point to one segment of the population (usually the richest) and say, "This one group of people will have to pay higher taxes, but not the rest of you." Naturally the other four fifths of the population will eagerly vote in favor of this "social justice." Therefore, even people who do not receive any government benefits are starting to play plunder politics.

This sort of class warfare escalated under President Barack Obama. In 2008, only 32% of American adults failed to pay federal income tax, either because they did not work at all, or because they earned too little. However, after Obama's 2010 tax cuts for the poor and middle class were implemented, suddenly 52% of American adults no longer paid federal income tax.[472] This means that after 2010, *the majority of the voters* had a strong financial motive to vote for politicians who *would increase the federal income tax on everyone else*. A majority of American voters suddenly had more motive than ever to play plunder politics.

Previously, property owners in old England protected their wealth from socialism by strictly limiting the right to vote. For several centuries, only land owners, men with titles, and wealthy merchants could vote for representatives in the House of Commons. Furthermore, the House of Lords was composed of hereditary title holders. These wealthy aristocrats naturally opposed socialism because it went against their financial interests. Yet during the 19th century, social agitation from the masses for wider voting rights became overwhelming. By the end of the 19th century, the right to vote was extended to nearly all adult male English subjects. By the 1960's (about three generations later), England had become a socialist state. England is the classic example of the natural tendency for democracy to spawn socialism.

The American Founding Fathers also wanted the right to vote for their leaders. Yet they also wanted to protect property rights (and prevent socialism). At first, the Founding Fathers also restricted the right to vote to only property owners. Yet they created an additional defense against socialism. The Founding Fathers also tried to prevent socialism by means of the Constitution. The Founding Fathers especially tried to prevent any sort of federal income tax on individuals. Article One, Section Eight requires that all direct federal taxes must be *"uniform throughout the several States."* Article One, Section Nine also requires, *"No Capitation or other direct tax shall be laid unless in proportion to the Census..."* Taken together, these two requirements mean that any direct federal tax on individuals must be proportional to the population of the state where the tax-payer lives.[473]

In other words, if Virginia has ten percent of the population, then the people of Virginia would have to pay exactly ten percent of the total federal income tax burden, (no more and no less). This effectively prevented any kind of federal income tax on individuals. So the Founding Fathers intended for the federal government not to have any type of income tax at all. In fact, for nearly a hundred years, the federal government was financed mostly by tariffs on imported goods. This kept the federal government fairly small. Historically, for our first hundred years, the Supreme Court only tolerated the federal income tax during wartime, as an emergency measure.

FEDERAL INCOME TAX: THE BEGINNING OF THE END

All of this changed in 1894, when Congress first passed a federal income tax *in peace time*. This progressive income tax on individuals was challenged and the controversial case went to the Supreme Court. In a convoluted decision the Court upheld the federal income tax on *earned* income (i.e. on wages or salaries) but struck down the federal income tax on *unearned* income (i.e. on rents, interest, and dividends).[474] In order to tax all forms of income, the supporters of big government passed the sixteenth amendment in 1913, giving constitutional protection to all federal income taxes.

After the Supreme Court accepted a federal income tax on wages and salaries in 1895, the relationship between the people and the Federal government changed forever. With the power to tax individuals, the federal government grew and grew. This could never have happened without a federal income tax. Modern Liberals could have dreamed about socialism, foreign aid, government-run health care, food stamps, and farm subsidies forever. Yet none of these things would have been possible without the federal government's new power to tax individual citizens.

In America it only took about two generations (after 1895) for socialism to become completely entrenched. America has been living under socialism (extensive government control of the economy plus transfer payments) since 1938, when the Supreme Court started to accept new federal powers, in violation of the Tenth Amendment. Without a strictly enforced constitution, we cannot prevent socialism. It is a natural animal instinct to survive while doing as little work as possible, even if it means sponging off other people. Education, patriotism, even appeals to religion, can never influence human beings as much as their basic instincts will. In 1931, Dr. Adrian Rogers warned us:

"When half of the people get the idea that they do not have to work because the other half is going to take care of them, and when the other half gets the idea that it does no good to work because somebody else is going to get what they work for, that my dear friend, is about the end of any nation. You cannot multiply wealth by dividing it…You cannot legislate the poor into freedom by legislating the wealthy out of freedom."

THE BURDEN KEEPS GROWING

Back in 1894, when the federal income tax law passed, the maximum rate was only 2%. In 1909, one Senator suggested a constitutional amendment to limit the income tax to a maximum of 10%. This idea failed because most Senators thought it was not even conceivable that the tax would ever get that high. Others feared that if such a maximum were established, then it might encourage future law makers to raise the tax that high. Both groups were pitifully wrong. As early as 1920, the maximum rate for federal income tax reached 77%. At its height in the 1970's, it was over 90%.

This explosion in government greed was inevitable after the federal government gained the ability to tax its citizens directly, regardless of apportionment. Yet as we saw in Chapter Four, the total federal tax burden (as a percentage of GDP) stabilized after 1952, with the middle class paying slightly more taxes to the federal government in the 1970's and less in the 1980's. Then the middle class paid more in the 1990's and slightly less from 2000 to 2010.

However, the burden of state and local taxes kept on increasing during the 1960's as the federal government's "Great Society" legislation imposed new welfare obligations onto the states. By 1977, state property taxes and state income taxes were taking away 10% of the average middle class family income. After the 1996 Welfare Reforms went into effect, welfare recipients dropped by 60%.[475] Yet the state tax burden did not decline! It stubbornly remained at about 10% of income all the way from 1977 to 2009.[476] State taxes remained high mostly to pay for a significant increase in the number of state and city employees, along with their overly generous retirement systems.

According to the Americans for Tax Reform, when you consider all types of taxes from all levels of government (federal, state and local), along with the cost of government imposed regulations, then the average family of four now works from January 1st to about June 25th for the government. This means the average family is really working for the government almost half of the year. Compare this to the medieval French peasants, who complained bitterly about having to work just *three months* out of the year for their feudal lords.

THE PERFECT PARASITE

In nature, the perfect parasite is one that takes all of its energy from its host, without actually killing the host. Many contemporary politicians seem intent on achieving this perfect parasitic state. Some of them openly talk about taxing as much as possible without actually killing off the economy. This is perfect parasitism. Our modern leaders are little better than the Japanese shogun who said:

"Peasants are like sesame seeds; the more they are squeezed the more they will produce."[477]

Some well known Modern Liberal scholars in academia share this desire to squeeze as much as possible out of working Americans. Harvard's John Kenneth Galbraith and MIT's Lester Thurow both openly argued that working-class people have a set idea about how much money they need in order to enjoy a decent lifestyle. Once they earn that amount, they will not work any more. So by raising taxes, *the government can force people to work longer hours* in order to still have the same amount of money they need for a decent lifestyle.[478]

If this sounds similar to the Japanese shogun squeezing peasants like sesame seeds, you are correct. If it sounds brutal and exploitative, please note that no conservative scholar has ever proposed such a thing. Only cold-hearted socialists such as Galbraith and Thurow could dream up such an exploitative formula, which turns regular people into beasts of burden for the state.

Working-class people do not pay much (if any) income tax, per se. However, they are still squeezed hard by many regressive taxes such as the sales tax, gasoline tax, social security tax, and property tax. *Everyone pays property taxes, even if they are renters.* The amount of money their landlord needs to pay his property tax is simply included in their rent.

Sales taxes were originally begun at low levels, usually one percent on the sale of luxury goods. Now sales tax is approaching 10% in some states. In many states, it is levied on the purchases of all goods, even some foods. Some states are now taxing the payment of services. So now a sales tax may be added to your plumber's bill for unclogging the sink.

The various government taxes on gasoline hurt working-class people the most. The combined federal and state taxes on gasoline currently amount to about sixty cents per gallon in most states. It should be noted that the oil companies only earn about 6% profit from every gallon of gasoline sold. At four dollars per gallon, the oil companies earn about twenty-four cents. However, the government takes in more than double that amount, for doing nothing whatsoever. At four dollars per gallon, the government (combined state and federal) makes a windfall profit of sixty cents on every gallon.[479]

HIGH TAXES HURT CHILDREN

In Chapter Four we saw how taxes destroy wealth, and hurt the economy. Taxes also damage society, because high taxes make it more difficult for parents to spend time with their children. Because all forms of taxes and government regulations eat up almost half of the average family's income, millions of married couples are both forced to work, while trying to raise their children as well.

This means the government is forcing millions of mothers to work outside the home, in order to have enough money to live on after paying off the government. This creates serious social problems and even medical problems. Numerous studies have shown that children who are raised by full-time mothers tend to be happier, better adjusted socially, and even physically healthier than children who are left with babysitters or at day care centers.[480] An important 2001 study showed that children left in day care displayed more aggressive behavior than children who remained under the care of a parent. This was true regardless of the quality of the day care center.[481]

The Big Picture

Children left in day care are also at much higher risk for serious medical illnesses. These children are far more likely to contract medical conditions such as meningitis, otitis media, bronchitis, hepatitis A and B, impetigo, measles, epiglottis, whooping cough, body lice, rotavirus, RSV, shigellosis, and tuberculosis. One epidemiologist described day care centers as; *"...the open sewers of the twentieth century."*[482]

Modern Liberal feminists support day care so adamantly that they are trying to censor any criticism of it. In 1991, Dr. Louise Silverstein wrote in the prestigious journal *American Psychologist*, *"...psychologists must refuse to undertake any more research that looks for negative consequences of other-than-mother care."*[483] When Dr. Benjamin Spock published his first book about baby care, he advised mothers against day care centers because of the medical and psychological risks associated with day care. After pressure from radical feminists, he deleted this material from later editions of his book. Later in life, Dr. Spock confessed regret for having caved in to their pressure tactics.[484]

Marriages where both parents work also suffer from a higher divorce rate, which creates additional psychological problems for children. Yet our political leaders appear to feel no guilt over forcing both parents to work in order to feed the great government beast. Our masters really are squeezing us "like sesame seeds."

ASSAULT ON THE FAMILY

Because high taxes hurt families with children, some conservatives allege that high taxes are a deliberate assault on traditional families. Modern Liberals invariably dismiss this charge as paranoia. Yet a review of Modern Liberal scholarship reveals that conservatives may not be paranoid at all. The world's first social engineer was Plato. He certainly wanted to destroy the nuclear family. In his book *Republic*, Plato argued that adults should breed children only when authorized by the state. Furthermore, Plato said that these children should be raised collectively, in giant orphanage halls. Plato figured this would prevent any man from knowing who his own son might be. This (Plato thought) would encourage older men to treat all younger men as their own sons. Therefore, parental compassion would be spread throughout society.

However, common sense tells us that in this situation, the older men would tend to treat *no one* as their own son. So parental compassion would be *eliminated* from society. This is exactly what Aristotle pointed out in Book Two of his classic work, *Politics*. Plato was an idealist, and that made him much more liberal than Aristotle. Aristotle was a realist, and that made him more conservative.

At first it may be difficult to understand why some Modern Liberals are so antagonistic towards the traditional nuclear family. Perhaps these Modern Liberal collectivists fear that a mother and father will impart their own moral values upon their children. Parents might teach children that moral values should be followed even if it means violating the law. In effect, parents might teach their children that it is sometimes morally justified to disobey the state.

Another fear may be haunting Modern Liberals. A child who grows up in his nuclear family naturally learns to care more about his own family than he cares about other people in society. So the family unit might lead many people to reject the social welfare system.

Either of these explanations is plausible. However, Modern Liberal collectivists have not openly admitted their precise motive for seeking to destroy the traditional family unit. Stalin and Hitler both wanted to replace the family with the state. Neither of them was courteous enough to tell us exactly why. However, Hitler implied that his motive was to increase government power:

"If the older generation cannot get accustomed to us we shall take their children away from them, and raise them as needs be for the Fatherland."[485] **(Hitler, 1933.)**

Of course this would explain why brutal tyrants such as Hitler, Stalin, and Pol Pot wanted to destroy the family unit. But why did such seemingly civilized men as the scholar H.G. Wells (the intellectual champion of both socialism and globalism), Dr. Arthur W. Calhoun (the most eminent sociologist before WWII), and George Bernard Shaw (perhaps the 20th century's greatest propagandist for socialism), all want to destroy the traditional family unit?

The answer is simple. These Modern Liberals may have been respected scholars, but they were also revolutionary collectivists. Instead of using bullets and bombs, these tenured rebels used books and plays to change the world to their liking. A smart revolutionary is one who sits safely in his home writing and publishing, to influence others. A foolish revolutionary is the one who mans the barricades to put some new leader in power. Furthermore, radical intellectuals can foment a cultural revolution. And a cultural revolution is longer lasting than a mere coup d'etat. Cultural revolutions last longer because they tend to be self-sustaining, so long as the armchair rebels keep control of the schools and the mass media.

In case you find it hard to believe that Modern Liberal intellectuals such as H.G. Wells, Dr. Arthur Calhoun, and George Bernard Shaw really wanted to destroy the traditional family unit, here are some revealing quotations:

"Socialism is in fact the state family. The old family of the private individual must vanish before it."[486] (H.G. Wells.)

"The new view is that the higher and more obligatory relation is to society rather than to the family. The family goes back to the age of savagery while the state belongs to the age of civilization. The modern individual is a world citizen, served by the world, and home interests can no longer be supreme." [487] (Dr. Arthur W. Calhoun)

It is ironic of Calhoun to claim that the traditional family is associated with savagery, while government is associated with civilization. Actually, the opposite is true. Modern governments are responsible for the *savagery* of world wars, genocides, nuclear bombs, political prisoners, and forced sterilizations. By comparison, families have been far more civilized than governments. After considering the bloodthirsty history of governments, it is more accurate to say that society is civilized *despite* governments, not because of them.

George Bernard Shaw suffered a wretched childhood. His abusive and alcoholic father barely fed his children. Shaw's mother failed to protect Shaw from his cruel father. This ill treatment left lifelong scars. Shaw refused to attend the funerals for either of his parents, and admitted a nearly equal loathing for his brothers and sisters. No wonder that Shaw's prescription for women's liberation included an assault against the traditional family unit; *"Unless woman repudiates her womanliness, her duty to her husband, to her children, to everyone but herself, she cannot emancipate herself."*[488] All of these men (Wells, Calhoun, and Shaw) would have agreed with the following entry from Mussolini's Fascist Dictionary; *"Family; See Fascist State."*

The best known propagandist of communism was Karl Marx. Just like other radical Modern Liberals, he too despised the traditional family unit, calling it *"bourgeois claptrap."* Marx thought that parents only viewed their children as *"articles of commerce and instruments of labor."* Marx believed that women who were part of the traditional family unit (wives and daughters) were no better than *"common prostitutes."* From Rousseau, to Wells, to Marx, nearly all radical Modern Liberals condemned the traditional family unit.[489]

Many of today's Modern Liberals are not even aware that their ideology is working to destroy the traditional family unit. Yet every time Modern Liberals change some aspect of family life, the nuclear family suffers as a result. For example, in the 1960's, Modern Liberals were behind the effort to pass "no fault" divorce laws, which made it easier to terminate marriages. Today, Modern Liberals support homosexual marriage as an equal rights cause. They are deluding themselves into thinking that this will not lead to polygamy. Likewise, Modern Liberals support adoption by homosexual couples, unconcerned that this will further minimize the importance of the traditional family unit.

But the most damaging Modern Liberal assault on the family is also the most insidious. It comes from the Modern Liberal demand that we must "tolerate" all forms of sexual immorality. Specifically, it is the Modern Liberal support for unmarried girls who are having (and raising) bastard children out of wedlock. Modern Liberals have been behind the effort to "mainstream" these unwed pregnant teenagers back into high school, where (by example) they will encourage other girls to do the same thing.

In the past, conservatives successfully shunned these pregnant teenage girls, and imposed a social stigma on them for their "sluty" behavior. In the past, (to avoid this stigma) these girls were quietly sent off to live with a distant relative, where they would give birth and immediately surrender the baby for adoption. Only then could they return home.

Nowadays, Modern Liberals insist that we all must treat these irresponsible girls with respect, so as to protect their self-esteem. Conservatives are criticized if they "pass judgment" on their behavior. Modern Liberals tell us that passing judgment is "mean-spirited." Of course, with the disappearance of this social stigma, more and more girls are raising babies out of wedlock. Our socialist government even encourages them by giving monthly support money to these foolish girls. As a result, illegitimate births have become a national crisis. This social plague is worse now than at any other time in our nation's history, despite the modern availability of birth control.

NATIONAL SERVICE: FRIENDLY FASCISM

Earlier we saw that high taxes are a subtle form of slavery. Other forms of slavery are more obvious. One example is forcing someone to labor on a government project. Yet Modern Liberals in America are surprisingly enthusiastic about this old fashioned type of human bondage. In September of 2007, *Time* magazine ran a banner headline on its cover which read, "The Case For National Service." The New York Times has also eagerly endorsed this form of involuntary servitude.[490]

My own internet search in 2009 revealed 36 non-profit organizations that are all dedicated to spreading the gospel of *"mandatory volunteerism."* As a result of persistent lobbying from all of these groups, we now have a government funded "Corporation for National and Community Service." Like most government programs, the CNCS has developed its own vocal constituency to expand its scope and power. This constituency is led by a Modern Liberal umbrella group called Voices for National Service, which receives money from the big non-profit foundations.

Mandatory national service is another illustration of the Modern Liberal preference for collectivism and authoritarianism. Modern Liberals see no danger in government power so long as the people in charge have good intentions. This means they see nothing wrong with forced labor for "the common good."

Some Modern Liberals have argued that if conservatives accept the military draft, they should also be willing to accept mandatory national service. However, Libertarian Conservatives point out that the military draft is a special case. As we saw in Chapter One, Frederic Bastiat proposed that there are only two legitimate functions of government: (1) to prevent citizens from harming each other, and (2) to prevent invasion by foreigners. So the military draft would be morally justified under the government's duty to prevent invasion. In contrast, mandatory national service has nothing to do with either of the two legitimate purposes of government. Therefore, mandatory national service cannot be justified in the way that the military draft can be.

It is ironic that the same Modern Liberals who want to impose forced labor "for the common good," are the same people who oppose punishing criminals by putting them in chain gangs. In fact chain gangs make much more sense than national service does. In a chain gang, a criminal is forced to pay back his *actual debt to society*, i.e. the cost of keeping him fed and clothed in prison. However, with national service, the slave laborer is forced to pay back an *imaginary debt to society*. This imaginary debt to society only exists inside the minds of the friendly fascists who support national service. If the most fundamental characteristic of fascism is government control over the individual, then national service is a huge step toward fascism.

THE WISE OLD ORGANISM

Modern Liberals who want to change the world claim that they merely want to make society more orderly and better organized. Modern Liberals believe that a society which is left to its own will result in chaos. What they fail to understand is that society is already *self-regulated* by all of its individual members. Here we must draw an analogy from nature. Every ecosystem on earth is so inherently complex that humans can never fully understand every nuance of it. Any attempt by man to alter part of an ecosystem inevitably leads to some unforeseen harm. The best thing that humans can do for any ecosystem is to leave it alone, thereby letting the ecosystem remain in its natural state.

The same holds true for the complex society that mankind has evolved for itself over the centuries. Society is far too complicated for any committee of sociologists or politicians to understand all of its nuances. Any attempt by social engineers to change part of society inevitably leads to some unforeseen harm. The best thing that government can do for any society is to leave it alone, thereby letting society remain in its natural state.

The collective wisdom of the great organism we call society is phenomenal. We usually don't notice it simply because we are immersed in it. This invisible wisdom was perhaps best described by Herbert Spencer, the father of modern social statistics:

"The turning of land into a food-producing surface, cleared, fenced, drained and covered with farming appliances, has been achieved by men working for individual profit, not by legislative direction.... village, towns, and cities have insensibly grown up under the desires of men to satisfy their own wants...spontaneous cooperation of citizens have...formed canals, railways, telegraphs and other means of communication and distribution...And supplementing these come the innumerable companies, associations, unions, societies, clubs... serving...philanthropy, culture, art, amusement...all of them arising from the unforced cooperation of citizens. And yet, so hypnotized are nearly all by fixedly contemplating the doings of ministers and parliaments, that they have no eyes for this marvelous organization, which had been growing for thousands of years without government help—nay, in spite of government interferences."[491]

Perhaps the greatest historians of our modern era, Will and Ariel Durant, agreed:

"No one man, however brilliant or well-informed, can come in one lifetime to such fullness of understanding as to safely judge and dismiss the customs or institutions of his society, for these are the wisdom of centuries of experiment in the laboratory of history."[492]

Another reason to trust the collective wisdom of the organism, (instead of social engineers), is because the organism tends to be naturally *self-correcting*. Nearly all of its members are able to regulate themselves. For example, let's say a young man fails to attend college because he wants to devote his time and energy to his high school rock and roll band. After a few years, he realizes that the band is not a success. He also sees many of his former peers graduating from college and then working at high paying jobs. Now the young man realizes his error and finally enrolls in a decent college. He understands his mistake and takes steps to correct it.

In contrast, the social engineers who work for the government lack any motive to admit that their plans have failed. Such an admission might cause them to lose funding. Also, if a politician admitted to any failure, he might lose an election.[493] Another danger is that the bad social policy might become politically protected, because it is supported by a special interest group. So the government has several perverse incentives to maintain bad policies, long after they have proven harmful. These factors all seem to justify Hobbs' famous observation:

"A plain husband-man is more prudent in the affairs of his own house than a privy counselor in the affairs of other men."[494]

In reply, Modern Liberals often point to a few Supreme Court decisions in the 1950's that "forced a reluctant society" to abolish racial segregation in education. This, they claim, is justification for social engineers, (such as the Supreme Court), to force their enlightened will upon a reluctant society. Yet this example is highly misleading. It is true that back in the 1950's, Modern Liberal social engineers persuaded the Supreme Court to force the desegregation of public schools. However, American society was already headed in that direction on its own, regardless of the Supreme Court. It might have happened ten or so years later, but the end result would have been the same.

In fact, only about a decade after the Supreme Court desegregation decisions, the American people elected a Congress that passed the Civil Rights Act of 1964, banning racial discrimination in education and employment. Therefore, we can infer that by 1964 the majority of Americans wanted *equal economic opportunities* for all races. The next year, this same elected Congress also guaranteed black Americans the right to vote. This indicates that the majority of our society also wanted *equal political rights* for all races. There was no need for the Supreme Court to take matters into its own hands. The organism has intelligence. The organism can change. Our masters should learn to be patient.

SUMMARY OF POLITICAL HISTORY

The authoritarian ideas of Plato were largely ignored in Western culture for over two thousand years, until the French Revolution. In the meantime, Anglo-Saxon culture had evolved its own unique tradition of limited government and personal freedom, based upon the three foundations of liberty:
1. Government by consent,
2. The law of the land, and
3. Property rights.

The zenith of this Anglo-Saxon progress towards individual liberty occurred in 1787, with the creation of the US Constitution. However, in 1712, Saint-Pierre (inspired by Plato) went in the opposite direction. His new goals for society were:
1. Global government,
2. All-powerful government run by elite social engineers,
3. Government-run schools without any Christian teachings,
4. Social-welfare programs, and
5. High taxes based on a progressive scale.

The frightening thing is, if you implement all of Saint-Pierre's goals you will produce a totalitarian government, in which the government controls all aspects of your life. Under Saint-Pierre's plan, the government controls the economy (see items four and five above). The government also controls the culture (see item three above). Finally the common people are helpless to change government policy (see items one and two above). In attempting to implement the goals of Saint-Pierre, Modern Liberalism has given us governments that are collectivist, authoritarian, globalist, elitist, and socialist. Therefore, history has shown that Modern Liberalism leads to totalitarianism.

Let's briefly review the historical record. The French philosophes picked up the radical ideas of Saint-Pierre and passed them on to both the Illuminati and the Jacobins. The Jacobins succeeded in creating a revolutionary government in France, based upon the Modern Liberal ideas of Saint-Pierre. The result was Robespierre's brutal Reign of Terror.

Karl Marx tried to inspire the revolutionaries of 1848 with his Communist Manifesto, which was really just an expanded version of Saint-Pierre's original plan. The Libertarian Conservative response by Frederic Bastiat had far less emotional appeal than either communism or socialism, and so it was largely ignored. Still, the monarchies of Europe were able to put down the uprisings of 1848 without much difficulty. In the end, socialism was finally able to gain its first permanent foothold in Prussia under Bismarck, without bloodshed.

In England, at the dawn of the 20th century, the Milner Group began their effort to peacefully implement the two great goals of Modern Liberalism, i.e. socialism and globalism. By 1922 Lord Alfred Milner had established a permanent institutional structure to promote these two goals. This powerful structure consisted of the Milner Group, the CRF, the RIIA, and the large charitable foundations.

During this same time the Progressive movement in America briefly added a veneer of Christianity to Modern Liberalism. Woodrow Wilson was greatly inspired by the religious impetus behind the Progressive Movement. Wilson tried to use Christianity to support collectivism, or as he called it "the common good." Wilson also came dangerously close to implementing authoritarianism in America during the alleged emergency of World War I. Wilson created sweeping new government powers, including warrantless searches and arrests.

Meanwhile, Modern Liberalism in continental Europe had never been influenced by Christianity at all. Therefore, Modern Liberalism in Europe took a more radical and violent turn. In 1917 the Bolshevik Communists implemented totalitarianism in Russia, following the ideological path laid out by Saint-Pierre, Rousseau, and Marx. Then in 1929 the fascists started to implement most of the five goals of Saint-Pierre in Italy. In 1935 the Nazis followed suit in Germany. The most important difference among these three groups was that the fascists and Nazis both favored *nationalism* instead of globalism. The Nazis also added a peculiar doctrine of racial hatred into the mix.

After the bloodbath of WWII, Modern Liberals all over the world rejected both the Christianity of the Progressives, and the nationalism of the fascists and Nazis. Instead, Modern Liberals went back to the atheism and globalism that were originally favored by Saint-Pierre when he created Modern Liberalism back in 1712. In the post WWII era, Modern Liberals have successfully used the mass media, Hollywood, public schools, and labor unions, to persuade the population at large to accept the original vision of Saint-Pierre. The three foundations of Anglo-Saxon liberty (government by consent, law of the land, and property rights) were virtually abandoned. They were replaced by the economic and political goals of Modern Liberalism, to wit: collectivism, authoritarianism, globalism, elitism, and socialism. Sadly, that is where we stand today.

WHAT HAVE WE LEARNED?

By reading this book, you have studied 2,400 years of history; including politics, economics, psychology, and religion. Now you know the most important developments of the past. In the next chapter you will find a detailed description of our current situation. Then in the final chapter you will see a glimpse into the future.

But right now, we can learn the most important lesson of all. We can finally compare the conservative and Modern Liberal models for society. The conservative model for society is: Patriotic, Representative, Autonomous, Capitalist, Traditional, Individualistic, Constitutional, Armed, and Libertarian. Let's briefly discuss what these terms mean.

"Patriotic" means we should teach our children to love this country, instead of encouraging them to belittle it.

"Representative" means that only Congress can make laws; not the President using executive orders, or the Supreme Court acting like a super legislature.

"Autonomous" means no international treaties should reduce any of our sovereignty or our Constitutional rights. It also means no global government should have jurisdiction over our people or our nation.

"Capitalist" means the free market should be left alone with as few restrictions as possible, and with the lowest taxes possible. It also means no more corporate welfare.

"Traditional" means preserving the values that have kept society safe and sane for generations, such as the two parent family, and parental control over what children are taught in school.

"Individualistic" means every innocent human life is sacred, so Modern Liberal innovations such as abortion and euthanasia must be stopped.

"Constitutional" means strictly limiting the federal government to the range of powers originally intended by the Founding Fathers.

"Armed" means that the people should be allowed to carry arms for self-protection, and also for possible resistance against tyranny.

"Libertarian" means the government should leave us alone in all things, so long as we do not trample on other people's rights. No more social engineering. No more fascism. No more socialism.

These nine conservative ideals for society may be listed under the acronym "P.R.A.C.T.I.C.A.L." (i.e. Patriotic, Representative, Autonomous, Capitalist, Traditional, Individualistic, Constitutional, Armed, and Libertarian).

On the other hand, the Modern Liberal model for society is based on very different ideals. As we have seen throughout this book, The Modern Liberal model for society is: Collectivist, Authoritarian, Globalist, Elitist and Socialist. These Modern Liberal ideals may be reduced to the acronym "C.A.G.E.S."

Which type of society would you rather live in; a society that is PRACTICAL, or a society that is made up of CAGES?

CHAPTER EIGHT

OUR PRESENT

"Men occasionally stumble over the truth, but most of them pick themselves up and hurry off as if nothing happened." Winston Churchill.

"THE LIBERAL ESTABLISHMENT"

The combination of the Royal Institute for International Affairs (RIIA) and the Council on Foreign Relations (CFR), together with the Rockefeller Foundation and the Carnegie Endowment, has enough power and influence that they may together be considered the unofficial "establishment" in both England and the United States. Henceforth we shall refer to these four institutions collectively as "the Liberal Establishment."[495] The Liberal Establishment consists of separate groups that are all working toward the same goals. These goals are nearly identical to the five goals of Saint-Pierre that we saw in Chapters Two and Three. Not surprisingly, the motivation behind the Liberal Establishment is also identical to the motivation of Saint-Pierre, namely to prevent war and revolution.

We should be honest with ourselves and admit that the Liberal Establishment constitutes a thinly veiled network of power which effectively controls politics, education, and the mass media, on both sides of the Atlantic Ocean.[496] In a rare and revealing article published on October 30[th,] 1993, even the Washington Post admitted that the CFR was *"The nearest thing we have to a ruling establishment in the United*

States." This eye-opening article gave just a few examples of the powerful positions that were held by CFR members at that time:

"The President is a member. So is his Secretary of State, the deputy Secretary of State, all five of the undersecretaries, several of the assistant secretaries and the department's legal adviser. The national security adviser and his deputy are members. The director of the CIA (like all previous directors) and the chairman of the Foreign Intelligence Advisory Board are members. The Secretary of Defense, three undersecretaries and at least four assistant secretaries are members. The secretaries for the departments of Housing and Urban Development, Interior, Health and Human Services, and the chief White House public relations person are members, along with the Speaker of the House and the majority leader in the Senate."

Nearly every powerful politician in America (at the national level) is a member of the CFR. In the early 1990s, while Republican Newt Gingrich was battling the Democratic Party for control of the US Congress, you could often find him and his Democratic foes attending meetings at the CFR building in downtown Washington. Back in the 1970's, political enemies Jimmy Carter and Gerald Ford were also contemporaneous members of the CFR. Just as party affiliation meant little to the old Milner Group, likewise it still means little to members of the Liberal Establishment today. Across the pond, most influential English journalists and English politicians of all political stripes are members of the RIIA. The RIIA holds power in Britain in a manner nearly identical to the CFR in America.

Only a few American elected officials have dared to complain about the inordinate power of the CFR. One of these brave souls was Congressman John R. Rarick:

"The Council on Foreign Relations—dedicated to world government, financed by a number of the largest tax-exempt foundations, and wielding such power and influence over our lives in the areas of finance, business, labor, military, education, and mass media – should be familiar to every American…Yet the nation's right to know machinery, the news media…remains conspicuously silent when it comes to the CFR…The CFR is the establishment."[497]

In the USA, the CFR focuses primarily on foreign policy matters. This leaves the two great charitable trusts free to work on US domestic policy as a means of changing society. The Rockefeller Foundation and the Carnegie Endowment have assisted nearly every important Modern Liberal organization in America. They still routinely support a wide range of Modern Liberal pressure groups such as the National Organization of Women, the National Education Association, the ACLU, the NAACP, PUSH, La Raza, The World Council of Churches, The National Council of Churches, People for the American Way, Planned Parenthood, the Sierra Club, the Nature Conservancy, the Center for Law and Justice, and various anti-gun organizations.

The Liberal Establishment has created several subsidiary organizations, to accomplish specific policy goals. In an effort to influence international trade and banking the Liberal Establishment formed the Bilderberger Club in 1954. Yes indeed, the Bilderbergers do exist. They really are a group of super wealthy bankers and industrialists who meet behind closed doors every year. Of all the daughter organizations created by the Liberal Establishment, this one has inspired more conspiracy theories than any other. This is mostly due to the Bilderbergers' own fault, because of their insistence on absolute secrecy. If their meetings really are entirely innocent (i.e. meetings where members discuss economic issues and world events), then they should be willing to invite independent journalists to verify that nothing else is going on.

However, if their meetings involve decisions about the monetary policies of sovereign nations (such as which currencies to inflate and which currencies to deflate), then one can certainly understand the Bilderbergers' motive for maintaining secrecy. Yet such decisions affect billions of people around the globe. Certainly these common folk have a right to know what is being planned for their economies.

By the 1970's, Japan had become an economic power house. In order to bring Japanese members into their deliberations, the Liberal Establishment founded another group, this time called, the "Trilateral Commission." Trilateral meant the new group would include members from three regions of the globe, namely Japan, North America and Western Europe. In the 1990's, members were added from Eastern Europe and mainland Asia. The Trilateral Commission was founded by members of the CFR under the guidance of David Rockefeller and

Henry Kissinger, with financial help from the Rockefeller Foundation. It became instantly powerful because of the influence possessed by its individual members.

While all of these daughter organizations are still helping to carry out the Liberal Establishment's agenda, millions of unaffiliated individuals are doing their part as well. Countless numbers of professors, journalists, politicians, labor leaders, teachers and wealthy industrialists around the Western world now support the twin foundations of Modern Liberalism: globalism and socialism. The most useful tools that the Liberal Establishment uses to encourage widespread support for its agenda are the mass media and education. This brings us to our next two topics.

THE MASS MEDIA

The Liberal Establishment has been prudent enough to influence the press for the same reasons that the old Milner Group did. By controlling a few key media outlets, their influence has become pervasive. As the Modern Liberal commentator Noam Chomsky correctly pointed out in his documentary "Manufacturing Consent," the New York Times world desk consists of a few men who sit around a desk each morning and decide what Americans will know about the entire world. Their influence is daunting. Nearly all the other American newspapers get their international news from the New York Times world desk. The big three television news shows also take their leads for stories from the headlines of the New York Times. Therefore, these few men decide what nearly all of America will know about the rest of the world every day.

The Times of London and the English news magazine *The Economist* together wield almost as much influence in England. They have long been staffed with supporters and members of the Milner Group and later of the Liberal Establishment that succeeded the Milner Group. The Liberal Establishment also influences the national information sources in both America and England, namely the American Corporation for Public Broadcasting and the British Broadcasting Corporation. So long as the Liberal Establishment can influence these key media outlets, they will continue to influence public opinion on both sides of the Atlantic.

This control over the media is no longer as blatant as it was eighty years ago, when Lord Alfred Milner had to ask the Astors to purchase the Times of London outright. Nowadays, American schools of journalism are overwhelmingly staffed with Modern Liberal professors. Therefore, the Liberal Establishment no longer needs to actually buy the printing presses. The vast majority of contemporary journalists are quite willing to promote socialism and globalism without actually being paid employees of the Liberal Establishment.

The overwhelming influence of Modern Liberalism over American schools of journalism is obvious for anyone who cares to look. However, this is not merely due to the leftward tilt of the faculty, which is considerable. It is more due to the fact that the vast majority of aspiring young journalists already possess a Modern Liberal point of view. For example, the most prestigious school for journalism in America is the Columbia School of Journalism. In 1999, there were over two hundred students in the graduating class. Out of all these students, only two were known to hold conservative beliefs. Their names were Stephen Hayes and Stacey Pressman. Hayes was frequently ridiculed by his professors for having conservative opinions. Hayes recalled his ordeal: *"I knew the school would be left-wing, but I really didn't anticipate the ferocity of the bias."* [498]

Stacey Pressman was persecuted after she dared to challenge a left-wing feminist professor for being biased. This feminist professor actually tried to punish Pressman for her conservative views, by assigning her extra work. Pressman concluded, *"It's a school full of the Stepford students,"* alluding to the popular movie about mindless robots. *"That's the way they want it. God forbid you challenge them or rock the boat…"*[499] These misplaced pilgrims barely survived the intellectual gulag of Modern Liberal academia. Their story is repeated all too often on today's college campuses. Conservatives are a tiny minority in schools of journalism, and they are simply not welcome.

This is not a new development. It has been going on for decades. In a moment of candor, ABC journalist Peter Jennings admitted; *"Those of us who went into journalism in the 1950's or 1960's, it was sort of a liberal thing to do. Save the world."*[500] Such idealistic young crusaders usually become eager supporters of both socialism and globalism. In this way the Liberal Establishment now exerts a powerful influence over our sources of information without actually having to purchase those sources. An "off the record" statement by the President of CBS News, Andrew Heyward, was more blunt:

"Of course there's a liberal bias in the news. All the networks tilt left."[501]

Modern Liberal readers will probably object to the thesis that the mainstream news media are biased in favor of Modern Liberalism. This is because Modern Liberals (generally) refuse to read any of the several books which document this embarrassing subject. For those people who still deny this Modern Liberal bias, I offer the following home test: Just keep a notebook and pen on your couch, and watch lots of mainstream television news shows, specifically those aired by ABC, NBC, CBS and PBS. If a story about a controversial social issue comes on (e.g. gun control, capital punishment, abortion, flag burning, prayer in public, school vouchers, illegal immigration, welfare reform, government health care, etc.), just draw a circle every time a person is interviewed who presents the Modern Liberal side of the issue. Draw an "X" every time a person is interviewed giving the conservative side of the issue.

Using this technique over several months back in 2003 and 2004, I discovered that the big three commercial television networks (along with PBS) have a strong bias in favor of Modern Liberal views. The first story I analyzed was a Bill Moyers piece on Public Television. It was about guns in America. Mr. Moyers interviewed twelve people. Nine of these people were anti-gun. Two of them were pro-gun. One was neutral. Mr. Moyers was obviously not neutral. Moyers' narration favored the Modern Liberal (anti-gun) point of view.

That story was fairly typical of nearly all the other news stories that followed. Of the 97 stories I analyzed, there were a total of 161 people interviewed who gave the Modern Liberal side of the issue. In all those stories, only 54 people were interviewed who gave the conservative view. This means that mainstream journalists were giving almost three times more opportunities for the Modern Liberal point of view to be heard.

The media's left wing bias is also obvious when you compare their unequal treatment of political candidates, depending on whether they are conservative or Modern Liberal. For example, the mainstream news media called conservative Sarah Palin stupid for not knowing about something called "the Bush doctrine." However, nobody else knew what "the Bush doctrine" was either. In fact, it turned out later that even the journalist who asked Mrs. Palin about it did not know what the phrase meant.[502]

In contrast, the mainstream media are mysteriously silent whenever a Modern Liberal makes a truly serious verbal blunder. For example, on May 12th 2008, while making a campaign speech in Beaverton Oregon, Mr. Obama said:

"Over the last fifteen months, we've traveled to every corner of the United States. I've now been in fifty-seven states. I think one or two left to go, Alaska and Hawaii."[503]

Barack Obama did not even know how many states were in the United States of America. He showed complete ignorance of the most basic knowledge about the United States. This was not unusual incident.[504] In his State of the Union speech for 2011, Obama actually said; *"…drawing on the promise enshrined in our constitution, the notion that 'we are all created equal.'"* Anyone familiar with American history knows that this idea is NOT found in the Constitution. It is found in the Declaration of Independence. This glaring mistake came from a man who supposedly taught Constitutional law. Yet in regard to his knowledge about the United States, Barack Obama is probably the most ignorant president in American history.

The point to all this is not simply to criticize Mr. Obama. The important point here is how the mainstream media covered up all of Obama's gaffs, while they screamed bloody murder every time Sarah Palin allegedly made a mistake. Conservatives like Palin oppose globalism and socialism. That is why the mainstream (Modern Liberal) news media attack conservatives at every opportunity, real or imagined. Whenever a conservative candidate runs for office, Modern Liberal journalists work hard to destroy them. They either try to make conservatives look like extremists (e.g. Pat Buchanan and Ron Paul), or fools (e.g. Dan Quayle and Sarah Palin).

The seminal book about left-wing bias in the mainstream news media is *Bias* by Bernard Goldberg. After working for CBS news for over twenty years, (and writing hundreds of stories for Walter Cronkite and Dan Rather) Goldberg finally documented in great detail the Modern

Liberal bias in the mainstream media. One example from his book will have to do. On Feb 8[th,] 1996 CBS news aired a hit piece which ridiculed Stephen Forbes' conservative plan for a flat federal income tax. The story presented three economists who said it was a bad idea. The story failed to show even one economist who favored the flat tax. In fact many respected economists were already on record as supporting the flat tax (e.g. Milton Friedman, Merton Miller, James Buchanan, Harvey Rosen, William Poole, and Robert Barro). Yet the story failed to include a single person who supported it.

The CBS journalist, Eric Engberg, mocked Forbes' plan, saying *"Steve Forbes pitches his flat tax scheme as an elixir, good for everything that ails us."* The CBS journalist went even further with his impertinence; *"Forbes' number one wackiest flat tax promise is that it would give parents more time to spend with their children and each other."* As Goldberg points out, can you imagine a CBS journalist ever calling a plan by Ted Kennedy or Barack Obama "wacky?" This hit piece was presented as a straight news story, not an editorial. In fact it was presented as part of the CBS "Reality Check" series. This was a series of exposé stories which supposedly revealed the truth behind various deceptions. It was just one example of bias from dozens which Mr. Goldberg documented in his book.

In response to all the evidence of left-wing bias, Modern Liberals claim that FOX News provides a conservative version of current events. They argue that this provides a counter balance to any possible left-wing bias in the rest of the news media. However, FOX News is not really conservative. It is simply not left-wing. Of course a few of their personality based shows are conservative, (such as Glenn Beck), but *FOX News programs are not.* FOX News only appears conservative when you compare it to the left-wing coverage provided by all the other television news programs. As the Democratic Governor of Pennsylvania (and strong supporter of Hillary Clinton) concluded during the 2008 primary campaign; *"FOX has done the fairest job, and has remained the most objective of all the cable networks."*[505]

Yet even if FOX News were conservative, very few people watch it compared to the rest of the television news shows. As of this writing, FOX News only averages 2.5 million viewers. However, the evening news shows presented by CBS, ABC, and NBC combine for a total of

22.6 million viewers.[506] When you add those viewers to the 2.7 million who watch "The Newshour" on PBS, along with the 1 million who watch CNN, then a grand total of 26.3 million Americans get their evening news from Modern Liberal sources. So the Modern Liberal news media is watched over ten times more often than is the allegedly conservative FOX News.

The bias toward Modern Liberalism is not limited to the media of television. It also pervades the written press as well. The most influential weekly news magazines (*Time* and *Newsweek*) and the most influential daily papers (*NY Times, L.A. Times*, and *Washington Post*) are all heavily influenced by the Liberal Establishment. The extensive influence of the Liberal Establishment on the American printed news media was once described in detail by the *Washington Post*. According to the *Washington Post*, the most prominent print journalists in America are not only members of the CFR, *journalists are often in charge of it:*

"In the past 15 years, [CFR] council directors have included Hedley Donovan of Time Inc., Elizabeth Drew of the New Yorker, Phillip Geyelin of the Washington Post, [and] Karen Elliott House of the Wall Street Journal...The editorial page director, the executive editor, the managing editor and the foreign affairs editor and various writers as well as the paper's principal owner represent the Washington Post in the Council's membership. The executive editor, managing editor and foreign editor of the New York Times are all members, along with executives of other large newspapers such as the Wall Street Journal, the Los Angeles Times and the weekly magazines, network television executives and celebrities—Dan Rather, Tom Brokaw and Jim Lehrer for example...."[507]

THE UNFAIRNESS DOCTRINE

At the time of this writing, (2010) Modern Liberals are trying to eliminate the last outpost of conservative ideas from the electronic media. Modern Liberals want to impose the so-called "fairness doctrine" on radio and television shows that offer conservative views. The FCC created the fairness doctrine in 1947. It required radio and television stations to make sure *"...that contrary views be presented."* In 1987 the FCC suspended the fairness doctrine, and Modern Liberals have been pressuring the FCC to reinstate it ever since. After the recent election of Barack Obama, their pressure has reached a crescendo.

The fairness doctrine is not just a regulation; it is really a clever form of censorship. Modern Liberal politicians know that radio stations *will cancel conservative talk shows* if the radio stations are also required to broadcast an equal number of *liberal talk shows*. This is due to simple economics. Liberal talk shows are money losers. The listener ratings for liberal radio talk shows are historically abysmal. That is why the Modern Liberal "Air America" radio network quickly went off the air. Look at all the famous Modern Liberal personalities who tried talk radio but failed: Al Franken, Allan Combs, Jim Hightower, Mario Cuomo, Jerry Brown, Phil Donahue, etc.

Modern Liberal talk shows have poor ratings because Modern Liberals already receive a left-wing version of the news from the three major television networks. If Modern Liberals want news from the radio, they can always hear the leftist version of the news from NPR. Conservatives do not have all these other options. The only truly conservative news source is AM talk radio. This explains why conservative talk radio consistently enjoys more listeners than Modern Liberal talk radio. Modern Liberals have many alternatives. Conservatives do not.

The other problem with enforcing the fairness doctrine against conservative talk radio is the *unfairness of selectively enforcing it only against conservative shows*. No one at the FCC or in the Obama administration wants to enforce the fairness doctrine against the three big television networks or NPR. Can anyone recall the last time Terrie Gross interviewed a conservative guest on her NPR show "Fresh Air?"[508] The people interviewed on NPR are usually *Modern Liberal activists* involved in environmentalism, homosexual rights, the anti-war movement, multiculturalism, feminism, abortion rights, minority rights, illegal immigrant rights, welfare rights, prison reform, etc. Yet no one is suggesting that the fairness doctrine be applied against NPR. No one suggests that Terry Gross should be forced to devote half of her shows to conservative guests. So the enforcement of the fairness doctrine will be very selective. Selective enforcement is the same as persecution.

Remember that CBS journalist Bernard Goldberg documented dozens of examples of left-wing bias in the mainstream news media. Yet no one ever complains to the FCC about left-wing bias in the mainstream news media. Certainly Modern Liberals do not invoke the fairness doctrine when the big three television networks give biased (left-wing) coverage. This is because Modern Liberals are perfectly happy with the left-wing bias of the mainstream media. Yet when conservative talk show hosts give biased opinions or biased information, suddenly Modern Liberals want to enforce "balance" and "fairness" with the hob-nailed boots of government censorship. Modern Liberal politician Chuck Schumer actually said that conservative talk radio should be regulated just as pornography is regulated.[509]

In 2009 President Obama began to explore alternative ways to silence talk radio, just in case his enforcement of the fairness doctrine might be recognized as censorship. At the time of this writing Obama is considering the creation of "community boards" and "citizen review committees" which would decide who could speak on AM radio, *based on the content of their speech*. Of course the members of these boards will be appointed by the government. This will just be another thin disguise for censorship.

For a healthy republic we need a free marketplace of ideas, not censorship. If the government gains control over the content of talk radio, then conservative opinions will be silenced. The people behind this effort know that very well. That is their goal. Modern Liberals want to eliminate conservative ideas from the public forum.

HIGHER EDUCATION

The Modern Liberal dominance over the American mass media is equaled by their control over higher education in America. According to a poll published in the New York Times, university professors who are registered with the Democratic Party outnumber professors who are registered with the Republican Party, by a ratio of seven to one.[510] It should be noted that thirty years earlier, this ratio was only three to one. So the nearly complete dominance of Modern Liberal ideas on our college campuses is still surging forward at remarkable speed.

Some prestigious universities now offer more courses in women's studies than they do in economics. In some class course guides, the number of courses in the "hard sciences" (engineering, mathematics, physics, chemistry, biology, botany, etc.), is less than half the number of courses in the social sciences.

Today it is virtually impossible for a conservative to get a professorship in teaching, sociology, English, African American studies, women's studies, philosophy, history, or political science. Mark Bauerlein is a professor of English at Emory University. He described an open secret among academicians; *"...the first protocol of academic society is the common assumption that at professional gatherings all of the strangers in the room are liberals."*

PRE-SCHOOL PROPAGANDA

The Modern Liberal dominance over education now extends all the way down to the pre-school level. The Modern Liberal producers of children's television are using television as a tool to indoctrinate very young children. For the sake of brevity, I will offer only three examples. In regard to socialism, there is a popular show for pre-school children on American Public Television. The show is called "The Big Comfy Couch." The only episode I happened to see presented a *socialist* version of Aesop's classic fable, "The Grasshopper and the Ant."

In the original fable, the ant works all summer storing up food, in preparation for the long winter. Meanwhile, the lazy grasshopper plays all summer long and laughs at the hard-working ant. Then, when winter comes, the ant is comfortable in his little home with plenty of food to eat. The lazy grasshopper is hungry, and he knocks on the ant's door begging for food. The ant tells him firmly, "You played all summer long while I worked hard all summer. Why should I give you anything? Your hunger is your own fault! Go away!" The lesson from this classic story is to work hard, so you will not sponge off other people.

However, the PBS program drastically altered the entire story to favor socialism. In their Modern Liberal version of the story, when winter comes the hard-working ant feels sorry for the poor hungry grasshopper. The grasshopper even offers to play music and sing to entertain the ant, in exchange for food. The ant agrees to feed the talented but lazy grasshopper. The narrator ends this socialist fairy tale for four year olds with the pregnant statement, *"The world needs more 'grants' for art."* (The grasshopper's name was Grant.)

Children's television has not forgotten about the other main goal of Modern Liberalism: globalism. Another popular show for young children is called "A Place of Our Own." Again, I only happened to watch one episode, and it was devoted primarily to global citizenship.[511] The obvious lesson was that our belonging to a global community was more important than being a citizen of the United States.

Yet socialism and globalism are not the only Modern Liberal ideas being spoon fed to our children. Non-traditional family values are being taught to children at very early ages. For example, another popular television program for pre-schoolers is "Sesame Street." Whenever it can, it also teaches children the Modern Liberal way to think about social values. Sesame Street frequently teaches children that the traditional nuclear family is no better than any other assortment of human beings. In this effort they teach children the following song:
First child: "I've got one Daddy."
Second Child: "I've got two [Daddies]."
Third child: "There's my Mom and me, and baby makes three,
And it works perfectly! Don't you see? We're a family!"[512]

After one or two years of such indoctrination, it should be easy for your child to accept the new children's classics that are standard reading in some public schools, such as *Heather has Two Mommies,* and *Daddy's Roommate*. You will be hard pressed to find any children's television program that promotes traditional values, Christian morality, or patriotism.

RE-THINKING PUBLIC EDUCATION

Modern Liberals and conservatives also disagree on who should be educating children. Modern Liberals prefer to place the vast majority of children into government schools, paid for by taxes and government debt. Conservatives prefer to let parents choose from either public or private schools, through a system of school vouchers. Conservatives argue that poor parents could use vouchers to give their children the same education that rich kids receive. Wealthy parents could still pay privately without a voucher.

One might think that Modern Liberals would support school vouchers. After all, Modern Liberals claim to be the champions of poor people. They also usually support all types of "leveling" schemes. However, on this issue the opposite is true. Modern Liberal politicians are mostly in lock step *against* school vouchers. The most cynical of conservatives claim that Modern Liberals want to keep poor black kids trapped in bad schools. They argue that Modern Liberals want to keep black people poor, so they will remain a permanent underclass, addicted to welfare and a loyal voting block for the Democratic Party.

In fact, the true explanation is only slightly less diabolical. Modern Liberal politicians oppose school vouchers because the powerful teachers' unions oppose school vouchers. The teachers' unions provide volunteer campaign work and huge campaign donations for the Democratic Party. Therefore, the Democratic Party will do everything it can to satisfy the teachers' unions. The ugly truth is, the Democrats believe that receiving campaign aid from the teachers' unions is more important than giving a decent education to poor children.

In fact, the creation of a federal Department of Education was a political payback to the teachers' unions from President Jimmy Carter. This agency employs burned out teachers so they can collect paychecks while they sit at desks going over useless data and otherwise pushing papers. Has the Department of Education improved education? Quite the opposite. SAT scores are now lower than they were before the Department of Education was created. To help conceal this embarrassing development, the SAT score system was changed in 1995. Now extra points are added to most scores, so that baby-boomer parents cannot accurately compare the scores of their children to their own scores.[513] One can only wonder how Modern Liberal politicians can continue to fund the Department of Education without blushing.

During every election cycle the teachers' unions call for more money to be spent on public schools. However, as we saw in Chapter Five, spending more money has little to no effect upon the quality of education. Other factors are far more important. These more important factors are: 1) the number of days a child is absent from school, 2) the amount of television watched in the home, 3) the number of pages of homework completed, 4) the quality of reading material available in the home, and (most important of all) 5) whether there are two parents in the home.[514] None of these critical factors are improved by spending more money on education.

The history of wasted money in the public school system also supports the conservative view on school vouchers. Government schools waste vast amounts of money on administrators and other *non-classroom expenses*. As a result, government schools normally employ from *ten to twenty times more administrators* (per student) than do private schools. For example, the New York City public school system employs at least 7,000 administrators for about one million students. This means the government system employs one administrator for every 142 students. Meanwhile, in the privately run Catholic school system of New York City, only twelve administrators are used. This private system has 150,000 students.[515] This means the private system only needs one administrator for every 12,500 students.

WHY JOHNNY CAN'T THINK

Finally, there is a political reason for why the government should get out of the education business. It is dangerous for freedom if the government is allowed to groom our children for citizenship. The government has a vested interest in producing obedient, docile subjects. The government naturally wants to produce adults who would never think of civil disobedience, much less revolution. Therefore, schools run by the government are an unnecessary danger to civil liberty.

Concern about this danger is not mere paranoia. Ever since the 1930's, the largest teachers' organization in America has been controlled by radical Modern Liberals, who support every conceivable expansion of government power. In 1934, Dr. Harold Rugg and Dr. George Counts (with help from a handful of supporters, including California's influential School Superintendent Dr. Willard Givens) managed to gain control over the National Education Association (NEA).[516] These doctrinaire Modern Liberals were all zealous followers of the famous socialist, Dr. John Dewey of Columbia University. Ever since then, the NEA has done more to implement the educational theories of Dr. Dewey than any other group.

With their control of this powerful lobbying organization, Modern Liberals now influence educational policy from Washington DC all the way down to your local school board. The Modern Liberals who control the NEA affect decisions about curriculum, text books, testing protocols and even teaching methods. The NEA's influence is daunting, and it usually goes unchallenged. There is simply no comparable conservative organization to act as a counter weight.

Under Modern Liberal leadership, the NEA has supported the entire spectrum of left-wing causes, including socialism, gun control, abortion, high taxes, global government, amnesty for illegal aliens, government controlled health care, welfare, homosexual marriage, global warming, the Silly Putty Constitution, multiculturalism, feminism, nuclear disarmament, and any other leftist cause that comes along. According to former KGB agent Yuri Bezmenov, this push for left-wing indoctrination has seriously damaged American society:

"Marxism-Leninism ideology has been pumped into the soft heads of at least three generations of American students, without being challenged or counter-balanced by American patriotism."[517]

This is because the Modern Liberals who control the NEA are more concerned with changing the attitudes of our children than with educating our children. The Modern Liberals who run the NEA believe that the primary mission of teachers is not to teach academics, but rather to indoctrinate students to accept socialism, collectivism, and government control over their lives. Read what Dr. Rugg and Dr. Givens (two of the Dewey disciples who originally took over the NEA) openly said:

"...through the schools we shall disseminate a new conception of government—one that will embrace all of the collective activities of men; one that will postulate the need for scientific control and operation of economic activities in the interest of all people."[518] (Dr. Harold Rugg.)

"...we stand today at the verge of a great culture. But to achieve these things many drastic changes must be made. A dying laissez—faire culture must be completely destroyed, and all of us, including the owners, must be subject to a large degree of social control."[519] (Dr. Willard Givens.)

This arrogant desire to brainwash our kids instead of educating them in English, math and science, has resulted in three generations of under-educated Americans. Shockingly, John Dewey basically said that teachers should treat kids like cretins and not try to teach them anything challenging, lest this might *"violate the child's nature:"*

"We violate the child's nature...by introducing the child too abruptly to a number of special studies, of reading, writing, geography, etc. out of relation to his social life...the truer the correlation of the school subjects is not science, nor literature, nor history, nor geography, but the child's own social activities."

Due to this intentional "dummying down" of American schools, illiteracy is now worse than ever.[520] A few fortunate souls who were educated the old fashioned way have noticed that America's children are getting short-changed. According to the brilliant father of the US nuclear submarine force, Admiral Hyman Rickover:

"America is reaping the consequences of the destruction of traditional education by the Dewey-Kilpatrick experimentalist philosophy... Dewey's ideas have led to the elimination of many academic subjects on the ground that they would not be useful in life...The student thus receives neither intellectual training nor the factual knowledge which will help him understand the world he lives in, or to make well reasoned decisions in his private life or as a responsible citizen."[521]

So Admiral Rickover was not merely concerned about the lack of academic instruction being given to American school children. He also feared their lack of knowledge and intellectual training made them less capable of making decisions in their private lives. This sad state of American youth did not happen by accident. Dr. John Dewey and his followers purposely discouraged the independent thought process that might lead to individual decision-making. According to the so-called "dean of American education:"

"Children who know how to think for themselves spoil the harmony of the collective society which is coming, where everyone is interdependent." [522] (Dr. John Dewey.)

By now it must be obvious to anyone with common sense that Dr. John Dewey was a blathering fool. Sadly, Dewey's theories about socialism, globalism, and collectivism are still being taught in most of America's teachers' colleges. Therefore, his influence on American schools is still pervasive. This is largely due to the power of the NEA, which strongly influences the curriculums of America's teachers' colleges.

Thanks to the NEA, public education in America is based largely on the demented musings of a socialist crackpot.

MODERN BLACKLISTING

Education is just one part of Modern Liberalism's complete hegemony over Western culture. The writers of television programs, movies, and live theatre are all predominantly Modern Liberals. This is not entirely due to the natural Modern Liberal penchant for fantasy and self-delusion. The "blacklisting" of conservatives is also a factor. Modern Liberal blacklisting has been far more pervasive than conservative blacklisting was back in the 1950's during McCarthyism.

For over fifty years, Hollywood's blacklisting of conservatives has generally prevented them from achieving success in the film industry.[523] The few conservative actors who have managed to become successful were all careful not to reveal their conservative views until long after they had already established their acting careers. These discrete few include Mel Gibson, Jon Voight, Sylvester Stallone, and Tom Selleck.

We have already noted that college faculties across America are increasingly made up of Democrats (Modern Liberals). But why is this happening? Blacklisting explains how Modern Liberals have taken control of higher education in America. The number of conservative scholars who have been denied tenure, promotions, fellowships, and lecture chairs at American universities is astounding. For example, back in the 1920s, the great Austrian economist Ludwig Von Mises was repeatedly denied teaching positions for which he was eminently qualified. The problem was that the European universities were all run by socialists. Von Mises was a free market capitalist. His other handicap was being Jewish.

"For a Jew to get a professorship he had to have the support of his fellow Jews...But the Jews who were teaching were all socialists, and Mises was an anti-socialist, so he could not get the support of his own fellows."[524]

Finally, in 1945, Von Mises was permitted to lecture at the New York University School of Business. However, as his conservative (free market) views became better known, the University tried to quietly get rid of him. Instead of telling him that his laissez-faire ideas were too conservative, the administration told him they could not afford to pay his lecture fees any longer. A few wealthy conservative patrons stepped in and paid him a salary equivalent to what he had been receiving from the school.[525] Only in this way was he able to continue lecturing, i.e. without receiving a salary from the University.

During the 1950's and 1960's, the only major school of economics that had a significant number of conservative professors was the University of Chicago. This was not because the administrators at the University of Chicago went out of their way looking for conservative teachers. Rather, it was simply because Chicago was the only major school of economics that did not actively discriminate against conservative teachers. Therefore, by default, conservatives went to the University of Chicago because they had no other place to go.[526]

Modern Liberals throughout the rest of the American university system were mortified that conservative economists had found a safe haven in Chicago. The Liberal Establishment (e.g. the Rockefeller, Carnegie, and Ford Foundations) tried to isolate and even eliminate this last refuge of conservative thought. For example, as early as 1961, the head of the Ford Foundation's Economic Funding Program (Kermit Gordon) warned the University of Virginia's president that future funding might be cut off if the school hired or promoted any *conservative* professors in the field of economics:

"...additions should be made to the staff (faculty) of full professional members of different 'modern' outlook (sic)... care should be taken in making or renewing non-tenure appointments, as well as those of higher rank, to AVOID RECRUITMENT FROM THE CHICAGO SCHOOL."[527] (Emphasis added.)

As a result of this financial intimidation, the President of the University of Virginia (Edgar F. Shannon) got rid of conservative economists such as James Buchanan, Gordon Tullock, Ronald Coase, and G. Warren Nutter. Two of these academic refugees later went on to become Nobel laureates.

In 1950, the conservative professor F.A. Harper dared to have his students read a book written by the conservative economist Hayek. The book in question was *The Road to Serfdom*. It pointed out disturbing similarities between Nazism and communism. For this blasphemy against Modern Liberalism, Harper was summarily purged from Cornell University.[528]

Back in the 1960's at Yale law school, Robert Bork was one of only two conservatives on a staff of about forty-five people. This means that only 5% of the staff was conservative. Bork noticed that when a new candidate (a conservative) was being considered, he was quickly rejected, because, in the words of one professor, hiring a third conservative might *"tip the balance."*[529]

Some professors have been blacklisted simply for pointing out human rights violations committed by communist regimes. Steven Mosher, a highly qualified PhD candidate at Stanford was denied his doctorate degree because he made the mistake of telling the truth about human rights abuses in Communist China. The fact that he had lived in China and had first hand knowledge of the subject did not matter.[530] After Mosher exposed the communists' abuse of Chinese farmers with his book, *Broken Earth: The Rural Chinese*, he was effectively banished from academia.

Sometimes the Modern Liberal demand for intellectual orthodoxy reaches the absurd. For example, Jared Sakren of the Arizona State University Drama Department was denied tenure after he rejected a feminist's request to alter Shakespeare's language in "The Taming of the Shrew." Instead, the Drama Department put on the intellectual tour de force, "Betty the Yeti: An Eco-Fable."[531]

Blacklisting is a deliberate effort by one group of people *to exterminate the ideas of an opposing group*. Therefore, it is evil. It is the moral equivalent of book-burning. Blacklisting has turned our universities into very expensive indoctrination camps. Our tax dollars are supporting an intellectual gulag that demands conformity and punishes dissent. As a result, American universities are now the exact opposite of "a free marketplace of ideas."

THE VICTORY OF SOCIALISM

Education and the mass media are not the only fields dominated by Modern Liberals. In regard to the economy, Modern Liberals are winning on that battlefront as well. Socialism has triumphed over free market capitalism. Every industrialized nation in the West now has some sort of government-run (tax-payer funded) retirement plan, government health plan, government school system, welfare system, disability income program, and even a government food distribution system.

For example, US tax-payers pay for 30 million free meals *everyday for school children alone*. Yet even this expense is small compared to the Food Stamp program, which currently feeds 45 million Americans and illegal aliens every day.[532] No politician would dare try to eliminate any of these government assistance programs. These welfare programs have millions of recipients who depend on them for economic support. These people will certainly vote against anyone who tries to reduce their benefits. Furthermore, each welfare program would be doggedly defended by sympathetic journalists, who are overwhelmingly Modern Liberals.

THE FINAL OBSTACLE TO GLOBALISM

Surprisingly, a few Modern Liberal media outlets have already declared that they have won the struggle for global government. One of these outlets is the *New Republic*. On January 17th 2000, the cover of this Modern Liberal journal read in bold print; *"America is surrendering its sovereignty to a world government. Hooray."* In the text of the related article by journalist Robert Wright, conservatives were rudely admonished; *"World government is coming. Deal with it."*

In reality, Modern Liberals are being a bit premature if they are already celebrating the triumph of globalism. This is because the Supreme Court has been less willing to support globalism than it has been to support socialism. Surprisingly, the Supreme Court has generally defended US Sovereignty with an honest interpretation of Article VI of the Constitution. Article VI reads:

"This Constitution and the Laws of the United States which shall be made in Pursuance thereof; and all treaties made, or which shall be made, under the authority of the United States, shall be the supreme Law of the Land; and the Judges in every State shall be bound thereby, any Thing in the Constitution or the Laws of any State to the Contrary notwithstanding."

A superficial reading of this language would indicate that any treaty is a higher law than the US Constitution itself. In other words, it appears that international treaties can override the Constitution. However, this is a spurious interpretation of Article VI. When the Founding Fathers were writing the Constitution during the summer of 1787, they did not know how long it would take for the States to approve it. They did not know if the approval process ("ratification") would take a few months or several years. In fact, it ended up taking a year and a half for the Constitution to be ratified and then finally enacted.[533]

The Founding Fathers realized that during the ratification process, treaties with foreign nations and Indian tribes would still have to be agreed upon. Lingering British control over the Indian Territory had to be resolved. Some property disputes still festered after the Treaty of Paris. These conflicts could not wait for the Constitution to be ratified by the states. So the Founding Fathers intended that all of the treaties which might be signed during the ratification process, would still be honored after the Constitution was finally ratified. This is what they meant by *"all treaties made or which shall be made."* On the other hand, any treaties made after the Constitution became law on March 4th, 1789, would obviously be inferior to the Constitution.

Fortunately, in 1957 the US Supreme Court faithfully followed this historical interpretation of Article VI.[534] The Court ruled that the US Constitution was superior to any treaty made after the Constitution was ratified in 1789. So if any modern treaty contradicted the US Constitution, then that treaty was null and void. However, it remains to be seen if our current Supreme Court would still follow this logic. If any future Supreme Court decides to follow the literal language of Article VI, (and ignore its historical context) then American sovereignty will fall victim to the forces of globalism.

THE MODERN LIBERAL ADVANTAGES

We have already detailed the means by which Modern Liberalism has dominated the West politically, economically, and culturally. It has acquired this dominance through its control of the mass media, labor unions, teachers' unions, higher education, politicians, and both the television and film industries. But exactly how are Modern Liberals able to maintain their control over all these institutions? Why have conservatives failed to loosen the Modern Liberal grip on power? Conservatives have failed because Modern Liberals enjoy three great advantages:

#1. MODERN LIBERALISM IS MORE DYNAMIC

Modern Liberals are highly motivated by the positive goal of improving society. In contrast, Status-Quo Conservatives only have the negative motivation of preventing change. This inability to take the initiative puts Status-Quo Conservatives at a hopeless disadvantage. It puts them constantly on the defensive. They can only try to remain static, while Modern Liberals constantly push ahead to change society according to their latest plans. The 18th century American scion Fisher Ames recognized this inherent weakness of Status-Quo Conservatism:

"It is indeed a law of politics (as well as physics) that a body in action must overcome an equal body at rest."[535]

Because Modern Liberalism keeps moving away from traditional restraints on personal behavior, it is never satisfied. It never stops pushing. One illustration of this comes from the homosexual liberation movement. At first Modern Liberals only wanted to decriminalize homosexual behavior. Then after achieving this goal, they sought protection from discrimination in the work place. Next, they wanted to make sure homosexuals could adopt children just like heterosexual couples. Now they want homosexuals to be given the legal status of married couples.

We should not be surprised if in a few decades, Modern Liberals will seek to require that every teenager should have at least one homosexual experience, so as to "round off" their high school education. Does this sound ridiculous? Please remember that only ten years ago the idea of homosexual marriage was considered ridiculous.

Western civilization has long recognized that a man and a woman living together to raise children is the most stable building block for society. Marriage is an institution which honors that tradition. *Homosexual couples have nothing to do with that tradition.* Therefore, homosexuals should have nothing to do with the institution of marriage.[536]

Moreover, if homosexual marriage becomes legal, then polygamy would logically follow. After all, the homosexuals wanted us to change the definition of marriage to accommodate their alternative lifestyle. The polygamists want exactly the same thing. Polygamists want us to change the definition of marriage to accommodate *their* alternative lifestyle. In fact, polygamous marriage makes more sense than homosexual marriage, from both a historical and biological point of view.

Of course many long-term homosexual couples do have a legitimate complaint. They often cannot obtain medical or pension benefits for their partners because they cannot be legally married. The most prudent cure for this problem would be to merely change those discriminatory laws. The federal government should recognize and give benefits to any couple that is registered by any state as a "civil union." However, changing the definition of marriage to accomplish this purpose is over-kill. It's like setting off an atom bomb to kill a few mice.

This "never satisfied" trait of Modern Liberalism can also be seen in race relations. At first Modern Liberals only sought equal political rights for black people. Then, after they achieved this noble goal, Modern Liberals could not rest. They moved ahead and forced children to be bussed to far away schools, so that racial balance could be achieved inside the classrooms, (despite the fact that no academic benefits accrued for anybody). Then Modern Liberals demanded that racial quotas be imposed on employers and colleges.

Eventually Modern Liberals will probably seek "equality of outcome," i.e. that schools must graduate a certain percentage of blacks and Hispanics regardless of their qualifications. We should not be surprised if someday Modern Liberals will demand that a worker's pay should be determined not by his productivity, but merely by his race. This will be touted as "the only sure way" to prevent economic discrimination against racial minorities. Does this sound ridiculous? Remember that fifty years ago people thought the idea of racial quotas for jobs and education was ridiculous. Now these quotas are commonplace. Over time, the unthinkable becomes acceptable.

Another example of this never-ending quest for change is the feminist movement. A few decades ago, most people were shocked at the idea that under age girls might be given abortions without anyone telling their parents about it. Nowadays this is the law in many states. Over time, and with enough pressure from activist groups, the outrageous becomes normal.

Just as in a military struggle, when one side is always on the offensive, and the other side is always on the defensive, the outcome of the war is virtually assured. The side which maintains the offensive will nearly always triumph. In politics, Modern Liberals are constantly on the offensive. They keep moving from one conquest to the next, while Status-Quo Conservatives can only mount rear guard actions, because they are constantly in retreat.

Status-Quo Conservatives are also intellectually adrift, because they lack a permanent reference point from which to measure the leftward drift of society. This means they cannot observe their own leftward movement as well. Therefore, many Status-Quo Conservatives are not even aware that they are being carried along towards bigger, more powerful government. They certainly cannot swim against the current.

Only the Libertarian Conservatives possess a permanent standard which lets them consistently judge any government policy. Their permanent standard limits the government to only two functions; to prevent foreign invasion, and to prevent citizens from harming each other. Any other action by the government is illegitimate. This standard does not change over time, nor does it float along with the social current. This explains why only Libertarian Conservatives have not drifted leftward to support bigger government. However, Libertarian Conservatives are so few in number (and so shunned by the Modern Liberal news media) that they have virtually no influence on contemporary events.

Because Modern Liberalism is constantly changing it cannot be defined by its end goals. It can only be described temporarily, by the current goals it has in mind. As T.S. Eliot observed: *"It (liberalism) is a movement not so much defined by its end, as by its starting point, away from, rather than towards something definite."*[537] Yet what exactly is Modern Liberalism moving away from? According to Status-Quo Conservatives such as Robert Bork, Modern Liberalism is constantly moving away from the limits on immoral behavior which are imposed by religion, tradition, law, family, and society in general.

In contrast, Libertarian Conservatives such as Robert Higgs see Modern Liberalism as more of a political movement, constantly moving away from individual freedom and towards authoritarianism. Author Irving Kristol sees both movements happening simultaneously, towards moral anarchy on the one hand, and political repression on the other.

No matter where it is currently headed, Modern Liberalism cannot be defined by its values, because these values are always changing.

Recall that Herbert Croly declared, *"Liberalism is an activity."* He was probably correct. Modern Liberalism is essentially a call for action. It is a methodology that constantly generates new impetus for change, because Modern Liberals believe in social experimentation above all else. Some of the most ardent Modern Liberal scholars readily admit this:

"Liberalism is an attitude rather than a set of dogmas, an attitude that insists upon QUESTIONING ALL PLAUSIBLE AND SELF-EVIDENT PROPOSITIONS."[538] (Morris Raphael Cohen, Russian born Marxist scholar. Emphasis added.)

"The essence of the liberal outlook lies not in what opinions are held, but in how they are held." (Bertrand Russell, noted atheist.)

"Liberalism is a methodology. Liberalism is not what you believe. It is how you believe."[539] (David Baumbaugh, Democratic Party activist.)

Some very prominent Modern Liberal politicians agree. Adelia Stevenson said that the essence of liberalism was *"...being open to new ideas."* Likewise, John F. Kennedy defined a liberal in part as *"...someone who welcomes new ideas without rigid reactions..."*[540] Of course being open to new ideas is really just the same as being open to more change.

In Chapter Seven, we saw that some Modern Liberals define their ideology as *the pursuit of increased government power*. Now we see that other Modern Liberals define it as *the pursuit of change*. These two definitions are not contradictory. They are perfectly compatible. By combining these two definitions we finally arrive at a working definition of Modern Liberalism:

Modern Liberalism is the effort to change society through massive government power.

This definition fits perfectly with the five core values of Modern Liberalism: collectivism, authoritarianism, globalism, elitism, and socialism. This definition fits because all five of these values require *massive government power* before they can be implemented. Furthermore, these five values of Modern Liberalism also require *radical changes* in traditional Anglo-Saxon culture.

If Modern Liberalism's appetite for change is insatiable, then does this mean Modern Liberals seek change merely for the sake of change? Obviously they would deny this charge. However, because society can never be perfect, there is always room for more improvement. This means there is always room for more change.

The biggest disagreement that conservatives have with this thinking is that Modern Liberals believe *the government* should decide what changes are needed. In contrast, Conservatives would rather leave those decisions up to *the millions of individuals* who make up the gigantic organism we call society. So contrary to what many people believe, conservatives are not opposed to change. Conservatives just want change to occur naturally. In contrast, Modern Liberals prefer to see changes that are deliberately orchestrated by government leaders, who can change society as they see fit. This is all because Modern Liberals are the intellectual heirs of Saint-Pierre and Rousseau, while conservatives follow Burke and Bastiat.

Modern Liberalism's constant demand for change is politically dangerous, because it refuses to acknowledge that any of our rights are "off limits" from being changed. Under Modern Liberalism, no right is held sacred, and so any right can be taken away. Every tradition in our culture is subject to change. This is another reason why Modern Liberalism fails to honor the three foundations of Anglo-Saxon liberty, namely: government by consent, the law of the land, and the right to property. So the Modern Liberal support for powerful government is not the only reason that Modern Liberalism threatens individual freedom. Modern Liberalism's constant desire for change is another danger to our freedom.

#2. MODERN LIBERALISM HAS EMOTIONAL APPEAL

The second advantage that Modern Liberalism has over conservatism is that Modern Liberalism is far more appealing on an emotional level. As we discussed earlier, Modern Liberalism is an ideology, while conservatism is not. As an ideology, Modern Liberalism promises its followers that they are part of a noble movement to improve mankind. Modern Liberalism offers its followers the prospect of creating an earthly utopia. It is very tempting to believe that you are part of a movement that can "end poverty," and "change the world."

Modern Liberalism promises all this and more. As we saw in Chapter Six, it even offers spiritual meaning for people who lack a traditional belief in God. Modern Liberalism gives purpose to life for people who do not believe in an afterlife. Modern Liberalism (which includes socialism) also promises to achieve perfect fairness, via the redistribution of wealth. Modern Liberalism (which includes globalism) even alleviates the guilt some people feel for having been born into a wealthy nation.

Conservatism offers none of these emotional rewards. Status-Quo Conservatism offers only a sense of respect for our forefathers, and pride in Anglo-Saxon culture. This hardly compares to the heady promise of re-making a perfect world. Look how differently Modern Liberalism and Status-Quo Conservatism approach the problem of poverty. Modern Liberalism promises the lofty goal of ending poverty. To achieve this great feat, (they claim) we must take bold action, by directing money and social services into poverty stricken ghettos.

On the other hand, Status-Quo Conservatism dryly says that poverty can never be eliminated. At best, it can only be kept to a minimum. The best we can do is to reinvigorate the traditional social fabric (two parent families) and keep taxes low. Low taxes will permit one parent to stay home and properly raise children. Low taxes will also encourage investment that will create new jobs. Increasing jobs will reduce poverty. Not very exciting stuff!

Libertarian Conservatism is even less appealing. Libertarian Conservatism offers nothing at all emotionally. Instead it limits the government to only two functions: 1) to prevent people from harming each other, and 2) to prevent foreign invasion. So under Libertarian Conservatism, the government would never get involved in any sort of war on poverty. Libertarian Conservatism protects both economic and political freedom. This economic freedom produces the most wealth possible. So the problem of poverty is automatically addressed by Libertarian Conservatism.

These sober concepts only appeal to the rational part of the human mind. Unfortunately, it appears that in our modern era, the rational part of the human mind is not the dominant part. The emotional part of the brain seems stronger. This may also partly explain the predominance of Modern Liberalism over the past hundred years.

#3. MONEY IS POWER

The third advantage that Modern Liberalism enjoys over conservatism is that the Modern Liberal movement is much better funded than the conservative movement. The Modern Liberal movement has always had extremely wealthy benefactors to help finance its progress. In the beginning of the Milner Group, Lord Rhodes and fellow African Tycoons Abe Baily and Alfred Beit gave the modern equivalent of millions of pounds sterling to support the group's efforts. Then after WWI, these two wealthy Afrikaners were forced to curtail their donations. To fill this void in funding, Lord and Lady Astor endowed the Milner Group up until World War II. After the center of financial influence shifted to the United States in 1945, the two great American charitable trusts began to foot more and more of the bill. In 1927, the Rockefeller Foundation began pouring generous annual contributions into both the CFR and the Institute of Pacific Relations.[541]

The 1960's and 1970's saw significant support from international trader Armand Hammer. Instead of giving money, Hammer arranged trade between the West and Russia that was crucial to sustaining the Soviet economy throughout the 1970's and early 1980's. In the 1990's Modern Liberalism got a financial boost from Modern Liberal tycoons such as Warren Buffet, Bill Gates, Ted Turner, and especially from George Soros. In 2008, Forbes magazine estimated Soros' personal fortune to be 62 billion dollars. It was Mr. Soros who put up the money to create "MoveOn.org," a Modern Liberal political organization which supports the twin goals of globalism and socialism. He also started a news organization which supports Modern Liberalism. It is known as "Media Matters."

Everyone in America is familiar with the tens of thousands of dollars that Hollywood celebrities perennially donate to Modern Liberal political candidates and to Modern Liberal political causes. However, these donations are a pittance compared to the tens of millions spent by men like Soros and Gates, not to mention the hundreds of millions spent by the Rockefeller and Carnegie foundations every year. Since the 1980's, other charitable trusts have begun giving substantial sums in support of globalism and socialism. The most notable of these new-comers are the John D. & Catherine T. MacArthur Foundation, the Woods Fund, the Pew Foundation, the Joyce Foundation, and the Annenberg Project.

One would tend to think that the super rich would be interested in preserving the status quo (i.e. conservatism). Therefore, they would naturally want to keep taxes lower, in order to better preserve their comparative wealth. However, just the opposite seems to be true. The wealthiest people in the world (e.g. George Soros, David and Nelson Rockefeller, Bill Gates, Warren Buffet, etc.) inexplicably support socialism. Why is this?

Modern Liberals assume that the super rich have only altruistic motives. Modern Liberals believe that the super rich support socialism because they are compassionate, and so they sympathize with poor people. This theory cannot be proved or disproved, because it is based entirely on the inner motives that exist inside the minds of the super rich.

In contrast, most conservatives claim that the super rich embrace socialism because it will prevent new-comers from joining their ranks. Socialism (with its high income taxes) will prevent moderately wealthy people from becoming extremely wealthy. The super rich do not fear a high income tax for two reasons. First, as we saw from our discussion of Hauser's law in Chapter Four, the super rich are very adept at sheltering their income from high income taxes. Second, the super rich already possess their vast piles of wealth, so they fear a tax on assets much more than they fear a tax on income.

Regardless of which explanation is correct, the fact remains that Modern Liberalism has long been supported by most of the super rich. In contrast, the conservative movement has had very few wealthy patrons behind it. Aside from the late David Goodrich and a few eccentric Texans (e.g. Ross Perot and the Hunt Brothers), the conservative movement has received little help from the truly super rich. This explains why conservatives have never funded anything as ambitious as the CFR or the RIIA. Furthermore, a few conservative billionaires cannot compete with the massive funding that the big charitable foundations dole out every year to various left-wing causes.

A few wealthy conservatives have set up their own charitable foundations. In fact, two of today's biggest charitable foundations were started by conservatives. These are the Ford Foundation and the John D. & Catherine T. MacArthur Foundation. However, these two foundations were quickly taken over by Modern Liberals. In both cases, Modern Liberals gained control of the foundations and diverted the funds to causes that the original benefactors would have found shocking. In Ford's case, the transition happened while Henry Ford was still alive. He quickly decided he wanted nothing more to do with the foundation he had begun. In the MacArthur case, the original benefactor was a freedom-loving capitalist. However, after John D. MacArthur died, his leftist son changed the foundation into a Modern Liberal support fund. This explains why the MacArthur Foundation's famous "genius grants" are invariably given out to Modern Liberals.

Modern Liberals point out that sometimes the Republican Party manages to collect more political contributions that the Democratic Party.[542] However, this is irrelevant for two reasons. Firstly, (as we will discuss later in this chapter), most of the candidates in the Republican Party are actually Modern Liberals. So whether the Democrats or the Republicans raise more money, America will still continue down the same path, to more collectivism, authoritarianism, globalism, elitism and socialism. Secondly, even if the Republican Party were ever to become truly conservative, it could still never compete financially with the billion dollar budgets of the great charitable foundations, which fund Modern Liberal advocacy groups.

MODERN LIBERALISM TRIUMPHANT?

For the past sixty years, the only real opposition to the Modern Liberal goals of globalism and socialism has come from poorly funded conservative groups such as the John Birch Society, the Eagle Forum, the Club for Growth, and the Cato Institute. With Modern Liberals controlling most of the mass media and virtually all of the institutions of higher education, it is most likely that conservative ideas will soon be left in the dust bin of history.

For the past eighty years, the Modern Liberal members of the US Senate have kept effective control over America's highest court. Since 1932, very few truly conservative judges have been appointed to the US Supreme Court. By truly conservative judges I mean "originalists," i.e. judges who follow the original intentions of the Founding Fathers when interpreting the Constitution. As we have already seen, the originalist interpretation is the only way to prevent the creation of new government powers. Sadly, ever since 1938, the majority of the judges have preferred the "Silly Putty" Constitution, which lets them approve any new government power, and impose any social policy they see fit.[543]

Modern Liberals have controlled the Presidency as well. For the past eighty years, only one truly conservative president has been elected. Even after Ronald Reagan was elected in 1980, his domestic agenda was almost entirely frustrated by a Modern Liberal Congress. All of the other attempts by conservative candidates to become president failed miserably, either in the primaries or in the general election. These include Alf Landon (1936), Robert Taft (1952), Barry Goldwater (1964), Ronald Reagan (1976), Pat Buchanan (1992, 1996, 2000), and Ron Paul (2008).

Conservatives have failed to get any significant part of their agenda passed into law. Conservatives have lost on the issues of abortion, school prayer, a balanced budget amendment, getting the U.S. out of the UN, getting back on the gold standard, abolishing the Federal Reserve Bank, ending federal welfare programs, and closing down the departments of Commerce, Education, the EPA, and the Export-Import Bank.

In contrast, Modern Liberals have triumphed with their control of the mainstream media, popular culture (movies and television), education (both higher and lower), and labor unions. Modern Liberals also control most of the organs of government, all the way from the Presidency down to the city councils of every large city in America. Conservatives only control rural counties, small towns, and a sprinkling of governorships.

Conservatives are clearly losing the demographic battle against Modern Liberals. In the Republican primary election of 2008, there were three truly conservative candidates; Duncan Hunter, Ron Paul and Fred Thompson. Together they garnered only about 14% to 22% of the total Republican vote. The percentage varied from state to state, but it averaged roughly 18%. This estimate is consistent with a poll taken by the Pew Foundation, which found that 17% of Republican voters said they would not vote for their party's Modern Liberal candidate, John McCain.[544] Therefore, within America's conservative party (which accounts for approximately 40% of the US population), only about 18%

of the party membership is truly conservative. This means that at most, only about 8% of the American population is truly conservative. (18% of 40% equals 8%.)

Demographically speaking, true conservatives are becoming extinct. This is not happening due to a lack of sound ideas. If conservative ideas (reduced government power, lower taxes, more individual freedom, and free market economics) were ever implemented, we would certainly enjoy a new era of prosperity and freedom.

However, the cards are so thoroughly stacked against conservatism that it is doomed to oblivion. Modern Liberals control the educational system, the labor unions, teachers' unions, the mass media, the government, the entertainment industry, and even most of the corporate board rooms. How can conservative parents teach their children conservative ideas when their children are being taught Modern Liberal ideas everyday at school, in theaters, and on television? So we should not be surprised that during the election of 2008 only 8% of America was still conservative. Instead, we should be surprised that there were still that many conservatives left.

TWEEDLEDEE VS TWEEDLEDUM

The mere fact that most of our presidents for the past fifty years have been Republicans is of no importance. Even the Republicans in Congress are only nominally more conservative than the Democrats. As Dr. Carroll Quigley documented, the Liberal Establishment does not care which political party is in power. The basic movement towards globalism and socialism still moves right along. The movement towards globalism and socialism may be slightly slower during a Republican administration, but the general direction of the movement never changes.

For example, most Americans believe that Richard Nixon was a conservative. In reality, Nixon was far more "liberal" than most people think. Under Nixon, globalism and socialism made significant gains. In regard to globalism, Mr. Nixon established diplomatic relations with Communist China, while breaking off relations with the free market nation of Taiwan. He was also instrumental in helping Communist China obtain a seat on the UN Security Council. Nixon's foreign policy was run by Henry Kissinger, a zealous supporter of global government.

Nixon also failed to reverse any of the social welfare programs begun by his Modern Liberal predecessor, Lyndon Johnson. Instead, eligibility for these social welfare programs was expanded. In 1972 Nixon even generously signed into law an automatic cost of living increase for anyone living on federally funded welfare programs. He spent significantly more money on social services than he did on the Vietnam War. It was Nixon who signed the executive order to create the first racial quotas for federal contracts and employment (the so-called "Philadelphia Plan"). Worst of all perhaps, it was Nixon who took the US dollar off the gold standard, killing the most sacred conservative cow of all.

The power of the central government also grew during Mr. Nixon's tenure. Nixon imposed central planning on the economy just like his fascist and communist predecessors. He arrogantly tried to freeze wages and prices across the entire country by his own personal decree. Finally, Nixon expanded the federal government when he created two brand new agencies, the Environmental Protection Agency and OSHA. Nixon was not a conservative by any meaningful standard.

For the past sixty years, the only difference between the two American political parties has been on highly emotional issues such as abortion and gun control. Of course these issues are important, but they tend to distract the public from much broader issues, such as the battle between socialism and freedom, and the conflict between globalism and sovereignty. Emotional issues such as abortion and gun control give voters the illusion that they have a real choice during elections.

But the truth is, the overall policies of the two American political parties are almost identical. Both parties support free trade agreements, which erode American sovereignty. Both parties support the United Nations and its plan for global government to replace the nation state. Both parties support the main components of the social welfare state, such as Social Security, Medicare, poverty welfare, and corporate welfare. The Republicans claim to be the party of lower taxes, but they only want to tax income at a few percentage points lower than the Democrats do. The differences between Republican and Democrat tax policies (in terms of the average American household) are truly negligible.

The only important issue that divided the two political parties over the past sixty years has been the recent dispute over Obama's health care take-over. Yet even in this controversy, the question was not whether we should abolish federal control of health care (such as Medicare and Medicaid). Instead the question was merely, *how far shall we expand federal control of health care?* Neither party even considered the idea of getting the federal government out of the health care business completely. So the truly conservative position was not even considered.

The late Dr. Carroll Quigley was one of the shrewdest American political scientists of the 20th century. Quigley was also a Modern Liberal. He openly supported the idea that *the candidates of the two parties should only appear to be different.* He admitted that the Liberal Establishment prefers to have nearly identical candidates from both parties. In this way, the American people can vote merely to vent their frustrations, without having any real impact on long term policy.

"...the two parties should be almost identical, so that the American people can 'throw the rascals out' at any election without leading to any profound or extensive shifts in policy."[545]

The Liberal Establishment is able to exert strong influence over both political parties primarily through its control over the mass media. The Modern Liberal mass media works hard to demonize conservatives, while portraying Modern Liberals in a positive light. This biased reporting is how the mass media effectively prevents true conservatives from being nominated for office by either political party. That is why the candidates from both parties have nearly always been Modern Liberals, ever since the 1930s.

Of course, this explains why the vast majority of elected politicians in America have shifted inexorably to the left. Ideas that were considered liberal fifty years ago are now accepted as "middle of the road," or even conservative. For instance, when President John F. Kennedy was elected he was the darling of the left-wing. However, by today's standards, JFK would be viewed as extremely conservative. Recall that JFK cut taxes, supported anti-communist regimes, tried to overthrow the communist Fidel Castro, and dramatically increased our nuclear arsenal.

On the other hand, ideas that were considered conservative fifty years ago are no longer taken seriously by anyone with power or influence. These include abolishing Social Security, Medicare, federal welfare, and the Federal Reserve Bank. Furthermore, many so-called "neoconservatives" today are even more liberal than the old English

Liberal Party was just one hundred years ago. *Virtually everyone in power has moved further to the left.*

The last gasp for American conservatives was in 1953, the first year of the Eisenhower administration. During his campaign, Eisenhower called for an end to virtually all federal welfare programs. Even Social Security was on the chopping block. Eisenhower also pledged his support for the Bricker Amendment, which would have explicitly made the US Constitution higher law than any international treaty. After less than one year in office, Eisenhower gave up on all of these conservative goals. Instead, Eisenhower accepted both globalism and socialism.[546] Eisenhower even sabotaged the Bricker Amendment in the Senate, causing it to fail by just one vote. Conservatism in America has never recovered since.

In the general election of 2004, the two parties were almost identical. The Republicans originally wanted to make 10% of the Social Security fund subject to individual direction. The Democrats wanted the government to pay for the prescription drugs of the elderly (Medicare Part D). In the end, the Republicans adopted the Democrats' plan for Medicare Part D. Also, the Republicans dropped their idea about privatizing part of Social Security. There was no more disagreement.

More recently, during the primary elections of 2008, there were three serious candidates running for the nomination of the Democratic Party (Barack Obama, Hillary Clinton, and John Edwards). All three were doctrinaire Modern Liberals, supporting every aspect of the social welfare system. The Republicans were similar. Of the nine serious candidates for the so-called "conservative" Republican Party, fully six of them shared *nearly identical support for the same social welfare system.* As we discussed earlier, the few truly conservative candidates, such as Fred Thompson, Duncan Hunter and Ron Paul, received very little voter support across the nation.

The presidential election of 2008 clearly demonstrated how identical the two parties have become. Both Obama and McCain opposed President Bush's tax cuts. Both men fervently believed in man-made global warming. Both men supported expensive "cap and trade" restrictions on carbon dioxide emissions. Both men favored a general amnesty for illegal aliens. Both men promised to prevent any suspected terrorists from being tortured. Both men supported the infamous Bush Bailouts for reckless commercial bankers. Both men failed to offer any plan or timetable for rescuing American troops from the quagmires in Iraq and Afghanistan. The only significant issue they disagreed on was how far to extend government-run health care. And even this issue did not come up until a full year after the election was over. So it is no exaggeration to say that conservatives have not had a presidential candidate to vote for since 1984.

CONCLUSION

Despite the similarities between the two American political parties, and their mutual shift to the left, the past few American presidential elections were fought very bitterly…over almost nothing at all. Recent elections in America have been fought with such rancor that one would think the fate of the nation was being decided. It was not. The fate of the nation was already decided back in 1922 when the CFR was founded. America's fate is to move toward greater socialism and more global government.

At least that was the course that America *was* following, until Islam declared holy war upon the West on September 11, 2001. Muslim terrorism has disrupted the best laid plans of the Liberal Establishment. The attack on September 11, 2001 sounded the death knell for Western civilization, including both Modern Liberalism and conservatism. This brings us to our final chapter.

CHAPTER NINE

THE FUTURE

*"In a time of universal deceit, telling the truth
becomes a revolutionary act."*
George Orwell.

ISLAM INVADES THE WEST

Ever since the 7th century, Muslims have been waging holy war (on and off) against the rest of the world. World War I ended with the collapse of the last Muslim empire, which had been ruled by the Ottoman Turks. For half a century after this defeat, Muslims were unable to do much of anything against the European colonial powers. For a half century, they lacked both technology and money.

This situation began to change during the 1960s. The technology needed to kill non-Muslims (bomb-making) became cheaper and easier to manufacture. Also, the Muslims began demanding far more profits from their oil fields. Now, after the Millennium, forty years of huge profits from oil sales have provided Islamic terrorists with ample resources to finance their holy war against the West.

Because of this, Modern Liberalism is now facing a greater threat than a thousand Rush Limbaughs. In the past, conservatives had merely tried to slow down the Modern Liberal advance toward globalism and socialism. In contrast, Islam seeks to destroy Modern Liberalism completely. Islam is an aggressive ideology that seeks to exterminate every other belief system on earth, including both Modern Liberalism and conservatism. Islam seeks to destroy any belief system that is not based upon the Koran.

Had it not been for the resurgence of militant Islam, then this book would have been much easier to write. It would have simply been about the death of conservatism and the danger of liberalism. However, Modern Liberalism has opened up a hole in the armor of Western civilization, a lethal opening that the Islamic sword will penetrate.

MODERN LIBERALISM'S ACHILLES' HEEL

This hole in our armor was created when Modern Liberalism adopted a new precept: multiculturalism. Multiculturalism is one of the many tertiary movements spawned by Modern Liberalism's overwhelming urge to achieve equality. This burning desire for equality has inspired numerous Modern Liberal "leveling" policies, such as socialism (equality of wealth), women's rights (equality of gender), racial desegregation (equality of race), homosexual rights (equality of sexual preference), public education (equality of knowledge), and national health care (equality of medical treatment). Tragically, the desire for equality also led to multiculturalism, i.e. the belief that all cultures are equally good and equally valuable. This is a pernicious ideological trap. It forces the multiculturalist to tolerate even those cultures that are bent on destroying his own culture.

This is exactly the situation we face with Islam. The doctrine of multiculturalism is preventing us from defending Western culture against a dangerous and implacable enemy: Islam. As a result, multiculturalism threatens to bring down the entire edifice of Western civilization. Every time a serious scholar tries to warn the West about the threat of Islam, the multiculturalists who dominate the news media condemn him with opprobrious clamor. For example, Bernard Lewis is a highly qualified authority on both Islam and the Middle East. Yet he has been vilified beyond all reason merely for speaking the truth; that Islam seeks to destroy the West. The mainstream media cannot refute his arguments or his evidence. So instead they attack him personally, and variously imply that he is hateful, hysterical, or bigoted. Other critics of Islam, such as Daniel Pipes and Robert Spencer, receive similar mistreatment.

Multiculturalism is the offspring of an intellectual movement called "Cultural Marxism," which was conceived by the German communist,

Herbert Marcuse. Most authors prefer to call Marcuse a "socialist." However, Marcuse's slavish obedience to the policies of the USSR, under both Stalin and Khrushchev, indicate that he was really a communist. For example, after the fascists had been defeated in WWII, Marcuse still insisted:

"The Communist Parties are and will remain the sole anti-fascist power...the realization of the theory [of socialism] is only possible through the Communist Parties, and requires the assistance of the Soviet Union."[547]

And just like his Soviet masters, Marcuse believed that free speech should be taken away from anyone who spoke out against socialism, or anyone who even called for limiting social welfare benefits:

"They (the steps needed to implement socialism) include the withdrawal of toleration of speech and assembly from groups and movements which promote aggressive policies, armament, chauvinism, discrimination...or which oppose the extension of public services, social security, medical care, etc."[548]

This total disregard for freedom of speech shows us once again that communists and fascists are nearly identical. And yet, despite his fascist mentality, Marcuse is a household name among Modern Liberals in Continental Europe. His writings have also influenced millions of Modern Liberals in the United States. Marcuse spent some thirty-five years disseminating his authoritarian ideas at various universities across America from the early 1950's until his death in 1979. A darling of the radical left, Marcuse lectured regularly at Harvard, Yale, Brandeis, and at the University of California at San Diego, where he held his professorship. The Modern Liberal militant Angela Davis praised Marcuse, gushing, "...*among the pure scholars he had the most direct and profound effect on historical events of any individual in the twentieth century.*"[549]

Marcuse was one of the leaders of the "Frankfurt School" of socialism. The influence of this small group of ideologues over today's Modern Liberals is comparable to the influence of the French philosophes two hundred years earlier. Since the 1970's, the radical ideas of the socialist Frankfurt School have dominated the departments of history, sociology and political science at nearly every major university in the Western World.

Most members of the Frankfurt School combined Marxism with psychology. Men such as Erich Fromm, Theodor Adorno, and Max Horkheimer, believed that the eternal class struggle was not only a battle between competing economic interests. They also believed that the people who supported property rights and opposed socialism *were mentally ill.* So they saw the great class struggle as a conflict between rational socialists and mentally ill conservatives. In effect, the Frankfurt school claimed that conservatives were crazy, and in sore need of either therapy or medication.[550]

The Frankfurt School abandoned orthodox Marxism because it had obviously failed as an economic theory. As we saw in Chapter Three, Karl Marx had completely underestimated the power of capitalism to generate new wealth and even to spread wealth throughout society. Besides, socialism was already being implemented gradually, without the need for violent revolution by the proletariat, which Marx had insisted upon.

Unlike the other members of the Frankfurt School, Marcuse understood that merely calling conservatives insane was not really Marxism. It had nothing to do with the historical dialectics upon which Marxism was based. So Marcuse decided to alter Marxism into a new ideology, called "Cultural Marxism." This new ideology would preserve the historical dialectic (class struggle) of Marxism, but without relying on economic struggle. Karl Marx had originally blamed the world's problems on an economic class enemy called the bourgeoisies, (capitalists). However, Marcuse now blamed the world's problems on a new class enemy: *white males.* He denigrated white males and made it appear that their influence upon society had been entirely negative. So while the rest of the Frankfurt School combined Marxism with psychology, Marcuse combined Marxism with anthropology.

The truth is, white males are capable of both great good and great evil, just like any other human group. Marcuse could only remember nuclear war, slavery, economic exploitation, and colonialism. He seemed to forget about the positive contributions of white males, such as: democracy, the scientific method, the industrial revolution, electricity, nuclear power, telecommunications, modern medicine, and even civil rights.

The real danger with Cultural Marxism is that when you begin to denigrate white males, you inevitably start to devalue their entire culture as well. All the elements of traditional Western culture were soon rejected by major universities in Europe and North America. The Western literary classics (from Homer to Hemmingway) were scorned. Entire new departments were founded, such as Feminist studies, African American studies, and Hispanic studies, just to counter the perceived over-empowerment of the "white male establishment."

Several American universities now have "White studies" departments, in which students are taught all the negatives (and none of the positives) of the white race. Even the religion of Western culture, Christianity, was (and is) ridiculed beyond reason at Western universities. It has been arbitrarily subjected to critical methods that were never applied to any other religion.

Just as the multiculturalists who dominated our universities began to devalue Western culture, they also began to *over-value* non-Western cultures. Their intent was to level the cultural playing field. The Modern Liberal urge to make everyone equal now went beyond economics and was applied to culture as well. Western culture was now considered no better than any other culture. A band of stone-age headhunters who chew each others' toenails under a tree in New Guinea was now considered every bit as worthy as the culture that produced William Faulkner and the internet. This is the specious ideology we now call "multiculturalism." Sometimes it is called the "diversity movement," or "cultural tolerance."

If multiculturalism had remained merely a harmless fad, then it might have been just a minor attribute along side the far greater triumphs of Modern Liberalism, such as racial equality, the labor movement, women's rights, child labor laws, environmentalism, etc. However, with the rise of Islam, multiculturalism has proven to be extremely dangerous. In fact, multiculturalism will almost certainly bring about the death of Western civilization. Herbert Marcuse was very clever but he was also fatally unwise. When Marcuse invented cultural Marxism, he inadvertently planted within Modern Liberalism the seed of its own destruction.

How will multiculturalism destroy the West? If a majority of Westerners do not see any special value in their own culture, then they will not try to protect Western culture from being destroyed by Islam. Multiculturalism demands absolute tolerance of any non-Western culture. This dogmatic tolerance prevents Modern Liberals from seeing Islam for the perilous threat that it really is. This explains why Modern Liberals have actually welcomed Muslim immigration to the West. Multiculturalism is nothing more than cultural suicide.

ALLAH: THE GOD OF WAR

To understand why radical Muslims want to destroy Western Civilization, just read a good book about Islam, such as Robert Spencer's *Islam Unveiled,* or Don Richardson's *Secrets of the Koran.* For those readers who are unwilling to do that, I offer the following short-hand explanation:

Islam is the only religion on earth that calls for killing non-believers, who are called "infidels" in the Koran. Here are just a few of the deadly verses from the Koran that you will never hear about from the mainstream news media:[551]

"Fight and wage war against the infidels, even if they are your neighbors." Koran 9:125.

"Kill the infidels wherever you find them..." Koran 2:191.

"When you encounter the infidels, strike off their heads until you have made a great slaughter among them, and the remainder of them shall be bound as slaves." Koran 47:4.

"Holy War is mandatory. If you do not fight, your punishment will be grievous and Allah will put others in your place." Koran 9:39.

"It is not fitting for a prophet of Allah to take prisoners of war, but the unbelievers should be killed until they are wiped out from the land, and the believers have the upper hand..." Koran 8:67.

"I will cast a fear in the hearts of the infidels. Strike off their heads then, and cut off their fingertips." Koran 8:12.

"You shall do battle against them (non-Muslims) or else they shall profess Islam." Koran 48:16.

"Lord thou art our protector, give us victory over the Infidel nations." Koran 2:285.

"Fight against them until there be no more discord, and the only worship be that of God." Koran 2:187.

"He shall make Islam victorious over every other religion." Koran 61:9.

"Lord, leave not one single family of infidels upon the earth." Koran 71:27.

"Fight against them until disagreement be at an end, and all religion shall be of God's only." Koran 8:40.

These last four verses are the most troubling of all. They clearly state that Islamic holy war shall not end until the entire world worships only Allah. These verses are a mandate for world conquest. They are a fascist demand for complete intolerance against any religion except Islam. The Koran is in fact a declaration of war against the entire global population of non-Muslims. That is why Muslims have been waging war against the rest of the world for fourteen centuries. Muslim clerics are constantly reminding Muslims that these war verses apply in our own time just as much as when Muhammad was alive.

Of course most Muslims are not suicide bombers. Most Muslims are decent people. However, the fact is that most Muslims are decent people *despite their religion,* not because of it. Islam takes naturally good people, and then it teaches them some very evil ideas.

COMPARE TO THE BIBLE

Muslim apologists and Western multiculturalists argue that the Bible also contains a lot of violence. Indeed, in the Old Testament, Yahweh ordered his people to kill the Canaanites, Amorites, Perizites, Hivites and Jebusites. However, those peoples no longer exist. So the Old Testament cannot be used to justify killing in our modern age.

Furthermore, all those commands to fight were given during a savage and barbaric era. To preserve their religion, the Jews had to have their own land to build permanent settlements. If Yahweh had not told the Jews to fight for their own land, the Jewish tribes probably would have dispersed. The Jews would have been assimilated into the various pagan cultures of the day, and the precious seed of monotheism might have been lost forever. It is important to note that Yahweh only gave the Jews a very *limited* order to fight. It was limited to: (1) only fight certain people, (2) only fight during a critical time period, and (3) only fight for a limited geographic area (Canaan).

In contrast, Muhammad has ordered his followers to fight *all the peoples of the earth, for all time*, until every nation on earth worships only Allah. (See the last four Koranic quotes listed above.) For Muslims there is no limit in time or place, because the vast majority of Muslim clerics still teach that these war commands (like the rest of the Koran) are intended to be obeyed forever.[552]

This brings up the crucial difference between the Koran and the Bible. The Bible contains relatively few quotations from God. Instead, the Bible is mostly a narrative history of events. The Bible records both good and evil behavior. We can choose to follow any example we find in the Old Testament, depending on whether we think it is appropriate for us today. This is very different from the Koran. Muslims believe the Koran is one long quotation of God's own spoken words. So Muslims believe that all of the Koran is strictly binding on them. Therefore, all true Muslims are fundamentalists.

Most Muslim scholars admit that Islam is necessarily a fundamentalist religion. For example, one candid Muslim professor who teaches in America wrote:

"To a considerable extent, all Muslims are fundamentalists, that is, they believe that the Quran…is God's final, complete and perfected revelation for all mankind. The Quran is the supreme guide for the human race."[553]

TOLERANCE IN ISLAM

There are only five verses in the Koran which seem to offer tolerance for non-Muslims:

"Let there be no compulsion in religion." Koran 2:257.

"If they (infidels) become Muslims then they are guided aright; but if they turn away (reject Islam) thy duty is only preaching." Koran 3:19.

"What? Wilt thou compel men to become believers?" Koran 10:99.

"Tell the believers to pardon those who hope not for the days of God…" Koran 45:13.

"We know best what the infidels say; and thou art not to compel them." Koran 50:44.

Unfortunately for humanity, virtually all orthodox Muslim scholars agree that these tolerant verses have all been cancelled out by the 109 verses which demand violent holy war against non-Muslims. Muslim scholars all over the world employ the same method for resolving contradictions in the Koran. Whenever Muslim scholars come across conflicting verses, they try to decide which verse was pronounced earlier by Muhammad, and which verse was pronounced later. They believe that the later verses of Muhammad are binding, and the earlier verses are cancelled out. Unfortunately, Muslim scholars agree that the famous "Sword Verse" of Koran 9:5 was the last verse in which Muhammad addressed the subject of holy war vs. tolerance.[554] Therefore holy war is binding on all Muslims. This bloody verse reads:

"And when the sacred months are past, kill those who join other Gods with God (i.e. Christians) wherever you find them. And seize them, and lay siege to their homes, and lay in waiting for them with every kind of ambush. But if they shall convert, and observe the prayers…then let them go their way, for God is Gracious, Merciful." Koran 9:5.

There is another reason that Muslim scholars believe the bloody verses about holy war are still binding. Muslim scholars agree that any public statements which Muhammad made after the Koran was completed *cannot possibly contradict the Koran*. So they look to Muhammad's later public statements for guidance. Sadly, in Muhammad's last public speech (which he made a full two years after he had finished dictating the Koran), Muhammad repeated his call for violent holy war against non-Muslims.[555] So for virtually all orthodox Muslim scholars, Muhammad's last public statement confirmed the Koran's bloody verses about holy war, and cancelled out the tolerant verses...forever!

Unfortunately, the Modern Liberal news media seem determined to only let Westerners hear about the tolerant verses from the Koran. To know the truth about Islam, you cannot rely on the mainstream news media. The mainstream news media never tell us about all the many Muslim leaders in America who call for abolishing all other religions. According to Omar A. Ahmad, head of the supposedly mainstream Council on American Islamic Relations, no other religion but Islam should be permitted:

"Islam isn't in America to be equal to other faiths, but to be dominant. The Koran...should be the highest authority in America, and Islam the only accepted religion on earth."[556]

Even tenured professors who teach at American universities are boldly calling for Islam to be forced upon unwilling populations. A.J. Abraham is a professor of Middle Eastern Studies at the New York Institute of Technology. In his own book, he arrogantly proclaimed; *"Islam is for everybody, whether they want it or not."* [557]

Islam is determined to destroy all other ideologies and cultures on earth. Therefore, Islam does not deserve to be tolerated as Christianity, Buddhism, and Hinduism deserve to be tolerated. Yet our slavish adherence to multiculturalism prevents us from seeing Islam for the cultural pestilence that it really is. As a result, our great-great-grandchildren will probably witness the death of Western civilization.

WHO IS THE ENEMY?

We are facing a potent and malevolent ideology that is determined to destroy our culture and our way of life. In response, we have done little more than bury our heads in the sand, trying to pretend that "Islam is not our enemy." We pretend that only the Islamic terrorists are the enemy. As a result, we ignore and even patronize the very ideology that continues to generate new terrorists every year. Our real enemy is the source of Muslim terrorism: the Islamic religion itself.

Peter W. Hauer

THE SILENT INVASION

The main reason for the spread of Islam is the generous immigration policies of the Western nations. In fact, Islamic immigration to the West is an even greater threat than Islamic terrorism. Islamic immigration and over population will indeed let Islam conquer the world. Look at Europe. Back in 1945, there was only one mosque in all England. Fifteen years later, England was supporting 25 mosques. In 1976 England was hosting 200 mosques. By 1989 there were over a thousand mosques in this land that has an official Christian religion.[558] Ironically, many of these mosques were converted Christian churches. As a result of both loose immigration and the high Muslim birth rate, Islam is now the second largest faith in England.

The Muslim invasion of England is typical for most of Europe. Germany will soon have similar problems due to its growing population of Turkish Muslims. In 1950 Germany had only three mosques. Now Germany has over 2000 mosques.[559] Muslims now comprise 7% of the population in the Netherlands. Muslim immigrants to Spain are so numerous that they are openly talking about re-establishing "Andalusia," i.e. the old Muslim state that ruled Southern Spain for nearly 800 years. It is no coincidence that most Muslim immigrants to Spain now decide to settle in this exact location. It is part of an open plan to re-capture "Muslim territory."

France is in more trouble than any other European nation. In 1960 there were already one million Muslims living in France.[560] Most of these Muslims came from one former French colony, Algeria. Now Muslims in France are estimated to account for six to eight million people. This represents almost 10% of the population. Modern Liberalism's lenient immigration policies are finally putting into practice the charitable teachings of the Sermon on the Mount. However, the teachings from the Sermon on the Mount (humility, compassion and charity) were intended as a guide for *individual behavior*, not as a guide for government policy. The feminine religion of Christianity (passive, compassionate, and charitable) is finally falling victim to the masculine faith of Islam, (violent, ruthless, and rapacious).

THE POPULATION BOMB

It took half a century of political struggle before Western women finally won the right to use birth control devices such as condoms and the birth control pill. However, Islamic law condemns any action taken by married couples to avoid pregnancy. All forms of birth control, (condoms, hormones, and even premature withdrawal) violate Allah's exclusive prerogative to decide when life will occur. Islamic law completely takes away a woman's right to control her own body. Under Islamic law, a woman has no more control over her reproductive organs than a farm cow. Worst of all, Islamic law is permanent and cannot be changed, because it is based on the original teachings of Muhammad.

As a result, Islamic nations are suffering from the highest birth rates in the world. In fact, according to the population data available from UNESCO, the forty-one nations with the highest birth rates in the entire world are all Muslim nations. Niger tops the list with 6.9 births per female, and Yemen is right behind with 6.8 births. As a reference for comparison, even the Catholic nations are lagging far behind the Muslims. The highest fertility rate among Catholic nations is 4.8 births per female in Haiti. But Haiti is only number 42 on the worldwide fertility list. Next come Honduras and Paraguay, both with four births per female. So Islam is indeed the "world's fastest growing religion," but this is due mostly to the *explosive birth rates* in Muslim nations.

From Morocco to Indonesia, Islam is quietly precipitating an environmental crisis that could imperil the earth's fragile eco-system. Hindu India and Buddhist China have both curbed their population problems with remarkable success. Islam stands alone as a true impediment to curbing the overpopulation of our planet. While the native French, German, Spanish and Dutch populations are seriously declining, Muslims are reproducing at remarkable speed in Europe. If current trends continue, then by 2090 Western Europe will have a majority Muslim population.[561]

WHY WE WILL BE DESTROYED

Muslims are not the largest group of immigrants to the USA. Therefore, America will probably not be conquered demographically. We will be conquered through terrorism. This conquest will probably take the form of crippling terrorist attacks that bring down our economy. American immigration policy has failed to restrict the influx of Muslims. In a suicidal gesture of tolerance, both George W. Bush Jr. and Barack Obama have permitted Muslims refugees to settle in America, without any serious effort to screen out militant Muslims.

Because of America's growing number of Muslims, we now harbor a huge pool of potential terrorists inside our own country. There are three million Muslims living in the United States. According to a 2007 poll conducted by the Pew Research center, 8% of these people believe that suicide bombings can be justified under Islam.[562] That means 240,000 Muslims living in America believe that suicide bombings can be justified in order to serve Allah. Five percent of all Muslims surveyed said they support Al-Quaida. So 150,000 Muslims living in this country as our neighbors support a vicious terrorist group that has killed at least three thousand American civilians.

The most effective way to prevent the coming disaster is for Western nations to begin deporting Muslim immigrants immediately. Of course we will not do this, because such an act would "offend" Modern Liberals. Deportations would be decried in the Modern Liberal mass media, and condemned in the schools and universities. We common folk would not be allowed to hear even one rational voice in favor of deportation. Instead we would be told that deportation of Muslims is a "fringe idea" and "hateful." We would be told that message so often that most of us would believe it. Just listen to the propaganda already spewing from the mouths of our Modern Liberal rulers: *"Americans respect and honor Islam." (Bill Clinton)*[563] *"Islam is a religion of peace." (George W. Bush Jr.)*[564] *"It (the Muslim call to prayer) is one of the prettiest sounds on earth..." (Barack Obama).*[565]

Multiculturalism has so brainwashed us that we are unwilling to even criticize a foreign faith like Islam. We are certainly too civilized to begin mass deportations based upon religious belief. Sadly this means we have become too civilized to protect ourselves from a cultural invasion. *We have become too civilized for our own good*. While Modern Liberals eagerly embrace cultures that are foreign to the West, Muslims are determined to destroy cultures that are foreign to Islam.

We Westerners are the first people in history to passively accept the destruction of our culture merely because we think it would be immoral to take the steps needed to protect our culture. This is quite different from the fall of ancient Rome. The 5th century Romans knew they were in danger, and they desperately wanted to stop the invading barbarians. However, they were unable to defend themselves because they had grown so weak militarily.

The reverse is true today. We Westerners are quite able to defend ourselves. To defend ourselves culturally, we could ban Muslim immigration and deport Muslims. To defend ourselves militarily, we could easily bomb every Muslim army on earth into oblivion. To defend ourselves from Muslim terrorists, we could threaten to obliterate *several* Muslim cities in retaliation for any *one* American city that is attacked.

However, unlike the ancient Romans, we are *unwilling* to defend ourselves. We are unwilling to take any of the unpleasant steps that are necessary for our defense. Instead, we are taking the pacifist ideas from the Sermon on the Mount and implementing them as national policy. This is not something to be proud of. Our obsequious tolerance of Islam will be our undoing. As a result of our excessive tolerance, Modern Liberalism and conservatism will both vanish from the earth.

TORTURE

One example of our deliberate failure to defend ourselves is the Modern Liberal refusal to use torture as a way to obtain information from suspected terrorists. In terms of human lives saved, torture is morally justified. For example, if torturing one thousand suspected terrorists had prevented the 9/11 attack, then we would have saved over three thousand innocent lives. One Modern Liberal friend of mine replied to this logic by saying "Morality is not determined by mere numbers." Why not? What other criteria makes more sense? If our government refuses to torture terrorists, and more civilians are blown up as a result, how is this "moral?"

It is ironic that Modern Liberals object to making a policy decision based on the number of people it can save. On nearly every other social issue, Modern Liberals are quite utilitarian. Remember, they nearly always support Jeremy Bentham's collectivist goal of, *"the greatest good for the greatest number of people."* As a result, most Modern Liberals also accept the closely related idea, "The ends justify the means." However, on the issue of torture, Modern Liberals suddenly become moral absolutists. They display a level of self-righteousness that Jerry Falwell would have admired.

Unfortunately, this atypical devotion to moral absolutism is badly misplaced. Muslim terrorists are already fighting us with the most unconventional warfare known to mankind. They are purposely targeting civilian victims. They are not following any of the rules of warfare normally observed by civilized nations. It would be extremely foolish for us to obey those same rules when our enemy is not. We would be fighting at a great disadvantage, and so we would probably lose the war.

Imagine you are in a boxing match, and suddenly your opponent pulls out a knife. Would you feel morally obligated to continue following the normal rules of boxing? Of course not. You are now in a fight for survival, and you can fight back in any way necessary. The same principle applies when a nation is fighting for its survival against an opponent who does not follow any rules. Muslim terrorists must be fought *by any means necessary.*

Modern Liberals who oppose torture also claim that information obtained under torture is unreliable, because "the victim will give false information just to end his suffering." In fact the opposite is generally true. *So long as the prisoner is still held in captivity,* he has every motive not to lie. You see, if the information he gives proves to be false, then his captors can torture him even more severely than they did the first time. This threat of increased torture will prevent most prisoners from lying in the first place. It will certainly prevent almost any human being from lying twice.

Empirical evidence shows that torture is very useful. As of this writing, the CIA has only used torture on three individuals.[566] One of these was Kaleed Shiek Muhammad, one of the masterminds behind the 9/11/01 airplane attacks. After just two and a half minutes of a mild form of torture called "water-boarding," this terrorist revealed critical information about several planned terrorist attacks. All of these planned attacks were prevented because of the information he gave under torture.[567] Dozens if not hundreds of innocent lives were saved because stout hearted men had the resolve to torture this evil madman.

Another success story was the mild torture given to Zayn Abidin Muhammad Hussein Abu Zubaida, another Al-Qaida terrorist. Before the water boarding, agents described him as *"ideologically zealous, defiant, and uncooperative."*[568] In fact, after several weeks of conventional interrogations, Abu Zubaida refused to give any information. However, after just 35 seconds of riding a water board Abu Zubaidah gave up the names of other Al-Qaida operatives, and also information about several planned terrorist attacks. Once again many innocent lives were saved, because tough men were willing to do an unpleasant job just to keep the rest of us safe.

Unfortunately, Western culture has become so feminized that unconventional methods such as torture will not be used. Because of this, we will probably lose the military battle against Muslim terrorists. Eventually they will start destroying entire cities in America, with nuclear bombs probably obtained from either the Russian mafia or sympathetic elements within the Pakistani or Iranian military.[569]

OUR ONLY HOPE

If we are unwilling to take the unpleasant steps necessary to protect ourselves, is there any hope for us? Couldn't we just convert Muslims to Christianity, or even to atheism? According to Islamic law, anyone who attempts to lead a Muslim away from Islam must be killed. This barbaric law is actually enforced in some Muslim nations, most notably Saudi Arabia, Iran and Pakistan. Under Islamic law, any Muslim who leaves Islam is also subject to the same death penalty.

There is virtually no hope that Muslims will ever become "Westernized" enough that they will accept non-Muslim cultures and institutions. This is true for two reasons. First, the Koran forbids Muslims to marry outside their religion. This is the same stumbling block that prevented the Jews from being assimilated into European culture for almost two thousand years. Of course this begs an obvious question: "Why were the Jews such a peaceful minority compared to Muslims?" The crucial difference is that the Torah never tells Jews to kill all the non-Jews in the world. However, the Koran does indeed tell Muslims to kill all non-Muslims in the world, in 109 verses.[570]

The second reason that Muslims will not accept Western traditions and institutions is because Muhammad demanded that all laws must be based solely on his own teachings. To Muslims, any Western law that conflicts with Muhammad's teaching is illegitimate, and must be abolished. For example, Muhammad taught that no one can preach in public about any religion except Islam. This teaching violates our right to free speech under the Constitution. So to any orthodox Muslim, the First Amendment must be abolished, because it conflicts with the teachings of Muhammad.

According to Muslim scholars, all "true Muslims" support the enforcement of Islamic law, over the entire population. However, Islamic law would destroy most of our rights under the Bill of Rights.[571] Therefore, according to Muslim scholars, a true Muslim cannot be a good American citizen.

Finally, we should not delude ourselves into hoping that moderate Muslims will convince radical Muslims to reform. The few Muslims who dare to publish books which criticize either holy war or Islamic law live in hiding, for fear of their lives. Even Muslim governments are often held hostage by Muslim militants. As one Muslim professor explains:

"No government can oppose the fundamentalists without seeming to oppose Islam or to quiet them unless they commit a criminal act, and then they cite religion in their defense to intimidate the judicial process. Meanwhile the liberal scholars and politicians constantly come under attack for deviating from the faith, and have little support, so that they continue to lose ground to the radicals."[572]

Perhaps our only hope is if Modern Liberal teachers and professors begin to analyze Islam with the same logical scrutiny that they have used against Christianity for decades. If Western universities begin to use objective and critical techniques to study Islam, then it will be found extremely lacking as a religion.

The most fatal flaw within Islam is a self-contradiction in logic, one which cannot be resolved. The Koran says you must believe in every word of it or you will go to Hell. (Koran 2:79.) However, the Koran contains many verses which contradict each other. Of course it is *logically impossible* to believe in contradictory verses. Therefore, it is logically impossible to believe in the entire Koran. Yet the Koran says you must believe in every word of it or you will go to hell. Therefore it is *logically impossible for any Muslim to avoid going to hell.* So Islam is not merely a religion that is based upon faith; it is a religion that is based upon a logical impossibility. As a belief system, Islam is nonsensical. Incidentally, the

Bible does not contain this sort of "all or nothing" clause. Christianity is based on faith, but not on a logical impossibility.

If Western scholars would only have the courage to treat Islam with the same intellectual scrutiny that they have inflicted upon Christianity, many Muslims would see the truth, and they would abandon Islam. Unfortunately, multiculturalism prevents the West from criticizing Islam. Multiculturalism demands that only Western traditions should be broken down and reduced to absurdity. Under multiculturalism, foreign traditions like Islam must be coddled, appeased, and even supported.

Islam is poised to defeat Modern Liberalism precisely because Islam is *not* multicultural. The Koran teaches Muslims that their religion is superior to all others. The Islamic "hadiths" (teachings of Muhammad that were written down, but not placed in the Koran) teach that the culture of 7th century Arabia is superior to every other culture on earth. This encourages Muslims to destroy cultures that preach tolerance and diversity. So long as Modern Liberals insist on tolerating all cultures, they are condemning Western culture to extinction.

Islam will destroy conservative traditions, such as government by consent, equal rights for all, limited government, property rights, the right to bear arms, and freedom of speech, press, and association. Islam will also kill off Modern Liberalism's most cherished dreams, including: socialism, secularism, environmentalism, women's rights, homosexual rights, racial quotas, and multiculturalism itself.

CONCLUSION

A century ago, the Modern Liberals of the old Milner Group were "liberal" *without* being blindly tolerant of foreign cultures. They fought for Modern Liberal causes, such as socialism, labor rights, women's rights, public education, and global government. Yet they never supported multiculturalism. In fact, the pioneering Modern Liberals of the Milner Group understood that Western culture was valuable and worthy of imitation. Those early Modern Liberals worked hard to spread Western culture around the world in an honest effort to improve the human condition. For most of the 20th century, pride in Western culture was perfectly compatible with Modern Liberalism. During those years, no one ever condemned this pride in Western culture as "ethnocentric."

Multiculturalism changed all of that. It has persuaded Modern Liberals to tolerate a foreign culture that is determined to destroy our own culture. To save Western civilization, we must reject multiculturalism. We must rekindle the ethnocentric spirit of the Milner Group. We must persuade today's Modern Liberals to once again value Western culture. Persuading conservatives will be useless, because conservatives do not control the levers of public opinion. Modern Liberals do. So we must persuade Modern Liberals to embrace a fact that they are reluctant to admit: Western culture really is superior to other cultures. Therefore, it deserves to be protected from invasion by Muslims.

If Modern Liberals do not begin to defend Western culture, then it will soon be replaced forever, by the barbaric culture of a 7th century Arab warlord.

REFERENCES

1. I have chosen these dates because they cover the time span from when Anglo-Saxons first began establishing their own rule of law in eastern England to the time that Parliament began to seriously and consistently violate the old precepts of Anglo-Saxon common law. The legal precedent for this was established in 1648, but Parliament did not become truly tyrannical until 1774, when it passed "The Intolerable Acts."
2. Will Durant, *The Age of Voltaire* (Simon & Schuster 1965), p. 788.
3. The most notable difference between the two types of law was that the Danelaw gave more rights to non-Danes than the Anglo-Saxon law gave to non-Anglo-Saxons. The Danes established the "wereguild." This was a "man price" which made killing any human being a crime. This means that the Danes gave some legal protection for Saxons living in their domain. The Anglos-Saxons did not return the favor. The Anglo-Saxons did not care if a Dane was killed in Anglo-Saxon territory. The Anglo-Saxon legal system treated all Danes as enemy invaders.
4. Jared Diamond, *Guns Germs and Steel* (W.W. Norton & Co. Publishers 1999), p. 63.
5. Will Durant, *Rousseau and Revolution* (Simon & Schuster 1967), p. 737.
6. Jim Powell, *The Triumph of Liberty* (The Free Press 2000), p. 60.
7. M. Stanton Evans, *The Theme is Freedom* (Regnery Publishing 1994), p. 298.
8. See Will Durant, *Our Oriental Heritage* (Simon & Schuster 1954), pp. 1-89.
9. The communal living arrangements in some Polynesian cultures was also probably due to a lack of fire wood on small islands. With so little fuel, communal cooking became a necessity. With communal cooking came communal living. Furthermore, on the smaller islands, agriculture was not as important as fishing for producing food. Therefore, establishing land ownership was not critical. However, in the interior regions of larger islands such as New Guinea, agriculture was much more important than fishing, and so property rights were recognized and land ownership was strictly observed. In Mesopotamia, some of the early settlements had communal areas to store food and some did not. However, the earliest written records from Mesopotamia indicate that people did own separate plots of land and owned separate flocks. So the communal storage of food was probably maintained for emergency use, e.g. as preparation in case of drought or siege. See Hans J. Nissen, *The Early History of the Ancient Near East* (University of Chicago Press 1988).
10. http://quotes.liberty-tree.ca/quotes_by/cato Letter 62 (1722) of Cato's Letters (1720-1723), quoted by Ronald Hamowy, "Cato's Letters, John Locke, and the Republican Paradigm", in Edward J. Harpham (Ed.), John Locke's Two Treatises of Government: New Interpretations (Lawrence: University Press of Kansas, 1992), p. 157.

11   http://libertyandculture.blogspot.com/2007/03/cicero-on-private-property.html
12   In fact, in an act of defiance, the warrior threw the chalice to the ground, smashing it to pieces. Apparently the warrior was angered by the King's request, and he intended to show the King his extreme displeasure. Of course Clovis was insulted, but he could still do nothing. Remember, the chalice was the warrior's property. However, several months later, Clovis (who never forgot an insult) saw this same warrior at a military inspection, and noticed that his sword was rusty. Clovis struck him down on the spot for this military offense.
13   As quoted by M. Stanton Evans, *The Theme is Freedom* (Regnery Publishing 1994), p. 86.
14   As quoted by Jim Powell, *The Triumph of Liberty* (The Free Press 2000), p. 22.
15   John Adams, *A Defense of the Constitution of the United States* (1787), as found in *The Political writings of John Adams* (Liberal Arts Press 1954), p. 148, as quoted by M. Stanton Evans, *The Theme is Freedom* (Regnery Publishing 1994), p.298.
16   Sadly we have regressed recently by permitting abortion. This is because our modern politicians have chosen to follow the moral precepts of secular humanism instead of Christian morality.
17   http://www.eadshome.com/QuotesoftheFounders.htm
18   http://www.errantskeptics.org/FoundingFathers.htm
19   Fulton J. Sheen, *Philosophies at War* (Charles Scribner's Sons 1943), p. 115.
20   M. Stanton Evans, *The Theme is Freedom* (Regnery Publishing 1994), p. 192.
21   I did not include Heritage Foundation, the Hoover Institute, or the American Enterprise Institute because these groups are generally neo-conservative.
22   Jim Powell, *The Triumph of Liberty* (The Free Press 2000), p. 410.
23   It should be noted that on the issue of the draft, not all Libertarian Conservatives agree with Bastiat. Some (e.g. Robert Higgs and the late Lysander Spooner) believe that military conscription is the worst form of slavery of all, to wit; *"I order you to serve me, even if it kills you."* However, most Libertarian Conservatives favor the draft in cases where our borders are actually attacked. On the other hand virtually all Libertarian Conservatives oppose the draft for military adventures on other continents in which American interests are vague at best.
24   Craig Schiller, *The (Guilty) Conscience of a Conservative* (Arlington House 1951), p. 42, quoting the National Review from Nov 19, 1955, p. 6.
25   Unpublished essay by Stephen Klink, dated June 4, 2003, with permission.
26   David Kelly, director of the Objectivist Institute (Ayn Rand think tank), as quoted in Jim Powell, *The Triumph of Liberty* (The Free Press 2000), p. 67.
27   Daniel J. Flynn, *Intellectual Morons* (Crown Forum 2004), p. 5.
28   Thomas Sowell, *The Vision of the Anointed* (Basic Books 1995), p. 241, quoting Jean-Francois Revel.
29   In a secular ideology, the promised utopia will be enjoyed here on earth. In a spiritual ideology, the utopia will be enjoyed in the afterlife.

30 Of course political parties had existed previously in European culture, notably the green and blue parties of Byzantium. However, the true political party did not exist in Anglo-Saxon culture until the 17th century.

31 It should be noted that Tory is still just a nickname. The official name of England's conservative party is the "Conservative and Unionist Party."

32 Specifically the ruling Liberal Party was blamed for failing to adequately defend the English colonial outpost at Khartoum.

33 Will Durant, *Caesar and Christ* (Simon & Schuster 1944), pp. 113-127.

34 Julius Caesar was by no means the first to do this. A half dozen other ambitious politicians did the same in the hundred years before Julius Caesar. These were Tiberius Gracchus, Caius Gracchus, Gaius Marius, M. Livius Drusus, Cornelius Cinna, and Catiline. See Will Durant, *Caesar and Christ* (Simon & Schuster 1944), pp. 11-145.

35 William Ebenstein, *Two Ways of Life* (Holt, Reinhart & Winston 1962), p. 133.

36 Conservative sources for this quotation are numerous, but it should also be noted that Mr. Ickes later denied making this remark.

37 In 1415 AD, near the beginning of the Renaissance, the Greek scholar George Gemistos Plethon tried to persuade the Greek Government of Morea (the Byzantine province which occupied nearly the same boundaries as the ancient kingdom of Sparta) to implement socialism with high taxes on accumulated wealth. Plethon also wanted all land to be owned in common. However, Plethon had no plans for international government, so he cannot be seen as the creator of Modern Liberalism. Moreover Plethon has been largely forgotten, while the philosophes were widely read across Europe and America, and still influence us today.

38 The Renaissance was spurred on because of four separate events. First, the crusades exposed Europeans to some of the knowledge of classical culture. They obtained this both from Constantinople and also through contact with the Muslims. Second, the Christian re-conquest of Spain revealed thousands of ancient Greek texts that had been preserved by the Muslim rulers of Spain. (The library at Cordoba alone was reputed to have contained 400,000 volumes.) Third, in 1396 the energetic Greek scholar Manuel Chrysoloras was appointed to the newly founded chair of Greek literature in Florence. He quickly ushered in a wide-spread appreciation of classical Greek philosophy among the intelligentsia of northern Italy. Fourth, most of the Greek scholars who somehow survived the Muslim slaughter of Constantinople in 1453 fled to Venice for refuge, bringing with them additional classical learning.

39 European monks had already been reading Plato for centuries before the Renaissance. Aristotle was also well known and gave birth to the scholastic movement, also before the Renaissance. However, statism was not an acceptable concept until the Renaissance.

40 Some scholars claim that an "Age of Reason" occurred in between the Renaissance and the Enlightenment. For the sake of simplicity I am not including the Age

of Reason as a separate movement in this text. I am combining it with the Enlightenment.

41   M. Stanton Evans, *The Theme is Freedom* (Regnery Publishing 1994), p. 41.

42   This is such a basic idea that I am surprised it has not been expressed so simply by any other author. Therefore, please indulge me as I christen this idea, "Hauer's Law."

43   The earlier Peace of Westphalia did nothing to erode national sovereignty. In fact it reinforced national sovereignty by assuring that the ruler of each independent state could determine the religion of his state without external interference. Therefore it was merely a peace treaty, not a step toward global government.

44   William Norman Grigg, *Freedom on the Altar* (American Opinion Publishing 1995), p. 8. The original sources Mr. Grigg used for the policies of Saint-Pierre are Will & Ariel Durant, *The Age of Voltaire* (Simon and Schuster, New York 1965), p. 336. It should be noted that Saint-Pierre also included as one of his social goals the equal education of both men and women. I did not include this idea on the list with his other goals because this idea is no longer the least bit controversial. No rational conservative today opposes equal education for women. However this support for equal education is makes Saint-Pierre also qualifies Saint-Pierre as one of the earliest supporters of feminism.

45   Some scholars have tried to trace the inspiration for socialism back to the Albigensian heresy of the early 13th century. This is not justified. The Albigensians were only partly interested in social reform. Indeed, they looted some churches for the benefit of the poor. However, the Albigensian heresy was first and foremost a religious movement, not a social or economic movement. The Albigensians believed there were two supreme beings; one good and one evil. Likewise, (for similar reasons) efforts to connect socialism to the Waldensian heresy are also not justified. The Greek intellectuals Dionysiacs of Ionia and Pythagoras also had some socialist ideas, but their movements died out long before Saint-Pierre published his essays. Even though Saint-Pierre was well educated by the Jesuits, it is uncertain whether Saint-Pierre ever read anything by Dionysiacs or Pythagoras. However, under Jesuit tutelage, he almost certainly read Plato; and Plato's *Republic* probably inspired Saint-Pierre's thinking about the appropriate power and scope of government. But it was Saint-Pierre who proposed to tax the wealthy to pay for the social welfare system. Furthermore, the Greeks never supported globalism, because the ancient Greeks viewed the rest of the world as barbaric. In fact, each Greek city-state tended to view itself as superior to every other Greek polis.

46   Will Durant, *Rousseau and Revolution* (Simon & Schuster 1967), pp. 30 and 174. But see also pp. 32 and 174. Rousseau sometimes supported socialism and sometimes he criticized it.

47   Will Durant, *Rousseau and Revolution* (Simon & Schuster 1967), pp. 1-26.

48   Will Durant, *Rousseau and Revolution* (Simon & Schuster 1967), p 891.

49   Will Durant, *Rousseau and Revolution* (Simon & Schuster 1967), p 891.

50   M. Stanton Evans, *The Theme is Freedom* (Regnery Publishing 1994), p. 105.

51 M. Stanton Evans, *The Theme is Freedom* (Regnery Publishing 1994), p. 105.
52 M. Stanton Evans, *The Theme is Freedom* (Regnery Publishing 1994), p. 52.
53 The Masons still continue to use some of the original practices of the 18th century Illuminati movement. During their ceremonies, Masons still only use a certain number of lights, depending on the Masonic rank of the person who is the subject of the ceremony. For example, if a 2nd level Mason is being promoted to third level, they will begin the ceremony with two lights, and finish it by lighting a third. In this way the member is becoming "more illuminated." Some Masons claim their group invented this practice, and that the Illuminati copied it. Who borrowed the idea from whom is a mystery for some other historian to solve.
54 A more complicated theory is that the name Jacobin came from the fact that these French free thinkers greatly admired the Scottish Masons, who claimed to have secret knowledge of mankind's future. The Scottish Masons enthusiastically supported the royal claim of James II of England, whose name in Latin was "Jacob." Hence these Scottish Masons called themselves "Jacobites." They were living in France after being exiled from Great Britain. The radical French Masons may have adopted the name "Jacobin" in deference to their Scottish Masonic brethren.
55 "The Writings of George Washington," as quoted in Archibald E. Roberts, *Emerging Struggle* (Betsy Ross Press 1979), p. 148.
56 John Robinson A.M., *Proofs of a Conspiracy* (The Americanist Classics 1967), p. 18.
57 Dee Zahner, *The Secret Side of History* (LTAA Communications Publishers 1994), p. 38.
58 John Robinson A.M., *Proofs of a Conspiracy* (The Americanist Classics 1967), p. 218. See also Will Durant, *Rousseau and Revolution* (Simon & Schuster 1967), pp. 955, 956.
59 John Robinson A.M., *Proofs of a Conspiracy* (The Americanist Classics 1967), p. 74.
60 M. Stanton Evans, *The Theme is Freedom* (Regnery Publishing 1994), p.33.
61 M. Stanton Evans, *The Theme is Freedom* (Regnery Publishing 1994), p.35.
62 M. Stanton Evans, *The Theme is Freedom* (Regnery Publishing 1994), p. 185.
63 Whether they actually met on the docks or at an inn is a matter of speculation. I have written a fictional description of one possible setting.
64 Their web site says that in 1010 the federal government spent an amount equal to 35% of the GDP. This is what I mean by 35% control over the economy.
65 According to USA Today, (August 30th, 2010) only 15% of all Americans receive government "help" for living expenses (including Medicaid). This 15% includes the 40 million people who receive food stamps, and the 50 million people who receive Medicaid benefits. However, these numbers cannot be simply added together because most of the food stamp recipients are also on Medicaid. Yet this 15% number is far too low, because it does NOT include people who are receiving Social Security retirement checks. In fact there are an additional 58 million people receiving Social Security or Supplemental

Security Income (according to http://www.ssa.gov/policy/docs/quickfacts/stat_snapshot/). When you add this to the number of people who depend upon Medicare, Medicaid, and all the various forms of welfare (ADC, Food Stamps, section eight housing, etc.) then the total number of people who rely on the government for assistance is about 74 million people. Once again, the total number of government beneficiaries is not simply the sum of 40 million and 58 million, because some people receive both SS benefits and food stamps. It would be misleading to count them twice. Yet even this grand total of 74 million people is still slightly low because it does not include persons who are receiving federal disaster assistance. Nor does it include people receiving federal grants for education.

66 The Daily Bell April 16th 2010, article by Phyllis Schlafly. Her article did not say if this number included government employees.
67 A few socialists later modified the second half of this slogan to read "and to each according *to his work.*" Oddly enough, the USSR adopted this variation on the socialist slogan. It may have been an admission that their centrally planned economy did not produce enough wealth to take care of those who were unable to work. Of course the change might instead have been a sincere change in ideology. We can only speculate.
68 As quoted in Mona Charen, *Do-Gooders* (Sentinel 2004), p. 92.
69 Dec 3rd, 2010, as reported by the Huffington Post. See http://www.huffingtonpost.com/sen-dianne-feinstein/millionaires-dont-need-ta_b_791687.html
70 http://etext.virginia.edu/jefferson/quotations/jeff1550.htm
71 http://www.rcarterpittman.org/essays/misc/Equality_v_Liberty.html
72 The Writings of Lincoln, vol. 7 p. 33, as quoted in *Private Property and Political Control* (anonymous) (The Freeman Classics 1992), p. 108. See also http://www.classic-literature.co.uk/american-authors/19th-century/abraham-lincoln/the-writings-of-abraham-lincoln-07/ebook-page-33.asp - 9k -
73 The Founding Fathers only failed to follow Christianity on one issue: slavery, an institution which was condemned by St. Paul. Not surprisingly, this one failure to follow Christianity ended up causing America's only nation-wide bloodbath, the Civil War.
74 As quoted by Will Durant, *The Age of Voltaire* (Simon & Schuster 1965), p. 154.
75 Jan Kozak, *And Not A Shot Is Fired* (Robert Welch University Press 1999), p. viii introduction by Robert R. Eddlem. See also *Private Property and Political Control* (no author listed), (The Freemen Classics, 1992), p. 22, quoting Robert G. Anderson, *Two Ways of Life*.
76 These statistics are available easily from the internet, and I found similar differences (but not quite as dramatically different) for breast cancer, prostate cancer, and brain cancer. I picked colon cancer because the statistical disparity was the largest.
77 CBS Sixty Minutes, October 25, 2009.
78 China had twice previously attempted to create a national pension system during the Han and Sung dynasties. However, these experiments were very

short-lived, with each attempt lasting less than one generation. See Will Durant, *Our Oriental Heritage* (Simon & Schuster 1954), pp 701-730.
79 Winston Churchill was favorably impressed with the health insurance benefit in the German "work exchange" program during his 1909 tour of Germany. Before WWI, the young Churchill was flirting with the socialist aspects of Modern Liberalism, and he was even recruited (unsuccessfully) by the Milner Group. Instead, Churchill went on to become a powerful Status-Quo conservative.
80 John Robinson A.M., *Proofs of a Conspiracy* (The Americanist Classics 1967), p. 29.
81 Dr. Carroll Quigley, *The Anglo American Establishment* (G.S.G. & Associates Inc. 1981), p.137.
82 Times Books, *The Times History of the World "New Edition"* (Harper Collins 1999), p. 272.
83 Times On Line, (Sunday Times of London) January 7th 2007.
84 Archibald E. Roberts, *Emerging Struggle* (Betsy Ross Press 1979). p.186.
85 The Saturday Review, July 19, 1952, in an article ironically entitled "The Climate of Freedom."
86 As quoted by Archibald E. Roberts, *Emerging Struggle* (Betsy Ross Press 1979), p. 201. In fact, the NEA was already advocating for world government even before the UN was created. Way back in 1942, the NEA adopted (and has never recanted) the following official position; *"To keep the peace and ensure justice and opportunity we need certain world agencies of administration, such as: A police force; a board of education, (etc.)"* See William Norman Grigg, *Freedom on the Altar* (American Opinion Publishing 1995), p. 37.
87 As quoted by Steve Bonta, *Inside the United Nations* (The John Birch Society 2003), p. 7, referencing *Foreign Affairs*, April 1974.
88 James Madison at the Virginia ratifying convention on June 16 1788, see http://www.revolutionary-war-and-beyond.com/james-madison-quotes-5.html
89 Archibald E. Roberts, *Emerging Struggle* (Betsy Ross Press 1979). p. 194.
90 Margaret E. Hirst, *Life of Friedrich* List (Smith Elder & Company 1909), p. xix, introduction.
91 Dee Zahner, *The Secret Side of History* (LTAA Communications 1996), p. 156, quoting the research of Professor R.J. Rummel. Roughly the same figures have been tallied up by other historians as well.
92 Dr. Carroll Quigley *The Anglo American Establishment* (G.S.G. & Associates Inc. 1981), p. 269.
93 The fascinating (but depressing) book about military abuses by UN troops is by Steve Bonta, *Inside the United Nations* (The John Birch Society 2003).
94 Archibald E. Roberts, *Emerging Struggle* (Betsy Ross Press 1979), p. 199.
95 Some sources note that the foreign (English language) press in Greece published details of their affair after the two lovers boldly sailed on a cruise through the Eastern Mediterranean. However, the coverage by domestic American newspapers (after Lord Lothian's leak) was the real breakthrough in the story.

96 Carroll Quigley noes that this was the first time that members of the Milner group were divided on a major policy issue. Not only does Carroll Quigley document this mistake by some members of the Milner Group, but so does Michael Bloch in his biography *Ribbentrop,* (Crown 1993) p. 81. Amazingly, important members of the Milner Group (George Bernard Shaw, Sir Austin Chamberlain, Lady Astor, Lord Cecil, and Lord Lothian) all gave friendly assurances to Nazi diplomat Ribbentrop that Britain would accept Hitler's territorial ambitions in central Europe. Of all the Milner Group members, Lord Lothian and Lady Astor were the most sympathetic to Adolph Hitler, but for different reasons. Lady Astor was notoriously anti-Jewish and Anti-Catholic. She cared nothing for the fate of German Jews or Catholic Poles. Lord Lothian was motivated by the desire to avoid war at all costs. Like many other Englishmen, he was still anguished by the bloodbath of WWI.

97 Carroll Quigley, *The Anglo-American Establishment* (C.S.G. Associates Publishers 1981), p. 49.

98 China did not exactly follow the model of Karl Marx because China was an agrarian society, not an industrial society. In China, there simply was no proletariat class to speak of. Furthermore, China's attempt to impose Marxist economics (no private property, central planning of the economy, etc.) lasted from only 1949 to 1990.

99 Some historians are still embracing this "single theory" approach for history. For example, Jared Diamond (*Guns Germs and Steel,* W.W. Norton & Co. Publishers 1999), claims that all the important differences among human cultures today can be explained by the types of food and domestic animals their ancestors possessed thousands of years ago.

100 I am focusing on Lord Milner and his circle because their influence upon modern liberalism was more profound (and longer lasting) than any other set of intellectuals or politicians ever since. Obviously there were other men and women who also contributed to the Modern Liberal support of socialism and globalism. As early as the 1890's, American social scientists were flocking to spend at least one year of their studies at the fashionable German universities. In Germany they were steeped in the socialism of post-Bismarck Germany. Famous sociologists from the turn of the century who made this intellectual pilgrimage included Edward A. Ross, Henry Carter Adams, Simon Patten and Richard T. Ely. These men influenced several generations of American college professors and in turn their students. Their ideas found fulfillment in the policies of men like Edwin Witte and Harry Hopkins, the socialist architects behind FDR's "New Deal." See Jim Powell, *FDR's Folly* (Crown Forum 2003).

101 Dr. Carroll Quigley, *The Anglo-American Establishment* (C.S.G. Associates Publishers 1981), p. 185.

102 Dr. Carroll Quigley, *The Anglo-American Establishment* (C.S.G. Associates Publishers 1981), p. 16.

103 For example, according to Dr. Quigley, James Arthur Salter was a member of the Milner Group's outer circle. He was also the Director of the Economic and Finance section of the League of Nations from 1919 to 1931.
104 Lord Lothian (Phillip Henry Kerr) was the editor of the highly influential journal, Round Table Quarterly. Earlier he had been the private secretary to Prime Minister David Lloyd George, and later he became ambassador to the United States from Great Britain. It was Lord Lothian who revealed the sexual affair between Edward VIII and Wallis Simpson to the Washington Post.
105 Dr. Carroll Quigley, p. 191.
106 John Robinson A.M., *Proofs of a Conspiracy* (The Americanist Classics 1967), p. 168.
107 John Robinson A.M., *Proofs of a Conspiracy* (The Americanist Classics 1967), p.69.
108 G.N. Volkov et al, *The Basics of Marxist Leninist Theory* (Progress Publishers 1979).
109 John Robinson A.M., *Proofs of a Conspiracy* (The Americanist Classics 1967), p. 91.
110 John Robinson A.M., *Proofs of a Conspiracy* (The Americanist Classics 1967), p.70.
111 Dr. Carroll Quigley, *The Anglo American Establishment* (G.S.G. & Associates Inc. 1981), p. 129.
112 See John Robinson A.M., *Proofs of a Conspiracy* (The Americanist Classics 1967), p. 38 and compare to Dr. Carroll Quigley, p.34. Both admit to a heavy initial influence from the Jesuits.
113 Dr. Carroll Quigley, *The Anglo-American Establishment* (C.S.G. Associates Publishers 1981), p. 32.
114 Ibid, p. 40.
115 Ibid, p. 114
116 Ibid, p. 222.
117 Archibald E. Roberts, *Emerging Struggle* (Betsy Ross Press 1979), p.149, quoting a letter from Sir Winston Churchill to the Illustrated Sunday Herald, dated February 8th, 1920.
118 There are too many examples of such cross-membership to discuss or even list here. For a full partial description of the cross membership I recommend *The Anglo American Establishment*, by Carroll Quigley.
119 New York Post, June 30th 2004. See also Washington Times June 30th 2004, as quoted by Jonah Goldberg, *Liberal Fascism* (Doubleday 2007), p. 357.
120 The fascists alone gave their judicial system some autonomy. However, only common criminals benefited from this. The political enemies of the fascist regime were often killed without a trial. Though to their credit, the fascists did not slaughter all Italian dissidents. Many were merely exiled.
121 Fulton J. Sheen, *Philosophies at War* (Charles Scribner's Sons 1943), p. 23.
122 Fulton J. Sheen, *Philosophies at War* (Charles Scribner's Sons 1943), p. 24.
123 As quoted from M. Stanton Evans, *The Theme is Freedom* (Regnery Publishing 1994), p. 48. It is also interesting to include the other great collectivists of

the 20th century, the Japanese Shinto-Imperialists. According to the Japanese Imperial Ministry of Education, the individual was so worthless that he did not even exist: "The individual is not an entity, but depends upon the whole arising from and kept in being by the state." Source: Fulton J. Sheen, *Philosophies at War* (Charles Scribner's Sons 1943), p. 24.

124 Fulton J. Sheen, *Philosophies at War* (Charles Scribner's Sons 1943), p. 19. This idea can be traced back to the Modern Liberal philosophes, such as The Marquis d'Argenson, see Will Durant, *The Age of Voltaire* (Simon & Schuster 1965), p. 279.

125 Fulton J. Sheen, *Philosophies at War* (Charles Scribner's Sons 1943), p. 20. It is no coincidence that the fascists, communists, and Nazis all shared this same rationalization to justify their grasp on absolute power. After all, this rationalization (to protect the weak), was invented by the very first Modern Liberals: the French philosophes. Just like 20th century collectivists, many of the philosophes favored a government with absolute power. As the philosophe Rene d' Voyer said; "*...only an absolute monarchy can protect the people from oppression by the strong.*" See Will Durant, *The Age or Voltaire* (Simon & Schuster 1965), p. 297, describing the views of the philosophe Rene Louis d' Voyer, (the Marquis d' Argenson.

126 Jonah Goldberg, *Liberal Fascism* (Doubleday 2007), p. 71. It should also be noted however that Hitler had Strasser killed in a power struggle within the Nazi Party. Furthermore, as he was closer to gaining power, Hitler began to see Strasser as a liability, because Strausser still wanted to confiscate all privately owned factories. Strasser was an idealist, and he refused to compromise on this point. Hitler was a pragmatist, and he needed the cooperation of both the conservative army and the great industrial tycoons.

127 Jonah Goldberg, *Liberal Fascism* (Doubleday 2007), pp. 134,135.

128 Ibid.

129 Jonah Goldberg, *Liberal Fascism* (Doubleday 2007), p 11.

130 This transition is covered well by Jonah Goldberg, *Liberal Fascism* (Doubleday 2007).

131 This is my own definition. It is better than anything else I have found.

132 Jonah Goldberg, *Liberal Fascism* (Doubleday 2007), p. 4.

133 Thomas J. Dilorenzo, *How Capitalism Saved America* (Crown Forum 2004), p. 192.

134 Jim Powell, *FDR's Folly* (Crown Forum 2003), p. 76.

135 Jonah Goldberg, *Liberal Fascism* (Doubleday 2007), p. 98.

136 Jonah Goldberg, *Liberal Fascism* (Doubleday 2007), p. 120.

137 As quoted by F.A. Hayek, *The Road to Serfdom* (The University of Chicago Press 2007) p. 70.

138 Jonah Goldberg, *Liberal Fascism* (Doubleday 2007), p. 87.

139 MTV April 19, 1994, as quoted by William Norman Grigg, *Freedom on the Altar* (American Opinion Publishing 1995), p. 77.

140 FDR's statement about choosing twenty-one because three times seven is a lucky number is exactly how Morgenthau remembers the conversation, according to

      Jim Powell, *FDR's Folly* (Crown Forum 2003), pp. 71, 72. I added only a few embellishments, such as the bad weather and baby blue pajamas.

141 The wonderful author to read who exposes false economics is Henry Hazlitt, *Economics in One Lesson* (Three Rivers Press 1979), p. 15.

142 The best modern author on this subject is P.J. O'Rourke, *Eat the Rich* (Atlantic Monthly Press 1998). It takes the classic ideas of Adam Smith and presents them in an entertaining way. O'Rourke explains both how wealth is created and how it is destroyed.

143 Jim Powell, *FDR's Folly* (Crown Forum 2003).

144 Thomas J. Dilorenzo, *How Capitalism Saved America* (Crown Forum 2004), p. 199.

145 NAM Newsletter, April 30th 1938, p.1, Quoted in Jim Powell, *FDR's Folly* (Crown Forum 2003), p. 76.

146 To see these charts for yourself, just search, "historical income tax rates" and "historical estate tax rates."

147 See http://www.taxpolicyventer.org/briefing-book/background/numbers/revenue.cfm

148 "If the government took 100% of all taxable income beyond the $75,000 tax bracket, it would get only 17 billion dollars, and this confiscation (which would destroy productive enterprise), would only be sufficient to run the government for seven days." From the Grace Commission Report, "President's Private Sector Survey on Cost Control," submitted on Jan 12th 1984. Found at http://wwww.uhuh.com/taxstuff/gracecom.htm

149 American Enterprise Institute, See http://www.american.com/archive/2007/november-december-magazine-contents/guess-who-really-pays-the-taxes

150 http://www.cbsnews.com/8601-18560_162-7114229-1.html?assetTypeId=30 Please note that our total for federal revenue does not include the 1.1 trillion "new dollars" that the Treasury Department printed in 2009. The Treasury Department must issue bonds to cover this printing of money. Therefore it is carried on the books of the federal government as a debt, which must be repaid to bond holders. Therefore it is not an asset. This means it cannot be fairly considered part of federal revenue.

151 Some writers claim Bush Jr. spent over 30% of GDP in 2008, but my own research only identified 3.77 trillion dollars for all federal spending (2.9 trillion for the official federal budget PLUS .87 trillion (870 billion) for "special appropriations" to fund the war in Iraq and Afghanistan. (See NY Times, Feb 2, 2008.) The GDP for 2008 was 14.5 trillion dollars, and 3.77 trillion dollars is 26% of 14.5 trillion dollars.

152 See http://www.usgovernmentspending.com/federal_spending The federal budget for 2010 was 3.72 trillion dollars, and this did not include the "special appropriations" for the Iraq/Afghan wars, which have not been tabulated as of this writing. The federal budget in 2008 (under Bush Jr.) was 2.9 trillion dollars.

153 Thomas Sowell, *The Vision of the Anointed* (Basic Books 1995), p. 257.

154 This argument was made by Governor Huckabee during a televised debate in February of 2008, but the point was lost upon most Americans.
155 Nov 3, 2009, Lee Rogers Show, KSFO Radio news, ABC affiliate.
156 Dick Armey, *The Freedom Revolution* (Regnery Publishing 1995), p. 155
157 Dick Armey, *The Freedom Revolution* (Regnery Publishing 1995), p. 155.
158 Washington Post, October 6th 2006.
159 US Bureau of Economic Analysis, as quoted by category/pubs/tbbl/tbb-0605-35.pdf
160 Actually I had to visit both the government web site and a private web site to figure out these numbers. The government still hides 4.37 trillion dollars of debt as "Intra-Governmental holding" (accounting transfers from the Treasury to the Fed and back again, sort of like check kiting.) The government only acknowledges a privately held debt of 7.174 trillion. According to seekingalpha.com, 3.162 trillion of this 7.174 trillion is held by US banks and US citizens. This is where the 44% figure comes from. (3.162 is 44% of 7.174.)
161 As of January 2009 General Electric had total assets of nearly 48 billion dollars. This amount goes into 509 billion dollars 10.6 times.
162 Dick Armey, *The Freedom Revolution* (Regnery Publishing 1995), p. 155.
163 http://www.rightpudits.com/?p=1121
164 Jim Powell, *FDR's Folly* (Crown Forum 2003), p. 76.
165 Ibid.
166 Ibid.
167 Los Angeles Times, April 3rd 2008, article by Donny Malhoney and Kim Murphy, data from a graph produced by the Associated Press. This article was published in the Oakland Tribune on the same day.
168 Will and Ariel Durant, *Christ and Caesar* (Simon & Schuster 1944), pp. 220, 221.
169 Ibid, p. 219.
170 Jim Powell, *The Triumph of Liberty* (The Free Press 2000), p. 37.
171 Jim Powell, *The Triumph of Liberty* (The Free Press 2000), p. 131.
172 Jim Powell, *FDR's Folly* (Crown Forum 2003), pp. 247,248.
173 Dick Armey, *The Freedom Revolution* (Regnery Publishing 1995), p. 37.
174 Ibid, p. 35.
175 As quoted by Jim Powell, *The Triumph of Liberty* (The Free Press 2000), pp. 438, 439.
176 As quoted by P.J. O'Rourke, *Eat the Rich* (Atlantic Monthly Press 1998), p. 208.
177 See John Julius Norwich, *Byzantium, The Early Centuries* (The Folio Society 2003), pp.192-196.
178 Dee Zahner, *The Secret Side of History* (LTAA Communications 1996), p. 63.
179 Rene Costales, Comments on *'Some Ideas for Taxation During Cuba's Transition'* found at http://lanic.utexas.edu/la/ca/cuba/asce/cuba9/cos_comm.pdf.
180 P.J. O'Rourke, *Eat the Rich* (Atlantic Monthly Press 1998), pp. 93, 97.
181 P.J. O'Rourke, *Eat the Rich* (Atlantic Monthly Press 1998), p. 96.
182 Ibid, pp. 77-103.

183 http://beltwayblips.dailyradar.com/video/obama_admits_cap_trade_will_cause_electricity_rates_to_1/
See also http://www.theminorityreportblog.com/blog_entry/steve_foley/2009/03/04/obama_admits_cap_trade_will_cause_electricity_rates_to_skyrocket

184 My thanks goes to Professor Douglass Woodhouse for pointing out this European factor.

185 The sad tale of how the railroad barons swindled the tax-payers can be found in several books. I recommend Thomas J. Dilorenzo, *How Capitalism Saved America* (Crown Forum 2004), p. 194.

186 NationMaster.com – Encyclopedia, *List of Recessions*, accessed on Jan 17, 2009. These were 1819-24, 1837-43, 1857-60, 1873-79, 1893-96, and 1907-08. I also added the recession of 1910-12 for a grand total of seven recessions before the Federal Reserve Bank was created. I did this in the interest of objective scholarship, even though this recession was not included by NationMaster.com, and its inclusion obviously does not support my thesis. Furthermore, the recession of 1819-1824 was caused by an earlier central bank, very similar to the current Federal Reserve Bank. So it really should not be included in the list of "pre-Fed" or "free market" recessions.

187 CNBC.com, *A History of Recessions*, accessed on Jan 16, 2009. I combined three of the listed recessions in the 1930's and early 1940's into one long Great Depression. The CNBC site actually listed eighteen recessions, but to be fair, I used the number sixteen, because most historians view the Great Depression as one long slump instead of three separate recessions.

188 Friedman's great work on this subject was *Theory of the Consumption Function* (1957) and Kuznet's contribution was *A Monetary History of the United States*, (1963). Both works are summarized nicely by Jim Powell, *The Triumph of Liberty* (The Free Press 2000), pp. 381-383.

189 There is one important difference between interest rates and other prices. If the price of hats is forced down below the free market price, then the result is a shortage of hats. Suppliers will offer fewer hats than consumers want to buy at the artificially low price. Some consumers will have to leave the market without a hat. However, the Fed will not permit a shortage of credit to develop. When the Fed forces interest rates below the market price, the Fed is actually *increasing the supply of money* in the loan market. So even though bank depositors are not willing to supply more money for investors to borrow, the Fed provides the extra money *by creating it out of thin air*, and making the money available for banks to lend to investors. As a result, investment spending will quickly exceed the amount of savings available to support the many new projects that are undertaken with all of this "cheap" money. See The Daily Bell January 9th, 2010.

190 All of the preceding nine paragraphs about the Fed were based on an article published in The Daily Bell on January 9th 2010. I did not quote the article directly, because it was too long. I condensed the most important ideas, but full credit for them goes to the writers of The Daily Bell.

191 From The Daily Bell, January 9th, 2010. To the Fed's credit, the Fed actually tried to prevent the crisis of 2008 by raising short term interest rates before the meltdown happened. The Fed raised short term rates 17 times in a row, in quarter-point increments from roughly 1% in 2004 to 5.25% in 2007. But unfortunately it was all too little too late. The Fed's tighter short term interest posture had virtually no effect on the mortgage market, which was already spiraling out of control. The Fed has strong control over short term interest rates, but the Fed has less influence over long term interest rates, such as mortgages.
192 Dee Zahner, *The Secret Side of History* (LTAA Communications 1996), p. 100.
193 Jim Powell, *FDR's Folly* (Crown Forum 2003), pp. 27, 28.
194 Clarence B. Carson, *The Welfare State* 1929-1985 (American Textbook Committee 1986), p. 11.
195 Jim Powell, *FDR's Folly* (Crown Forum 2003), p. 55.
196 Dee Zahner, *The Secret Side of History* (LTAA Communications 1996), p.101.
197 Clarence B. Carson, *The Welfare State* 1929-1985 (American Textbook Committee 1986), p. 13.
198 Jim Powell, *FDR's Folly* (Crown Forum 2003), p. 80.
199 Jim Powell, *FDR's Folly* (Crown Forum 2003), p. 49.
200 Jim Powell, *FDR's Folly* (Crown Forum 2003), p. 80.
201 Jim Powell, *FDR's Folly* (Crown Forum 2003), p. 89.
202 *Imprims*, January 2009, vol. 38, number 1, a publication of Hillsdale College. See also Burton Folsom Jr., *New Deal or Raw Deal* (Simon and Schuster Inc. 2008), p.248, which partially quotes the same statement.
203 Jim Powell, *FDR's Folly* (Crown Forum 2003), p. 43.
204 Jim Powell, *FDR's Folly* (Crown Forum 2003), p. 231.
205 Thomas J. Dilorenzo, *How Capitalism Saved America* (Crown Forum 2004), p. 195.
206 Clarence B. Carson, *The Welfare State 1929-1985* (American Textbook Committee 1986), p. 123. The wonderful book for great detail on this subject is Robert Higgs, *Against Leviathan* (The Independent Institute 2004).
207 Website of Congressman Ron Paul, Dec 14th 2009. This paragraph is a summary of his thoughts.
208 Thomas Sowell, as quoted on the editorial page of Investor's Business Daily, Sept. 28th 2010.
209 WorldNetDaily, posted on March 9 2009, quoting an article from the London Financial Times in January 2007.
210 WorldNetDaily, posted on March 9 2009.
211 Oakland Tribune March 19th 2008.
212 Ibid.
213 http://en.wikipedia.org/wiki/Ethanol_fuel#energy_balance
214 The Daily Bell, December 29, 2009.

215 Gretchen Morgenson & Joshua Rosner, *Reckless Endangerment: How Outsized Ambition, Greed and Corruption Led to Economic Armageddon* (Henry Holt & Co. 2011).
216 Washington Post Feb 2, 2009, editorial by Amity Shlaes.
217 Jim Powell, *The Triumph of Liberty* (The Free Press 2000), p. 363.
218 In California, most public safety personnel (police and fire) currently retire at 50. Nearly all other public employees can retire at 55.
219 http://blogs.sfweekly.com/thesnitch/2011/02/heather_fong_pension.php Earlier articles reported an annual pension of "only" 229,500, but these were not accurate.
220 Press Democrat.com April 30th 2010. http://www.pressdemocrat.com/article/20100502/OPINION/100439950
My own case may help illustrate the situation. After working for the Oakland Police Department for only 16 years I retired at age fifty. I now receive two thirds of my pay, which is triple what I would receive under Social Security. Most retired public employees worked longer, and so they receive much more. Most of my retired police officer friends receive five times more than the standard Social Security benefit.
221 http://www.ssa.gov/policy/docs/quickfacts/stat_snapshot/
222 Thomas J. Dilorenzo, *How Capitalism Saved America* (Crown Forum 2004), p. 55.
223 P.J. O'Rourke, *Eat the Rich* (Atlantic Monthly Press 1998), pp. 58, 59.
224 Ibid.
225 Ibid.
226 Will Durant, *Our Oriental Heritage* (Simon & Schuster 1954), pp. 700-701.
227 Will Durant, *Our Oriental Heritage* (Simon & Schuster 1954), p. 725.
228 Will Durant, *Our Oriental Heritage* (Simon & Schuster 1954), pp. 724-726. In fairness Durant points out that bad harvests and a suspicious comet were also factors in Wang An Shih's fall from power.
229 This quote is an honest attempt to recall the exact words of Mr. Perata. If one or two words may be wrong, the general meaning of the statement is undeniable. I heard it played on the radio news. However I did not have the opportunity to tape record the statement.
230 Dec 1st 2010. http://www.politicsdaily.com/2010/12/01/democrats-rally-to-support-unemployment-insurance-extension/
231 M. Stanton Evans, *The Theme is Freedom* (Regnery Publishing 1994), p. 108.
232 James Lewis was the first conservative I know of to suggest this "perfect parent" theory, in an article for The American Thinker, (Americanthinker.com) January 9th, 2008.
233 Howard E. Kershner, *Dividing the Wealth* (Devin-Adair Co. 1971), p. 17-28.
234 Robert Higgs, *Against Leviathan* (The Independent Institute 2004), p. 339.
235 Jim Powell, *FDR's Folly* (Crown Forum 2003), p. 8.
236 Clarence B. Carson, *The Welfare State* 1929-1985 (American Textbook Committee 1986), p.56.
237 Jim Powell, *FDR's Folly* (Crown Forum 2003), pp.84-87.

238 Clarence B. Carson, *The Welfare State* 1929-1985 (American Textbook Committee 1986), p. 80.
239 Jim Powell, *FDR's Folly* (Crown Forum 2003), p. 127.
240 Jim Powell, *The Triumph of Liberty* (The Free Press 2000), p. 360.
241 Peter Schweizer, *Makers and Takers* (Doubleday 2008), p. 24.
242 Thomas E. Woods, *The Politically Incorrect Guide to American History* (Regnery Publishing 2004), p. 171. Other prominent communist spies who rose to high levels in the federal government were Harry Dexter White (Assistant Secretary of the Treasury and author of the infamous Morgenthau Plan), John J. Abt, Henry H Collins, Charles Kramer, Nathan Witt, and Harold Ware. See W. Cleon Skousen, *The Naked Communist* (Ensign Publishing Co. 1962), pp. 144, 145.
243 William Ebenstein, *Two Ways of Life* (Holt, Reinhart & Winston 1962), p. 189.
244 Thomas E. Woods, *The Politically Incorrect Guide to American History* (Regnery Publishing 2004), p. 161.
245 W. Cleon Skousen, *The Naked Communist* (Ensign Publishing Co. 1962), p. 146.
246 I am not including Hillary Clinton in this group because she had already converted to liberalism before she had graduated from college. Her graduation speech was ample proof of this fact. Her brief appearance as a "Goldwater Girl" was her last contribution to conservatism.
247 Bernard Goldberg, *Arrogance* (Warner Books 2003), p. 224.
248 Ibid, p. 225.
249 M. Stanton Evans, *The Theme is Freedom* (Regnery Publishing 1994), p. 65.
250 Craig Schiller, *The (Guilty) Conscience of a Conservative* (Arlington House Publishers 1978), p. 133.
251 Jim Powell, *The Triumph of Liberty* (The Free Press 2000), p. 220.
252 Thomas Sowell, *The Vision of the Anointed* (Basic Books 1995), p. 250.
253 As reported in the Boston Globe Feb 3 2005.
254 http://www.youtube.com/watch?v=KAmtBiruW5E See also Human Events, June 8 2011, Keith Olberman as quoted in an article by Ann Coulter.
255 Collected by Jeff Jacoby, and published in the Oakland Tribune Newspaper on December 29th 1995.
256 Ibid.
257 Ibid.
258 Ibid.
259 Ibid.
260 Ibid.
261 Wall Street Journal, March 27 2009.
262 Bernard Goldberg, *Bias* (Regnery Inc. 2002), p. 181.
263 American Guardian, August 1999.
264 Alec Baldwin was speaking on the Television show "Late Night with Conan O'Brien" and this quote was published in the American Guardian, August 1999.

265 Washington Examiner, May 23 2011 and May 26 2011.
266 Human Events, March 24 2010.
267 Peter Schweizer, *Makers and Takers* (Doubleday 2008), pp.84, 86.
268 Peter Schweizer, *Makers and Takers* (Doubleday 2008), p. 86.
269 The revealing book which documents this is by Arthur C. Brooks, *Who Really Cares* (Basic Books, 2006).
270 Ibid, pp.17 and 21.
271 Ibid, p. 31.
272 Ibid, pp. 35-39.
273 Peter Schweizer, *Makers and Takers* (Doubleday 2008), p. 53.
274 Ibid, p. 64.
275 Ibid, p. 65.
276 Ibid, p. 218.
277 A few conservatives have grown to accept big government as a necessary evil in the war on terrorism, (most notably George Will, Fred Barnes, and David Brooks). However, it is doubtful whether these men can still be considered "conservative," because the most fundamental tenant of conservatism is to favor a smaller, less powerful government.
278 The fascinating conservative confession to read is by Craig Schiller, *The (Guilty) Conscience of a Conservative*, (Arlington House 1978).
279 Mona Charen, *Do-Gooders*, (Sentinel 2004), pp. 180-185.
280 Personal email from the author.
281 Both the McGovern quote and the Cuomo quote come from Peter Schweizer, *Makers and Takers* (Doubleday 2008), p. 157.
282 Peter Schweizer, *Makers and Takers* (Doubleday 2008), p 158.
283 Ibid.
284 Ibid, p. 161.
285 Ibid, p. 12.
286 I borrowed most of this list from Daniel J. Flynn, *Intellectual Morons* (Crown Forum 2004), p. 22.
287 Ibid, p. 173.
288 Ibid, p. 169.
289 Peter Schweizer, *Makers and Takers* (Doubleday 2008), pp. 169, 170.
290 Ibid, p. 171, 172.
291 Ibid, p. 173.
292 Ibid, p. 161.
293 Ibid.
294 Peter Schweizer, *Makers and Takers* (Doubleday 2008), p. 172.
295 People who fail to distinguish between intelligence and education usually lack both. Earlier we observed that Modern Liberals earn slightly more money than conservatives. Yet Modern Liberals have slightly less education. How can this be? After all, isn't education a strong indicator of income? The answer to this riddle may be motivation. According to nonpartisan research sources such as the World Values Survey and the General Social Survey, *conservatives are generally less concerned with making money than Modern Liberals are.* See Peter

Schweizer, *Makers and Takers* (Doubleday 2008), pp. 88-104. So much for the stereotype that conservatives are money grubbing materialists. The higher motivation of Modern Liberals to make money may be due to their being less religious than conservatives. After all, it would seem that the less religious a person is, the more materialistic he is likely to be. This stronger motivation to earn money probably explains why Modern Liberals earn slightly more than conservatives (on average), yet paradoxically conservatives have slightly more education than Modern Liberals (on average). So while education is a strong indicator of income, it is certainly not the only factor that determines income. The motivation to earn money is apparently even more important.

296 Dick Armey, *The Freedom Revolution* (Regnery Publishing 1995), pp. 198-293.
297 Peter Schweizer, *Makers and Takers* (Doubleday 2008), p. 166.
298 MTV April 19, 1994, and printed by William Norman Grigg, *Freedom on the Altar* (American Opinion Publishing 1995), p. 77.
299 Jim Powell, *The Triumph of Liberty* (The Free Press 2000), p. 161.
300 Jim Powell, *The Triumph of Liberty* (The Free Press 2000), p. 60.
301 Robert Bork, *Slouching Towards Gomorrah* (Regan Books 1996), p. 24.
302 These Modern Liberals include: Helen Hunt, Sean Penn, Ben Affleck, Barbara Streisand, Warren Beatty, Julia Roberts, Whoopie Goldberg, Jane Fonda, Ellen Degeneres, Alec Baldwin, Bea Arthur, Brad Pitt, Leonardo DeCaprio, Sarah Jessica Parker, Harrison Ford, Richard Dreyfuss, Allan Alda, Woody Allen, Winonna Ryder, Carl Reiner, Danny Glover, Ed Asner, Jeanne Stapleton, Carroll O'Conner, Gregory Peck, Tom Hanks, Kim Bassinger, Al Lewis, Martin Sheen, Henry Fonda, John Travolta, Tom Cruise, George Clooney, Sidney Portier, Meryl Streep, Lily Tomlin, Woody Harrelson, Robert Redford, Paul Newman, Christina Applegate, Chevy Chase, Bill Murray, Dan Akroyd, and Richard Gere.
303 Bernard Goldberg, *Arrogance* (Warner Books 2003), p. 102.
304 This popular left wing protest song was appropriately titled "I'd Love to Change the World."
305 Robert Bork, *Slouching Towards Gomorrah* (Regan Books 1996), p. 75.
306 As quoted in Robert Bork, *Slouching Towards Gomorrah* (Regan Books 1996), p. 74.
307 John Robinson A.M., *Proofs of a Conspiracy* (The Americanist Classics 1967), p. 75.
308 Robert Bork, *Slouching Towards Gomorrah* (Regan Books 1996), p. 68.
309 Robert B. Reich, *Reason, Why Liberals Will Win the Battle for America* (Alfred A. Knopf 2004), pp. 135, 136.
310 Robert B. Reich, *Reason, Why Liberals Will Win the Battle for America* (Alfred A. Knopf 2004), p. 136.
311 John Robinson A.M., *Proofs of a Conspiracy* (The Americanist Classics 1967), p. 258.
312 Benjamin Rush, March 28th 1787, "To the Citizens of Philadelphia: A Plan for Free Schools." http://www.errantskeptics.org/FoundingFathers.htm

313   Another factor which tended to keep early homo-sapien bullies under control was that in early human groups, everybody was equally vulnerable to assassination while they slept. Unlike other social mammals, only man has the ability to instantly incapacitate another member of the group in their sleep, by dropping a large rock on their head. This universal sense of vulnerability probably kept the strongest males from being too overbearing. Together, these two factors (spoken language and mutual vulnerability), set the stage for persuasion to replace brute force as the primary means for gaining power over other people.

314   Today it is fairly well accepted that Neanderthal men did not share their hunting kills with their women. Therefore the females suffered from protein deficiencies. Furthermore, Neanderthal women were also buried haphazardly, and without any ceremony. All of this indicates that Neanderthal women were not considered important. This brutish male domination probably resulted from the fact that Neanderthal women were not able to express complex ideas to their men, due to their small vocal cords. It may well be that the survival of our own species was because our larger vocal chords gave our women a superior ability to nag us.

315   The Casey Report, April 24 2010 www.CaseyResearch.com, Weekend Edition "Into the Lifeboats" The article did not carry an author's credit, but it was probably written by David Galland. I edited this passage slightly for the sake of simplicity and brevity.

316   Carroll Quigley *The Anglo-American Establishment* (C.S.G. Associates Publishers 1981), p. 68.

317   Thomas E. Woods Jr., *The Politically Incorrect Guide to American History* (Regnery Publishing 2004), p.162.

318   Two excellent books document this phenomenon in great detail. The first is by Marvin Olasky, *The Tragedy of American Compassion* (Regnery Publishing 1992). The more recent book is Mona Charen, *Do-Gooders* (Sentinel 2004).

319   M. Stanton Evans, *The Theme is Freedom* (Regnery Publishing 1994), pp. 229, 233.

320   Marvin Olasky, *The Tragedy of American Compassion* (Regnery Publishing 1992), p. 171.

321   John A. Andrew III, *Lyndon Johnson and the Great Society*, p. 81.

322   Clarence B. Carson, *The Welfare State* 1929-1985 (American Textbook Committee 1986), p. 207.

323   Thomas J. Dilorenzo, *How Capitalism Saved America* (Crown Forum 2004), pp. 160,161.

324   Jim Powell, *The Triumph of Liberty* (The Free Press 2000), p. 145.

325   Mona Charen, *Do-Gooders* (Sentinel 2004), p. 91. My statement "we must provide whole communities for the poor" comes almost straight from Mona Charen. I could not put it better.

326   Quoted from Bernard Goldberg, *Arrogance* (Warner Books 2003), p. 194.

327   Ibid.

328   Ibid.

329 New York Times May 24, 2000, as quoted from Bernard Goldberg, *Arrogance* (Warner Books 2003), p. 193.
330 Ibid. Once again I did exactly the same averaging of both the Kleck and Lott studies.
331 Gary Kleck, *Social Problems*, vol 1 Feb 1988. See also John Lott *More Guns Less Crime* (University of Chicago Press 1998). I averaged the results (percentages) from both studies to arrive at my estimate of "approximately half."
332 USA Today, Friday Aug 2nd 1996, citing a study from the University of Chicago by John R. Lott & David B. Mustard, *Crime, Deterrence and the Right-to-Carry Concealed Handguns*, (University of Chicago Press 1996).
333 Ibid.
334 The finest review of all the relevant literature is John R. Lott, *More Guns Less Crime* (University of Chicago Press 1998).
335 American Rifleman, April 1995, citing data from Florida Department of State, Division of Licensing, Concealed Weapons/Firearms License Statistical Report for Period 10-01-87 through 01-31-95.
336 Gary Kleck, *Social Problems*, vol. 1 Feb 1988. See also Journal on Firearms and Public Policy vol. 6, Fall 1994.
337 American's First Freedom, July 2008, p. 25.
338 Ibid.
339 The FBI originally published data which detailed the fact that certain races commit the vast majority of crime in America. However, the FBI no longer publishes this data for fear of being politically incorrect. However, you can still find this data on line by doing an internet search under "the color of crime."
340 These last remarks from Abzug are quoted from a source that I cannot now recall. My apologies and thanks to the original source.
341 Pat Robertson, *The Turning Tide* (Word Publishing 1993), pp. 308, 309.
342 Washington Times, Dec 25 2009.
343 http://www.commentary magazine .com/viewarticle.cfm/religion-and-liberalism-12730 accessed on 03-03-09, quoting from Mr. Bell's book *The Contradiction of Capitalism*.
344 John Robinson A.M., *Proofs of a Conspiracy* (The Americanist Classics 1967), p. 26.
345 Jonah Goldberg, *Liberal Fascism* (Doubleday 2007), pp. 222,223.
346 Robert Higgs, *Against Leviathan* (The Independent Institute 2004), p. 37.
347 Christopher Walton, from http://www.uuworld.org/ideas/articles/2728.shtml accessed on 03-032-09.
348 Robert Bork, *Slouching Towards Gomorrah* (Regan Books 1996), pp. 26, 27.
349 Robert Bork, *Slouching Towards Gomorrah* (Regan Books 1996), pp. 28, 29.
350 Terry H. Anderson, *The Movement and the Sixties: Protests in American from Greensboro to Wounded Knee* (New York, Oxford University Press 1995), p. 413.
351 Pat Robertson, *The Turning Tide* (Word Publishing 1993), p. 74.
352 Pat Robertson, *The Turning Tide* (Word Publishing 1993), p. 74.
353 Ibid.

354 P.J. O'Rourke, *Eat the Rich* (Atlantic Monthly Press 1998), p. 62.
355 John Robinson A.M., *Proofs of a Conspiracy* (The Americanist Classics 1967), pp. 93, 94.
356 Modern Liberal economist and journalist Stuart Chase, as quoted by Thomas E. Woods Jr., *The Politically Incorrect Guide to American History* (Regnery Publishing 2004), p. 163.
357 Thomas E. Woods Jr., *The Politically Incorrect Guide to American History* (Regnery Publishing 2004), p. 159.
358 Jonah Goldberg, *Liberal Fascism* (Doubleday 2007), p. 133.
359 Thomas Sowell, *The Vision of the Anointed* (Basic Books 1995), p. 113.
360 Thomas Sowell, *The Vision of the Anointed* (Basic Books 1995), p. 122.
361 Jonah Goldberg, *Liberal Fascism* (Doubleday 2007), p. 42.
362 Teddy Roosevelt also favored strong central government, but he was not a globalist. He was too much of a nationalist to be considered a true Modern Liberal. In contrast, Wilson embraced all five core values of Modern Liberalism: collectivism, authoritarianism, globalism, elitism, and socialism.
363 Jonah Goldberg, *Liberal Fascism* (Doubleday 2007), p. 88.
364 Jonah Goldberg, *Liberal Fascism* (Doubleday 2007). Apparently Wilson established federal control over information just weeks before the Germans.
365 Jonah Goldberg, *Liberal Fascism* (Doubleday 2007), p. 89, quoting from Wilson's frightening essay *Leaders of Men*.
366 Jim Marrs *The Rise of the Fourth Reich* (Harper-Collins 2008), p.179.
367 William J. Miller, *The Meaning of Communism*, (Time Life Books 1963), p. 34. Chernishsky wrote before the Bolshevik Party was formed, so he never called himself a "communist," because that term was not yet widely known in Russia. Yet the type of revolutionary socialism he advocated was later adopted by Lenin as a model for the Bolshevik revolution. Chernishkey's influential book on revolution was entitled *Chto Delat*, or *What Is to be Done?* Lenin read the book so many times he memorized portions of it.
368 Robert Bork, *Slouching Towards Gomorrah* (Regan Books 1996), p. 86.
369 Robert Bork, *Slouching Towards Gomorrah* (Regan Books 1996), p. 87.
370 Will Durant, *Rousseau and Revolution*, (Simon & Schuster 1967), p. 174.
371 Thomas Sowell, *The Vision of the Anointed* (Basic Books 1995), p. 122.
372 Thomas Sowell, *The Vision of the Anointed* (Basic Books 1995), p. 122.
373 Ibid.
374 Ibid.
375 This is not meant to imply that Obama is significantly stupider than any other Modern Liberal of his era. I am only exposing Obama's delusions about his intelligence because (as President) he is the most influential Modern Liberal at the current time. Of course Al Gore, Joe Biden, Nancy Pelosi, and Hillary Clinton are equally deluded about their own mental capacities. In contrast, Bill Clinton and Jimmy Carter are Modern Liberal political figures who possess truly high intelligence. Even so, their superior intelligence did not seem to have imparted wisdom.
376 Thomas Sowell, *The Vision of the Anointed* (Basic Books 1995), p. 124.

377 Some state election laws required that all absentee ballots must be postmarked by a certain date to show when they were mailed. However, many military bases overseas do not have the equipment to make these postmarks.
378 PJTV June 28th 2010, interview with Christian Adams, former USDOJ attorney, who resigned as a result of this shocking policy. Under the previous President (George W. Bush Jr.) all races were protected equally. Under Obama, this policy was officially abandoned by the USDOJ. favorehttp://www.pjtv.com/?cmd=mpg&mpid=174&load=3751
379 Dee Zahner, *The Secret Side of History* (LTAA Communications 1996), p. 119.
380 Dee Zahner, *The Secret Side of History* (LTAA Communications 1996), p. 48.
381 Dee Zahner, *The Secret Side of History* (LTAA Communications 1996), p. 117.
382 M. Stanton Evans, *The Theme is Freedom* (Regnery Publishing 1994), p. 48.
383 M. Stanton Evans, *The Theme is Freedom* (Regnery Publishing 1994), p. 50.
384 http://en.wikiquote.org/wiki/Robert_Owen
385 William Norman Grigg, *Freedom on the Altar* (American Opinion Publishing 1995), p. 157.
386 Ibid.
387 Ibid.
388 John Robinson A.M., *Proofs of a Conspiracy* (The Americanist Classics 1967), p. 26.
389 M. Stanton Evans, *The Theme is Freedom* (Regnery Publishing 1994), p. 70.
390 As quoted by M. Stanton Evans, *The Theme is Freedom* (Regnery Publishing 1994), p. 70.
391 As quoted by Will Durant, *The Age of Voltaire* (Simon & Schuster 1965), p. 775.
392 Fulton J. Sheen, *Philosophies at War* (Charles Scribner's Sons 1943), p. 138. His actual words are: "Once man had to know why he was living in order that he might know how to live; now he is told how to live without ever knowing why."
393 Fulton J. Sheen, *Philosophies at War* (Charles Scribner's Sons 1943), p. 141.
394 M. Stanton Evans, *The Theme is Freedom* (Regnery Publishing 1994), p. 317.
395 Pat Robertson, *The Turning Tide* (Word Publishing 1993), pp. 306, 307.
396 In Federalist Paper #2, John Jay carelessly refers to Americans as having "the same religion." However, he was clearly not using the term "religion" as it was later used in the First Amendment. John Jay did not even attend the Constitutional Convention. In addition, Federalist Paper #19 (written by James Madison and Alexander Hamilton, both of whom *did attend* the Constitutional Convention) more accurately reveals the attitude among the Founding Fathers. Federalist Paper #19 makes no claim of religious unity, but instead warns us that the newly created states must try to avoid violent religious conflicts. It cites the "violent and bloody conflicts" among the Swiss cantons (Protestant vs Catholic) as an example that we must try hard to avoid. Madison and Hamilton understood that our new nation was burdened by religious rivalry.

397 John Marshall, in a letter to Jasper Adams May 9th 1883. http://www.errantskeptics.org/FoundingFathers.htm
398 http://www.eadshome.com/QuotesoftheFounders.htm
399 John Jay, in a letter to Jedidiah Morse February 28th 1797. http://www.errantskeptics.org/FoundingFathers.htm
400 Incidentally, the expression "In God we trust" has been used ever since the days of our Founding Fathers, but it did not officially become the national motto until 1956. It was taken off our currency only briefly by Teddy Roosevelt, not because he was a misotheist, but rather because he thought it might be blasphemous to put "God" on money.
401 Clarence B. Carson, *The Welfare State 1925-1986* (American Textbook Committee 1986), p. 267.
402 William Ebenstein, *Two Ways of Life* (Holt, Reinhart & Winston 1962), p. 184.
403 M. Stanton Evans, *The Theme is Freedom* (Regnery Publishing 1994), p. 105.
404 CNSNews.com October 23 2009, article by Matt Cover.
405 Kevin R.C. Gutzman, *The Politically Incorrect Guide to the Constitution* (Regnery Publishing 2007), p. 207.
406 M. Stanton Evans, *The Theme is Freedom* (Regnery Publishing 1994), p. 68.
407 Sam Adams, 1768, as quoted in M. Stanton Evans, *The Theme is Freedom* (Regnery Publishing 1994), p. 256.
408 Thomas Jefferson, Draft of the Kentucky Resolution, October 1798.
409 http://thinkexist.com/quotation/do_not_separate_text_from_historical_background/212529.html
410 Thomas Jefferson, letter to William Johnson of 1823.
411 South Carolina v. US, 199 US 437, 448 (1905).
412 Lincoln as quoted by William H. Rehnquist, "The Notion of a living Constitution," Texas Law Review, vol. 54, p. 702, 1976. As quoted by William Eaton, *Who Killed the Constitution*, (Regnery 1988), p.186.
413 Philadelphia Trumpet, January 2009. See also National Review On Line Oct 27, 2998.
414 http://writ.news.findlaw.com/hilden/20081112.html, published on November 12 2008, and accessed on February 11 2008. It quotes a statement made by Obama on a liberal blog called Volokh Conspiracy from February 2008. It only received passing mention in the legal press, and was completely ignored by the mainstream media.
415 As quoted from M. Stanton Evans, *The Theme is Freedom* (Regnery Publishing 1994), p. 401.
416 As quoted in M. Stanton Evans, *The Theme is Freedom* (Regnery Publishing 1994), p. 402.
417 Up until 1949, a special committee in the House of Lords called the "Law Lords" would occasionally try to limit a law made by Parliament without actually overruling Parliament. In 1949 Parliament took away even this small power from the Lords. In October of 2009, Parliament created a new "Supreme" Court for England. Sadly, this court is little more than a bad joke. The court has

no more power than the House of Lords had after the 1949 Parliament Act. All they can do is ask Parliament to reconsider their law, and delay its enforcement for one year. Lately the World Courts (both the ICJ and ICC) has seen fit to review English laws. However, this is merely transferring absolute power to a higher level. There is no appeal from the World Courts, and Parliament does not control their jurisdiction (unlike the US Supreme Court).

418   The European Union currently does claim to have power over national legislatures such as the English Parliament, but as we will see in Chapter Seven, the European Union is very undemocratic, and it also has no limits on its power. So it is simply another tyranny which dominates a larger territory.
419   As quoted by Jim Powell, *The Triumph of Liberty* (The Free Press 2000), p. 56.
420   As quoted from www.liberty-page.com/quotes/dem.htm accessed on May 5 2009.
421   From Jan 4th 2007 to Oct 24th 2010, according to the Bureau of Public Debt, a division of the US Treasury Dept., as their report was read on KSFO Radio News, on October 25th 2010.
422   A few Republican Senators and Representatives voted for the bailouts of 2008 and 2009, but the vast majority of votes in favor of the bailouts came from Democrats, at the urging of Democratic President Barack Obama.
423   http://www.federalreserve.gov/generalinfo/faq/faqfrs.htm
424   For the best overall review of the Fed's abuse of power, see Rolling Stone, at http://www.rollingstone.com/politics/story/26793903/the_big_takeover Posted on March 13 2009.
425   Ibid. p. 10.
426   Ibid. p. 3. These were initially called CDOs for Collateralized Debt Obligations. Then AIG created a new financial instrument called a CDS (Credit-Default Swap). This was the device which became the source for multiple bets to be placed on the same mortgage. AIG touted the CDSs as a form of insurance, but as later events revealed, they were "insurance" with no assets to back them up. It was like being insured by a homeless beggar.
427   Wall Street Journal Dec 5 and 6, 2009, Page W2.
428   Rolling Stone magazine, April 5th 2010.
429   The case is called Kelo v City of New London. It can be found on the internet. Justice Alioto wrote a brilliant dissenting opinion.
430   M. Stanton Evans, *The Theme is Freedom* (Regnery Publishing 1994), p. 65.
431   Jonah Goldberg, *Liberal Fascism* (Doubleday 2007), p. 132.
432   Woody Allen as reported by Fox News, May 17th 2010
433   Prudhon, Demokratie und Republik, S. 10.
434   Bernard Goldberg, *Bias* (Regnery Publishing 2002), pp. 138-143.
435   However, if the Constitution had been strictly followed, this injustice would have been prevented. The "due process" clause of the Fifth Amendment guarantees your right to a hearing in any case where the government makes a claim against you. The bigger the government's claim against you, then the more "process" you are entitled to. Being forced to support a child for eighteen

years is a huge claim. So a regular mail notice with no right to appeal hardly qualifies as "due process of law."
436 For polling sources and minority response data see Bernard Goldberg, *Arrogance* (Time Warner 2003), pp. 106,107.
437 Steve Bonta, *Inside the United Nations* (The John Birch Society 2003), p. 38
438 See Madeline Morris, *ICC Jurisdiction over Nations of Non-Party States*, Duke University School of Law, May 25, 1999. See also Steve Bonta, *Inside the United Nations* (The John Birch Society 2003), p. 81.
439 For a summary of New York Times scare stories about climate, See Christopher C. Horner, *The Politically Incorrect Guide to Global Warming*, (Regnery Publishing 2007) pp.182-184.)
440 As quoted by Christopher C. Horner, *The Politically Incorrect Guide to Global Warming* (Regnery Publishing 2007), p. 85.
441 As quoted by Christopher C. Horner, *The Politically Incorrect Guide to Global Warming* (Regnery Publishing 2007), p. 22.
442 As quoted by Christopher C. Horner, *The Politically Incorrect Guide to Global Warming* (Regnery Publishing 2007), p. 55.
443 See the film documentary by Noam Chomsky, "Manufacturing Consent."
444 See the film documentary by Lord Christopher Monckton, science advisor to the English government, "Apocalypse? No!" at http://video.google.com/video play?docid=5206383248165214524
445 See the film documentary by Lord Christopher Monckton, science advisor to the English government, "Apocalypse? No!" at http://video.google.com/video play?docid=5206383248165214524
446 Ibid.
447 Christopher C. Horner, *The Politically Incorrect Guide to Global Warming* (Regnery Publishing 2007), p. 96.
448 As quoted by Christopher C. Horner, *The Politically Incorrect Guide to Global Warming* (Regnery Publishing 2007), p. 83.
449 Christopher C. Horner, *The Politically Incorrect Guide to Global Warming* (Regnery Publishing 2007), p. 87.
450 http://www.c3headlines.com/global-warming-quotes-climate-change-quotes.html It should be noted that Houghton has since denied making this statement.
451 See the film documentary by Lord Christopher Monckton, science advisor to the English government, "Apocalypse? No!" at http://video.google.com/video play?docid=5206383248165214524
452 Ibid.
453 Ibid.
454 Christopher C. Horner, *The Politically Incorrect Guide to Global Warming* (Regnery Publishing 2007), p. 119.
455 See the film documentary by Lord Christopher Monckton, science advisor to the English government, "Apocalypse? No!" at http://video.google.com/video play?docid=5206383248165214524

456 Associated Press, Sept 24 2006, as quoted by Christopher C. Horner, *The Politically Incorrect Guide to Global Warming* (Regnery Publishing 2007), p. 104.
457 Ibid at p. 59.
458 As quoted by Christopher C. Horner, *The Politically Incorrect Guide to Global Warming* (Regnery Publishing 2007), p. 79.
459 Ibid at p. 38.
460 Ibid at p. 91.
461 United Kingdom Telegraph, Nov 3 2009. http://www.telegraph.co.uk/earth/energy/6491195/Al-Gore-could-become-worlds-first-carbon-billionaire.html
462 Christopher C. Horner, *The Politically Incorrect Guide to Global Warming* (Regnery Publishing 2007), pp. 192-207. However, in 2010, BP decided to drop their support for the IPCC.
463 Christopher C. Horner, *The Politically Incorrect Guide to Global Warming* (Regnery Publishing 2007), p. 6.
464 Ibid, p. 31.
465 Ibid, p. 35.
466 Ibid, p. 6.
467 Ibid, p. 6.
468 Ibid, p. 294.
469 Ibid, p. 214, quoting from Al Gore's interview with Grist Magazine.
470 Ibid, p. 35.
471 Ibid, p. 40.
472 Sean Hannity Radio Show, Jan 22nd 2009.
473 To know what these terms originally meant (and still mean) see Charles Adams, *Those Dirty Rotten Taxes* (The Free Press 1998).
474 See Pollock v Farmers' Loan & Trust Company, 158 U.S. 601 (1895).
475 New York Times, 02-02-2009, article by Jason Departe, accessed by Wikipedia on 02-12-2009. See http://en.wikipedia.org/wiki/Welfare#cite_note-nytimes_tanf-17
476 http://www.taxfoundation.org/taxdata/show/335.html
477 *Times History of the World, "New Edition"* (Times of London), p. 175.
478 This idea was best described by M. Stanton Evans, *The Theme is Freedom* (Regnery Publishing 1994), p. 32.
479 The figure I used for the total government take represents the current situation in California, where I am writing. The higher the price of gasoline, the more money that state and local governments make on taxes. The federal tax on gasoline is a fixed mount, currently (July 2009) set at fourteen cents per gallon.
480 Children left in day care centers become more emotionally insecure, and they develop unnecessary psychological problems. Abnormally aggressive behavior is the most frequently observed problem. See Arizona Republic, April 19, 2001. See also Bernard Goldberg, *Bias* (Regnery Inc. 2002), p. 172.
481 Ibid.
482 Brian C. Robertson, *Day Care Deception* (2003), p. 887.

483 As quoted by Jonah Goldberg, *Liberal Fascism* (Doubleday 2007), p. 352.
484 Jonah Goldberg, *Liberal Fascism* (Doubleday 2007), p. 352.
485 William Norman Grigg, *Freedom on the Altar* (American Opinion Publishing 1995), p. 66.
486 H.G. Wells, *New World's for Old* (New York: The McMillan Co. 1919), p.128.
487 Arthur W. Calhoun, *A Social History of the American Family* (Cleveland Oh. The Arthur H. Clark Co. 1919), pp. 162, 163.
488 As quoted by Fulton J. Sheen, *Philosophies at War* (Charles Scribner's Sons 1943), p.119.
489 The only noteworthy exception was the French socialist Pierre-Paul Prudhon. Prudhon was also the only prominent socialist who did not favor large scale (national) socialism. Prudhon was wise enough to see that socialism on a national scale would lead to an unhealthy concentration of power. It is significant that the only famous socialist who opposed the all powerful state was also the only socialist who supported the traditional family unit. This indicates that weakening the family unit is part and parcel with statism.
490 New York Times, Opinion Editorial piece from Jan 25th 2009. This article is by no means the only one.
491 Herbert Spencer, *Principles of Sociology*, as quoted by Jim Powell, *The Triumph of Liberty* (The Free Press 2000), p. 272.
492 Will and Ariel Durant, *The Lessons of History* (New York: Simon & Schuster, 1968), p. 35.
493 Thomas Sowell, *The Vision of the Anointed* (Basic Books 1995), p. 196.
494 Thomas Sowell, *The Vision of the Anointed* (Basic Books 1995), p. 128.
495 The first person to use the term "Liberal Establishment" was probably M. Stanton Evans, although it may have been coined by Clarence B. Carson.
496 The RIIA and the CFR give the Liberal Establishment substantial control over the foreign policies of both the United States and England. However, this control is by no means complete. For example, this control over foreign policy was substantially challenged during the Reagan administration, when Reagan insisted on developing his missile defense program widely known as Star Wars, and his invasion of the sovereign state of Granada. The Liberal Establishment initially supported Reagan's policy to deploy Pershing missiles in Europe, but then tried to persuade him to reverse that decision. Their effort failed.
497 Archibald E. Roberts, *Emerging Struggle* (Betsy Ross Press 1979), p. 203.
498 For a tragically funny retelling of their persecution see Bernard Goldberg, *Arrogance* (Warner Books 2003), pp. 211-217.
499 Ibid, p. 214.
500 Bernard Goldberg, *Bias* (Regnery 2002), p. 213.
501 Bernard Goldberg, *Bias* (Regnery 2002), p. 43.
502 The journalist, Charles Gibson of ABC, thought "the Bush Doctrine" meant going into Muslim nations to bomb terrorists. Instead it was an obscure phrase coined by a mid-level state department bureaucrat to describe nation building and planting democracy in the third world, not just in Muslim nations.

503 See http://www.youtube.com/watch?v=EpGH02DtIws for a video tape. Or type in the following internet search: Obama 57 states. This gaff by Obama was even confirmed by the liberal fact-check site, Snopes.com. However they tried to obfuscate it by claiming it was a "mixture of true and false information." There was nothing false about it. Snopes.com was merely clouding the issue by saying that conservatives were incorrect to claim that Obama was referring to 57 Islamic states. However, conservatives were not even claiming this. Conservatives were simply claiming that Obama did not even know how man states were in the USA. Their "claim" was 100% correct.

504 On November 10th 2010, President Obama told a delegation of foreigners that our national motto was, *"E pluribus unum."* Of course the national motto of the United States is "In God We Trust."

505 The Huffington Post, accessed on Dec 14, 2009. This story was first published on 3-31-08.
http://www.huffingtonpost.com/2008/03/31/clinton-surrogate-ed-rend_n_94280.html

506 NBC news averages 9.4 million viewers. ABC news averages 8.1 million. CBS news averages 5.1 million. I did not include MSNBC because their ratings are currently negligible, at 788,000.

507 Richard Harwood, Washington Post, Oct. 30th 1993.

508 There was one occasion I recall when Terry Gross interviewed conservative actor Charlton Heston. However, this does not really count because Miss Gross carefully limited the conversation to his Hollywood life and acting career. She did not give Heston any opportunity to express his political views, despite his long time relationship with the National Rifle Association and his support for the right to bear arms.

509 CNCNews.COM, Nov 4 2008, showing a tape recording of Schumer on FOX television.

510 New York Times, Nov. 18th 2004.

511 For this show I did not see an episode number on the credits, but this show was produced in 2006 by KCET and aired numerous times since then. I happened to see it on August 4, 2008 on KQED, Public Television in San Francisco.

512 Mona Charen, *Do-Gooders* (Sentinel 2004), p.132.

513 This deceptive change in SAT scoring was begun back in 1995. The new system adds (on average) about 35 points to a student's final score. This scam has continued ever since 1995. See John A. Stormer, *None Dare Call it Education* (Liberty Bell Press 1999), p. 11.

514 Newsweek, March 23, 2009, p. 64, in an article by George F. Will.

515 Mona Charen, *Do-Gooders* (Sentinel 2004), p. 196.

516 John A. Stormer, *None Dare Call It Education* (Liberty Bell Press 1999), p. 39-42.

517 http://www.youtube.com/watch?v=zeMZGGQ0ERk&feature=related

518 Dr. Harold Rugg, as quoted by John A. Stormer, *None Dare Call It Education* (Liberty Bell Press 1999), p. 40. This shocking statement is still being quoted with approval by highly educated "experts" on education. It was even re-printed

in *Philosophical Foundations of Education* by Howard Ozman and Craver. See John A. Stormer, *None Dare Call It Education* (Liberty Bell Press 1999), p 42.

519   John A. Stormer, *None Dare Call It Education* (Liberty Bell Press 1999), p 42.
520   John A. Stormer, *None Dare Call It Education* (Liberty Bell Press 1999), p 93.
521   John A. Stormer, *None Dare Call It Education* (Liberty Bell Press 1999), p 43.
522   Ibid, at p. 46.
523   For example, the beautiful and talented Bo Derek made a sensation when she appeared in the 1979 hit movie, "10." However, she then made the fatal mistake of admitting some conservative views. Suddenly Bo Derek virtually disappeared from the silver screen. With the aid of her film-directing husband, she only obtained some "B" movie roles. By virtue of her husband's Hollywood connections, Bo Derek played Jane in a sexy 1981 re-make of Tarzan. This film had backing from MGM, but the studio put up a mere six million dollars to make the film, and then did very little to promote it. Despite these barriers, the movie grossed 36 million dollars. This was her last "major" work.
524   Jim Powell, *The Triumph of Liberty* (The Free Press 2000), p. 355.
525   Jim Powell, *The Triumph of Liberty* (The Free Press 2000), p. 359.
526   This situation has improved slightly with the creation of the Patrick Henry Institute. Also, a few other universities specialize in teaching a conservative economics curriculum, such as George Mason University and Hillsdale College.
527   Jim Powell, *The Triumph of Liberty* (The Free Press 2000), p. 434.
528   Jim Powell, *The Triumph of Liberty* (The Free Press 2000), p. 449.
529   This anecdote can be found in Robert Bork's fascinating book, *Slouching Towards Gomorrah*.
530   Dee Zahner, *The Secret Side of History* (LTAA Communications 1996), p. 154.
531   Daniel J. Flynn, *Intellectual Morons* (Crown Forum 2004), p. 225.
532   http://news.yahoo.com/s/ac/20110302/hl_ac/7980606_45_million_receive_snap_benefits_monthly_a_history_of_the_food_stamp_program_1
533   Some legal scholars and historians differ on exactly when the new Constitution took effect as the highest law of the land. On September 13 1788, New Hampshire was the ninth State to ratify the Constitution. This is important because at the Philadelphia convention of 1987, the drafters agreed that nine states would be sufficient to ratify the new Constitution. However, in 1787 these men were still operating under the Articles of Confederation, which required all the states to agree to any change, unanimously. In fact, Rhode Island was the last of the thirteen States to ratify the Constitution on May 17, 1790. However, in the meantime (after the New Hampshire ratification) the Continental Congress voted on September 13 1788 to implement the new Constitution as of March 4th, 1789. Therefore, this last date is considered by

most historians to be the actual start of both our nation and our Constitution. Most legal scholars ignore May 17, 1790 (the date of Rhode Island's ratification) for two reasons: 1) The first Congress which met under the new Constitution convened before May 17 1790. So the first Congress would not be legitimate if it met before the new Constitution took effect. 2) These scholars view the 1787 convention in Philadelphia as a separate government all on its own, not merely a creature of the Articles of Confederation. Therefore the delegates were not bound by the old requirement for unanimous agreement of all the States.

534   See Reid v. Covert 354 US 1 (1957). "These debates, as well as the history that surrounds the adoption of the treaty provision in Article VI, make it clear that the reason treaties were not limited to those made in "pursuance" of the Constitution was so that agreements made by the United States under the Articles of Confederation, including the important peace treaties which concluded the Revolutionary War, would remain in effect. It would be manifestly contrary to the objectives of those who created the Constitution, as well as those who were responsible for the Bill of Rights -- let alone alien to our entire constitutional history and tradition -- to construe Article VI as permitting the United States to exercise power under an international agreement without observing constitutional prohibitions. In effect, such construction would permit amendment of that document in a manner not sanctioned by Article V." See also Geofroy v Riggs 133 US 258 (1890).

535   Fisher Ames, *Dangers of American Liberty* (1809), p. 434.

536   Homosexual activists point to older men and women who get married without the possibility of raising children. They argue, "If heterosexuals can have marriage for companionship, why can't we?" However, older heterosexuals who get married are still honoring at least half of the traditional building block for society. When homosexual couples get married, they are not honoring any part of it. Older heterosexuals who marry are also imitating the example of their parents. Homosexual couples are not.

537   As quoted by Robert Bork, *Slouching Towards Gomorrah* (Regan Books 1996), p 61. See also *Cliches of Socialism,* by various authors (The Foundation for Economic Education 1963), pp. 71-73.

538   Morris Raphael Cohen was a Russian born Marxist scholar who settled to teach in the US. He died in 1947. This particular quote from Cohen comes from bartleby.com.

539   David Baumbaugh from http://www.celestiallands.org/wayside/?tag=liberal-faith accessed on 03-04-09.

540   Speech before the American Liberal Party, Sepermber 14th 1960. Accessed from www.liberalparty.org/JFKLPAcceptance.html on April 14 2009.

541   For the Astor contributions, see Dr. Carroll Quigley, *The Anglo-American Establishment* (GSG Associates 1981). For the Rockefeller contributions, see John Steinbacher *The Conspirators Against Man and God* (Orange Tree Press Inc. 1972), pp. 78-90.

542   Recent history indicates that the Democrats raise more money than the Republicans anyway. For example, in the national election of 2004, Modern

Liberal political action groups (properly called "section 527(c) organizations") received far more money than conservative political action groups. The Republican Party itself sometimes receives slightly more "hard money" than the Democratic Party. However, the "soft money" (i.e. the money given to 527(c) organizations) that Modern Liberal groups donate more than makes up the difference. Of the twenty richest section 527(c) organizations, fifteen of them are pro-Democrat. See American Spectator, April 10, 2006, p. 16. Furthermore, in 2008, the Democrats raised significantly more funds *(in both soft and hard money)* than the Republicans did. A 2010 Supreme Court decision gave greater freedom for campaign contributions, and for 2010 the conservative 527(c) organizations may have collected more money than those on the left. At the time of this writing (Oct 20, 2010) the total amounts for the November 2010 election have not yet been tallied.

543 Astute readers will notice that I refer to the members of the Supreme Court as judges, not "justices." That's what they are; judges. I will start calling them "justices" when they actually start to produce some justice.

544 This poll was reported in NPR on March 9th, 2008.

545 Dr. Carroll Quigley, *Tragedy and Hope*, as quoted in The New American, Dec. 12 2007.

546 Conservatives such as Robert Welch of the John Birch Society suspect that Eisenhower never intended to fulfill the conservative promises he had made during the campaign of 1952. They believe that Eisenhower made empty promises to conservatives in order to take delegates away from Robert Taft (a true conservative) during the Republican Convention of 1952. Others believe that after Eisenhower was elected, he began to see increased federal spending as his way to get re-elected. See Clarence B. Carson, The Welfare State, 1929-1985 (American Textbook Committee 1986), pp. 194-195.

547 Daniel J. Flynn, *Intellectual Morons* (Crown Forum 2004), p. 17.

548 Ibid, at p. 24.

549 Robert M. Young, *Negations: Essays in Critical Theory* (London, Free Association Books 1988), p.viii.

550 Jonah Goldberg, *Liberal Fascism* (Doubleday 2007), p. 227. Modern Liberals are not alone in calling their opponents crazy. At least one conservative writer has laid the same charge against Modern Liberals. See Lyle H. Rossiter, Jr., M.D., *The Liberal Mind: The Psychological Causes of Political Madness*.

551 A word of caution. If you try to verify these verses from the Koran, all of the translations use slightly different verse numbers. The verse numbering of the Koran is not standardized (unlike the Bible). My verse numbers come from the translation by J.M. Rodwell.

552 R.C. Sproul & Abdul Saleeb, *The Dark Side of Islam* (Crossway Books 2003), p. 89.

553 A.J. Abraham, *The Warriors of God* (Wyndham Hall Press 1989), introduction.

554 Norman L. Geisler and Abdul Saleeb, *Answering Islam* (Baker Books 1993), p. 97.

555 Albert Hourani, *A History of the Arab Peoples* (Warner Books 1991), p.19.
556 This statement by Omar A. Ahmed was made to the Muslim crowd attending the 1998 annual meeting of C.A.I.R., in Fremont California. It was reported in the Fremont Argus newspaper in an article by journalist Lisa Gardiner, who attended the meeting. It has also been published on World Net Daily web site at http://www.wnd.com/news/article.asp?ARTICLE_ID=53303. This quote by Ahmed was ignored by the mainstream press. Years later, under pressure from more moderate Muslims, Mr. Omar Ahmed denied making this statement. However, his denial was transparently unconvincing. He claimed that the journalist (Lisa Gardiner) could not possibly have remembered a statement that he had made "years ago." However, Ms. Gardiner actually wrote the article the very same evening that she heard Mr. Ahmed make the statement. The only thing that occurred "years later" was Mr. Ahmed's denial.
557 A.J. Abraham, *The Warriors of God* (Wyndham Hall Press 1989), introduction.
558 Dr. Henry Malone, *Islam Unmasked* (Vision Life Publications 2002), p. 28.
559 Don Richardson, *Secrets of the Koran* (Regal Publishers 2003), p. 196.
560 Albert Hourani, *A History of the Arab Peoples* (Warner Books 1991), p. 347.
561 This estimate has been taken from tables provided by UNESCO, and it has been re-published across the internet only by conservatives such as Pat Buchanan, Robert Spencer, and Michael Savage. At current birth rates, Muslims will be the majority by 2090 in Spain, France, England, Netherlands, and Germany. However Muslims will still be a minority in Ireland, Italy and Norway. Norway (by law) wisely limits the number of ethnic foreigners to only one percent of the total population.
562 Poll results quoted from *Imprimis*, January 2011, article by Brian T. Kennedy.
563 Robert Spencer, *Islam Unveiled* (Encounter Books 2002), p.7.
564 Ibid.
565 NY Times interview of March 6 2007 with journalist Nicholas D. Kristof.
566 ABC Radio News, Nov 2, 2007.
567 Ibid.
568 Washington Post, Dec 11, 2007, by Joby Warrick and Dan Eggen. See also Washington Post article of August 29, 2009, which mentioned that over a month of sleep deprivation was used before the water boarding of these men.
569 KSFO Radio news Aug 4, 2004, interview with former FBI consultant Paul L. Williams. The frightening book to read is *Osama's Revenge: The Next 9/11*, (Prometheus Books 2004).
570 Don Richardson, *Secrets of the Koran* (Regal Books 2003), pp. 21-29.
571 Another example is freedom of association. In his Koran, Muhammad tells his followers never to make friends among nonbelievers: *"Thou shall see many of them (bad Muslims) take infidels for friends...God is angry with them, and in the torment of Hell shall they live forever."* Koran 5:84. "Oh believers, take not infidels for friends rather than believers. Would you furnish God with a clear reason to punish you?" Koran 4:143. "Oh believers, take not the Jews

or Christians as friends…If any of you take them for friends, he is surely one of them! God will not guide the evil-doer." Koran 5:56. Muhammad even tells his new converts to stay away from *their own family members* who are not Muslims: "Oh believers, make not friends of your fathers or your brothers if they are non-believers. And whoever of you shall make them his friends, you will be sinners." Koran 9:23. The 4th Amendment protects individuals from "unreasonable searches and seizures." There is no basis for this idea in the Koran or the hadiths. Therefore, it has never been a part of Sharia. Anything that restricts the government of Allah from enforcing Sharia will be pushed aside. So the Fourth Amendment will simply be abolished. The Fifth, Sixth, Seventh, Eighth and Ninth Amendments will also be eliminated for exactly the same reason. These amendments are obstacles to enforcing the will of Allah. Islamic law would even eliminate the right to self-defense for non-Muslims. Sharia prohibits non-Muslims from owning any weapons with which they might protect themselves. Under Sharia, a non-Muslim simply cannot raise a hand to protect himself from a Muslim. Under Sharia, if a non-Muslim kills a Muslim (whether in self defense or even by accident), then the non-Muslim absolutely must die. See Don Richardson, *Secrets of the Koran* (Regal Books, 2003) pp. 155,156.

572 A.J. Abraham, *The Warriors of God* (Wyndham Hall Press 1989), p. 10.